ANALYTICAL BEHAVIOURAL GEOGRAPHY

CROOM HELM SERIES IN GEOGRAPHY AND ENVIRONMENT
Edited by Alan Wilson, Nigel Thrift, Michael Bradford and
Edward W. Soja

ANALYTICAL BEHAVIOURAL GEOGRAPHY

REGINALD G. GOLLEDGE
and ROBERT J. STIMSON

CROOM HELM
London • New York • Sydney

© 1987 Reginald G. Golledge and Robert J. Stimson
Croom Helm Ltd, Provident House, Burrell Row,
Beckenham, Kent, BR3 1AT

Croom Helm Australia, 44-50 Waterloo Road,
North Ryde, 2113, New South Wales

British Library Cataloguing in Publication Data

Golledge, Reginald G.
    Analytical behavioural geography.
    1. Anthropo-geography 2. Human behaviour
    I. Title II. Stimson, Robert J.
    304.2   GF50
    ISBN 0-7099-3844-6

Published in the USA by
Croom Helm
in association with Methuen, Inc.
29 West 35th Street
New York, NY 10001

Library of Congress Cataloging-in-Publication Data

Golledge, Reginald G., 1937–
    Analytical behavioural geography.

    Includes index.
    1. Anthropo-geography — Methodology. 2. Spacial
behavior. 3. Geographical perception. 4. Environmental
psychology. I. Stimson, R.J. (Robert John) II. Title.
GF21.G65 1987   304.8   87-9118
ISBN 0-7099-3844-6

Printed and bound in Great Britain by
Biddles Ltd, Guildford and King's Lynn

CONTENTS

List of Tables
List of Figures
Preface
Acknowledgements

1. THE EVOLUTION OF A BEHAVIOURAL APPROACH IN HUMAN GEOGRAPHY

2. DATA COLLECTION BY SURVEY METHODS

3. PERCEPTION AND ATTITUDES

4. SPATIAL COGNITION

Contents

Contents

LIST OF TABLES

List of Tables

LIST OF FIGURES

List of Figures

To Allison and Geri

PREFACE

The proliferation of highly specialised sub-areas of all disciplines now makes it difficult for any book to be all-encompassing. We have accepted this fact, even though our chosen problem area - behavioural geography - has been a focus of research attention for less than three decades. In this volume we have deliberately chosen only a sub-set of the problem areas open to today's researcher interested in spatial behavioural problems. Our choice of sub-area has been conditioned not the least by our desire to stress sub-areas that have forced development of new theories, new forms of data or data collection practices, and, most of all, by our preference for analytical approaches. The dominant theme of this book is tied to this analytical emphasis, for we believe that research requiring an analytical mode has produced the greatest academic and applied knowledge contributions in the entire area of behavioural research in geography. We also believe that it is this research that has been most widely accepted, referenced, and used by our peers in other disciplines. Finally, we believe that this research mode has been instrumental in expanding the research frontier in geography, leaving few, if any, "dead ends" behind.

No doubt there will be equally strongly reasoned arguments by adherents of other approaches. We neither deny the existence of other approaches, nor reject the potential insights and advantages that they may offer. We prefer the approach stressed in this book, because it seems to us that analytical reasoning modes give greater return on time and effort than do any of the others. We further believe that benefits accrue, not only in terms of academic research, but also in terms of instruction and teaching at all levels (Golledge, 1986). Readers looking for a broadly based introductory behavioural text will not find it here, unless their courses - like the ones we teach - emphasise only analytically based work. We believe there is a sufficient base represented in this book, however, either to structure a quarter or semester length advanced undergraduate course, or to provide sound preliminary material for a post graduate course or seminar.

The Scope and Content of the Book

This book is written with instructional needs in mind. Each chapter emphasises concepts, theories, methods, models and examples. For convenience, references are collected in alphabetical order at the end of the book. References are selective and not exhaustive, but should provide adequate back-up material for more in-depth reading and for a greater range of empirical examples.

The opening chapter of the book introduces our point of view, stressing the analytical base of both philosophy and reasoning modes adopted in the book. We emphasise the substantial change from the original logical positivist base of early analytical behavioural research, emphasising the strengths that have been retained and the weaknesses that have been eliminated. This chapter should dispense with the bone-wearying criticisms tied to the spectre of the logical positivist straw man. For those who see the logical positivist shadow behind anything statistical, mathematical, or generally analytical, we urge a thorough reading of this chapter.

Our first chapter stresses that behavioural research in geography required many "innovations". Among these was a need to go beyond existing publicly compiled data sets (e.g., censuses) in an attempt to uncover or generate the individually based behaviours and explanatory variables on which behavioural research relies. The second chapter stresses the need to identify different types of data, and acquaints readers with what we see as an area of ever increasing significance in behavioural research - the use of survey methods of data collection. For those familiar with the enormous amount of time and effort involved in designing and conducting surveys, the significance given this chapter should come as no surprise. How many of us, however, have been present when someone uninitiated in these areas blithely proposes that a problem be solved by "doing a quick and dirty survey"! The words "quick and dirty" and "survey" are to us completely incompatible! We feel that many geographers would benefit from this book - even if they read only this chapter. It introduces the tasks, the problems, and the sources of error and bias, that plague every survey researcher. These problems are an integral part of the question - "what is the validity and reliability of your survey data?" We even suggest that many physical geographers (who have long appreciated the time and effort required to produce data in the field) would benefit from a reading of this chapter - even if only to point to the similarity and immensity of problems involved in undertaking surveys to collect data from unresponsive human populations!

Analytical behavioural research in geography is process oriented. Among the first behavioural processes seen to be of importance were those of perception and attitude formation. Given the historical significance of this emphasis, our third chapter examines spatially relevant aspects of the perceptual process, and, following the lead of early researchers in the area, examines the tie between perception and the formation of attitudes. Although much of Chapter 3 is conceptual rather than empirical - an emphasis that runs counter to much of the published work in this area - we feel that the importance of understanding the spatial properties of the senses is of sufficient magnitude to warrant this early emphasis. We have drawn on real world examples to illustrate concepts and to point to the vast unexplored areas that await future research activity.

A distinction was drawn in Chapter 3 between sensory perception and the general process of cognition. We emphasise this difference by focusing in Chapter 4 on the cognitive processes. In particular, we outline many areas of concern in a rapidly growing interdisciplinary research effort devoted to uncovering the components of spatial cognition. Although for some years at the forefront of research on spatial cognition, geographers have fallen somewhat behind in this area - surpassed by the concentrated efforts of many more researchers in areas such as environmental psychology, cognitive science, computer science and artificial intelligence modelling. Much of this other research focuses on restricted laboratory settings. With their emphasis on complex large-scale real environments, geographers have managed to stay at the forefront of research in areas such as cognitive mapping, spatial preferences, and spatial choice and decision making. This chapter illustrates some areas of spatial cognition where geographic research is generally acknowledged to be at, or near the research frontier.

Much behavioural research admits (implicitly or explicitly) that it is based on learning. Whether this takes place in the context of general knowledge accumulation associated with spatial interaction, or whether it is a conscious effort to learn (as in choosing a route to work or a place to shop), the learning base is of critical importance. Chapter 5, therefore, discusses a range of learning theories and learning processes which dominate our spatial behaviour. The chapter extends more conventional learning models and theories into the modern arena of artificial intelligence modelling, inquiry into the nature of spatial knowledge accumulation, and the structure of human decision processes.

A long-established stream of behavioural analysis in geography is the investigation of human activities in a time-space framework. In Chapter 6 we focus on activity and action spaces in an intra-urban setting, linking their development and characterisation to cognitive mapping. Factors influencing daily activity patterns are discussed, and a number of modelling approaches to activity analysis are outlined.

Chapter 7 focuses on the use of time-path analysis, developed by the Lund School in Sweden, which places human activity studies within the framework of time, as well as physical and societal constraints. Applications of time-path analysis are discussed, and some attention is given to the study of time-space budgets. We emphasise that defining their characteristics represents considerable methodological challenges for data collection.

Consumer spatial behaviour was among the first problems investigated by behavioural geographers. It continues to occupy much research effort, and is taken as the theme in Chapter 8. The traditional economic and marketing bases are acknowledged early in this chapter, but in essence it "starts" with the change of behavioural assumptions from economic and spatial rationality initiated by David Huff. His argument that choice is a probabilistic rather than a deterministic process, and that it depended to a large degree on cognition of the choice environment, was a major theoretical and empirical departure from established research norms. The evolution of work on preference, choice and decision-making by consumers is traced through two decades of research. Major analytical departures, such as were necessitated by the disaggregate choice theorists and their various logit models, are reviewed. Examples of the use of the multinomial logit model is then articulated. The chapter also examines the use of more general stochastic models of buyer behaviour such as the NBD (negative binomial distribution) model, and outlines an example of the use of construct theory and repertory grids to elicit cognitive images of stores and shopping centres. A final section discusses the increasing volume of research on store and shopping centre image, from both consumer and retailer points of view, and discusses several new and promising research trends in the area.

A major area of application of disaggregated behavioural models has been in the area of spatial choice and activity patterns, with a focus on travel. Chapter 9 reviews the use of individual behavioural models in travel studies and transport planning, including the development in recent years of a situational approach to modelling individual travel behaviour. Reference is also made to recent attempts to investigate repetitive travel behaviour in a cognitive spatial choice paradigm.

Another prominent area of behavioural research in human geography has been in the field of migration and mobility studies. In Chapter 10 we review the evolution of approaches to the study of migration in a behavioural framework. A major focus is the modelling of aggregate flows and the search for explanation. This involved the development of probabilistic gravity and simulation models, and the investigation of the motivational basis underlying migration.

In Chapter 11 we focus on the residential location decision process at the intra-urban scale. Location decision choice processes are examined in the context of a framework of urban social spaces, and we trace the development of modelling approaches from micro-economics and micro-behavioural models to decision-making and search probability modelling.

The basic elements of the residential location decision process are elaborated with numerous empirical illustrations in Chapter 12. Aspirations, preferences, achievement, and the role of stressors are discussed, as is the nature of the search process in individual relocation.

We neither claim to have covered all the various behavioural approaches in geography, nor to have covered all the different analytical approaches currently in existence. Our final chapter pays lip-service to some other dominant points of view, epistemological bases, and reasoning modes that appear in the general literature, but we leave the development of such areas to others more firmly committed to them. The final segment of the book does, however, emphasise what we see at this stage to be promising lines of research for the current as well as the next generation of analytical behavioural geographers.

Despite many protestations from disillusioned casual researchers that "behavioural geography is dead", we hasten to assure readers that this is not so. Such pronouncements, we assume, are either the result of an inadequate knowledge of the field itself, or of a lack of acquaintance with some of the more vibrant and progressive research areas, such as those outlined in this book. There are so many research tasks open at this stage to the behavioural geographer, that a concerted effort by our entire discipline would probably make only a little headway. Since many problems and tasks have almost of necessity become the prerogative of researchers in other disciplines, we repeat the earlier message in our first chapter. Behavioural research in geography was part of a general interdisciplinary movement which transgressed disciplinary boundaries. Today's behavioural geographer should continue to actively search other disciplines for up-to-date information on theories, methods, and models relevant to any defined research task.

ACKNOWLEDGEMENTS

We could not have produced this book without the tremendous efforts of Patty Fenwick-Miller and Karen Harp, both of the University of California, Santa Barbara (UCSB), and Bev Flynn, formerly of the Flinders University of South Australia. We deeply appreciate their efforts in compiling drafts from rough handwritten scripts; in developing trans-Pacific communicative skills and the tolerance to deal with problems ranging from telephonic hook-ups to unravelling the many paper sizes, type styles, and reproductive formats of a variety of idiosyncratic and incompatible word processors in Australia and the USA. Their skills as editors, indexers, and general advisers are greatly appreciated. The efforts of Karen Harp are particularly acknowledged across all the final segments of the project, when the loss of sight by co-author Golledge forced her and co-author Stimson to carry additional major production burdens. In particular, we appreciate her cartographic efforts. Almost all of the tables, diagrams and maps used in the book were produced by Karen Harp using an Apple Macintosh computer - which she first had to learn to use! All learning, trials and finished production took less than four months - a remarkable achievement for someone with no cartographic background!

This task has, like many books, taken much longer than we anticipated. There are many reasons for this. In Australia it was the lure of Fosters Lager and Doyles Watson Bay Restaurant. In Santa Barbara, L'Espana's margaritas and Sea Landing's fishing expeditions perhaps added a year to the production time of the book!

There are many other persons whose help should also be acknowledged and we offer apologies to many who have helped us but whose names might not appear here. At UCSB for example, members of Geography 153 (Introduction to Human Spatial Behaviour) in several years were (willing?) subjects on which to try most of the ideas in this book. Also at UCSB, Dr. Nathan D. Gale and Dr. William C. Halperin were responsible for developing a variety of examples, particularly in the cognitive mapping and consumer behaviour areas. A major contribution was also made by Sucharita Gopal, graduate researcher at UCSB, who took on the massive taks of checking and compiling the final bibliography - many thanks, Suchi!

As co-workers on several projects mentioned in the text, co-author Golledge also recognises and acknowledges the critical help and advice of Professors T. Smith, H. Couclelis, and W. Tobler (Geography) and Professors L.J. Hubert and J. Pellegrino (Graduate School of Education). Finally, Professor Golledge would like to acknowledge the financial and technical support of Provost David Sprecher of the UCSB, the Los Angeles Braille Institute, and the Santa Barbara Division of the Californian Department of Rehabilitation, particularly Mary Sanders, for helping obtain the complex set of equipment that enabled him, a severely vision-impaired person, to break the print barrier and contribute to the production of this book.

Co-author Stimson is indebted to former colleague, Dr. Les Heathcote, at the Flinders University of South Australia, Cartographer Andrew Little, and numerous years of students in the course Environmental Perception and Behaviour who spurred his belief that this type of text was needed.

We are also indebted to the various agencies and organisations which gave us permission to reproduce material for the book. Acknowledgement is due to National Science Foundation (NSF) for partial assistance (Grant # 82-19830) provided by the U.S.-Australia Co-operative Science Program, which though primarily focused on a different problem, had important spinoff consequences for this book (e.g., the addition of Chapter 2). And finally, we acknowledge the help and advice of Nigel Thrift and Peter Sowden of Croom Helm, publishers of this book, whose advice, guidance and comments were invaluable.

Chapter One

THE EVOLUTION OF A BEHAVIOURAL APPROACH IN HUMAN GEOGRAPHY

1.1 THE EMERGENCE OF BEHAVIOURAL RESEARCH IN GEOGRAPHY

For much of this century, geographic research has been dominated by a search for definitive structures in both the human and physical environment. This search was undertaken by inventorying, describing and cartographically representing the spatial and temporal facts of existence. An ever increasingly important component of this research was oriented towards the human and built environments and, in this case, the search was for regularities in the form or structure of activity patterns (physical and human) associated with those environments. It was assumed that activity patterns could be given substance and stability by regarding them as relatively invariant and repetitive events within any time-space context.

At various times, isolated researchers in human geography pointed to the need for expanding the geographer's horizons. They talked of imaginary maps (Trowbridge, 1913), the world of the imagination (Wright, 1947; Kirk, 1951), perceived spatial orientation (Gulliver, 1908), and the perception of natural hazards (White, 1945). The message emanating from these early researchers was that the subjective component of human spatial existence was equally as important as the objective component. For example, cities were not only the structures in which urban populations were housed and performed their daily activities, but the city was the people who lived in the structures and gave life to this objective form by means of daily interactions and activities.

By the early 1960s a growing number of geographers realised that, in order to exist in and to comprehend any given environment, people had to learn to organise critical subsets of information from the mass of experiences open to them. They sense, store, record, organise and use bits of information for the ultimate purpose of coping with the everyday task of living. In doing this, they create knowledge structures based on information selected from the mass of "to whom it may concern" messages emanating from the world in which we live. Different elements from these various environments are given different meanings and have different values attached to them. It was the explicit recognition of the relationship between cognition, environment, and behaviour that initially helped to develop behavioural research in geography.

The 1960s and early 1970s saw a surge of interest in behavioural research. One stream of thought, now identified as the **humanist approach**, investigated the relevance of imagination (Lowenthal, 1961), values and beliefs (Buttimer, 1969; 1974), environmental meanings (Tuan, 1971), and in a variety of literary contexts examined the varied meanings associated with place and space. Another stream, one which we emphasise in this book, followed first the **positivist** and then a more general **scientific/analytic** line, and examined attitudes and expectations (White, 1966; Saarinen, 1966), risks and uncertainty (Wolpert, 1965), learning and habit (Golledge and Brown, 1967), decisions and choice (Pred, 1964; Burnett, 1973), preferences for places (Gould, 1966; Rushton, 1969), cognitive maps (Downs, 1970; Stea, 1969), and the general process of acquiring spatial knowledge (Golledge and Zannaras, 1973). This analytic mode of behavioural research also tied strongly into earlier work on migration and innovation diffusion (Hagerstrand, 1952; 1957), which emphasised the critical role of space in the processes of diffusion and adoption.

Looking back, it can be seen that many of these research activities represented a desire to increase the geographer's level of understanding of particular types of problems. This intention appeared to be part of a general and widespread academic desire to gain a deeper level of understanding of problem situations than was possible within the context of narrow disciplinary boundaries. The consequent cross-disciplinary interactions and sharing of epistemologies, theories, methods, concepts, models and so on, exposed many academic areas to different points of view. Part of this involved the formation of cross-disciplinary academic institutes and associations which proved to be fertile grounds for the widening of our knowledge horizon.

1.2 PROCESS ORIENTATION

Traditionally, geographers had achieved a facility to observe, record, describe and classify environmental phenomena, both physical and man-made. Perhaps the single most important feature of the 1960s for the human geographer was the change in emphasis from **form** to **process**.

The emphasis on **form** had long been a geographic tradition and this emphasis was strengthened by the powerful theoretical and quantitative revolutions of the 1950s and early 1960s. An emphasis on form or structure allowed the researcher to focus on objectively identifiable characteristics and patterns and to use the many and varied tools and languages of mathematics, statistics, and scientific explanation generally in their research. In the context of human geography, however, it soon became obvious that the geographer's usual laboratory - the world of **objective reality** - was far too complex to be incorporated into a comprehendable mathematical or statistical model. A process of simplification and generalisation was undertaken so that problems could be made tractable. In doing so, a critical assumption involved removing much of the individual variability of human kind and replacing it with **normative rational beings** (economically and spatially rational man).

However, as a wider range of probabilistic methods, innovative statistical techniques, topological languages, nonparametric measurement techniques and analytic measures became more readily available to the geographer, there emerged also a message that superficial and general descriptions of the natural, human, or built environments (whether verbal, cartographic, or mathematical) were no longer enough. What was required for both understanding and explanation was insight into why things were where they were. This theme has become known as a **process-driven** search for explanation and understanding.

Within the space of a decade, therefore, a large segment of research in human geography changed from one that was interested primarily in classifying and categorising phenomena on the earth's surface through a theoretical and quantitative revolution that sought to build normative models of where things ought to be and to define ideal patterns that were abstractions from reality, to a process-driven search for knowledge of the various aspects of our spatial existence. In particular, the processes on which researchers focused were behavioural, and included things such as learning, thinking, forming attitudes, perceiving, sensing, giving meaning and value, imaging, representing, and using spatial knowledge.

1.3 DOMINANT CHARACTERISTICS OF BEHAVIOURAL RESEARCH

Apart from being primarily process-driven, human spatial behaviour research can be said to have a number of distinguishing characteristics. Some of these were evident in the earliest analytical behavioural research, while others emerged in response to research barriers or hostile criticism. Since not all of these characteristics have been generally recognised, we will outline them briefly.

1.3.1 New Models of Man

Over the centuries writers, thinkers and scientists have either implicitly or explicitly proposed models of man's behaviour which have incorporated assumed internal determinants plus the effects of interpersonal influences, social interactions, motivations for group membership and decision-making logic. In human geography, traditionally the focus was on the model of **economic man** proposed by classical and neo-classical economic theorists. They posed man as a totally rational being influenced in his decision-making as objective external factors of which he had perfect knowledge. Man was either a consumer or an entrepreneur, the former seeking to maximise his utility, the latter seeking to maximise his profit. Not surprisingly, models of economic man failed to account for variation in human behaviour.

An alternative model of man was introduced in the late 1950s by Simon (1957). He saw man as behaving within the bounds of rationality in a complex world. It was the objective weighting of alternative criteria which led to the principle of **bounded rationality**. Behaviour thus generated may appear to be irrational but, merely reflects the outcomes of man's individually variable ability to cope with and store information which is fragmented and incomplete under severe time constraints. The result is that man satisfices, taking a course that is "O.K. for him at that time" insofar as he comprehends the situation. Simon (1957: 261) suggested that:

> however adaptive the behaviour of organisers in learning and choice situations, this adaptiveness falls far short of the ideal 'maximising' postulated in economic theory. Evidently organisers adapt well enough to 'satisfice'; they do not, in general, 'optimise'.

It is largely out of this model of man as a **satisficer** that the behavioural approach in human geography developed. It was a solution to the geographers' search for a model of man that was a viable alternative to the omniscient economically or spatially rational being incorporated into many

3

predictive and explanatory models during the theoretical and quantitative revolution. Such beings were found to be an inadequate base for those interested in the variability of behaviour, as well as its uniformity. In their articles on game theory and decision theory, Gould (1963) and Wolpert (1964) exposed the discipline to a variety of behavioural criteria other than that of complete rationality. Thus, notions of conservative low risk behaviour, minimum regret, satisficing, bounded rationality, and risky and uncertain behaviour, appeared with increasing frequency as the human characteristics that ought to be included in our explanatory schemas.

1.3.2 New Models of Environment

Along with this search for a new model of man came an understanding that there existed environments other than the observable external physical environment. The increased interdisciplinary interaction clearly indicated to geographic researchers that there were multiple constraints imposed by economic, social, political, legal, and other environments that were equally as real as the physical constraints imposed by the objective environment. Thus, there developed an interest in the perceptual, cognitive, ideological, philosophical, sociological and other environments that were all part of the dialectical relation between humanity and the realities in which they lived.

1.3.3 Micro Level Focus

For many researchers, the idea of dealing with artificially aggregated masses of humanity was unappealing. While it was recognised that macro- (or aggregate) levels of analysis could produce some interesting general trends - and, in fact, were a necessary part of the geographer's search for explanation - it was also felt that a focusing of attention at the micro-level would give higher levels of understanding and explanation than could otherwise be achieved by the macro level approach.

It must be remembered, however, that while some researchers pursued a disaggregate or behavioural approach in their attempts to obtain more satisfactory levels of understanding and explanation, it was also implicitly understood that a major aim of analytic behavioural research was to search for new and improved generalisations. The generalisations would be tied to aggregates based on behavioural responses rather than on arbitrary criteria, such as location, demographic, or socio-economic indices of uniformity.

1.3.4 New Data

The new focus on the individual and the subjective evaluation of phenomena in various environments meant that the majority of existing data banks used by geographers were no longer useful or accessible. Researchers had to create new data sets by survey research or other interactive methods. The creation of new data sets was paralleled by an emphasis on different methods of data analysis, including non-parametric analytic measures, multi-dimensional and multivariate methods for the representation and analysis of phenomena, the use of complex experimental designs and incomplete data sets, and the search for new graphic and cartographic modes for presenting mixed metric data.

To a large extent, the search for new variables, data, and measurement methods meant the development of strong ties to the discipline of psychology, which complemented existing ties with other social and behavioural sciences.

1.3.5 The Basis for Generalisation
The search for a new basis for generalisation was undertaken by attempting to find sets of human actions, internal or external, about which researchers could make legitimate, general, realistic, and appropriate statements. It was generally felt that many of the analyses of existing objective data sets represented the methods of collecting the data (e.g., the census structure) more than they represented human behaviours and actions. Behavioural researchers, therefore, reorganised their thought processes from the base up, starting with the individual, searching for commonalities across groups of individuals, aggregating on the basis of commonalities, and then searching for potential generalisations that might be used to modify existing theory or to develop new ones.

1.4 BEHAVIOUR IN SPACE VERSUS SPATIAL BEHAVIOUR

Geographers are, and have always been, interested in **overt behaviour.** They have mapped, classified and described these behaviours of man in a spatial context, ignoring the complicated decision-making process underlying those overt activities. The elements of spatial structures and their behaviours were described in terms of quantities of movements, distances apart of origins and destinations, and other physical properties of spatial acts. The geographer thus produced abundant descriptive data, and, in addition normative based theories, on the properties of distributions, interactions, network connections, patterns, nodes, surface properties and hierarchical elements of spatial systems. Figure 1.1 illustrates these basic **elements of spatial systems.**

While the geographer became good at describing what was there, in seeking to explain why or how it was there, he would usually search for physical correlates within the spatial structure in which the phenomena were distributed or where the spatial behaviour occurred. Thus, spatial behaviour acquired a very loose meaning. As noted by Amedeo and Golledge (1975: 348):

"it was used to describe on the one hand the physical manifestations of directed acts of human beings, and on the other it was used to describe fluctuations of systems or systems elements, such as regional growth, commodity flows, population growth, and so on. Such uses lumped together human spatial behaviour (i.e. those behaviours that are caused, have directedness, motivation, action and achievement), and fluctuations of nonsensate system elements."

An important advantage of adopting a **process-oriented** behavioural approach is to distinguish between goal-directed human behaviours and the movement of **nonsensate** system elements which are generated by exogenous forces. Thus, we seek to find process-oriented explanations concerning spatial phenomena rather than cross-sectional explanations that correlate elements of the physical structure of systems with human actions in those systems.

It is important to understand the above proposition. It is the basis on which the process-oriented behavioural approach is differentiated from other approaches. It incorporates the belief that the physical elements of existing and past spatial systems represent the manifestations of a myriad of past and

5

Figure 1.1
The Elements of Spatial Systems

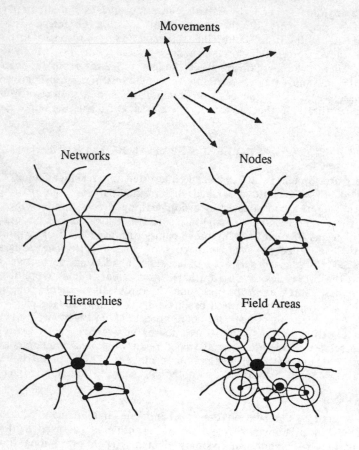

Source: After Haggett, 1965: 18

present decision-making behaviour by individuals, groups and institutions in society. The outcomes are the observable landscapes and built environments that comprise a system or set of systems and the spatial behaviours that occur within them. The total environment encompasses both physical (or natural) environmental phenomena plus the built environment that derived from individual and collective decisions and activities. In the context of human spatial behaviour, we tend to focus on the built environment as manifest in a city. The search for geographic understanding and explanation is via an examination of the processes that produce them and not the spatial phenomena themselves.

If spatial behaviours deduced by mechanistic examination of the properties of spatial systems do not match the empirical reality of behaviour of people acting in those systems, then it is presumed that factors other than the physical characteristics of those structures need to be considered in developing explanatory models. We need to incorporate variables derived from analysis of **behaviour within the system**. Consider an example such as the movement of passengers by air in a country. Aggregate flows (or movements) are not strictly goal-directed, but they are the results of individual sensate behaviour occurring in response to a multitude of needs. While it is possible to seek description of the movement of airline passengers over the air route network of a country, in terms of gravity model postulates about interaction between cities of specific sizes and attractiveness and their intervening distances (i.e. the physics of the structure over which the flow occurs), to achieve explanations we need to look beyond to other variables which are relevant and which may include behavioural processes, such as the goal-directedness underlying the movements.

Thus, while we may use gravity models to describe and even predict with considerable accuracy aggregate flows and movements of goods, people and messages over networks connecting hierarchically-arranged nodes, nonetheless we can furnish nothing towards explaining individual behaviours. The problem is that regularities that are apparent at aggregate levels of scale may lead us to believe that spatial behaviour is equally predictable at finer scales. But, at less aggregate levels all we can manage is to assign ranges of probabilities to individual decision choices. Even at the aggregate level there was a tendency for geographers in the 1950s and 1960s to fall into the trap known as the **ecological fallacy**. In so doing they inferred cause-effect relationships between area-based spatial variables via correlation and regression models, while all that one could conclude with validity was that there was a high degree of spatial association between component variables. To infer that there was explanation of behaviours, as portrayed by surrogate ratio-type data variables, was invalid.

It may be that the behaviour of spatial system structures and elements is directly related to behaviour occurring within those structures over time. We need, then, to ask the question "are there processes which operate regardless of the specific spatial structures in which given acts take place?" Thus, a change in the system characteristics changes the forces operating within it, but the behavioural processes themselves may remain unchanged over time.

An example will clarify this proposition. Imagine an economically rational man being placed first in a spatial system that is compact and then in one that is diffuse. If we examine the mechanics of the behaviour of such a "Marshallian man", we may find that his spatial behaviour was different in the two systems, and that this was due to the different arrangements of the opportunity set in each structure. However, his goals remain the same - that of a rational, utility-maximising economic man. We would need to explain his apparently different spatial behaviour by carefully specifying the rules of behaviour under which he operates and to assess the behaviour-directing effects of the structures in which he is placed.

This leads us to a definition of the **behavioural process** as "a mechanism for including a temporal unfolding of a behavioural system" (Amedeo and Golledge, 1975: 351). It enables us to use the distinction between **sensate** and other types of behaviour as the basis for distinguishing between the types of processes that are relevant in searching for explanations of these behaviours. Thus, the human behavioural process induces a **temporal sequence** of **directed acts** by individuals, groups and institutions in a society. The mechanistic processes that describe the operations of the spatial system over time are not able to explain the behaviours themselves, but only the geometric or physical properties of the system.   It is the examination of goal-directed spatial behaviour, as one manifestation of sensate behaviour per se, that may furnish us with explanation of spatial behaviours.

1.5   THE EPISTEMOLOGICAL BASES OF BEHAVIOURAL RESEARCH

1.5.1 The Positivist Tradition
Analytical research in geography, including a good part of research on human spatial behaviour, was strongly based on the positivist tradition. **Positivism** was a critical part of the quantitative and theoretical revolution that swept the discipline in the late 1950s and early 1960s. It combined with the use of quantitative methods and the desire for generalisation, via normative theory, to push the discipline into an era of scientific thought. However, it soon became obvious that, while some of the fundamental principles of positivism are ingrained in much of the analytic work in human geography, the limitations and constraints in the philosophy itself were also quite confining. By detailing some critical characteristics of positivism, it should at once be obvious that this philosophy in its entirety was not readily adaptable to human behavioural research.

The critical **elements of positivism** are as follows:

 (a) a physicalist view of the flux of existence
 (b) a characterisation of reality as a collection of atomistic facts
 (c) an emphasis on the objective and the observable
 (d) the critical importance of hypotheses testing within that mode of reasoning called "scientific method"
 (e) an empiricist base
 (f) the dominant theme of searching for generalisations and the ultimate aim of producing process theory
 (g) a need for public verification of results
 (h) the necessity of logical thought
 (i) the separation of fact and value
 (j) the assumption of the scientist as a passive observer of an objective reality
 (k) the principle that value-judgments must be excluded from science.

Obviously, a substantial part of behavioural research in the past two decades was born in the positivist tradition and still reflects some of its underlying principles. However, the bulk of recent analytic research has progressed well beyond its original positivist base, and it is increasingly difficult to identify that research with traditional positivism (Couclelis and Golledge, 1983). Analytical behavioural research has, in fact, evolved by shedding many of the classic positivist tenents.   For example, as the importance of cognition as a mediating factor between man and environment was recognised, the critical positivist tenent of the nonsense of the unobservable was quickly perceived to be untenable. With this loss came a weakening of the principle of reductionism and the physicalist interpretation of human behaviour.   In behavioural geographic terms, spatial behaviour became differentiated from behaviour in space (Cox and Golledge, 1969).

The increasingly criticised tenet of the scientist as a passive observer of an objective reality also came under criticism as it was recognised that humans and environment interact constantly in all time/space contexts, and it was these ongoing transactions that provided the essential structure and meaning of the relationship between human and environment. In turn, this meant that alternative epistemologies, such as the transactional or constructivist positions, based as they were on the dynamics of interaction between humanity and environment, were strengthened as alternatives to positivism. As alternative epistemological positions were taken, then the classic positivist separation of **value** and **fact** became less tenable, and the attempt to interpret values and beliefs in a scientific manner increased. Much research on human spatial behaviour began to accept that values must indeed be facts since they help determine overt spatial behaviours. This ongoing interactional epistemological debate also laid to rest the original positivist position of an a priori given world, and its replacement with an assumption that mind and world are in constant dynamic interaction.

For the last two decades, analytical behavioural research has made major advances by leaping barriers imposed by positivist philosophy while retaining fundamental and important principles of scientific research - principles that have endured the rise and fall of many philosophies.

What is contained in current analytic behavioural geography is what is truly positive in positivist thought:

(a) the importance of logical and mathematical thinking
(b) the need for public verifiability of results
(c) the search for generalisation
(d) the emphasis on analytic languages for researching and expressing knowledge structures
(e) the importance of hypotheses testing and the importance of selecting the most appropriate bases for generalisation or theorising.

1.5.2 Behavioural Research Today

The trend away from classical positivism has accelerated over the last decade. This has occurred for several reasons, including the advantages that alternate epistemologies provide for undertaking human behavioural research, and their suitability for exploring new areas of the subjective and unobservable.

To some, this move from positivism has signalled a flight to **humanist** alternatives. We interpret it not in this way, but as a search for the development of an appropriate analytic mode of discourse that serves well the original aims of behavioural researchers in geography.

Despite a variety of vigorous attacks on behavioural research from within the field of human geography, there has been an ever-increasing trend to incorporate much analytic behavioural research into the day-by-day practice of geographers. Increasingly, introductory textbooks have incorporated behavioural concepts into a variety of conventional geographic sub-areas, and have stressed that the understanding of spatial problems is incomplete without the inclusion of the behavioural dimension.

A significant development since the early 1970s has been the forging of stronger and stronger links between human geography and psychology. While many of the earlier links between these two disciplines were conceptual, of late they have been strengthened by common use of measurement procedures, model building activities, experimental designs useful for handling large and incomplete data sets, and by the more widespread use of segments of the real world as the scientist's laboratory. One indirect result of this tie has been an increased interest by geographers in the spatial problems of populations other than normal adults, including those of children, the poor, the elderly, and disadvantaged sub-groups (such as the blind, the deaf, the mentally ill, the mentally retarded, and the physically handicapped or infirm). Thus, the research undertaken by analytic behavioural geographers can span many traditional and non-traditional subareas of their discipline and provide strong links to hitherto poorly connected subsets of other disciplines.

Current analytical behavioural geography, therefore, can be characterised by a concern for scientific rigour. This concern covers topics such as:

(a) experimental design
(b) data collection procedures
(c) the search for validity and reliability
(d) the selection of appropriate analytical methods
(e) the choice of a modern, analytical, epistemological basis
(f) the innovative use of models of man and models of environment.

Research areas dominated by scientific approaches include:

(a) studies of cognitive mapping and spatial behaviour
(b) attitudes, utility, choice, preference, search, learning
(c) consumer behaviour
(d) location decision-making
(e) mode choice and travel behaviour
(f) and mobility and migration behaviour.

Since these areas appear to lend themselves more to the process of measurement, model building, abstraction, generalisation, and theory building than other areas of human geography, we will be focusing on them in this text.

Adoption of an analytic mode of discourse has brought geographic researchers to a stage where they can freely interact with, and comprehend researchers in a large number of other disciplines. In turn, those researchers can fully appreciate the contributions made from the particular viewpoint of the geographer. This **cross-disciplinary** interaction has been extremely fertile in the search for solutions to many problems of human spatial behaviour. Thus the geographer's knowledge and skills have contributed significantly to the current state of the art in environmental cognition, environmental learning, and the general process of modelling human decision processes. This latter area, sometimes known as artificial intelligence modelling, is one of the several active growth areas for the analytic behavioural geographer. By focusing on the process of acquisition, storage and recall of spatial knowledge, the geographer is able to use all his particular skills - his cartographic and graphic representational modes, and his particular analytic methods - in a context comparable to researchers in disciplines such as computer science, psychology, electrical engineering and cognitive science.

Since the geographer's entry into the general field of behavioural research has been relatively recent, there are still significant problems involved in terms of creating appropriate experimental designs, selecting appropriate survey research procedures for data collection, selecting appropriate methods for data analysis, and ensuring that research undertaken is verifiable and reliable. Like other scientific researchers, the analytical behavioural geographer must make a long term commitment to his research with no guarantee of successful results. However, we are so convinced that significant progress is being made, that we devote the rest of this book to discussing the evolution of, and illustrating the state of the art of, a selection of human behavioural research areas.

1.6 A PARADIGM FOR UNDERSTANDING MAN-ENVIRONMENT RELATIONSHIPS

A **paradigm** for enhancing behavioural human-spatial settings encompasses a complex set of the variables and their functional relationships. It includes the physical and man-made aspects of environment; it allows for roles of culture and its related social and political systems and institutions; it identifies the evolution of culture over time through technology; and it recognises intervening psychological processes as filtering mechanisms in how man perceives his environment and acts within it. The complexity of the inter-relationships between these variables within the operational milieu of modern western society is demonstrated in Figure 1.2.

Figure 1.2

The Man-Environment Behavioural Interface

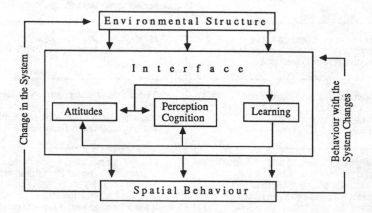

However, we have argued earlier in this chapter that it is the psychological variables intervening between man and his environment that are all important in expanding the behavioural outcomes of this interaction. They provide a paradigm for investigating the behavioural bases per se of these relationships which manifest themselves as spatial movements and location decisions. Thus, we may propose a man-environment behavioural interface model in the simple form of that in Figure 1.3.

The **behavioural interface** is the black-box within which humans form the image of their world. The schemata, or the basic framework, within which past and present environmental experiences are organised and given

Table 1.1

Beliefs Inherent in the Proposition of the Mind
as Mediator between Environment and Behaviour

BELIEF	ELABORATION
Minds exist and constitute valued objects of scientific enquiry.	We are more concerned with the description of preferences and perceptions than the description of conditions of neurons and nerve fibres.
Minds are described in psychological and not neuro-physiological language.	Minds do not have peculiarly mental, non-material, or ghostly properties which would place them outside the realm of acceptable scientific discourse.
There is an external world of spatial stimuli with objective places outside the mind.	These include things such as industrial agglomerations, central places, residential sites, etc.
Minds observe, select, and structure information about the real world.	Minds have processes corresponding to spatial learning and remembering and have streets somewhat corresponding to mental maps, perceived distances, awareness spaces, environmental cues, multi-dimensional image of shopping, residential and other locations, and more or less imperfect spatial knowledge.
Mental events or processes occur that correspond to thinking about or evaluating spatial information.	Minds have states describing action spaces and space preferences and utility functions.
Minds are the seat of emotions and sensations, and are the seat of attitudes, needs, desires and motives.	Minds thus are the producers of satisfactions and dissatisfactions, environmental stress, and aspirations to optimize or satisfice in making location decisions.
Spatial choices are made by thinking according to decision rules which are made in the mind and result from prior mental states, events and processes.	Choices are made among perceived alternatives. The decision rules may be viewed as methods of relating collated and evaluated information about alternatives on the one hand to motives on the other.
Spatial choice decisions are the cause of an overt act, and over time sequences of spatial choices by individuals and groups cause overt behavioural processes; which in turn cause changes in spatial structures in the external world. Thus, ultimately location processes are explained (caused) by mental states, events and processes.	An overt act is such as a search for a new residence, purchase of a new industrial site, or a shopping trip. Sequences of choice over time are such as intra- and inter-urban migrations. Changes in spatial structures are like transitions in urban land use.

Source: Tabulated presentation of material from Burnett, 1976: 25-26

Figure 1.3

A Paradigm of Individual Behaviour, Spatial
Cognition and Overt Spatial Behaviour

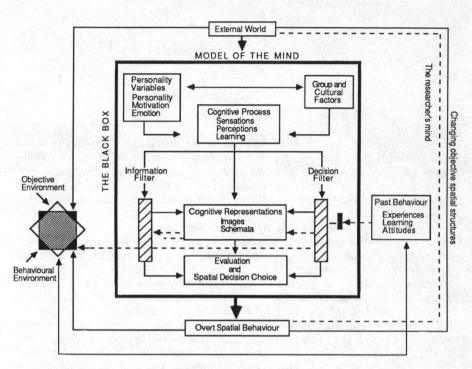

Source: Derived from both Gold, 1980: 42; and Burnett, 1976:27

locational meaning is the **cognitive mapping process**. The key psychological variables intervening between environment and human behaviour within it are a mixture of cognitive and affective **attitudes, emotions** or affective responses, **perception** and **cognition**, and **learning**. As Figure 1.3 demonstrates, these are linked. It is with the understanding of these relationships that the process-oriented approach is concerned.

The paradigm is applicable to the analysis of everyday behaviour of humans in their environment. It is based on what Burnett (1976 pp. 25-26) lists as nine beliefs about the mind as a mediator between the environment and behaviour in it (Table 1.1). The paradigm postulates both casual and non-casual connections between the overt behavioural process and the external world of changing objective spatial structures. The individual is simultaneously part of both the objective and the behavioural (or subjective) environments, receiving locational and attributive information from the latter.

Chapter Two

DATA COLLECTION BY SURVEY METHODS

2.1 INTRODUCTION

To our knowledge, no public agency collects or distributes individually based behavioural data. The reasons for this range from violation of disclosure rules to the excessive time and effort involved in designing and administering surveys to collect such data, coding it in an anonymous format, and making it available through some public information dispensing agency.

Nevertheless, the behavioural researcher **must** have access to such individually based subjective data sets. In many cases it is the perception, the preference, the attitude towards an event or a phenomenon, or a probed analysis of how a decision is made that is of dominant interest. Such variables do not come in prepackaged form dispensed by a public agency. They must be solicited from people via a selection of creative experimental behaviours and carefully contrived collection procedures. Data comes in many forms from unstructured responses to verbal prompts, to judgments made about the properties (spatial and otherwise) of things, people and events. By far the greatest volume of behavioural data is **soft**: i.e., it has few of the properties of **hard**, fully parametric data. It may consist of a binary recording of events (Yes/No) or subjective rating scalings based on bi-polar adjectives or rankings of preferences, or similarity measures.

In Chapter 1 we emphasised that behavioural approaches forced geographic researchers to become aware of "different" types of data; that it encouraged exploration of complex questions of complete and partial experimental designs; and that it necessitated the development of knowledge of survey research procedures and a host of "new" analytical devices, ranging from simple non-parametric inferential statistics to complicated "distribution free" methods of analysis (e.g., multidimensional scaling and quadratic assignment procedures). We pay homage to all those methodological innovations in this chapter by discussing some characteristics of types of data and examining some fundamental questions relating to survey research.

2.2 TYPES OF DATA

2.2.1 Creating Data
The collection of data represents a creative act on the part of a researcher. Things and people exist and events occur and they can be regarded, noticed, observed or monitored in their natural state. But when an experimenter or observer wants to record phenomena, there is a need to decide the form in which such observations are recorded. There is, therefore, an attempt to

"map" a set of observations into a set of data. The data has to have "truth preserving" qualities, such that a given quantity, volume or number of observations are represented faithfully and accurately by the data format chosen. In other words, data are made **objective** in the sense that the same transformation of phenomena or events into **recordable form** would be achieved by any observer. A good data set therefore produces interpersonal agreement about the way it is represented. Even **subjective evaluations** or **judgments** can achieve a level of interpersonal agreement about what a bit of data represents and how it can be manipulated. Thus an **isomorphism** or "equivalence of form" is required between that which is observed and that which is recorded. This isomorphism is produced through selecting a **measurement** procedure which can satisfy both the necessary and sufficient conditions for making an admissible transformation of observations into data. Depending on the success in achieving such an assumption, data is categorised as being "good" or "bad". At times we require a good representation (e.g., a count of the number of males or females in a room) while at other times a rough equivalent may be satisfactory (e.g., the average volume of water passing through a pipe of specified dimensions over a given time period). Data in a real sense then is created - primarily so that it can be **analysed**.

There are many ways to build a set of data about a phenomenon or event. For example, a city can be recorded in terms of its physical size, its population, its socio-demographic characteristics, its activity patterns, and so on. Depending on what a researcher has in mind (e.g., what problem or task is being investigated) one or more of these potential measurements or descriptions can be selected to represent the appropriate data to be analysed. In many behavioural situations it becomes of critical importance to select a type of data that will ensure that an admissible transformation has been made and that the resulting data is meaningful and interpretable.

Once a representation is made between an empirical situation and a data set, questions arise as to the extent to which the resulting data is **unique** and whether or not it retains properties such as identity, order, and additivity of the original system. Identity preservation requires distinct mappings of phenomena into single or multiple feature classes, and the maximisation of clarity in the allocation process. **Order** preserves the sequencing properties of the phenomena (e.g., on temporal, spatial, or qualitative dimensions) such that rankings can be produced which conform to a chosen monotonic rule set. **Additivity** preserves the manipulative qualities of the phenomena such that metric manipulations (e.g., adding, subtracting) can be undertaken in a meaningful way. Internal consistency within the elements of the data set must be capable of being maintained.

It is sometimes argued that there are three types of measurements that relate to the identity, order and additivity constraints. In many behavioural situations, a procedure known as **measurement by fiat** is used. Thus a single index may be derived to account for the complex variable "socio-economic status". Of course there may be an infinite number of these "fiats" produced, and with each one, the results of analysis might change. Such is the base of the social and behavioural scientist.

2.2.2 Types of Measures
In more general terms, we will find occasion to come across data produced by different types of measurement procedures. For example:

(a) **Nominal** data preserves only the **identity** of the phenomena it represents (e.g., A = trip to store 1; B = trip to store 2, etc.).

(b) **Ordinal** data preserves both identity and order. The statement A > B > C implies that there are three classes of phenomena and that class A is greater than (or comes before) class B which is in turn greater than (or comes before) class C. It is not possible under this condition of strong monotonicity for C > A. This violates the principles of triangle inequality. But in many behavioural data sets, this type of violation occurs and can be accepted to some level of tolerance. It also requires, however, a reformulation of the strong metric axiom constraining the monotonic property of data.

(c) **Interval** and **ratio** data is perhaps the most rigorous (but the most common) form of data with which behavioural researchers deal. Interval data assumes an arbitrary zero point but then allows all forms of additive manipulation. Ratio data gives to zero the precise meaning that absolutely nothing exists at that point. Thereafter all its additive properties have a special and powerful meaning.

2.2.3 Collecting Data
As we proceed with this book we will be exposed to a wide variety of data types. The behavioural researcher must be familiar with all these, recognising their strengths and weaknesses and becoming aware of those situations where some level of measurement may not be achieved. Mapping measurement level to data type to analytical tool, is a skill that must be mastered before the behavioural researcher can have confidence in the validity and reliability of his work. But what is also needed is a knowledge base covering how to go about collecting required data. It is to this task we now turn by examining questions relating to carrying out successful survey research procedures.

2.3 DATA COLLECTION USING SURVEY RESEARCH METHODS

Here we deal with the general principles that one needs to be aware of in conducting surveys and the steps one needs to go through. We also refer to some of the problems that result from the procedures which are involved and especially the types of errors and biases one gets in collecting data through survey methods.

2.3.1 Some General Choices and Constraints
It is convenient to commence by constructing the general question of **choices** and **constraints** that one has in conducting a survey as part of a research project. Some of the important choices and constraints facing us in contemplating conducting a survey are elaborated on below:

(a) First, what might seem an obvious point, but one which is apparently far from obvious for many clients and users of survey research is the need to **logically formulate and clearly specify the research problem** that is being investigated. One cannot emphasise too strongly the importance of having a very clear and specific statement of what it is that one wants to investigate before even contemplating conducting a survey. One must be aware of

(i) the theoretical questions involved in a particular process or behaviour that is to be investigated

(ii) other related empirical studies

(iii) specifically what type of phenomenon it is that we want to investigate.

Without clearly formulating and defining the research problem, it would be difficult to make rational choices in terms of the necessary data collection and the appropriate survey approach.

(b) Second, there is the question of **study design**. Two aspects of the design of the study are important. These relate first to the **research setting**, and second to the type of **research strategy** that might be followed. The research setting refers to a range of factors, including the population category to be investigated and the geographic location in which the study will take place. For example, it could be a national study, a city study, or the study of a particular population subgroup at a particular level of spatial scale (such as people who are registered voters in a state, people who belong to a particular age group, or people who live in a specific town). Thus, setting the geographic **scale** and sector of the population for the study is important and needs to be clearly defined.

The design should also be concerned with identifying and defining the appropriate **research strategy** that is going to be used. One needs to determine whether or not it is necessary to do a survey to address adequately the research question, or whether alternative approaches, such as an experimental or laboratory study or secondary data analysis, would be more appropriate.

(c) Third, there is the issue of choosing between **survey and non-survey** approaches. Quite often non-survey approaches are more appropriate than a survey. So often we find that people and organisations will respond to a particular problem that is confronting them by saying, "We'll approach that really easily; we'll just conduct a survey and find out all about it." If one delves through the library, looks at consultant reports and asks questions of public agencies, often one finds that there is already an enormous amount of available data that has been collected, or that other surveys have been conducted which are quite appropriate and sufficient for the particular purpose one might have. **Secondary data analysis** is often a cheap and fruitful means of addressing a research problem, provided the data is of good quality and contains the type of variables required to test the research hypothesis.

Non-survey approaches, some of which which may or may not involve data collection methods, may be appropriate. For example, one might choose to use other sources, such as newspaper reports, or just confine oneself to using other **secondary data**, such as the census. One might want to collect information through specific types of literature searches, and so on.

(d) Next is the question of **aggregate** versus **disaggregate** data and its analysis. Often, particular groups of social scientists are not concerned with disaggregate analysis, but are more concerned with aggregate sectoral analyses, e.g., how the economy is performing with respect to a set of specific measures. Data collection for aggregate analysis of macro-level economic data usually relates to national accounts or industry sector data. Other social scientists, such as psychologists and anthropologists and also geographers, to a large extent are concerned with disaggregate analysis. Here the concern is with looking at behaviours at an individual or a small group level and at this level it is more likely than not that specific purpose data sets need to be collected.

Table 2.1

Tasks Involved in Conducting a Survey

1. Definition of the research question:
    formulating hypotheses for testing.

2. Budget and time constraints

3. Target population:
    primary sample units

4. Parameter definition

5. Data variable specifications

6. Sample design issues:
    Type of sample, sample frame,
    sample questions, error estimates

7. Instrument design issues:
    mode, validity and
    variability considerations

8. Administrative procedures:
    field and office arrangements,
    training materials and
    programs, monitoring procedures

9. Pilot survey or pre-testing

10. Data processing:
    coding manuals, establishing
    a clean data set

11. Data analysis:
    dealing with non-responsive and missing data,
    cross-tabulation of data variables, statistical
    testing of research hypotheses

12. Report writing and data presentation

(e) Increasingly in western countries, there are excellent opportunities for analysing existing data sets (such as census data) and particularly in the USA, there are many existing survey data sets which are widely available through the ICPSR at the University of Michigan and the National Opinion Research Centre at the University of Chicago. Data archives make it possible to obtain such national (and other) data from surveys. One can obtain very good data sets and subject them to one's own particular secondary data analysis to address your own particular research problem. But, increasingly all social scientists are being encouraged to deposit their specific population, and often spatial scale-specific, data sets with data archives. In this way it may be possible to avoid the costs and effort involved in collecting a specific new set of data.

(f) Finally, there is the question of **executing the study design**. This involves two processes: the first is **operationalising the variables** that are relevant to the research problem, and the second concerns the **data collection process**. Details of the process are discussed later in this chapter.

The above are some general issues of concern in the making of choices and the constraints that operate when considering undertaking a survey. These points are just as relevant to research in general as they are to research that involves a survey component.

2.3.2 Tasks Involved in Conducting a Survey

It is particularly important to develop a check list of the tasks that are involved in conducting a survey.

Over the years many excellent books have been written on survey research. In general, the authorities list somewhere between 8 and 12 tasks that are involved in conducting surveys. Table 2.1 lists the specific tasks which we see as being vital in survey research. Some are points particular authors combine together, so do not necessarily think that a fixed number of tasks are involved.

(a) **Definition of the research question**. This involves formulating the **hypotheses** to be tested using data collated in the survey. It is very important when using survey methods to adopt an **analytical framework** in which to conduct the investigation. In social survey research, this usually means adopting a **quasi-scientific approach**, involving the development of precise measures on a set of **parameters** to make clear statements and **inferences** from the sample data, about how the surveyed populations behave with respect to the problems or phenomena under investigation. The aim is to develop **accurate** and **reliable measures**. This involves operating in a scientific/quasi-scientific framework because all the variables are not being controlled, as would be the case in a laboratory experiment. The distinction between the truly scientific approach and the quasi-scientific approach is important, and the latter predominates in most social survey research situations because of the difficulty of controlling the independent variables.

(b) **Budget and time constraints**. There is a need to look at the tasks involved in conducting a survey in the context of the constraints imposed by the **budget** that is available for conducting the study. The world is certainly not perfect, and researchers need to become very adept in terms of operating within imposed budget and time constraints. As with most resources, they are limited. These constraints will be very important factors influencing, or even determining, how decisions are made about the following sets of tasks involved in conducting a survey.

(c) **Target population and primary sample units.** A very important early decision we need to make is to identify the **target population** which we are to survey, and to specify what are called the **primary sample units** (PSU's).

For example, if a survey of travel patterns of the elderly were to be conducted, one would first specify what is meant by "elderly". This would probably involve setting a parameter with respect to age, and the elderly might be defined as people over 60 years. We probably would not have the resources to conduct a survey of the travel patterns of the elderly on a national basis, so we might have to limit our target population of elderly people to a specific geographic area. This might be determined, too, in terms of the particular purposes of the study, and it might be related to finding travel patterns and needs of the elderly in a particular transit or public transport regime.

Thus a process of refining and defining more precisely the target population is mitigated. In terms of the above example of the elderly and their travel, having defined what is meant by elderly, and having determined the geographical area for a specific elderly population, decisions have to be made about what constitutes the primary sample unit. Is it the individual? The households containing elderly people? There is a significant difference between these.

Generally, in social survey research the PSU is individuals, household units, or dwelling units. Sometimes there are complications, such as having a number of household units in specific dwellings. In some survey research, PSUs might be individual companies or institutions or classes. In conducting an education survey, the PSU might be the class rather than individuals, or it might be schools in a region.

(d) **Defining parameters.** Defining the parameters and data variables specifications are the fourth and fifth tasks that are involved in conducting surveys as set out in Table 2.1. Parameter definition and variable specification are important factors in analytical social research in general, and not just in survey research.

Hypothesis formulation and **testing** is central in survey research. It involves adopting an analytical approach to social inquiry. It means we have to specify variables and look at the relationships between them. Thus the parameters which enable hypotheses testing must be defined most carefully.

Usually in survey research a wide range of parameters must be specified. These can be measured by collecting data on very specific variables. In general, social investigations are concerned with differentiating populations and their behaviours on a number of broad parameters, such as age, sex, occupation, class, income level, ethnic origin and so on. One needs to ensure that data which will furnish measures on those parameters are collected. For example, in the case of travel, one would need to define a set of other variables that relate to specific parameters (such as locations that people travel to and from), and the mode of transport used. It would be necessary to make sure that questions are incorporated in the survey design that cover variables relating to the different modes of travel that people might use, such as private car, friend's car, walking, public transport, different types of public transport, and so on, and to do this for trips made for different types of functions, such as journey to work, shopping, recreation, and so on.

(e) **Sample and instrument design issues**. Having specified a target population and defined the PSUs, decisions must be made about the type of **sampling** design that might be appropriate. There are a wide range of sampling designs that have been developed over the past 40 to 50 years during which survey research has evolved.

Decisions must also be made with regard to the appropriate type of sample; the **sampling frame**; the **sampling fraction**; how to **estimate error** in choosing the sample; and the **type of instrument** (or **survey mode**) to be used to collect the data. Furthermore, questions **of validity** and **variability** and **reliability** in data must be addressed.

These questions involve making choices between **survey modes** for collecting data, such as a household or face-to-face survey, a mail survey, a telephone survey, and so on.

(f) **Administrative procedures**. Surveys are very complex; they are usually quite costly, and they involve the need to have very close coordination between the activities of the many people that are involved in the survey. This involves putting into place administrative procedures to do with tasks such as:

(i)   survey design staff selection
(ii)   maintaining field offices
(iii) preparing training materials and programs
(iv)   monitoring the performance of interviewers
(v)   coding data and key punching
(vi)   data analysis.

Setting up cost accounting procedures is important to ensure that one operates within budget. The field forces involved in conducting national surveys, for example, are really enormous, and there are significant management problems that need to be solved.

(g) **Pilot testing**. Having gone through all of the above steps, the stage has been reached where the survey instrument has been designed, a sample has been drawn, data collection procedures are in place, and administrative arrangements have been completed. Now comes the **pre-test** (or **pilot survey**). The pilot survey is a very important phase, because it enables us, through surveying a relatively small number of PSUs, to run a check to see that everything is going to work as planned. On the basis of a pre-test we can go back and do some redesign work, if necessary. We might even decide to scrap the whole survey if it is not going to work. It is really essential to go through the pilot survey. From it we can judge if, in fact, all the survey design efforts have been fruitful, if they will work, if they will furnish valid and reliable data, and if the administrative procedures will be effective.

(h) **Data processing and analysis**. Another task involved in survey research is **data processing**. In order to process the data collected, it is necessary to develop coding manuals, procedures whereby the data that is collected can be put into a computer, programs to clean the data, and programs that will format the data so that it is suitable for statistical analysis.

Data analysis involves looking at questions of non-response and missing data. It is very rare in any survey to obtain a 100 percent response rate. It is also certain that some respondents will not complete the questionnaire in full, so that we have to deal with missing data or item non-response. These are important aspects of surveys for which survey statisticians developed elaborate procedures to handle.

Decisions also need to be made about the **cross-tabulations** between the data variables that will be necessary. This brings us back to the first point: that is, the specification of research questions and the hypotheses that are to be tested. Unless these are clear, it will not be possible to make sensible decisions about the cross-tabulations that should be run.

If one runs a survey of common questionnaire length (say, a 15 or 20 minute survey), then it is quite likely to generate something in excess of 100 pieces of information about the people or households that participated in that survey. One could cross-tabulate every variable one with the other, and in doing so generate reams of computer output which are never going to be able to be accessed in any meaningful way. An early process of hypothesis formulation and testing is thus crucial in order that data analysis can be properly structured and be efficient in time, cost terms, and also research terms. It enables us to be clearly directed in the data analysis when we have clearly specified many of the things we are looking for in the data, so we know the types of cross-tabulations that must be undertaken. This can then guide us over further tabulations that should be run.

Data analysis also involves the choice of appropriate **statistical tests** in order to test the research hypotheses.

(i) Report writing. The final step is that of report writing. This includes data presentation, interpretation, and the formalising of results and recommendations.

It is important when writing up a report on a survey to be very specific in the report on the type of survey design and data collection methods that have been used to generate the data set. One must be very clear and precise about:

      (i)   the sampling procedures used
      (ii)   the target population
      (iii)   the PSUs
      (iv)   the mode of survey used to collect the data
      (v)   the response and non-response rates
      (vi)   non-response and missing data variables
      (vii) reasons for choosing methods of data analysis used.

People who read the results of surveys need to be able to appraise the degree to which that survey has generated reliable and valid data. One cannot judge that unless one has a good understanding of the data collection and design procedures that have been used. While a lot of surveys are worth doing, the results from many are meaningless, and the data might as well have been inverted when bad data collection methods have been used. Furthermore, we need to be aware that the research and data collection process involving survey methods is usually directed towards making estimates and evaluations about the population from which the sample data was drawn. As far as possible, we want to be able to make evaluations and inferences that are reliable and valid.

2.4 PROBABILITY AND NON-PROBABILITY SURVEY SAMPLING APPROACHES

A clear distinction must be made between non-probability and probability sampling approaches in survey research. The most fundamental point to remember is that **probability sampling** is an approach in which every PSU in the target population which has been specified has a stated and **equal** chance of selection in the sample. If a random sample from people in a town is to be drawn, a probability sample would mean that all of the town people would have a stated and equal chance of being selected. A **non-probability** sample would be one in which this is not the case, where biases in selection could occur. For example, if one decided, "I will choose blondes because they are nicer than brunettes"; or "I won't choose that person because I don't like scruffily dressed people", a known and equal chance of being selected does not exist.

2.4.1 Non-Probability Approaches

It is difficult, and often not appropriate, in many investigations in social research to use probability methods of choosing samples. Thus, **non-probability sampling** methods need to be considered. Sometimes we cannot clearly define the PSU or the target population. Cost constraints will often limit the scope of a study and rule out probability sampling. If we are adopting an experimental design approach, often it does not matter too much if we have a non-probability sampling approach, as the basic concern may be control for a whole set of independent variables, and/or we may need to get an adequate number of people with specific characteristics that fall into different types of groups in order that we can compare those groups. Quite a lot of the research that has been conducted in the field of spatial behaviour, such as consumer behaviour and cognitive mapping, has used non-probability sampling approaches, where the aim has been to test for differences between specific groups of people differentiated on a common set of characteristics.

Non-probability sampling methods have been characterised by a number of approaches:

(a) **Haphazard, convenience,** or **accidental sampling**. The aim is to obtain what is supposed to be a cross-section of people or a group of interested people. A lot of media surveys on topical issues use this approach, through procedures such as phone-ins, or a reporter approaching people in the street for their views. A report on the results of this type of survey - which may be marred by self-selection of respondents - is very haphazard - and it does not have reliability with respect to persons other than those surveyed. All it does is give an idea of what the people who just happened to take part in the survey thought about an issue, and the results may well report views of a prejudiced group on a particular topic, especially if respondents are self-selected.

(b) **Purposive, judgmental,** or **expert choice sampling**. Here the researcher decides there is a group of people who have a lot of experience and who can give expert views on a topic, and so they are brought together. It is surmised that they will represent an expert view on that particular problem. Market research is often done this way.

(c) **Quota sampling**. This includes setting a quota, such as a hundred people in a particular age category with a particular income, who might also have other common characteristics. Much social research is based on small group quota samples, whereby sets of clearly specified groups of 30 or 40 people are compared to test for differences between those sets with respect to certain behavioural characteristics.

More could be said about non-probability sampling approaches. They are widely used; used for very good reasons, often related to cost, and they are used in relation to the necessity of having a very strict experimental design in order to compare specific subgroups of a population on a set of parameters.

2.4.2 Probability Sampling Methods

Non-probability sampling approaches do **not** permit us to collect sample data from which to make **inferences** and statements about the **total population** from which the sample is drawn. This is the difference - the fundamental difference - between probability and non-probability sampling approaches. If one wants to make inferences about the total population from which that sample is drawn, it cannot be done unless one uses a **probability sampling** design. Probability sampling also means that the probability of each PSU in the population being chosen in the sample is known: there is a fixed probability, an **equal** probability over the members of the population, or within each stratum into which the population has been divided.

There is a copious literature on probability sampling designs. They have been widely used in geographic research. A number of common designs will be discussed here. For a detailed analysis of sampling, see Kish (1965), and for an excellent short book, see Kalton (1983).

(a) **Simple random sampling.** A simple illustration would be to draw a sample of, say, fifty households in a 500 household suburb. Each household is identified and numbered 001.....500. A slip of paper representing each house is put in a barrel, and 50 slips are drawn. This would generate a simple random sample. Alternatively, one can draw a random sample using tables of random numbers.

(b) **Systematic sampling.** This has been widely used in geographic research. What is done here is to list the population PSUs, select the sampling fraction, randomly choose a starting point, and then use a fixed skip interval to choose in a systematic manner the required sample. For example, in the 500 suburb case above, one would list the PSUs, 001.....500. Using the **sampling fraction** of 1 in 10 to give a sample size of 50, one would randomly select a **starting point** between 1 and 10 (say, 2); then commencing with household 002 in the list, select the required fifty household sample using a **skip interval** of 10 (i.e., households 002, 012, 022,....472, 482, 492) to generate the systematic sample.

Often in geographic sampling, and particularly in selecting spatial **point** or **area** samples, the procedure is to place a grid over an area. This enables us to sample points by choosing all the grid interactions, or to sample areas by systematically choosing, say, every 5th grid square in all directions (north, east, south and west) from a randomly selected starting grid area.

(c) **Stratification.** This is often used in sampling. What is meant by stratification is that a population is divided into categories. One might be interested, for example, in particular age and income groups in a population, and one might wish to focus primarily on a specific group, such as the poor aged. If one has age and income data for a population, one could stratify the sample into a number of age/income groups. This sets the categories, or **strata**, into which the population is sorted. In other words, the population has been **stratified** into a specified number and type of categories, each of which is a stratum within the population. Stratification is undertaken when wishing to specifically compare the particular strata of PSUs, and choosing a sample from within each stratum.

Sometimes it is desirable to sample over all the strata in order to have representation within each of the strata **proportional** to each stratum's representation is the total population. Thus, different size samples using the same sampling fraction would be chosen from within each stratum. Alternatively, it may be desirable to have either equal or specified representation in the sample across all strata in order, for example, to carry out particular non-parametric tests for differences between the strata. This would require setting a quota sample within each stratum, and randomly selecting PSUs from each stratum using different sampling fractions to ensure that both probability sampling and an equal or minimum specified quota of PSUs exist in each stratum. This latter type of approach is commonly used in much of the behavioural-based geography research discussed in this book. It requires comparison of behaviours between clearly specified groups of the population that are differentiated on the basis of specific independent variable parameters, such as sex, age, income, location of residence and period of residence. Furthermore, the non-parametric statistical techniques commonly used to test for differences between sub-groups of the population thus differentiated often require minimum numbers in cells of contingency tables which may be quite large when 2 and 3-way cross-tabulations between variable parameters are used in testing.

(d) **Cluster and multi-stage cluster sampling.** Probability sampling design is of particular interest in geographic research. The purpose is to obtain cost savings in large scale samples, such as a national sample, or even a metropolitan city-level sample, of households, by sampling intensively in a limited number of areal clusters, such as census tracts. In this way interviewer effort can be clustered. For example, in a city of one million population, a 1 percent probability multi-stage cluster samples frame will typically focus sampling in about 100 to 140 clusters. The clusters are chosen by weighting each census tract in the city by its number of dwellings (where the PSUs are dwellings), and the probability of choosing any census tract is proportional to its share of the total number of dwellings in the whole city. Within the census tracts - which are selected according to the sampling fraction and systematic sampling procedure discussed above, whereby every census tract is limited in some type of administrative units order - it is usual to divide the tract into further clusters or blocks. A field count of dwellings is conducted within each of those clusters. Then one or two clusters within that tract are selected proportional to size (i.e., number of dwellings). In this way, a multi-stage cluster sample frame is developed. Within the chosen block(s) in the chosen census tract, a systematic listing of dwellings is made to generate the list of PSUs in that cluster which from the sample.

It is important, however, to note that both clustering and stratification sampling designs introduce increased sampling error. This is particularly so in clustering designs, where the greater the degree of clustering, the greater the degree of error.

(e) **Other sampling designs.** There are many other commonly used sampling designs in social survey research, including **two-phase designs, replicated sampling designs, panel designs, block designs, network designs,** and so on. Of them the **panel design** is of particular interest in spatial behavioural research, particularly where configurational travel and activity data, in a time-space activity framework, needs to be collected. The use of panel designs is discussed in later chapters in both consumer behaviour and time-space budget studies. In panel studies, a sample of PSUs is requested to be re-interviewed over a period of time.

2.5 MODES OF SURVEY DATA COLLECTION

In considering **modes of survey data collection,** budget and the time constraints are the overriding factors affecting the type of survey mode to be used.

But first a decision must be made as to whether to run an **enumeration** (which is a census) in which an attempt is made to survey every member of that target population. For very small populations, often one wants to conduct a complete census on whether to take some form of sample survey. If the latter is decided upon, the feasible modes of data collection involve often difficult choices. The general modes of survey include the following:

2.5.1 Compulsory Registrations
Many government agencies have compulsory registrations (for example, car or alien registration). But most researchers who want to collect data through surveys do not have the official clout in order to enforce people to participate.

2.5.2 Self-Completion Questionnaires
Self-completion questionnaires are a commonly used mode of survey data collection. It is usual for someone to drop off the questionnaire and then to come back and pick it up. This method is widely used in market research, and it is the way in which the census data is collected in many countries. Sometimes the person doing the distributing and collection of the questionnaire might explain to the respondent how to fill it in, but basically the respondent fills it in unaided.

2.5.3 The Mail Survey
The mail survey is probably the most commonly used mode. This might be a straight mail survey where a list of primary sampling units by address is obtained, and you send a questionnaire to each address, along with a

covering letter telling people how important the survey is , and asking them to participate in it. You hope they will return the questionnaire with all the questions filled out according to instructions. Usually a reply-paid envelope is supplied. It is best to have a reply-paid registered mail box with the post office rather than stick stamps on the return envelopes, because about 60 percent of the people to whom you send a questionnaire simply are not going to return it, thus you might as well only be paying for those that are returned.

Thus, the mail survey is a mode in which there is no contact at all between the people conducting the survey and the potential respondent. You mail the questionnaire out, and hope people will cooperate by completing it and mailing it back. But, a major problem with the mail survey mode (as with non-compulsory forms of self-completion data collection) is that **response rates** are fairly poor - usually around 20 percent to 30 percent. It is essential to use second and third (or even additional) **phases of mailing** to increase the response rate. Normally each successive mailing results in a return rate to about half the number returned in the previous mailing phase. In this way it may be possible to build up response rates to approaching 50 percent, which is considered good for a mail survey. Specialised mail surveys focusing on an issue of particular interest for a special group have been known to have response rates of up to 70 percent, but this is extremely rare.

It is advisable in mail surveys to interview a random selection of non-respondents to a mail survey as invariably they display different characteristics to respondents to mail surveys (see, for example, Stimson and Ampt 1972).

2.5.4 Face-to-Face (or In-House) Interviewing
This is the standard mode for collecting survey data. While costly, and requiring skilled, trained interviewers, it is the most flexible and reliable method in survey research. Here the interviewer goes to the primary sampling unit (e.g., dwelling), talks to the chosen person within it, and conducts the interview face-to-face. The interviewer goes though a series of questions which the respondent answers, and the interviewer records those answers.

2.5.5 On-Site Interviews
Here an interviewer goes to the particular site where the activity being investigated is occurring, and the people who are participating in that activity are interviewed. **Shopping surveys** are a good example of on-site interviews. Developing random selection methods of who is selected in the sample poses a difficult problem in on-site surveys. Random selection is difficult, and usually is tackled by having a pre-determined number of shoppers pass the interview point before the next potential respondent is approached. Furthermore, it is necessary to have some form of procedure for selecting sites at which to station interviews in the shopping centre, and to determine (often in accordance with shopper volume variations) - the time distribution of interviews.

2.5.6 Telephone Interviews
Telephone interviewing techniques have been developed in the last couple of decades (see Groves, 1979). While they involve intricate designs to generate **random digit dialling**, selection of telephone numbers for area-based surveys, they are becoming more and more important for a number of reasons. First, they are cheaper to conduct. Second, especially in the USA., the response rate of face-to-face and in-house surveys has declined quite remarkably over the past 20-odd years, particularly in bigger cities where there are lots of apartments and security systems - while telephone interviews are achieving as high as 70 percent response rates. However, a problem is that one cannot cover households without a telephone, and inevitably one will miss out on some part of the population. This is not too big a problem now because of the widespread nature of telephone ownership. It is about 95 or 96 percent throughout the United States. But there are some subgroups of the populations where telephone ownership is much lower. In Australia, for example, ownership is considerably less - about 80 percent in cities and as low as 50 percent in some rural districts. So, one has to be aware of the coverage problems, particularly with respect to specific groups of the population, where telephone survey methods are used.

2.5.7 Relative Advantages and Disadvantages of Survey Modes
The various modes of collecting survey data discussed above have advantages and disadvantages in terms of **cost, efficiency, coverage problems, data validity**, and so on. For example:

(a) Mail surveys have the very great advantage of being quite inexpensive to run, but have the disadvantage of low response rates.

(b) Telephone interviews are apparently cheaper to run than face-to-face interviews, but they require elaborate computer facilities for random digit dialling sampling designs and computer-assisted interviewing systems, they require specialised interviewer training; and they have coverage deficiencies in some contexts.

(c) Ideally, one would choose **face-to-face interviewing** to keep non-response as low as possible to maintain maximum flexibility in questionnaire design, and to take advantage of techniques of interviewer probing of respondents.

What needs to be remembered is that the mode of survey data collection used will influence the type of questions that can be asked. The mail survey, in particular, restricts the range of question types that can be used.

What has not been discussed above is the mode of collecting data using **laboratory testing** of **experimental designs**. These procedures are being used increasingly in some areas of behavioural research which is described in this book, but in general, investigations of human spatial behaviour use survey methods and in-field modes of data collection. However, laboratory testing may sometimes use subjects that have been selected using probability sampling frames.

2.6 QUESTIONNAIRE DESIGN

The design of questionnaire schedules is a specialised field about which there is copious literature. Standard survey research texts usually devote one or two chapters to questionnaire design (e.g., Moser and Kalton, 1971). In general, there are a basic set of "do's" and "don'ts" concerning questionnaire design. Questionnaires or survey schedules are in fact the backbone of surveys, and it is essential that they are designed so as to minimise bias in reporting and maximise reliability of data.

(a)   **Facts**, such as sex, age, occupation, income, and so on, which often relate to socioeconomic and demographic characteristics of respondents and the occurrence of actual events and activities.

(b)   **Opinions**, which are responses given by respondents on their views on specific topics or events, such as their assessment of a political leader, their preferred shopping places, and so on.

(c)   **Attitudes**, which are elicited from respondents, usually via the procedure of asking them to rate or rank the importance of a phenomena; rate or rank their preferences for, say, a set of shopping centres; and rating on a semantic differential such as a Likert scale their attitudes to a set of stimuli, such as attributes of a shopping centre.

2.6.1 Question Wording
There are a number of basic rules to follow in the design of questionnaires. A major source of error and bias in surveys comes from poor wording. The following are a set of fundamental principles to follow:

a.   avoid questions that are **insufficiently specific**
b.   use **simple language**
c.   avoid **ambiguity**
d.   avoid **vague** words
e.   avoid **leading** questions
f.   avoid **presuming** questions
g.   avoid **hypothetical** questions
h.   avoid **personalised** questions
i.   avoid **embarrassing** questions
j.   avoid questions on **periodic** behaviour
k.   avoid questions involving **memory**
l.   questions should be **relevant**
m.   short questions are best
n.   avoid **negative** questions
o.   avoid **biased** items and options

2.6.2 Open and Closed Questions
There has been much debate and research on the merits of open and closed questions. In **open** questions the respondent is given the freedom to decide the aspect, form, detail or length of his answer, and the interviewer must record as much as possible. In **pre-coded** and **closed** questions, either the respondent is given a limited number of answers from which to choose or

the question is asked as an open ended question by the interviewer, who then allocates the answer to the appropriate category. The latter may offer two or more attractive answers, in which case they are **dichotomores** or **multi-choice** questions. One risk in the pre-coded question is that it may force respondents into a category in which they do not belong. However, for cost and time reasons, pre-coded questions are preferable, and pilot testing using open-ended questions can enable the researcher to categorise the range of answers relevant for the purposes of the research so that closed questions are used in the survey proper.

2.6.3 Ordering Questions
It is important to realise that the order in which questions are asked can affect the answers respondents give as well as refusal rate. Thus, it is best to begin with questions that will set the respondent at ease and to build rapport between the interviewer and respondent. These early questions need to be interesting for the respondent. After these preliminaries, questions may proceed in a logical sequence so as to move from topic to topic in such a way as to indicate to the respondent the relationship between the questions, and when a break occurs, the interviewer should explain the shift of the topic.

An especially important topic in ordinary questions is the use of **funnel sequences**. Here one starts with a general broad question about the subject, and then narrows down on specific issues.

A further consideration is **randomising** the order of questions where respondents are asked about different aspects of a particular phenomena or belief. This overcomes the problem of one answer influencing a later answer. One can randomise the order in which, for example, a series of attitude scale items are given to each respondent.

Finally, one needs to be aware that **respondent fatigue** can occur when dealing with long lists of items. Here, randomising the order can be used to randomise the effect of the tendency to respond negatively to later items in a long list.

2.6.4 Other Issues in Questionnaire Design
There are obviously many other issues in this extremely complex area of questionnaire design. These include the important area of **formats** for responses, the use of **contingency** questions, the use of **matrix** questions, the use of **sketches** and/or pictures in the pursuit of symbolic responses, the use of **flashcards** by the interviewer, and the whole complex area of **interviewer instructions**.

As Moser and Kalton (1971:347) have pointed out, the problem of questionnaire design has no easy solution, and even if one follows all the accepted principles and rules, there still remains a choice of several question forms, what type of "language" to use, how to avoid "leading" words for the population being surveyed, and so on.

Detailed pre-testing and pilot testing can assist in overcoming many design deficiencies. To a large extent, question designing is a matter of common sense and experience and of avoiding the known pitfalls, but it is amazing how prevalent badly designed questionnaires are in surveys.

2.7 COMPONENTS OF SURVEY ERROR AND BIAS

2.7.1 Total Survey Error

We now examine the question of **total survey error** in conducting survey research. One must be aware that there are a whole set of sources of **error** and **bias** in surveys which affect the **validity** of data and the **reliability** of respondent responses. These terms have been discussed continually in the literature. However, it is extremely important to be aware of this phenomena in survey research data.

As shown in Figure 2.1, Kish (1965) has developed a classification schema for the various sources of bias and error in surveys. This is a model of **total survey error.** The errors and biases listed have been receiving increasing attention by survey research methodologists in the last two decades. In general terms, **errors** result from **design effects.** Errors occur in **sampling.** Where probability sampling is used, we can actually statistically measure and estimate the degree of error derived as a result of the sampling design. Statisticians have developed good procedures for estimating and correcting errors due to the sampling design.

Figure 2.1

Classification of Sources of Survey Error

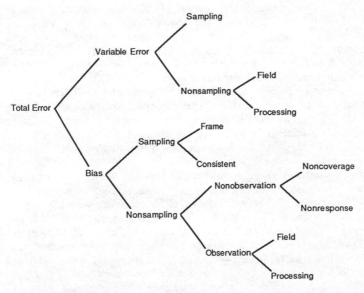

Source: After Kish, 1965

Bias has more to do with **non-sampling** types of problems. Biases come in particularly on the part of the respondent, but also on the part of the interviewer. **Validity** of data can be influenced by both design and by the respondents. **Reliability** of data can be influenced by misreporting on the part of the respondent (sometimes it is deliberate, but usually not), and it

31

can also be affected by differences in the way in which interviewers perform. These various sources of total survey error need to be identified and measured, if possible. What survey researchers are seeking is to develop procedures which will minimise errors and bias to ensure that valid and reliable data is obtained from surveys.

2.7.2 Non-Sampling Error and Bias

About 70 percent of total survey error is due to **non-sampling** errors. The main cause of bias is poor questionnaire design. There are a number of principles that need to be adhered to in questionnaire design. Second, biases arise due to **cognitive** and **motivational** difficulties respondents experience in answering questions. There has been much research in recent years, particularly by researchers in the Survey Research Center at the University of Michigan, on the question of cognitive and motivational difficulties which people face in answering questions. The respondent in a survey situation is in a very difficult situation. The respondent is likely to have problems of **recall**, and so on. It is necessary to motivate the respondent to get him or her interested in the survey.

Basically, in questionnaires are found questions which collect **factual** data, and questions which collect non-factual data. When collecting factual data, one wants to get very precise data, so the question design has to communicate to the respondent that clear, precise answers are desired. A problem that respondents often face in **giving factual data** is memory or recall loss. Most researchers are not aware of the magnitude of these problems - but Cannell, et al. (1981) has shown that reporting error is probable, even in simple questions (e.g., "When was the last time you consulted a doctor?"). Cannell and his colleagues have conducted experiments in health surveys. They noted very marked effects on errors in reporting as the recall time period increases.

Also, there are errors related to what is known as the **salience** of the particular event and its social desirability. For example, some people are not going to report the incidence of diseases that are perceived to be socially undesirable. Thus, the social desirability (or salience) of the event to people will influence the accuracy with which people give answers to factual questions.

There are many **question effects** that induce biases. We always need to allow a **don't know** category to question answers. The way in which we use open and closed questions, the effects of the ordering with which we put alternatives from which people have to choose one answer from a series of lists, all have potential pitfalls that can induce bias. We also have to make sure that, where we are trying to get respondents to categorise themselves, the **categories** are all **mutually exclusive** - sometimes they are not, and this introduces bias.

Bias may also come in through **misreporting** of characteristics such as the age, race, and education of respondents.

Problems of question bias have been the subject of much experimental work, and survey researchers are now able to propose means whereby its impact can be minimised. For example, it has been found that it is helpful to ask people at the outset to really commit themselves to a survey, and even to get them to sign a form to that effect. By saying, "Yes, I will participate in the survey", they thus undertake, to the best of their ability, to give factual and reliable data. All of these procedures of getting the respondent committed and motivated to participate in a meaningful way are having positive pay-offs.

There has been considerable research on how to obtain accurate answers to simple questions, like "When did you last go and see a doctor?" The use of **probes, feedback** from the interviewer to the respondent to reinforce the commitment and motivation, are also demonstrating good results.

One of the major sources of error and bias is a result of the effects of **interviewer performance.** It should not be surprising to have this pointed out. When people are involved in the interview process, they are exposed to many opportunities for problems, and for inconsistent behaviour. In a survey where many different interviewers are out in the field, it is essential to ensure that **the behaviour of interviewers is standardised,** otherwise there will be interviewer-induced effects. Cannell, et al. (1975) has furnished much light on this problem. These interviewer-induced effects are quite extraordinary, and the investigation of these effects shows that many interviewers do not even read the questions as they are written on the questionnaire! Interviewers go through various mannerisms - particularly eye-to-eye contact, expressions, the use of certain responses (like, "Oh, really?" or "Is that so?"), different voice inclinations - so it is not surprising that they can induce bias in the respondents' answers. Work has been done on the question of **reinforcement** and **feedback** aimed at reducing respondent misunderstanding and misreporting.

The interviewer situation is one in which there is **interaction** between the interviewer and the respondent, and feedback between them. In terms of feedback effects, we must decide when it is appropriate and not appropriate to have positive feedback versus no feedback, and when it is appropriate to eliminate negative feedback.

2.8 A MODEL FOR THE QUESTION-ANSWERING PROCESS

The complexity of the question-answering situation is demonstrated in Figure 2.2 (after Cannell, et. al., 1981), which models this process. It sets up a job description of what a respondent must go through to do a difficult task. It indicates that the interviewer situation induces a **cognitive processing of information** and an assessment of what information is needed to give an accurate response. It introduces the **retrieval of information,** and its **organisation** in response to the way questions are worded. It involves giving of a response judged to be **accurate** by the respondent. The respondent may modify his or her response based on both comprehension of the question, cues from the environment, and cues from the respondent's own beliefs and value system. The giving of accurate responses is characterised by conformity, desirability, acquiescence, incompleteness and other biases. Thus, the responding process is a most complex one.

The following chapters discuss theories, methods, and empirical research findings that relate to a selection of the major fields of investigating spatial behaviour. Most use data that is collected in specifically designed survey and/or experimental situations. It is essential that the student and researcher be aware of the nature of the data sets that have been used in testing theories of spatial cognition and spatial behaviour, and that these data sets, having been collected by some form of survey method, contain errors and

Figure 2.2

A Model of the Question-Answer Process

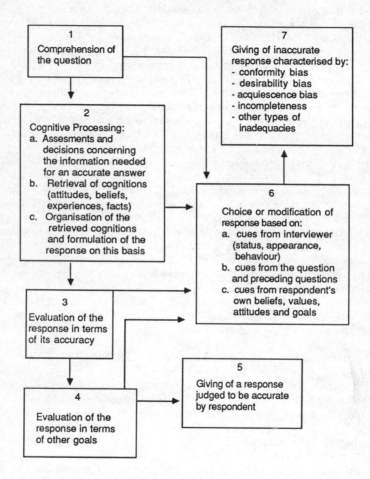

After Cannell, Miller and Oskenberg, 1981

biases. It is especially important to know something of the nature of these errors and biases – as discussed in this chapter – so that we may more properly evaluate the validity and reliability of data sets used in behavioural research. It is incumbent on geographers to use the most rigorous methods of data collection currently available to social scientists, and to make every effort to minimise errors and biases in collecting their data sets, and for them to be aware of the limitations imposed by the data they use.

Chapter Three

PERCEPTION AND ATTITUDES

3.1 THE EXPERIENCE AND CONCEPTUALISATION OF SPACE

Within the general objective geographical environment is a subset known as the operational environment consisting of the portion of the world which impinges on any given human. It influences behaviour either directly or indirectly. That part of the operational environment of which a person is aware is called **the perceptual environment**. Awareness of it may be derived from:

(a) learning and experience of a segment of the operational environment
(b) sensitivity to messages from environmental stimuli
(c) secondary information sources not necessarily related to direct experience.

At the level of the perceptual environment, therefore, part may be regarded as being symbolic rather than a mapping of an objective evaluation. Thus, when a person uses the word **space**, he is usually referring to what is being conceptualised. Space, as conceptualised, will be treated in later chapters in the context of environmental cognition. Space as experienced is often reflected in examinations of affective responses to environment, literary perspectives on environment, and in terms of the roles of attitudes, emotions, and personality factors of the person operating in an environment.

While in the past, geographers tended to emphasise the spatial structure and spatial relationships in the activities man undertakes in his environment, with the evolution of the behavioural or process oriented approach, it has been recognised that these structures and relationships do not appear the same to all people. Amadeo and Golledge (1975:381) have indicated that:

"the extent of our information about a system, the perception of barriers to movement in the system, the specific needs and values of the individuals and groups located therein will influence our cognitions of the spatial properties of such a system, distorting it in some places through illusion or incomplete information, and perceiving the structure very close to a scale model of physical reality in other places ...Recognition that different needs sets spawn different action spaces and that these action spaces are related to different elements of the objective world, has led to a search for an understanding of the processes that form the images of spatial reality that are retained in the human mind."

It is an understanding of the perceptual and cognitive processes that create this **image** or **cognitive map** of operational environments that has received much attention from behavioural geographers.

In this chapter we take a preliminary look at the nature of **environmental perception** and **attitudes** as factors in the man-environment behavioural interface paradigm proposed in Chapter 1. The details of the cognitive process and their outcomes as represented by cognitive maps, and the roles of cognitive maps in solving spatial problems are taken up in detail in Chapter 4.

3.2 A PROBLEM OF DEFINITION OF TERMS: WHAT IS PERCEPTION AND COGNITION?

The terms perception and cognition have been employed in a confusing variety of contexts.

3.2.1 Perception

Among geographers, the term **perception** has been used rather differently to the way it is used in psychology. Geographers have tended to use the term in the sense of how things are seen by people - especially with respect to perception of resources or hazards (see, for example, Burton, 1972; Burton & Kates, 1963; Saarinen, 1966). Designers have used the term to describe the mutuality of interests among various groups of actors in the design process (Rapoport, 1977: 30). However, psychologists have tended to treat perception as a sub-set of, or function of, **cognition**. For example, Werner and Kaplan (1963) see **perception** as an **inferential process** in which a person plays a maximal and idiosyncratic role in interpreting, categorising and transforming the stimulus input. Ittelson (1960) has emphasised the central role in perception of a person's assumption about the stimulus situation. As the real world is complex and is sending out millions of information signals about all aspects of life, we can only be aware of a small portion of this information. An individual receives these signals through his **senses** - by sight, hearing, smell, taste and touch.

The senses are viewed as functional systems designed to provide feedback to the body's motor system and to seek out information about the surrounding environment (Gibson, 1966). As active information seekers, the senses are thought to record only those stimuli that have a bearing on the needs of the individual and to ignore the rest. Occasionally, a strong stimulus may impose itself on the system, but normally the system decides what it will look for. Information is seen, recorded in the array of potential stimuli that presents itself to the body. It is contained in differentials of colour, heat, motion, sound, pressure, direction, or whatever else may be present in the environment and which is within range of the sense organs. The perception of two individuals vary as a function of the differences in the content of the information presented and the differences in the ability of the individuals to pick up the information messages.

These senses do not, however, play an equal part in spatial perception, as suggested in Figure 3.1, with only sight, hearing and smell being able to receive stimuli from parts of the environment beyond the so-called tactile zone. However, much of our environmental information is secondary, culled from the media and through hearsay via communication with fellow human beings. This is **perception**. It concerns the **immediate apprehension** of the environment (stimuli) by one or more of the senses. It occurs because of the presence of an object. It is closely connected with events in the immediate surroundings and is, in general, linked with immediate behaviour.

Figure 3.1
The Ranges of the Senses

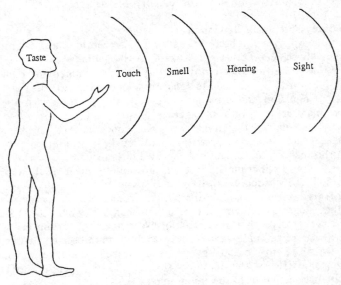

Source: After Gold, 1980

Figure 3.2
The Formation of Images

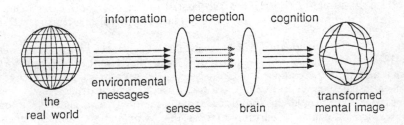

Source: After Hayes, 1980:2

3.2.2 Cognition

Cognition refers to the way information, once received, is stored and organised in the brain so that it fits in with already accumulated knowledge that a person has, and with his/her values. Thus, cognition is developmental. Wapner and Werner (1957) argue that as development proceeds, perception becomes subordinate to higher mental processes. Further, an organism's available cognitive structures influence perceptual selectivity, which leads to a reconstruction of the world through selected fields of attention. Thus, to give a simple example, one may perceive the street where we live by physically being there, but knowing the route to work depends on cognitive organisation of perceptions.

3.2.3 Immediacy and Scale Dependence

This distinction by the psychologists between perception and cognition is basically one where **perception** is linked to **immediacy** and is **stimulus dependent**, while cognition need not be linked with immediate behaviour, nor need it be directly related to anything occurring in the proximate environment. **Cognition** concerns how we **link** the **present** with the **past**, and how we may **project** into the **future**. Cognition is, then, the more general term, subsuming the more specific concepts and surrogates of sensation, perception, imagery, retention and recall, reasoning and problem solving, and the making of judgments and evaluations.

However, this distinction is not an absolutely clear dichotomy, the difference being one of degree and focus (Downs and Stea, 1973: 14). Stea (1969) has offered a more useful distinction from a spatial point of view, suggesting that cognition occurs in a spatial context when the spaces of interest are so extensive that they cannot be perceived or apprehended at once. Thus these large-scale spaces have to be committed to memory and cognitively organised to contain events and objects that are outside the immediate sensory field of the person. This is a scale-dependent difference and is intuitively acceptable to the geographer.

The end product of perception and cognition is a mental **image** of the objective environment. Thus, information signals are filtered through perception, then further filtered through the cognitive representation given to these in relation to previous cognitive structures in the brain, in the manner suggested in Figure 3.2. Thus, people respond not directly to their real environment, but to their mental image of it, and as a result, the location of human activities and the spatial pattern of their movements will be the outcomes of their perceived and cognitive structuring of their environment.

It is important to realise that all experiences with elements of environments external to the individual take place within a framework of space and time. Amadeo and Golledge (1975: 382) stress that the cognitive processes (such as perceiving, learning, formation of attitudes, etc.) operate to produce in people an individual spatio-temporal awareness or knowing about environments. Learning affects the completeness with which some things will be perceived and understood by individuals, and their attitude towards them helps determine their clarity and relevance to a person. Thus:

"the image of say, an urban environment, or of a shopping center, or of a hazard, is the product of both the immediate sensation experienced when confronted by an object and the memory of past experiences with the same or similar objects." (Amadeo and Golledge, 1975: 382)

Different people may thus give different interpretations to the same spatial structures and phenomena, which take on individual meanings. We may postulate that individuals impose a mental ordering on environmental information in order to provide identity, location and orientation for the elements perceived in the objective model, but it is the variations in the accuracy of these cognitive orderings that will furnish some explanation of the variations evident in the behaviour of different people in the same environment.

3.3 FACTORS INFLUENCING THE NATURE AND STRUCTURE OF THE PERCEIVED ENVIRONMENT

The roots of the concept of perception lie firmly in the realm of psychology, and within that discipline there are a range of interpretations given to this sensory process.

3.3.1 The Functionalist Approach
One school regards perception in functional terms, arguing that perception serves a function for individuals for converting information about what is "out there" into meaningful terms. It thus serves as a guide to action. This **functional** view includes the idea that perception is a matter of identifying something in the environment and anticipating its properties. The identification places phenomena into some category of equivalent objects, and by implication distinguishes it from other categories. The criteria used in identification may be single or multiple in nature.

3.3.2 Perception as an Encoding Process
An alternate viewpoint regards perception as an **encoding process**. It has been argued that the environment may be regarded as a mass of "to whom it may concern" messages. In this case, perception is a process by which we select those messages that are of concern to us. In other words, we use perception to encode input in the environment - we see a building and encode it as a house, or perhaps we see people acting boisterously and encode it as a riot. In this situation it is argued that through a vast amount of recurrent experience we build up sets of concepts that are like **templates**. Perceptual input is then compared to the set of templates stored in the mind. If the input fails to match a conceptual template or pattern, then it is compared with another and another until finally one is found that it matches sufficiently well to aid in categorisation. Input is assimilated in terms of this particular template and a bit of information is thus encoded in the brain. In selecting the appropriate templates for the pattern matching process, there is a preliminary sorting activity which eliminates many of the potentially irrelevant templates and concentrates on the few that are thought to be most suitable in helping with the current task. In artificial intelligence terms, this process relies on activation spread processes and the search for a potential pattern matching is undertaken via a complex hierarchically

organised network of encoded information.

Regarding this notion of perception as an encoding process, we would argue that the amount of information we are capable of encoding depends on the extent to which the concepts or categories with which we are familiar are elaborated and differentiated sufficiently one from another. While we may have difficulty distinguishing between a series of circles of approximately the same size or approximately the same shade of colour, we would not have the same degree of difficulty in differentiating between different parts of our general external environment. Critical components of the environment such as the distinction between large and small buildings, between commercial and non-commercial areas, between built up and non-built up areas, and so on appear to be readily perceived. Of course the templates used under these circumstances for the pattern matching process are relatively gross. It would be much more difficult to distinguish between every house on the basis of its size, age, value, colour, location, and other perceptual characteristics, although it is quite possible that, given a particular experimental context, such distinctions may be achieved. It is obviously easier, depending on cultural circumstances, to distinguish houses from factories, homes from parks, factories from schools, or houses from churches.

As we increase the scale at which information is collected for encoding purposes, there appears to be an increase in the tendency for selectivity to take place. Abstraction from reality becomes another common process, and incompleteness and generalisation processes also occur. In many cases, the accumulation of information consists of adding finer and finer detail to our initial gross template such that a more comprehensive picture of the attributes and dimensions of an external area is compiled.

3.3.3 The Concept of Scale in Perception

It is sometimes useful to study environmental perception according to the scale at which it is undertaken. This **scale** ranges from the most elementary level, the personal bubble, to perception of characteristics and features of units such as national groupings. Much recent work, for example, has been concerned with perception in unusual environments such as in space capsules. These artificial environments are precisely designed to fit the human physical form and its needs, with the aim of keeping stress at a minimum. Some of the most widely publicised and significant research in space perception today focuses on the perceptions of and reactions to environmental extremes. Thus, conditions of stress, conflict, crowding or abnormal cramping, are becoming more and more the norm in terms of research into the perception and use of space.

3.3.4 Perceptual Thresholds

When dealing with perception, one most frequently focuses on the visual senses. Regardless of which of the senses are the focus of attention, it is recognised that each has a minimum of sense organ stimulation that is necessary before sensory experiences are evoked - i.e., a **perceptual threshold** exists. Factors influencing the threshold level in any particular sensory situation include not only the physiological receptor limits, but also constraints imposed by social, economic, cultural, nationalistic, or other sets of factors. For example, when do we perceive something to be dilapidated?

When is something too far away? When do we perceive an area as a ghetto? When do we consider an environmental disturbance to be a hazard?

To answer the when, why, and how of these questions, it is necessary to incorporate the notion of a perceptual threshold. It is accepted that thresholds may vary between individuals, or may vary consistently across a broad class of individuals. Similarly, perceptual thresholds may be consistent across individuals at the same location.

A significant part of the discussion that follows, therefore, focuses on the effect that our position in both the physical and human environments has on the degree to which environmental stimuli impinge on our senses and are classified in various event categories.

3.3.5 Perception and the World of Identifiable Things
Perception assumes considerable importance to the geographer if we accept the argument that individuals are concerned with constructing a **perceived world** while maintaining, as far as possible, stability, endurance, and consistency of the images they develop. This argument suggests that there is an attempt to overlook some of the variableness of objective reality and to systematise knowledge of variableness along the line of greatest invariability.

In another context, it is argued that the man made environment is the spatial manifestation of human decision making, and that many of these decisions are related to the way in which we perceive space, evaluate elements of space, and image the potential use of it.

For example, considerable furore arose in the United States in the 1980s over the substantial differences in the way that environmental resources were perceived by Secretary of Interior, James Watt, on the one hand, and large segments of environmentally concerned individuals on the other hand. Obviously, the conflict over resource development and natural environmental preservation existed well before this particular controversy, but it did exemplify the degree to which conflict solutions may arise as perceptions of the worth of various segments of objective reality differ.

In general, it appears that any order retained in the perception of spatial reality is the result of perceiving enduring objects or the result of enduring socio-cultural interpretations or constraints. Perception, then, can be regarded as helping to build a world of identifiable things. Were the individual not sensitive and responsive to environment, he or she would be unable to satisfy needs, communicate with others, or derive pleasure from his or her surroundings.

3.3.6 Perceptual Constancy
When one considers the very complex problem of individual differences and also the complexity of objective reality, one cannot help but wonder about how we can obtain perceptual consistency across large groups of people. It is a fact, however, that the complex real world is handled by people with limited capacity for information storage, manipulation, and retrieval. It is also obvious that each individual must make certain simplifications and adjustments in his/her perceptions of the real world in accordance with needs and experiences. These simplifications and adjustments are a direct result of the way that reality is conceptualised.

There is no simple, unique one-to-one correspondence between a stimulus when presented to an individual and a stimulus perceived by an individual. But, the same stimulus presented to a large number of individuals will result in a similar type of perception across that group. For example, in many cases adults of similar social class and status perceive much the same things because their perceptions are constrained in similar ways by social mores. A more complete discussion of the nature of external constraints will be given in a later chapter.

Perception is thus a creation of the observer. The observer gives what is seen characteristics such as size shape, and position in accordance with information supplied to the senses. Perception can be thus seen as a critical component of the development of cognitive structure. We also see that perceptual characteristics are allocated to stimuli based in part on past experiences with the stimuli that help determine the known attribute dimensions.

3.3.7 Perceptual Focusing or Attention

Perhaps the most obvious factor influencing a perception is **attention**. This is sometimes called **perceptual focusing**.

At any given time, there are numerous potential stimuli impinging on our senses: all parts of the environment external to mind can potentially act in this way. We do not react equally to all stimuli: rather, we tend to focus on a few stimuli that are found relevant in a specific purposeful context. At any particular point in time, and at any given place for any individual, there is competition amongst stimuli for attention. Selecting one or more stimuli from the mass that are available represents the resolution of a form of conflict. The form of the conflict is to discriminate amongst the stimuli being presented and hopefully select those that are the most relevant and most significant in any given situation.

Some of the critical factors involved in the resolution of this conflict include the size, intensity, repetition, and clarity of any given stimulus. Sometimes the attention-getting qualities of stimuli are dependent on the context or situation in which they are presented. For example, a green lawn would stand out to a much greater degree in a semi-arid or desert area than in parts of Sussex or Iowa. Stimuli that stand out from the general contextual background appear to be perceived more clearly than those that merge with the background. Stimuli that are unique or rare in an environment appear to have more attention-getting qualities than those that are common in the environment - the maxim "one can't see the forest for the trees" is a good example of this problem.

3.3.8 Momentary Interest

Another factor influencing the attention-getting qualities of a perceived object includes the **momentary interest** or purpose of a potential perceiver. For example, a mechanic who specialises in transmission problems may be able to pick out the sounds of transmission trouble in the midst of a confusion of other mechanical and human noises. This is a result of an ability to focus on a particular type of noise even in a situation where the extraneous "white" noise accompanying the presentation of the stimuli is quite acute.

3.3.9 Preparatory Sets
"Preparatory sets" comprise a further influence on perception. Here, anticipatory changes take place prior to the presentation of a stimulus and influence the ways things are perceived. In other words, the preparatory sets influence preconceptions of a given stimulus.

For example, we all have ideas of what a ghetto looks like even if we have never actually experienced such a thing. Our preconceptions, then, influence the type of characteristics that we expect of a stimulus such as this and in turn, may influence the degree to which we characterise a given situation as ghetto-like. Thus, many people would reject the possibility of living in a certain place because they associate with it the undesirable characteristics of a ghetto-like existence - even if they never have the opportunity to confirm these preconceptions. Similarly, shopping behaviour is frequently a result of the preparatory information sets that people have about places. These sets are a major reason why advertising is such a significant factor in selling goods, locations, and store images. The same factor appears to be of some significance in the process of residential site selection. In that context, it is frequently incorporated in the notion of levels of expectation. These levels of expectation about a given house type or potential living environment appear to have a major influence on search patterns and the eventual choice of sites. Of course, search activity itself may be undertaken, if guided by an interested third party (such as an estate agent) in order to overcome sets of preconceptions and to assist in the site selection process.

3.3.10 Individual Needs and Values
Perception is also regarded as a function of the **needs** and **values** of individuals.

Social values may accrue to objects or places in an objective environment and, as such, may influence the probability of a stimulus passing a perceptual threshold. For example, it has been shown that poorer children overestimated the size of coins that were presented as stimuli, while children from richer families were able to estimate coin sizes much more accurately. Deprivation, in this case, appears to have influenced the nature of a perceptual image. It is often argued that it is better to own the poorest house in a rich area than to own the richest house in a poor area. In both cases, the attributes of the area imputed to the house in question and may inflate or deflate, respectively, its value.

3.3.11 Cultural Values
When individual differences are manifested in human behaviour and are not assignable to structural causes, the question arises as to whether and to what extent the differences are assignable to **cultural values** and to the nature of social interaction. This factor appears of some importance in determining perceptual thresholds. It is readily accepted that physiological needs, and conditioning, along with other motivational forces, influence what may be perceived. Personal beliefs, social values, and other social connotations also appear to influence the attributes of what is perceived. Working in combination, these factors influence perceptual thresholds, or at times, determine the extent to which parts of an existing knowledge structure are retained, modified, or deleted.

3.3.12 Ecological and Anthropocentric Constraints

It is sometimes argued that one can classify the relevant attributes of a given stimulus into sets that are **ecologically constrained** and those that are **anthropocentrically constrained**.

Ecological factors include things such as the dominance of the perceptual form (e.g., visible dominance), clarity or degree of ambiguity, and simplicity of structure. Each of these factors are inherent in stimulus objects and their general environmental context.

Perhaps equally important, however, is the anthropocentric dimension which includes factors such as frequency of exposure to a given stimulus, the source of information about the stimulus, its relevance to the activity space of the perceiver, its position in the general knowledge structure of the perceiver, and its socio-cultural importance.

3.3.13 Location and Orientation of Individuals

The **location** and **orientation** of individuals, as well as the clarity of environmental phenomena, will affect the level of awareness we have of objects, places and events.

We have seen that people are selective in constructing their images of the environment. It is important that these images have stability, endurance, and consistency, because humans respond to environments to satisfy their needs, communicate with their fellows, and utilise their surroundings.

Two alternative approaches have been suggested concerning how man stores the information he perceives from his environment and the accuracy with which environmental elements are positioned in the cognitive representations of a large scale environment such as a city.

The first approach suggests that man gives elements in space **co-ordinate locations** on a large mental map, and additions to the cognitive structure get allocated their position, size, shape, and so on, with respect to an existing structure. Thus, the accuracy of the positioning of new elements will depend on the accuracy of the positioning of existing elements in this structure. Also, these new structural elements will have their attributes specified with respect to surrounding attributes within the structure - that is, they will be imputed to be larger than, smaller than, closer to, more distant from adjacent elements rather than being judged purely on their own.

The second approach argues that the building of a perceptual image of a large scale environment is tied closely to the determination of a series of **orientation nodes** which specify position accurately for a selected few elements, and that these provide a skeleton for large perceptual structures. Orientation nodes will be places such as home, work, shopping centres, and so on. Other elements in the cognitive field are then located with respect to these orientation nodes rather than with respect to surrounding elements. As direction varies from these nodes, various types of perceptual inefficiencies will emerge and will result in disparity of position between the objective and cognitive world. Such disparities should be least marked in the immediate vicinity of these orientation nodes.

Inherent in the above are a number of very specific spatial properties, such as locational constancy, proximity, similarity, position, continuity and closure.

"The degree to which each of the above elements is recognised and utilised by individuals will determine the accuracy and consistency with which an image is formed on successive trials. If information of any sort is given to an individual (or is obtained by him) which affects his perception of proximity, position, similarity, and continuity, or destroys or assists his desire for closure, then the resulting perceptual image changes and consequent spatial behaviour might change." (Amadeo and Golledge, 1975: 384)

3.3.14 Summary

If one were to stop and look around and ask the question "What do I see?", the answer is likely to be very complex and consist of a collection of people, events and things.

With perceptual focusing, one may pick out specific things instead of making a general statement such as the one above. In addition to selecting specific things, one might cite some of their individual characteristics or sensory qualities. We may see the green trees, the snowy road, or the ugly building rather than the greenness, the snowiness, or the ugliness of the entire scene. In making such an analysis, we record a perceptual experience of segments of the environment. Each experience focuses on parts or sometimes whole patterns of things and recognition of the interrelationships of parts and wholes helps to build the world of identifiable things.

After perceiving something, one may remove oneself from the perceptual field but still remember or think of the things perceived in their original places and context. The extent to which our recall of the initial stimulus situation reflects its true structure will, in turn, depend on our ability to extract critical elements of the perceived scene, and encode, store, and recall them in an appropriate and efficient manner.

On a superficial basis, we may be perceiving primarily the physical structure and be unable to determine the hidden structural dimensions of a scene - for example, the underlying socioeconomic structure, ethnic or other relations, and the interactions and activities that take place within that scene and give prominence and recognition to individual scene elements.

Of course, the way in which we perceive a situation may influence the way we react to it. Assume that we are standing on a busy street waiting for a gap in the line of traffic to occur so we can cross the street. The size of the gap judged to be sufficient to allow the street crossing to take place can vary with the intensity of traffic on the road. On a very busy street, a small gap may be perceived as adequate enough for a crossing to take place. On a street not so busy, a perception of the frequency of cars passing and their rate of progress may be such as to substantially change the size of a traffic gap imaged as being necessary before a crossing attempt.

In general, if we perceive a structure to be complex, it is possible that our behaviour, with respect to that structure, may also be complex; similarly, the perception of simplicity in a structure may influence the type of reactions toward it. An individual who daily experiences the complexity of life in the downtown area of a large metropolis may become so familiar with those activities that it appears to be quite uncomplicated. The newcomer to the same place, on the other hand, will be faced with the same spatial structure but may regard it as so complex an environment as to be almost impossible to negotiate.

Thus, if we accept the fact that perception is an important factor likely to influence behaviour, then we must pay attention to it, just as we would pay attention to any of the structural properties of a situation in which an explainable behaviour is undertaken.

3.4 ATTITUDES

Regardless of the exact definition chosen, it appears that perception involves an interaction or transaction between an individual and an environment. The individual receives visual, auditory, tactile, or other information from an external environment and codes, records, and uses this information to constrain or modify potential behaviours. While in the classic sense perceptions are regarded as flexible and transitory phenomena which occur only in the presence of the stimulus, Downs (1981) has pointed out that in the discipline of geography the concept has been interpreted in a broader context with a distinct evaluative component. In many cases, the term **perception** has been confused with the concept of **attitude**, which is seen to be a relatively permanent structure which may hold in the absence of any particular stimulus. Attitude, therefore, can be regarded as a **learned predisposition** to respond to a situation in a consistent way. In the case of much of geographic literature on "environmental perception", the concept of perception is interpreted in terms of this learned predisposition to respond.

3.4.1 Attitude and Uncertainty
We suggested in Chapter 1 that it is generally accepted that man makes his decisions in relatively uncertain environments. This uncertainty occurs because as a decision-maker, man has incomplete objective knowledge about the various environments in which he exists, so that decisions are made in an atmosphere of conjecture about the actions that, say, his competitors will take in a market situation. Man is thus faced with choosing between the alternatives of which he is aware, about which he has imperfect knowledge, and in the context of uncertainty as to what decisions other people are making that may affect him. However, he makes his choice or decision with an expectation as to what the outcome is likely to be. Thus, the attitude of the decision maker is a key variable influencing this decision process. The concept of attitude is important because it brings together the internal mental life of man (his cognition, motivations and emotions) and his overt behavioural responses; within one framework (Gold, 1980: 23).

The concept of attitude and the nature of attitude formation have received relatively little attention by geographers concerned with investigating human spatial behaviour. There were a number of references to attitude formation as a causal factor in the analysis of the economic behaviour of man in his location decisions in the 1960s. For example, in 1962, Isard and Dacey argued that as an individual's attitude toward his role in an economic system changed from one of optimising to satisficing, then he would adopt different strategies in coping with his environment. Attitudinal information was thus incorporated into models using the theory of games by Isard and Dacey in the context of investigating new approaches to central place theory and location theory; by Gould in his analysis of decision making in uncertain environments; and by various researchers including Hagerstrand, in the development of simulation studies in the field of diffusion of innovations.

An alternative approach emerged in the work of Golledge (1970) and Kotler (1965), who examined attitudes from a psychological and marketing view. If, for example, a producer regards his consumers as **Marshallian** (economically rational) men that are price conscious, then he will seek locations that will allow him to compete favourably in a competitive market, and the producer will manipulate price to penetrate adjacent market areas. However, if the producer regards his consumers as creatures of habit, then he may accept a less than economically optimal location, attract spatially rational customers, and not engage formally in aggressive marketing policies. Thus, the attitude producers adopt toward consumers will influence their choice of business locations and will affect any equilibrium pattern of producers that may emerge in a spatial system. Kotler (1965) similarly suggested that the attitude of consumers toward producers would directly influence their behaviour. In contrast, **Pavlovian** consumers will respond immediately to the introduction of a stimulus set, such as an exciting advertisement or a pressure salesman, and the behaviours of such consumers in space may become distorted from the patterns predicted by the rational economic man models. Yet different behaviour could be expected from a Veblenian consumer who will be very much influenced by his peer group, thus he will tend to patronise those outlets used by his peers, even though this strategy may produce some unusual spatial patterns of behaviour.

These types of behaviours may be seen as reflecting man's attitude toward a given situation. Kemeny and Thompson (1957:284) argued that man's attitude toward **risk-taking** under uncertain conditions can explain in large part his behavioural outcomes. Diagrammatic representations of various individual utility functions according to the attitude of the individual toward taking risks are shown in Figure 3.3. These are in the form of a function between perceived value and monetary pay-off. The differences between the individuals is clearly evident. For example, the reckless person (A) exaggerates gains and discounts losses, whereas the cautious person (B) tries to avoid large losses and tends to disparage and discount large gains as he faces further problems of making decisions for the future. The socio-economic status of a person is seen to influence attitude to risk, with the poor person (C) exaggerating both wins and losses, while the rich person (D) underestimates large gains and losses. The actual utility function of people is thus seen to reflect their attitudes to risk-taking and their perception of value or utility. In reality, man is likely to be a complex mixture of these simple extreme types of decision makers, and a common utility function is likely to incorporate elements of all the above, as demonstrated by person (E). The important point is that attitudes of individuals to specific spatial stimuli in choice behaviour situations are an important element in explaining the behavioural response and strategy thus adopted in coping with uncertainty, and attitudes are important in furnishing explanations of difficult-to-explain spatial behaviours in terms of the more deterministic models that geographers have used.

Figure 3.3

Individual Utility Functions and Attitudes to Risk-Taking

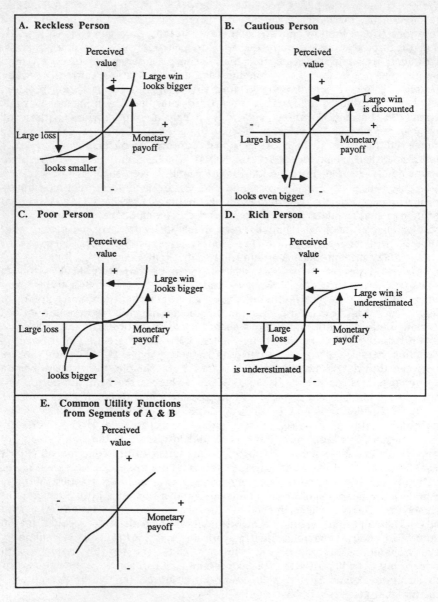

Source: After Kemeny & Thompson, 1957:284

48

3.4.2 The Nature of Attitudes and Attitude Formation

The concept of attitude is a complex one and there is considerable dispute over its definition. One widely accepted definition is:

> "Attitude is a learned predisposition to respond in a consistently favourable or unfavourable manner with respect to a given object, person or spatial environment." (after Fishbein and Aizen, 1975)

As such, **attitude** contains the notion that it is learned, that it predisposes to action, and that it is relatively invariant over time. Fishbein formalised this traditional view of attitudes specifically as having three components

    (a) **Cognitive** – involving perceiving, knowing and thinking a processes by which the individual knows his environment

    (b) **Affective** – involving his feelings and emotions about his environment, motivated by desires and values that are embodied in his image of his environment

    (c) **Conative** – involving acting, doing, striving and thus having an effect on the environment in response to (a) and (b). (This may also be termed a **behavioural** component of attitude.)

Figure 3.4 gives such a view of attitude components as intervening variables between stimuli and behaviour.

It is important to realise the limitations of this traditional view of attitude. In particular, the three components should be seen to interact. Thus, a person's feelings toward an environment will be determined, at least in part, by what he knows about it. Learning also plays a role, as all the components of attitude may change with experience. However, the view is useful, as it allows us to see what aspects of some total attitude we may be measuring at a given time in a particular situation. Furthermore, it points to possible sources of error if one is attempting to predict subsequent behaviour of persons exposed to certain situations. The view is generic, as it takes attitude to include a range of overlapping concepts – beliefs, biases, doctrines, faiths, ideologies, judgments, opinions, stereotypes, values, and so on.

Attitudes are evolutionary through the **learning process**, but it has been suggested that they are learned mostly in childhood and that once formed they are pervasive, and work cited by Altman (1975) demonstrates that attitudes can withstand extensive and concerted attempts to change them, as has been discovered in military propaganda and mass communication studies. O'Riordan (1973) suggests that even if attitudes are changed, there is not necessarily going to follow a change in behaviour because there is a gap between stated attitudes and actual behaviour. This is an interesting proposition, as it has important implications for the media, advertisers, the military, and governments, all of which tend to believe that attitude can be modified. It is, then, not surprising that attitudes and attitude formation is an area of considerable concentration of research in psychology.

Figure 3.4

The Three Components of Attitude

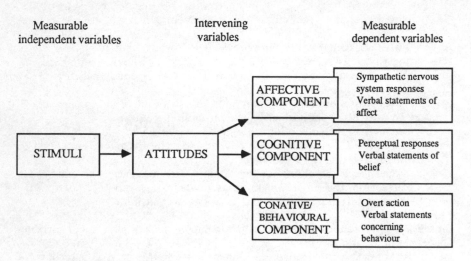

Source: After Triandis, 1971

3.4.3 Attitudes, Values and Stereotypes

Of the concepts that relate to the above generic view of attitudes, values and stereotypes are particularly important.

Values may be regarded as enduring beliefs that specific modes of conduct or specific outcomes are either personally or socially preferable to alternatives.

Stereotypes are sets of beliefs about something (people, places, events, objects, etc.) that contain no more than a "grain of truth", but which are the basis of opinions about them and are used to justify or rationalise our conduct toward that thing (Belcher, 1973).

Thus, values and stereotypes, as types of attitudes, may be seen to act as mechanisms whereby people erroneously come to terms with their complex environments. Through values and stereotypes we arrange information into categories and the individual items are assumed to have the same attributes of the category as a whole. For example, we ascribe certain values to areas that look basically the same, such as run-down housing areas being thought of as slums and rather unsavoury places to linger within. This is important in understanding people's attitudes to environmental phenomena, for, as Gold (1980:24) states:

"once a person can identify the category to which an entity belongs, he then has the basis for rapidly assimilating new information and rapidly reaching decisions about behaviour."

50

3.4.4 Attitudes, Motivation and Emotions

It is also useful to consider attitudes, and particularly their connotative component, to be linked to motivation and emotions, as these are central in man-environment interaction because our behaviour is said to be goal-oriented.

Motivation can be thought of as the force leading man to seek specific goals in order to satisfy his needs, and in doing so he will be motivated to pursue a specific strategy and take certain actions. The strength of motivation behind an act will depend on the level of need to attain that act. Thus, the notion of need is an important one and it has attracted considerable attention among social scientists. Evans (1976) suggested that man is motivated by a desire to overcome the problems posed and stresses imposed by his environment in order to reduce uncertainty and tension, whereas Wohlwill (1968) suggested that man desires novelty, excitement and stimulation and seeks to increase the level of tension in the environment.

Man has different **types of needs**, ranging from survival-type needs (for shelter, food, clothing) that must be satisfied to sustain life, to social and personal-type needs to do with acceptance and rejection and self actualisation that are not necessary to sustain life in a physical sense, but which can create mental anguish if they are unfulfilled. Maslow (1954) proposed a hierarchy of needs, with basic (survival-type) needs having to be satisfied before higher needs were sought by man. In this context, the link between needs and motivation is self-evident. But, there is considerable debate over whether man's needs are genetically determined or environmentally acquired through learning.

Linked to motivation is emotion which encompasses a wide range of both physiological and mental conditions. **Emotions** are a state of excitement that is characterised by strong feeling and usually definitive behaviour. Thus, emotion relates strongly to the affective component of attitude. Mehrabian and Russell (1974:8) have postulated the link between environment and behaviour through emotion, in which personality variables, combined with perceptions of environmental stimuli, arouse primary emotional responses, such as pleasure, arousal and dominance, leading to a behavioural response which may include physical action, affiliation and expression of preferences. These affective responses by people to their environment have been widely investigated in the context of design characteristics of the built environment and their impacts on human behaviour.

Chapter Four

SPATIAL COGNITION

4.1 THE NATURE OF SPATIAL COGNITION

In the domain of spatial cognition there has been a constant integration of **cognitive** and **developmental** approaches.   Much of the work in spatial cognition is based on the landmark paper by Tolman (1948), titled "Cognitive maps in rats and men," which explained the development of such a cognitive map whereby information was selectively extracted from the environment to build up a field map (mental map).

The psychologists Piaget and Inhelder (1967), in taking a somewhat different view, proposed that images developed with the intellectual development of the child, suggesting that as the child grows older, the view of space will be quantitatively different from when he was younger, thus proposing that spatial learning involves more than acquiring information, per se. The dominant processes suggested as being key elements of the process of acquiring spatial knowledge are those of accommodation and assimilation (Figure 4.1).

Figure 4.1

Piaget's Theory of Development of Spatial Schemata

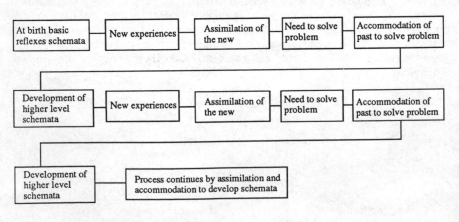

Source: After Kaluger and Kaluger, 1974:75

52

In this case, the critical factor is the emergence of the ability to organise information. Structural knowledge builds on existing cognitive structures, and is thus based on experiences. With development the child is seen to replace simple structures with increasingly complex ones.

Developmentalists argue that the stage of perceiving is important in determining the level of information that is absorbed and the structuring of the resulting cognitive image. This approach implies that persons who are more or less familiar with a given stimulus situation are able to construct more or less accurate images of that situation.

In the developmental context, several stages of perceiving can be identified:

(a) The first stage is one of **vague awareness**, when the perceiver is aware that something is impinging on the senses and that the sensory input appears to be coming from specific segments of the environment. At this stage, the geographer might develop expectations that the initial sensory input may relate to physical structure, location, or potential use of perceived objects.

(b) At the second stage of this developmental process, spatial characteristics are added to the perceptual set. Thus, the object is given an **existence** or **location** in space and time and is fitted into a class or category of objects which may have similar spatial characteristics. At this stage, the beginnings of differentiation among objects on the basis of spatial characteristics begins.

(c) A third stage involves **recognising** the relevant parts of the perceptual objects and being able to specify these components. Such components, or attributes, become differentiating characteristics used to distinguish a given object from others in its class. Thus, identity, size, condition, colour, function, and so on, are allocated to a stimulus object.

(d) A fourth stage is one of identification, or more realistically, the **attachment of meaning** to the stimulus object. The meaning and significance of an object apparently influences its durability and usefulness to an observer. Once an object becomes an identifiable entity, it may thereafter occupy a regular niche in the cognitive structure of an individual. It, along with other members of the set, can be used as a reference point against which new stimuli are matched.

Through much of the early work on cognitive representation of environment, the outcome of this process was known as the **image** (Lynch, 1960; Boulding, 1956). In this chapter we first develop the context of image at a variety of levels of scale, ranging from cities to neighbourhoods, then examine in more detail the nature and process of cognitive mapping.

4.2 METHODS FOR REPRESENTING ENVIRONMENTAL IMAGES

The first assumption required prior to any discussion of representing and measuring **images** is that information extracted from large scale external environments exists in an undetermined **psychological space**. This is the space in which characteristics, meanings, and configurational relations about elements in the world are held as mental constructs. A second assumption is simply that individuals must have **internal knowledge** about external environments in order to exist in them. A third assumption is that internal representations will be part **idiosyncratic** and part **common** in structure (i.e., people in general will know the difference between a street and a stream, the significance of a traffic light, and the difference between privately and publicly owned transportation systems).

Attempts to recover images of the spatial environment have taken forms ranging from written, verbal, and pictoral reports to second and third stage inferences made as a result of observing human behaviour. Studies of environmental image in the social sciences have frequently relied on survey research such as evaluative or attitudinal questionnaires, obervational methods, content and contextual analysis of written or verbal descriptions, analysis of personal constructs, and so on. The task is made more difficult if one conceives of images as possessing designative, appraisive, prescriptive, and evaluative components. Obviously, if we had to penetrate the unique experience barrier and to discover first the idiosyncratic general characteristics of image that are known by individuals, identify what structures they impose on environment, and interpret the meanings and significances of things which are retained in the image, we must have methodologies appropriate for extracting, representing, and interpreting this information.

Within geography, the most common problem concerning the measurement of representation of image relates to ignoring the different stages of development of individuals. Failure to match the skills required for representational form with the skills existing in a subject population has resulted in attempts to impute fully metric information (e.g., Euclidean distance concepts) to representational forms when subjects are known to have, at best, topological representational capabilities. Moore (1976) summarises the various levels of development, spatial organisation, and reference system, that are appropriate at different age levels. This schema, based on Piaget's developmental theories, provides a standard reference point, allowing a researcher to match required methodological skills with those likely to exist at each stage of development.

As indicated in Table 4.1, Golledge (1976) has categorised methods for extracting and representing imagery into the following classes:

(a) **experimenter observation** in naturalistic or controlled situations (Lynch 1960; Ladd 1970; R. Kaplan 1976; Ittelson 1951; Acredolo 1976; Hart 1974)

(b) **historical reconstructions** (Lowenthal 1961; Bowden 1975; Tuan 1976)

(c) **analysis of external representations** (Appleyard 1969; Craik 1970; Shemyakin 1962; Zannaras 1973)

(d) **indirect judgmental task** (Kelly 1955; Downs 1969; Harrison and Sarre 1976; Golledge, et al. 1975; Saarinen 1973).

The above conceptualisation includes a range of external representational formats, such as verbal reports, sketch maps, tables, profiles, word lists, analog models, slides, novels, poems, paintings, diaries, interviews, protocols, toy play, proximity judgments, scalings, and creative stories or writings.

Table 4.1 (continued)   Methods for Extracting Environmental Cognition Information

Method	Procedure	Subject Skill	External Representational Form	Example
	Subjects draw sketches or sketch maps representing environments	Affective Graphic Relational	Pictoral sketches Sketch maps Quantitative and Structural analyses	Lynch (1960) Shemyakin (1962) Stea (1969d) Appleyard (1970b) Ladd (1970 Moore (1973b) Wood (1973a)
	Subjects arrange toys or make models representing environments	Affective Cognitive Concrete Motoric Relational	Models Arrangements of toys	Piaget et al. (1960) Blaut and Stea (1969) Mark and Silverman (1971) Stea (1973) Hart (1974) Stea (1976)
	Subjects show existence, location, proximity, or other spatial relations of environmental elements; use of symbols to represent such elements	Cognitive Graphic Abstract Relational	Base maps with overlays Notation systems	Lynch (1960) Thiel (1961) Appleyard (1969a) Wood and Beck (1976)
	Subjects are asked to identify photographs, models, etc.	Affective Motoric Abstract Relational	Verbal Protocols	Piaget and Inhelder (1959) Laurendeau and Pinard (1970) Stea and Blaut (1973b) Zannaras (1973)

Table 4.1   Methods for Extracting Environmental Cognition Information

Method	Procedure	Subject Skill	External Representational Form	Example
Experimenter obervation in naturalistic or controlled situations	Experimenter observes of tracks movements through actual environments (e.g., crawl patterns, search behaviour, overt spatial activity, way-finding, etc.)	Cognitive Concrete Psychomotoric	Observations Reports Maps Tables	Lynch (1960) Marble (1967) Ladd (1970) Jones (1972) Devlin (1973) Zannaras (1973)
	Experimenter infers degrees of cognitive knowledge from behaviour in unstructured "clinical" situations	Cognitive Concrete Motoric	Charts Profiles	Werner (1948) Piaget and Inhelder (1956) Hart (1974)
	Subjects reveal environmental knowledge in the process of sorting or grouping elements of actual or simulated environments	Cognitive Abstract Relational	Lists Tables Composite maps	Downs (1970a) Wish (1972) Zannaras (1973) Golledge et al. (1975)
	Subjects adopt roles or perform acts in simulated and/or real environments	Cognitive Abstract Relational	Photographs Tables	Ittelson (1951) Milgram (1970) Saegert (1973) Acredolo (1976)
	Subjects arrange toys or objects representing environmental elements or model environments, and experimenter observes the sequence of acts in positioning elements and/or using the environment	Cognitive Concrete Motoric	Analog models	Piaget et al. (1960) Blaut and Stea (1969) Laurendeau and Pinard (1970) Mark (1972) Hart (1974)

Table 4.1 (continued)   Methods for Extracting Environmental Cognition Information

Method	Procedure	Subject Skill	External Representational Form	Example
	Subjects draw sketches or sketch maps representing environments	Affective Graphic Relational	Pictoral sketches Sketch maps Quantitative and Structural analyses	Lynch (1960) Shemyakin (1962) Stea (1969d) Appleyard (1970b) Ladd (1970 Moore (1973b) Wood (1973a)
	Subjects arrange toys or make models representing environments	Affective Cognitive Concrete Motoric Relational	Models Arrangements of toys	Piaget et al. (1960) Blaut and Stea (1969) Mark and Silverman (1971) Stea (1973) Hart (1974) Stea (1976)
	Subjects show existence, location, proximity, or other spatial relations of environmental elements; use of symbols to represent such elements	Cognitive Graphic Abstract Relational	Base maps with overlays Notation systems	Lynch (1960) Thiel (1961) Appleyard (1969a) Wood and Beck (1976)
	Subjects are asked to identify photographs, models, etc.	Affective Motoric Abstract Relational	Verbal Protocols	Piaget and Inhelder (1959) Laurendeau and Pinard (1970) Stea and Blaut (1973b) Zannaras (1973)

Table 4.1 (continued) Methods for Extracting Environmental Cognition Information

Method	Procedure	Subject Skill	External Representational Form	Example
Indirect judgmental tasks	Selection of constructs which reveal environmental information; adjective checklists, semantic differentials, repertory grid test, etc.	Cognitive Abstract Relational	Word lists Tables Graphs Grids	Kelly (1950) Downs (1973) Honikman (1976) Harrison and Sarre (1976) Golant and Burton (1976)
	Paired proximity judgments and other scaling devices that allow specification of latent structure in environmental information	Cognitive Abstract Relational	Maps Tables	Briggs (1973a) Lowrey (1973) Golledge et al. (1975) Cadwallader (1973) Golant and Burton (1976)
	Projective tests (e.g., T.A.T.)	Affective Abstract Relational	Verbal stories	Burton et al. (1969) Saarinen (1973b)

Thus, at various times individuals have been asked and have provided an impressive array of written and oral descriptions, pictures, sketches, cartographic representations, and grouped or clustered, scaled, and otherwise modified or transformed, bits of information.

One of the most widely referenced comprehensive works using a variety of the above methods was Kevin Lynch's (1960) pioneering work on the image of the city. In the next section we examine his concepts in detail and expand on them at different spatial scales.

4.3 IMAGES OF URBAN AREAS

4.3.1 The City as a Whole

Spatial components of the **city images** identified by Lynch in his book *The Image of the City* (1960) not only served to focus attention on perceptual and cognitive qualities of urban environments, but provided a conceptual framework for the discussion of the structural components of city images that still occupies a primary place in the literature on city images.

City images, or images of any given environment, can be recovered and represented in a variety of ways. In terms of the urban environment, Lynch proposed a five element classification system consisting of paths, boundaries, districts, nodes, and landmarks:

(a) **Paths** were the basic channels along which persons would occasionally or customarily move around a given environment.

(b) **Boundaries** were conceived as barriers tending to mark off or differentiate segments of space, with the barriers being more or less permeable, depending on whether they consisted of natural environmental features, (e.g., rivers, parks, freeways), or social, political, cultural features (e.g., boundaries of a gang turf, administrative boundaries, ghetto boundaries, and so on).

(c) **Districts** were the main areal component of the urban image and were defined as recognisable areas contained within sets of well-defined edges. Districts were generally larger than neighbourhoods and often were allocated an official or unofficial descriptive title such that they were readily recognisable by the local population and by many others living outside their boundaries.

(d) **Nodes** were defined as strategic spots which acted as foci for human behavioural activity. They may be things such as bus stops, outdoor luncheon or recreational areas, critical street corners, or specific buildings which had well known functions associated with them.

(e) **Landmarks** were visibly dominant and easily identifiable elements of the landscape and could be drawn from the natural, built, or cultural environments (e.g., an overlook, a major distinctive building, a place of historical significance, a place of religious significance, and so on).

Figure 4.2 shows the composite maps Lynch produced for Boston and Los Angeles which shows the above elements. While the initial research on city images incorporated fundamental concepts from the psychology of perception, such as figure-background, composition, clarity, singularity of form, visual dominance, perceptual closure, and so on, many of Lynch's

Figure 4.2
Los Angeles and Boston:
Compositional Sketch Maps of City Elements

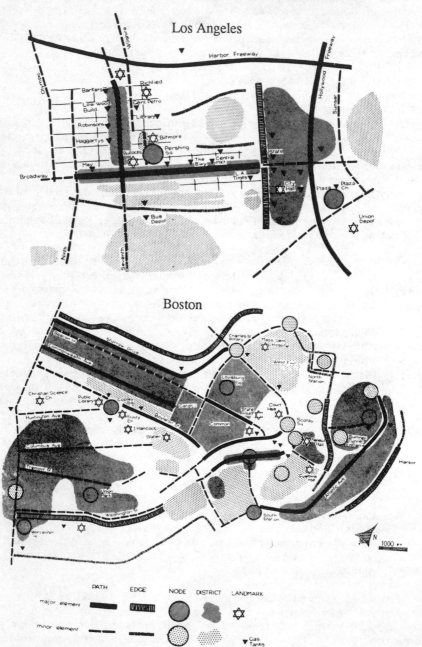

Source: After Lynch, 1960

imitators moved beyond these fundamental perceptual qualities to add the values, meaning,and significance of city elements in both a societal and a cultural sense. For example, Appleyard's (1969) research on why buildings are known included a discussion of basic characteristics such as singularity, level of visibility, community significance, and intensity, but he also emphasised societal and cultural context, historicity, and local significance as critical features of recognition. Other research focused on a search for reasons behind the departure from objective "accuracy" in city images and included things such as residential history of the respondents, levels of familiarity with places, basic elements of form, ethnic or cultural heritage or mode of travel (e.g., Maurer and Baxter, 1972; Orleans and Schmidt, 1972; Ladd, 1970; Ley, 1972). It must be remembered, however, that while the emphasis on affect and form dominated a considerable part of the research in this area, the research focused on attempts to refine modes of representing cognitive information other than via sketch maps and verbal descriptions (e.g., Golledge and Zannaras, 1973; Golledge, Rivizzigno and Spector, 1975).

The components of city structure were taken to be critical features of the urban environment by a new school of planners who were interested in the interactional relations between humans and elements in the built environment rather than the form of either the physical or built environments themselves. Their motto was "the city is the people, not the buildings"! Behind their beliefs was the argument that everyday episodic behaviours such as going to work, trips to the grocery store, giving directions to a stranger, or generally interacting with places in the environment, are, at least in part, dependent upon the characteristics and qualities of places and the connections between them that constitute part of the individual's spatial knowledge set. It was suggested that departures from optimality in a behavioural context could be accounted for by discrepancies between the information stored in the mind and the form and structure of the external world.

4.3.2 The City as a Trip
A transactionally based hypothesis concerning our knowledge of urban environments would be that one obtains knowledge about the city according to the type of interactions that one has with it. Thus, urban knowledge accumulates as a result of the various trips undertaken as part of the everyday process of living. Whereas other conceptualisations focus more on the node and landmark structure or areal pattern of urban knowledge, this conceptualisation is path based. As an example of a **path based view** of city images, we will summarise discussions of the city as a trip (Carr and Schissler, 1969).

In their study, Carr and Schissler interviewed a number of commuters, both car drivers and passengers, in the city of Boston in an attempt to identify the types of environmental cues noticed and used by individuals undertaking trips within an urban environment. In order to obtain information on the recognised and used cue structure, subjects were examined prior to the day of the field trip and asked to state their preconceptions of the trips they were to make - including regular trips undertaken by the individuals and specific tasks set them by the experimenters. In addition, subjects were laboratory tested to determine such things as the accuracy of recall and depth of memory, and the angle of eye movements. The next day, subjects were taken on a trip with a camera mounted on their head to record where they were looking, and optical devices focused on the corneas of the subjects' eyes to enable the researchers to identify the directions in which the subjects were looking at various places along the route. Thus, by establishing points of fixation and also requesting a verbal summary of what was noticed and used along the trip, the researchers attempted to define those elements of the city that were observed, recognised, and used in a trip making context.

The subjects were exposed to a variety of verbal, graphic and descriptive materials associated with the trips and films of the trip in order to provide a data bank. Data banks were then searched using content analysis to try to find those places, cues, or areas in the city that provided **anchors** for an individual's cognitive representation of the environment. The features recovered using these processes were then ranked according to the frequency with which they appeared in the subject's responses (Table 4.2).

Table 4.2

Individual Items Memory List for Drivers, Passengers and Commuters in Order of Best Remembered Item

Rank	Drivers	Passengers	Commuters
1	Mystic River Bridge	Mystic River Bridge	Mystic River Bridge
2	Toll Booth	Toll Booth	Overpass (early)
3	Overpass (late)	Prudential Building	Prudential Building
4	Sign for Haymarket	Three-Deckers: Chelsea	Bunker Hill Monument
5	Overpass (early)	Overpass (early)	State Street Bank
6	Second bridge	Bunker Hill Monument	Three-Deckers: Chelsea
7	Three-Deckers: Chelsea	Overpass (late)	Government Center
8	Billboard: John Hancock	Government Center	Custom House Tower
9	Sign for Downtown Boston	John Hancock Building	Soldier's Home
10	Sign for Charleston	Charlestown residences	Toll Booth
11		Custom House Tower	U.S.S. Constitution
12		Charles River Park Apts.	Naval Hospital
13		State Street Bank	Signs for Storrow Drive
14		Sign: Chelsea	William's School
15		North End residences	American Optical Co.
16		U.S.S. Constitution	John Hancock
17		Colored oil drums	Charles River Park Apts.
18		Billboard: John Hancock	Colored oil drums
19		Twin Tower Church	Sign: Fitzgerald Expressway
20		Billboard: Seagrams	Bradlee's Shopping Center
21		Residences on Soldier's Home hill	North Station
22			Sign for High Street
23			Sign for Dock Square
24			Sign for Chelsea
25			Grain Elevators
26			Wallpaper Factory
27			Barrell Factory
28			Cemetery

Source: After Carr & Schissler, 1969:21

Some of the results from this study focused on the difference between the number of items recorded by regular commuters, as opposed to newcomers in the area, and the number of features recorded by passengers, as opposed to drivers. For example, the average driver remembered only ten objects over a test section of four miles of road, but passengers remembered an average of twenty-one objects.

Commuters who regularly travelled the route remembered an average of twenty-eight objects. It was also found that individuals performing different functions tended to remember similar things in the same order of importance - thus the features remembered by drivers were included in the set of features remembered by the passengers, which in turn were contained within the set of features recalled by regular commuters. It appeared that familiarity with the route did change the range of things that were recorded in terms of adding more detail (and less significant features) rather than adding other major anchor points. This is indeed a critical feature, because it suggests that even newcomers to an area will focus on a fundamental set of primary cues or anchor points, which will then be commonly used to anchor cognitive maps and to provide detail in the vicinity of paths, such that expectations with respect to major decision points along the path can be defined with a great deal of reliability.

The above findings, in turn, suggest that some structural properties of a city impress themselves more on memory than do others. This appears to be the case either for casual or regular observers, and it appears likely that these points of fixation become **orientation nodes**, or focal points, in the structuring of a path dominated image of an area. Given that regular commuters observed and recalled the greatest range and variety of elements in the city, it appears that individuals learn about the environment over time and that they constantly modify their knowledge set as they travel throughout the local environment and accumulate further information. The connection of major nodes or landmarks by paths adds a critical spatial dimension, for it gives an individual an idea of spatial separation and connectivity that helps him define the concept of relative location amongst all points in the environment.

As represented in memory, and as evidenced by behaviour, the city as a trip appears to be a highly meaningful concept to all individuals. Whether it is the young child first exploring a neighbourhood, or the bored, long-time commuter, the structure, sequencing and dominance of features of the environment related to trip-making are critical in terms of specifying the spatial extent of knowledge at any given point in time. The acquisition of information as one selects and travels a subset of all possible paths in the city, helps define the concept of a node path structure which provides a basic framework for cognitive maps, as discussed later in this chapter. In short, for people to be able to relate to any given environment, they must be able to "read" it, or comprehend what is there. Apparently, this is what all individuals must do in their day-by-day interactions with the external environment. This helps them build coherent knowledge structures that, in turn, allow them to quickly store and access the information needed to operate on a day-by-day basis with a minimum amount of confusion and a minimum amount of effort. The path, or network, structure used in episodic activities thus becomes a critical feature of an image of a spatial environment.

4.3.3 The Neighbourhood

Here we concentrate on the imaging of **micro** spaces, particularly small scale social areas. The relationship between the cognitive processes and small local socio-cultural areas, such as **neighbourhoods**, has been summarised by Vernon (1962) as follows:

> "when we learn to find our way about a neighbourhood, we develop a system of images and ideas about the relative position and distance in roads, houses, and natural features. For instance, we know that when we come to such-and-such crossroads, we must turn right and proceed until we reach a certain house (which we image) and then branch left, and so on. Most people can acquire such patterns of images and ideas; and they also learn to relate them to plans and maps which symbolise those topological relationships."

Vernon's notions of the development of systems of images with specific geometrical or topological components has, as we have previously seen, been reflected in urban research literature such as that produced by Lynch (1960), Appleyard (1969), and so on. Approaching the study of urban images from an anthropological viewpoint, Gulick (1966) argued that imageability is determined by the beholder's perception of the visible form of an object, combined with consciousness of some social or behavioural significance which is associated with it. In a study of Tripoli, Lebanon, he found that the values of the Lebanese society and the social significance attached to the various districts of Tripoli greatly influenced their images of those districts. He concluded that urban imageability is thus a product of the perception of the visual form and of the conception of social significance. He did, however, warn that a purely visual approach to the elements of imageability cannot give a total answer to the notion of urban image, especially when the critical elements are defined purely by social and behavioural criteria.

In specific work relating to the imageability of areas defined as neighbourhoods, Bracey (1964), Lee (1964), and Michelson (1968), have emphasised specific subsets of residential characteristics in their studies of perceived neighbourhood space.

The neighbourhood is a form of spatial organisation and, as such, constitutes a valid concept for geographical research. Essentially, a neighbourhood is defined as a place where "neighbours" live, and combines both social and physical space. Traditional planning concepts of the neighbourhood vary from area to area and culture to culture. For example, Lee defines a neighbourhood using an areal concept (75 acres) in Cambridge, England. A more general planning concept for neighbourhoods in the US has focused on size, with about 10,000 people considered as optimum. Obviously, a neighbourhood in an affluent suburban area can differ substantially from a neighbourhood in an inner city ghetto. The older conventional mid-suburban neighbourhood may consist of multiple blocks of dwellings; the older inner city neighbourhood may focus on a single block or sections of a block; newer suburban areas may cover large tracts of residences irrespective of the area or density contained within them. A cross cultural explanation is sometimes used to account for the difference in the spatial size of neighbourhoods. This explanation relies on factors such as usual travel modes, average household density per acre, the extent of social interaction space, the degree of neighbouring activity, neighbourhood cohesiveness, ethnicity, nationalistic grouping, or cultural bonding. In general, neighbourhood studies have isolated the following dimensions:

(a) local involvement
(b) social class and ethnic or racial origins
(c) life cycle
(d) length of residence
(e) place of work.

The **local involvement** dimension focuses on three characteristics: the tendency for subjects to patronise local shops rather than those in other parts of the city; the number of friends and relatives located nearby, as opposed to in other parts of the city; and a number of affiliations with local clubs and social organisations. The neighbourhood space of any given household will vary according to the intensity of the household's local involvement. Thus, the number of friends and acquaintances a subject has in an area may influence the degree of recognition of a local area as having neighbourhood characteristics. Both perceptions of, and the attitude towards, a neighbourhood vary somewhat with **social class**. For example, Orleans and Schmidt (1972), focusing on the Los Angeles area, showed the relative poverty of the perceived size and complexity of inner city ethnic neighbourhoods compared to wealthy suburban neighbourhoods).

The concept of neighbourhood is usually defined as having two component parts. The first of these is a **physical area** that can be readily identified on a map and which has salience in terms of the environmental knowledge of any given respondent. The second component is usually called a **social neighbourhood**. This is defined by examining a range of human behaviours, spatial and otherwise, rather than determining individual interpretations of the physical limits of neighbourhood space. In the second interpretation of neighbourhood, the geographer's notion of **action space** becomes critical. Action space is generally defined as that part of the total area which an individual perceives and in which the most frequent episodic behaviours originate or take place. Although the degree of correspondence between physical and social neighbourhood space has rarely been examined, a study by Zannaras (1968) did indicate a remarkable correspondence between the two (Figure 4.3).

The general concept of neighbourhood has received a large volume of attention over the years in sciences such as sociology and anthropology. Anthropologists have at various times interpreted the neighbourhood in terms of the home range of pre-adolescent boys, as compared to the life cycle or social class definitions of the sociologists, while a combination of home range, life cycle and perceptual factors was used by Florence Ladd (1970) in her evaluation of the neighbouring characteristics and perceptual neighbourhoods of inner city black youths. Each of these approaches allows one to argue that variations in neighbourhood size depend on location of the neighbourhood, the size of the cities in which they are located, ethnicity, and cultural values. All appear to agree that neighbourhoods have definable boundaries, with the overwhelming single factor identifying boundaries being street systems. Cues that identify neighbourhoods appear to be predominantly physical (such as house types, land use change, and land use

Figure 4.3
The Social and Physical Neighbourhoods Compared

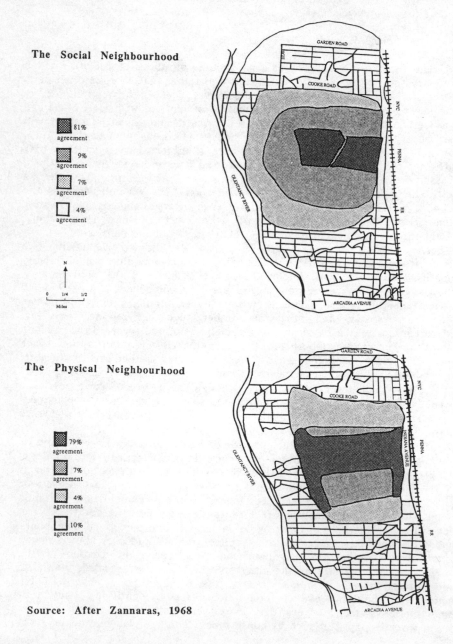

The Social Neighbourhood

81%
agreement

9%
agreement

7%
agreement

4%
agreement

The Physical Neighbourhood

79%
agreement

7%
agreement

4%
agreement

10%
agreement

Source: After Zannaras, 1968

```
┌─────────────────────────────────────────────────────────────────┐
│                         Table  4.3                                │
│                  Cues  Used  to  Identify  the  Defining          │
│                      Edges  of  the  Neighbourhood                │
├─────────────────────────────────────────────────────────────────┤
```

Physical Elements	% Respondents Citing	Number Citing
Housing Types	40.5%	161
Housing & Property Maintenance	33.4%	133
Land Use/Change in Land Use	27.9%	111
Housing Density/Lot Size	15.6%	62
Major Edges	13.3%	53
Vegetation	10.1%	40
Volume of Traffic	7.3%	29
Street Patterns	3.5%	14
Street Lighting	3.0%	12
On-Street Parking	2.0%	8
Topographic Features	1.3%	5
Utility Poles	0.3%	1
Social Elements		
Types of People	15.3%	61
Social Networks	10.8%	43
Familiarity	11.8%	47
Political Boundaries	1.8%	7

```
┌─────────────────────────────────────────────────────────────────┐
│                         Table  4.4                                │
│              Variations  in  Cues  Cited  by  Education           │
├─────────────────────────────────────────────────────────────────┤
```

	LEVEL OF EDUCATION			
Cues Cited	Elem. School	High School	4-yr College	Grad School
House Type	0.0%	37.7%	44.1%	47.9%
House Maintenance	25.0%	40.2%	28.7%	22.9%
Land Uses	0.0%	23.1%	28.0%	52.1%
Familiarity	37.5%	14.6%	8.4%	6.3%
Traffic	0.0%	5.5%	7.3%	16.6%

Source: From data collected by W. Sims in a study of neighbourhoods in Columbus, Ohio, 1975

density), but they also include social network cues (for example, a tendency to use local rather than global shops, friendship links, and patronage of local social organisations - see Table 4.3).

It is also apparent that the type and range of **cues** used to identify neighbourhoods varies by educational level (Table 4.4). For example, for those with a high level of education, housing types, land use, and traffic volumes are primary identifying characteristics. For lower levels of education, familiarity, or "a feeling of being at home", is dominant, along with household maintenance. Such a division is commonsensical. In general, less educated people tend to have lower incomes, lower mobility, and are consequently more likely to locate in areas of greater variability of housing quality, where the feeling of being part of the resident community is more a unifying factor than any external physical cue.

Attempts to recover **properties** of neighbourhoods from subjects frequently involve the process of **mapping**. For example, individuals may be given street maps and asked to indicate that area representing their neighbourhood. Alternatively, a free sketch mapping procedure may be used with a dominant node (such as the individual residence) being taken as a fixed central location. Appleyard (1969) has stressed that such sketchings or mappings of neighbourhood provide some information about topological and formal geometric properties. For example, he sees sketchings or mappings consisting of elements such as those that are:

(a) free-standing with no connecting substructures
(b) free-standing subareas with some connections to other components
(c) sequentially linked and partially rigid structures tied to travel mode and behaviour
(d) complex representations of a range of component parts with abundant links and meaningful individual relations.

When an individual is faced with the task of identifying the neighbourhood, it has been shown that the bulk (about 75 percent) of such populations try to attach a **name** to the area that they delimit. Since these names frequently differ from the widely accepted planning or community names, there can be major problems in terms of reconciling cognitive neighbourhoods with the labelled physical components of a city.

When switching from map descriptions of neighbourhood to verbal descriptions, social characteristics tend to increase in importance over and above physical characteristics and physical boundaries.

One of the more critical uses of the concept of neighbourhood is in a **planning** context. In general, the notion of neighbourhood is used to define a small subarea of the city; and the criteria used to define that subarea vary from place to place, from culture to culture, and from purpose to purpose. During the 1960s and thereafter, neighbourhoods achieved a .certain prominence by being touted as a solution to a wide range of urban ills. Thus, proponents such as Susan Keller (1965) and Jane Jacobs (1961), emphasised the loss of neighbourhood coherence and neighbouring activity as a part of the increasing patterns of decline in urban neighbourhood activities. They argued that the recognition of small cohesive subunits in an urban place, such as embodied in the concept of neighbourhood, would recapture the human scale of urban living. By refocusing attention on this local human scale, rapidly escalating problems of crime, violence, anomie, ethnic conflict, and the breakdown of social cohesion could be remedied. Thus, for some time there was a strong move in the planning context for the recreation of physically compact areas containing elementary or lower order goods and services and permitting close and informal social ties among the residents. The question that came out of this, however, was simply: does the small neighbourhood live only in the minds of moralists, poets, old men and city planners, or does it have an existence in fact and for all levels of society?

Associated with this were other comparable questions, such as: what is the meaning of size in a neighbourhood context?; and, perhaps more fundamentally, the question of whether neighbourhoods exist anymore, or whether they are outmoded concepts relevant only to the "big city" atmosphere of the nineteenthth and early part of the twentieth centuries?

In discussing this concept of neighbourhood, a number of other critical questions arise. For example, is stability of occupance an essence of neighbourhood? In general, it is regarded that such stability is necessary because it lies at the basis of the identification process for an area. Other questions concerning whether or not the neighbourhood is a **natural area** evoked responses that within urban areas one could readily find sections of homogeneous populations with a historic identity and strong social tradition which provides the considerable stability for a local area, thus giving some meaning and depth to the concept of neighbourhood. However, when one raises the question of whether there is any functioning component in neighbourhoods, the answers become far less clear. The question of whether or not neighbourhoods function as distinct spatial entities, or whether they have relevance only at the individual action space level, must be raised. Are they then submerged into the more formalised concept of community – which has relevance at the group level, with which individuals may more formally identify, and which planners may more formally recognise?

Given the above questions, it appears that even the most ardent partisans of the concept of neighbourhood as a purely spatial phenomenon would agree that the location of geographically demarcated areas is by itself no proof of the existence of actual neighbourhoods. Thus, planning subdivisions such as census tracts or community planning districts, may have no meaning with respect to the actual activity patterns of individuals, if they are delimited primarily on a locational basis or on the basis of similarity of physical form. Some additional information is usually considered necessary to ascertain whether the residents in such areas also perceive them to be distinct social and symbolic units and use them in a corresponding manner.

It is argued that purely subjective demarcations of neighbourhood are likewise unreliable guides, because when people are asked to draw the boundaries of their neighbourhood, relatively few of them draw identical ones. The Zannaras (1968) study tends to refute this by showing "core" areas which lie within the drawn neighbourhood boundaries of more than 85 percent of her sample population. Given the many findings concerning the salience of the neighbourhood concept, one would expect that subjective estimates of neighbourhood concept would tend to be among the more reliable ways of estimating their existence characteristics. A problem with this, however, is that many people do not ordinarily identify the subareas in which they live by any particular name, or by district boundaries, unless such areas are geographically or socially isolated, or unless they have a very definite social class structure, historic identity, or natural boundary.

Apparently, the boundaries recognised by individuals facilitate their subjective orientation to an environment. Most people have some type of environmental cue that tells them when they are "almost home", or entering their "home area". In many cases, such cues, and the boundaries formed by connecting such cues, can hardly serve as objective demarcations, since their locations also vary among households.

Evidence now tends to show that there is a high correlation between concentrated use of local areas or other special attachments to the local area and the subjective evaluation of neighbourhood space. Thus, while the concept of neighbourhood has surged and receded as a relevant one in the planning literature, in terms of city image, it seems an important subcomponent. It seems reasonable to assume that neighbourhoods:

(a) exist as a salient unit of cognitive space
(b) summarise spatial areal characteristics in the vicinity of major nodes, or anchor points, in an individual's image of place
(c) may have easily definable physical boundaries
(d) incorporate local social networks, focus local concentration on the use of areal facilities and have emotional and symbolic connotations for their inhabitants.

Under these circumstances, the concept of neighbourhood can be regarded as a viable one and an integral part of the total concept of urban image.

4.4 COGNITIVE MAPPING AND COGNITIVE MAPS

The foregoing discussion on images of urban areas largely focuses on description and inventory. We now turn to consider more structured analytical approaches using a variety of experimental methods, aimed at uncovering and representing the cognitive structure of large scale environments.

4.4.1 Definitions
Cognitive mapping is the process of acquiring, coding, using, and storing information from the multitude of environments external to mind. A **cognitive map** is, therefore, a person's model of objective reality. This model of reality is a complex one and should not be interpreted as a simple one-to-one mapping of discrete things that exist in the environment into the mind. Thus, it is not assumed that a cognitive map is an equivalent of a cartographic map, nor is it assumed that there is any one-to-one mapping between a piece of objective reality and a person's cognitive map of that reality. It is perhaps more appropriate, therefore, to regard the cognitive map as a set of stored propositions about the environment, each having been assigned a truth value by a given individual. In this sense, the cognitive mapping process is one designed to receive and code environmental information, store it in an accessible manner, and decode it in such a way as to allow spatial behaviour to take place.

Even tasks as simple as going from home to work, to school, or to a store, or directing newcomers to places they have never been, require information to be stored, accessed, and used in a convenient and easy way. In order to perform such tasks, it is necessary to use one's memory representations of spatial information - one's cognitive map. Over the past two decades scientists in a variety of fields have been examining questions relating to the nature of these cognitive maps, the process of acquiring and forming such mappings, and their role in everyday spatial activity. In what follows, we draw on concepts, theories and empirical evidence from a variety of disciplines as a means of examining the process of acquiring spatial knowledge (the cognitive mapping process) and illustrating the product of such knowledge acquisition – the sum total of environmental information stored in memory (i.e., the cognitive map).

The **process of cognitive mapping** is a means of structuring, interpreting, and coping with complex sets of information that exist in environments external to the mind. These environments include not only the observable physical environment, but also memories of environments experienced in the past, and the many and varied social, cultural, political, economic, and other environments which impinged both on those past memories and on our current experiences. The nature, structure, and content of these many environments also influence our expectations: whether these be in terms of immediate shortrun expectations which are essential to the more frequent episodes of our daily activity patterns (e.g., route selection in a daily trip to work or shopping), or those less frequent episodes with greater temporal intervals between their occurrences (e.g., annual holidays).

This mapping process requires each individual to undertake a cognitive taxomonic process which is culturally constrained and which results in the filtering of the varied "to whom it may concern" messages emanating from the many environments in which we live.

Cognitive mapping is constructive, develops throughout the lifespan, and is found in all levels of humanity (Siegel and Cousins, 1983). As will be seen in later sections, the mapping process changes with development: it can be studied through all ages from young children to the aged, from the intellectually exceptional to the profoundly retarded. There is with development a change from an emphasis on **declarative knowledge** (e.g., knowledge of place) to **procedural knowledge** (i.e., route or wayfinding knowledge), to a highly integrated form of **configurational knowledge** incorporating the major elements of place, past, area, or with appropriate directions and connectors attached to them.

Unlike much of the literature on perception that emphasises the acquisition of information through the senses in the presence of a stimulus, it is generally accepted that the process of cognitive mapping has no tie to a particular sensory modality, but instead spans all of them.

A particularly important component of cognitive mapping is **activation spread**. This procedure is one where sensory input provides a clue with which to search the memory for bits of information that might be related to the sensed data. Thus, when a bit of information impinges on the senses and begins processing that will allow it to become part of the general knowledge structure, there is put in motion a process by which the information may be organised, generalised, accessed and incremented. In other words, elements of a knowledge structure may be activated or excited to varying degrees. Activation may spread according to sets of principles or rules such that a bit of information may be classed as being similar to other bits previously sensed, and in that sense, instances of that sort may be incremented and the saliency of the incremented set increased, or the bit of information may be more difficult to interpret, such that it may be difficult to link it with relevant past experiences. Activation spread may be positive, thus increasing the salience of a set of instances, or it may be negative and be influential in suppressing the significance of an information subset. An increased salience is immediately translated into a more rapid real time accessing of information in the total structured information set. If it is assumed there is a **hierarchical structuring**, then an increase in saliency may result in a transition to a higher point or higher node in the hierarchical structure, or a strengthening in the link between the information set and others linked to it. The implication of this is that the closer together concepts are in a propositional network, the easier it is for them to foster each other's recall. Closeness, of course in the above context, implies the nature of **linkage** in the hierarchical structuring rather than physical proximity. Of course, **proximity** in a propositional network may foster mistakes; for example, being exposed to the word "bank", devoid of a specific context, would make one uncertain as to whether to include it with financial institutions or elements of a river basin.

4.4.2 Theories

A **cognitive map** may be defined as "long term stored information about the relative location of objects and phenomena in the everyday physical environment" (Garling, Book and Lindberg, 1979:200). Cognitive maps thus represent information about environments that are either known to exist or are imagined, but not necessarily present. Any given map, therefore, may be a mixture of information received at quite disparate time periods, and at any particular point in time may be incomplete, more or less schematised, or distorted, and may contain fictional or hypothetical information, or relics of the past which no longer exist.

It is, perhaps, simplest to view a cognitive map as a structure whose nodes and representations are prototypes (Kaplan and Kaplan, 1982). Some nodes are connected by paths expressing associative or predictive relations. In this way, the cognitive map can contain abstractions or gross simplifications, as well as some analog properties. The basic structure or structures contained in a cognitive map are built up over time through an associative learning process. Since they are built up over time, it is possible to develop a conceptualisation of the developmental sequence contained in this learning process.

Several embryonic **developmentally based theories** concerning the development of cognitive maps currently exist. Although each conceptualisation is based largely on the work of Piaget, separate and distinct hypotheses are attributed to Shemyakin (1963), Siegel and White (1975) and Golledge (1976, 1978).

Piaget's theories (Piaget and Inhelder, 1967) posit that knowledge progresses through different stages. His **developmental sequence** consists of an egocentric stage, an allocentric stage and a geocentric stage. In the **egocentric** stage, all spatial knowledge is referred to self. At the **allocentric** level, relative space is constructed independent of self and has critical topological and geometrical elements such as sequence, directionality, and some simple relational concepts. In the **geocentric** stage, a person constructs an absolute space, independent of self, of specific objects in which all components can be related one to another through general spatial principles. The essence of this developmental sequence is that as development proceeds, greater facility is obtained in symbolic and abstract thinking and there is an increased ability to recognise relationships between environmental features in their own right and quite distinct from self. Thus, a general understanding of geographic environment develops: it is this general understanding which is assumed to be present in all children and all adults.

As a supplement to the Piagetian hypothesis, Siegel and White (1975) have suggested the three phase sequence starting with the **identification of landmarks**, progressing then through the addition of **paths** to make **route knowledge**, and finally, a general **relational stage** in which **configurational properties** are understood.

Shemyakin (1963) postulates that the general transition occurs **from point to route to survey knowledge**. Apart from the earliest levels of egocentric orientation, which is similar to Piagetian levels, Shemyakin produces an explicitly spatial model which argues that route finding procedures necessarily predate any general spatial levels of comprehension (i.e., survey knowledge).

Somewhat parallel to the Siegel and White hypothesis, Golledge (1974, 1978) presents an **anchorpoint theory** of environmental cognition. In this theory, simple declarative knowledge (understanding individual nodes and landmarks in relation to self) is again followed by procedural knowledge in which primary nodes are linked by primary paths in a hierarchical linking of places as the primary node structure emerges. As information about place accumulates, spread effects in the vicinity of primary nodes and paths allow the development of simple aerial concepts such as neighbourhoods and community (Figure 4.4).

Figure 4.4

Descriptive Model of the Anchorpoint Theory

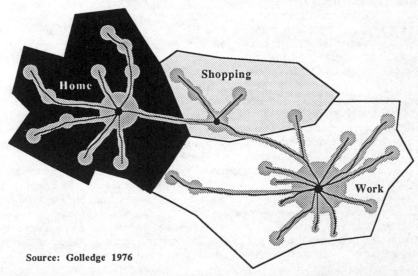

Source: Golledge 1976

Geometrically, the simple primary node oriented network properties, or **skeletal structure**, of the cognitive map begin to be filled out by the addition of intermittent areas surrounding the primary nodes and paths. **Distortions** in the relative location of primary nodes and their associated areas produce foldings or warpings in the general understanding of space. A lack of knowledge of segments of the environment may cause **folding in** which known places are drawn closer together in the cognitive map structure or the occurrence of holes or blank areas which can contribute to locational and relational errors in the spatial information required by any given individual. The final set of spatial information encoded, therefore, may include simple Euclidean properties among places that are well known, and hierarchically conditioned topological relations for those places less well known in a general spatial content. Given this conceptualisation, it is easy to see how a definition of a cognitive map as being incomplete, schematised, distorted and with regular metric or geometric structure, may emerge and be found acceptable.

4.4.3 Cognitive Maps as Semantic Long-Term Memory Structures

Each of the above theories stresses that a cognitive map need not be (and usually is not) interpreted as an attempt to do a one-to-one "mapping" of an object of reality. Spatial information may indeed be stored in the form of holistic images, semantic networks, or chunks and strings of information. For example, Garling, et al. (1982) suggest that a cognitive map is a **semantic long-term memory structure**, organised in a manner similar to that assumed by various network models of memory. This interpretation is compatible with information processing theory in psychology and much of current work in an artificial intelligence framework is based on this approach. In such a conceptualisation, critical processes underlying the control of information process of knowledge restructuring include pattern matching and activation spread. These processes are capable of operating on simple declarative knowledge, procedural knowledge, or more general configurational knowledge.

While we have presented a variety of alternative conceptualisations of the process of cognitive mapping and the nature of cognitive maps, it should be apparent that no definitive answer exists at this stage, and that the selection, storage, reconstruction, and use of cognitive information is a potentially fertile topic for geographers.

Within the context of cognitive mapping in artificial intelligence, Kuipers (1978, 1982) suggests that the idea of a cognitive map is more metaphorical than factual. Thus, rather than have information stored isomorphic to a cartographic representation, he suggests that knowledge falls into disconnected components which many times have little or no relation between them. This suggests that there is a critical spatial component to knowledge: for example, knowledge of routes may be asymmetric such that when information is stored, behaviour can take place easily in one direction, but not so easily in the other. Sadalla, Burroughs and Staplin (1980) also comment on the asymmetric nature of route knowledge and the critical importance of primary nodes or reference points in any given spatial structure. Kuipers thus suggests that information may be stored in the mind in a variety of metric or topological procedures so that little or no isomorphic representation is possible between knowledge acquired about an environment and an objectively derived representation of that environment. This, therefore, raises perhaps the most fundamental question in the cognitive mapping literature - how do we determine the correspondence between subjective and objective spatial knowledge?

4.5 COGNITIVE DISTANCE

In the cognitive mapping process, information is accumulated about relative locations and degrees of conductivity of environmental cues. The term **cognitive distance** has evolved to describe the relative spatial separation of objects in a cognitive map.

One of the earlier examples of applying the concept of cognitive distance occurred in the consumer behaviour area (Thompson, 1963). In this context, subjective distance estimates were incorporated into conventional gravity models in an attempt to help explain store choice. Along with this applied interest there developed a basic research interest in the concept of cognitive distance (Golledge, Briggs, Demko 1969; Briggs, 1969, 1972; Lowrey, 1970; Burroughs and Sadalla, 1979; Sadalla and Staplin, 1980). In most cases a curvilinear relationship was seen to occur between subjective and objective distance (see Figure 4.5), while authors such as Cadwallader (1975, 1981) and MacKay and Olshavsky (1975) and Pacione (1976) continued an applied interest in cognitive distance in the consumer behaviour context. In both basic and applied research, it soon became obvious that the type of procedure used to estimate subjective distance, or to convert objective to subjective distance, was of critical importance (see Table 4.5). Some studies (Briggs, 1972; Lowry, 1973; Thorndyke, 1981) supported Stevens' (1957) contention that a power function was the most appropriate transformation. Both Day (1976) and Cadwallader (1979) argued that the type of function likely to be found was significantly affected by the measurement procedure used in obtaining subjective estimates. Features such as whether estimates of distance were obtained in metric or non-metric units and whether the research question was specifically oriented toward spatial distance or temporal, social or functional, proximities or similarities, also proved to be critical.

Figure 4.5

**Relationship Between Cognitive Distance
and Physical Distance**

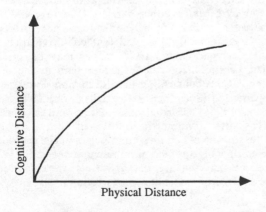

Source: After Cadwallader, 1985

Table 4.5

Relationship between Magnitude and Category Scales

	Pearson Correlation Coefficients for Relationship between Magnitude Scale and Category Scale	Pearson Correlation Coefficients for Relationship between Logarithm of Magnitude and Category Scale
Coefficients	Frequency	Frequency
0.40 or less	0	0
0.41 to 0.60	7	7
0.61 to 0.80	32	35
0.81 to 1.00	26	23

Source: After Cadwallader, 1979:568

Early investigations of cognitive distance produce some apparently contradictory results.   Lee (1962) found that distances outward from the centre of the British city of Dundee were overestimated more than inward distances.   Golledge, Briggs and Demko (1969), among others, found the distances toward downtown in US cities were overestimated, while those toward the periphery were underestimated.   Some reasons for the apparent differences were related to the size and functional complexity of the cities in question, and also possibly to their internal structure.   Thus, differences in the nature of the local environment and its regional or cultural setting also proved to be critical factors in the estimate of cognitive distance.

In examining the notion of cognitive distance, there have been suggestions made that differences occur on the basis of sex (Lee, 1970), and the nature and frequency of intervening barriers (Lowrey, 1970), the nature of the endpoints between which cognitive distances are estimated (Sadalla and Staplin, 1980).   It is generally accepted that cognitive distances may be asymmetric and that, in some cases, the distances may be interpreted in a functional, proximity, or similarity context rather than in a geometrical one. There have been speculations concerning the use of non-Euclidean metrics to represent cognitive distance (Spector, 1978; Richardson, 1979; Golledge and Hubert, 1981; Tobler, 1976).   Furthermore, Baird and Noma (1982) have suggested that, given the asymmetric nature of cognitive distance, its representation may be impossible in any known geometric space.

Along with the notion of distance asymmetry is the more general notion that cognitive distances may violate the axiom of triangle equality.   The three basic standard axioms of matricity are as follows:

(a) $a_{ii} = 0$ (identity)

(b) $a_{ij} = a_{ji}$ (symmetry)

(c) $a_{ij} \leq a_{ik} + a_{jk}$ (triangle inequality)

Depending on the point of view and purpose of recovering cognitive information, any of these three axioms may be violated. For example, a given place may be located at different points in a cognitive representation of space (violation of identity). This is more likely to occur if a given place is known by multiple labels and different labels are used in different contexts (e.g., a given location may be known by a street intersection name or the name of a major function located on one of the corners). Given that asymmetry of distance is quite possible (e.g., distance from a primary node to a secondary may not be equal to the subjective distance from the secondary node to the primary), then triangular inequality and translation invariance, other fundamental properties of space, are equally likely to be violated. Recent research on subjective directional associations also indicates the nonsymmetry of directional components.

4.6 METHODOLOGIES

Methodologies developed in attempts to recover cognitive configurations are as varied as the purposes behind such research. One of the earliest methods suggested by Lynch (1960) was the use of sketch map techniques. Other procedures include: requesting subjects to image scenes from different perspectives; to list the best recognised or most frequently visited places; to reconstruct images of unseen objects; to estimate lengths of streets and angles of intersections; to use various unidimensional scaling procedures to obtain interpoint distance judgments; and, by using proximity judgments in a paired comparison context, to develop cognitive distance estimates from multidimensional scaling configurations. More recently, table map modelling, and interactive computer experiments, along with the use of areal photos, all appear to be capable of producing reasonable configurational estimates.

4.6.1 Sketch Maps
Sketch mapping has long appeared to be a useful instrument for recovering information about environments if the maps are properly interpreted. This technique suffers from the assumption that the subject understands the abstract notion of the model and its relation to the real world, has the sufficient motor skills to accurately portray in sketch format what he is attempting to complete, and that a uniform metric is applied across the sketched information. Where violations of these assumptions occur, the best information that can be obtained would be topological in nature.

4.6.2 Multi-Dimensional Methods
Increased sophistication in specifying the design of experiments for recovering cognitive information, and the use of powerful multi-dimensional methods, have given researchers a great deal of confidence in their ability to

Figure 4.6

Examples of Axial Bias

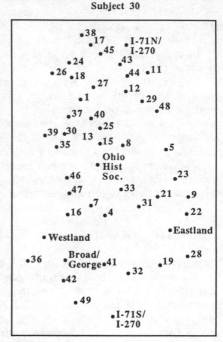

Subject 43

Subject 30

recover useful spatial information from knowledge structures. Many people have proven to be amazingly accurate in remembering the essential details of the spatial layouts of large scale environments with which they are familiar (Golledge and Spector, 1978; Golledge, Rayner and Rivizzigno, 1982). In particular, emphasis is being placed on the development of methods for comparing recovered configurations with some representation of objective reality (e.g., cartographic or other such representations).

4.6.3 Using Multi-Dimensional Scaling to Measure Cognitive Maps

As an example of multi-dimensional methods for recovering and interpreting cognitive spatial information, we will examine a set of experiments designed to try and recover cognitive spatial information and examine it for spatial properties.

This set of experiments was undertaken in the city of Columbus, Ohio (Golledge, Rivizzigno and Spector, 1974). Over a period of nine months, sets of subjects (subdivided into newcomers, intermediate residents, and long term residents) participated in an experiment involving the grouping or clustering of pairs of locational cues and the allocation of scale scores based on their subjective estimates of proximity of each pair (see Figure 4.6). The scale scores obtained from each subject were analysed using a nonmetric **multidimensional scaling** algorithm (KYST), in which interpoint distance estimates proportional to the scale scores were developed, then using an iterative procedure based on a gradient method for achieving convergence, a two dimensional point configuration was developed. The interpoint distance information contained in this configuration was monotonically related to the original scale scores, and the fit between the data and the developed configuration was assessed through a monotonic regression procedure, which minimised the error variances between recovered points and the original scale scores. To produce interpretable configurations, an initial configuration representing the actual locational arrangement of the cues in the city was used. Thus, the final configuration outputted from the scaling programme represented a distortion of the actual pattern based on the proximity scales developed by each individual. Samples of such configurations showing different types of axial biases are shown in Figure 4.7. The stress (badness-of-fit) statistic thus becomes an interpretable fit statistic proportional to the error obtained in the outputted configuration.

4.6.4 Correspondence Between Subjective and Objective Configurations
Each two dimensional output configuration obtained for each subject was matched with a two dimensional Euclidean configuration of the cues in their urban space via a process of standardising, centralising, and rotating the two configurations until the closest possible match had been achieved. The degree of coincidence associated with this procedure was recorded in the form of a bidimensional correlation coefficient (Table 4.6). Individual configurations that closely match the two dimensional Euclidean map, thus, would have high bidimensional coefficients.

A simple interpretation of the degree of correspondence between subjective and objective configurations can be obtained by warping a standard grid to fit the subjective configuration (see Figure 4.8).

Table 4.6

**Congruence Measures between
Subjective and Objective Configurations**

Control Group	T_1
C1	.891
C2	.952
C3	.855
C4	.944
C5	.938
C6	.882
C7	.889
C8	.901
C9	.709
C10	.882

Source: After Golledge, Rayner, Rivizzigno, 1982

The grids are obtained in a manner similar to the way one would compile a contour map - i.e., by interpolating grid lines between points and each configuration. Obviously, some of the finer displacements and distortions cannot be shown using this grid distortion technique, but the use

Figure 4.7

Distorted Grids for Sample Subjects' Columbus, Ohio, 1976

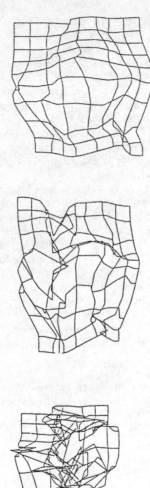

of a simple generalisation, such as this, helps the interpretation. Although each simplified grid has its own distinctive pattern of distortion, the use of these generalised procedures allows one to search for similarities repeated among many of the subjects and to consequently perform some basic grouping of subjects on the basis of similarity of distortions. Many grids, for example, indicated a pronounced exaggeration of the shorter distances. Overall, there was a pronounced localisation effect with distortion being least in the daily activity space of sets of individuals. Standard classes of distortions that could be achieved are illustrated in Figure 4.9.

Figure 4.8

Composite Cognitive Configuration Error Ellipses, Comumbus, Ohio, 1976

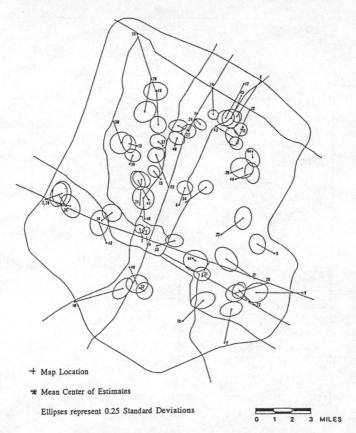

+ Map Location

✳ Mean Center of Estimates

Ellipses represent 0.25 Standard Deviations

0   1   2   3   MILES

The use of simple grid representations of the configurations provide further evidence that people's knowledge structures of urban information is incomplete, schematised, and filled with holes or folds or warps. Obviously, there are pronounced local effects, with the general knowledge surface declining exponentially away from places that could be designated as primary nodes.

4.6.5 Measuring Degree of Distortion and Fuzziness

In discussing the concept of correspondence, we have used the notion of bi-dimensional regression and the grid pattern matching as simple indicators of structural agreement. In a more precise context, it is possible to estimate the degree of distortion (or displacement of subjective cues from their objective locations), and fuzziness (or the degree of variability of subjective estimates of cue locations).

If we have an objective configuration C, defined by a set of xy coordinates, and a subjective configuration W, defined by a set of uv coordinates, the configuration matching problem is one of finding the

81

Figure 4.9

Standard Classes of Axial Distortion

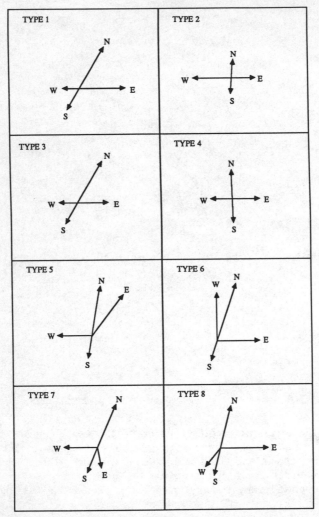

Source: after Rivizzigno, 1976

transformation $W = f(Z)$. Such a transformation would seek to undertake a translation to bring the mean location of the configurations into coincidence to rotations about this location, and a uniform change of scale. The parameters associated with these transformations can be estimated in a least squares fashion, so as to minimise the residual variance. A measure of the degree of coincidence is the root mean square error obtained by taking the square root of the residual variance (Gale, 1980). Alternatively, one may develop a procedure analogous to simple regression by taking the ratio of the explained variance to the total variance (see Tobler, 1977; Olivier, 1970).

Figure 4.10

Distortion Vectors, Columbus, Ohio, 1976

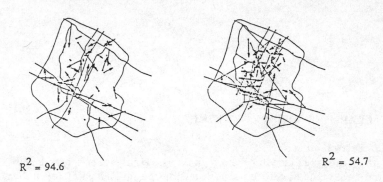

$R^2 = 94.6$

$R^2 = 54.7$

An alternative approach to structural correspondence is to consider the problem in a matrix matching framework. Here, one begins by defining the objective and subjective configurations by N proximity matrices (where N is the number of locations). The cell values matrix in each matrix are some measure of proximity between pairs of points. The question to be solved is one of assessing the degree to which the matrix structure for one configuration reflects that of the other. The technique involves producing a crossproduct statistic for the matrices, then using a randomisation procedure, iteratively changing the locations of rows and, simultaneously, columns in one matrix while holding the other constant, recalculating the cross-product statistic for each random iteration, and then assessing the degree to which all feasible cross-product statistics exceed or are less than the given statistic (Cliff and Ord, 1980; Golledge and Hubert, 1981).

Other ways of examining information on cognitive maps and/or assessing degrees of coincidence have been developed by Tobler (1977). For example, for the population as a whole, one may locate all subjective estimates of two locations, and summarise the resulting locational set in terms of error ellipses (Figure 4.10).

Such a construction indicates the degree to which the location of individual cues in the total set are more or less known by the subject population: obviously, the larger the ellipse and the more circular the ellipse, the less accurate is the general knowledge structure of the cues location. Similarly, by examining the magnitude of the distance displacement between a cue in a matched subjective and objective configuration pair, and estimating its directional distortion, the fuzziness component previously calculated can be complemented with an individual's distortional component (see Figure 4.10). In examining distortions of the cues used in the Columbus experiment, it appears that distortion is least in the cue set contained in an individual's activity space or associated with primary nodes, and greatest associated with places visited less frequently. Generally, a strong relationship exists between the amount of fuzziness associated with each location cue and the amount of distortion.

Chapter Five

LEARNING AND SPATIAL BEHAVIOUR

5.1 LEARNING AND BEHAVIOUR

5.1.1 Introduction

Whether they realize it or not, most geographers concerned with human spatial behaviour have been searching for the spatial habits of individuals or groups. Culture, for example, is little more than the common or shared habits of a society. In general terms we accept the fact that behaviour in any given environment is a direct function of the extent of learning about that environment and that gaps in our information set, or our inability to understand or comprehend a system, are a direct function of the extent of learning we have about the environment or the system at any given point in time. In building normative models we incorporate the notion of habitual responses: in defining optimizing behaviours we frequently rely on assumptions of complete information. The process of learning about any given environment in which human behaviour takes place is one that allows individuals to give meaning to what they see, to add distinctions and relations to the physical or other environmental structures in which people operate, provide identity, location, and orientation for elements of the spatial system in which they are located, and to suggest possible courses of overt activity designed to achieve any specified goal-set. Thus there appears little doubt that the learning process has an important spatial component and that there is a critical relationship between the extent to which we can learn about the components of a specific system and the extent to which we can behave "satisfactorily" within such a system.

There are many inherently spatial concepts in the general learning literature, and there has developed a complete subfield of psychology (environmental cognition) which has as a fundamental aim discovering the how, what, and where of learning activities in real and imagined environments. In this chapter therefore we shall pay attention to some inherently appealing spatial concepts from learning theory and then develop a conceptualization of the knowledge acquisition process in a spatial context.

Human spatial behaviour can be defined as any sequence of consciously or subconsciously directed life processes that result in changes of location through time. Although broad, this definition focuses on sensate behaviours, accepts the need for direction, eliminates behaviours that are fluctuations of inanimate systems elements (such as rocks rolling or rivers flowing), and covers all possible behaviours from the weakly motivated to the strongly stereotyped. Learning is the process by which an activity originates or is changed through responding to a situation - provided the changes cannot be attributed wholly to maturation or to a temporary state of an organism.

Learning is thus defined as a process which is involved in a wide range of acts from innovation to repetitive imitation, while discounting effects such as ageing, or the influence of temporary bodily system states.

5.1.2 Types of Behaviour
It makes little sense to try to categorize types of behaviours except in the grossest sense. We shall for convenience however, recognize three broad behaviour types:

(a) **Weakly Motivated or Random Behaviour.** These often are associated with the exploratory phase of a learning process. It is often accepted that apart from the first sensory motor experiments of the newborn child, there is probably no such thing as random behaviour. Within this context, however, we shall include weakly motivated behaviour for which it may be impossible to determine the critical derivative forces or which cannot meaningfully be differentiated from random acts, such that the behaviour might reasonably be called irrational, arbitrary, or relatively unpredictable.

(b) **Problem Solving Behaviour.** These behaviours occur when a sensate being is confronted with a problem requiring deliberate thinking in a specified direction prior to making a choice amongst sets of feasible alternative solutions to the problem. This type of behaviour may involve vicarious trial and error behaviour and uncontrolled or patterned search activities. A component of problem solving is the spatial manifestation of the process or the overt response.

(c) **Repetitive Learned Behaviours.** These are habitual behaviours which are relatively invariant, difficult to extinguish, frequently follow the paths of minimum effort, eliminate conscious consideration of alternatives, and are designed to reduce uncertainty and effort in the decision making process. This is behaviour assumed in virtually every geographic model involving human activity.

5.2 SPATIALLY RELEVANT LEARNING CONCEPTS

5.2.1 Contiguity, Concept Identifications, Paired Associate Learning, and Interactance Processes.
Almost every major psychological learning theory has important spatial implications, and some are inherently appealing to the geographer simply in terms of the concepts used. **Contiguity theory**, for example, has an empirical existence in the geographer's notion of spatial auto-correlation. **Concept identification** or discrimination learning appears potentially relevant to environmental cue recognition literature. The **stimulus sampling theory** might find a haven amongst those geographers that regard human and other systems largely in terms of linear difference equations. **Association models**, such as paired associate or linear operator models which represent hypothesis behaviour, have lead geographers to use associative methods and various scaling techniques to examine preference, choice, and spatial knowledge structures in ways that had never before been possible. Interactance process models have their parallels in locational choice, resource allocation, and

preference ordering. **Avoidance conditioning models** can be seen to have potential usefulness in examining repetitive choice situations such as consumer behaviour. Despite their obvious potential, relatively few of these models have been pursued in the geographic literature. Other learning theories and models, however, have become well entrenched in geography and now occupy a normal niche in our explanatory schemas. These include elements of field theory, place learning and spatial cognition, and incremental learning or habit theory.

5.2.2 Action Space

Geographers have found considerable value in the notions of **action space** or **activity space**. These are concepts developed in parallel with the notion of **life space**. Lewin (1935) regarded behaving organisms as geometrical points moving about in a comprehensive "life space". Such organisms were subject to the pushes and pulls or positive and negative **valences** which impinged on them at different locations and were part of the operation of the system of environments which make up the life space, as well as being subject to the pushes and pulls of personal and group expectations. In the course of their locomotions through space, individuals circumvented barriers of one sort or another (e.g., environmental, distance, political, legal, social, moral, etc.), and the state of their relationships with the life system at any point in space and time was the result of the forces impinging on them at that point in time. The presence of positive and negative valences in life space gives rise to various types of conflict situations such as:

(a) where two positive valences of equal force exist, leading to approach-approach conflict typified by choice amongst members of a feasible opportunity set

(b) where two negative valences exist, leading to avoidance situations, risk minimization, or minimizing regret or cognitive dissonance

(c) where there are simultaneously present positive and negative valences impinging on the individual, such as might be the case with attracting forces (e.g. number of vacant houses or number of vacant employment positions) as opposed to the friction forces (e.g. cost or distance or intervening barriers).

Ideas similar to the above appear in geography in terms of migration theory in particular, the push-pull hypothesis being a classic example of approach-avoidance behaviour. In market area analysis, one distinguishes which of a set of alternatives offering attracting forces are seen to be the most preferred or most highly attractive to a decision maker. The social gravity model embodies the notion of attraction and repulsion in each of the above three forms and has become one of the most critical and widely used generalizations across many fields of geography.

Within the total conception of life space the geographer distinguishes between **action space** (or the subset of the life space known by an individual) and **activity space** (or the subset of space containing daily interaction patterns). We will be dealing with these concepts of action space and activity space in greater detail in Chapter 6.

5.2.3 Place Learning

Whereas some of the initial interest in learning theory in geography was provided by stimulus response models which focused on learning movement sequences or movement habits, perhaps the most progressive stream of research using learning concepts has been firmly located in cognitive theory. Tolman's theory that organisms learn the location of paths or places is inherently appealing to the geographer. Place learning theory suggests that learning is a cognitive process guided by spatial relationships rather than by reinforced movement sequences. Given that an origin and destination is known, variable movement may be undertaken between the origin and destination with the same results in terms of goal gratification. Thus, there is a clear implication that places are learned, possible connections between them are built up over time, and that individuals develop a capacity for linking previously unknown destinations to given origins by referring to a general spatial schema which incorporates concepts of proximity, contiguity, clustering or separateness, sequence, and configuration or pattern. Tolman, in fact, argued that sensate organisms develop "mental maps" which allow them to navigate in any given environment. We shall be relying heavily on place learning concepts later in this and also in following chapters.

5.2.4 Incremental Learning and Habit Theories

The basis of this line of theorizing is that rather than contribute a maximum influence on one trial, reinforcement adds an increment to the habit strength of a particular behaviour on each trial occurrence. Habit strength is defined as a positive growth function of the number of trials and can be represented by the formula (Hull, 1964):

(1)

$$H_{sr} = 1 - 10^{-aN}$$

where

H_{sr} = habit strength
N = the number of trials
a = an empirically defined constant
(.03 in Hull's work)

This theory includes the notion that behaviour changes over time from motivated search to fully learned activities. Obviously, such a transition can be spread out over greater or smaller lengths of time depending on the type of behaviour, the purpose of the behaviour, and the system constraints. If we were examining the responses of an individual in terms of achieving a particular goal, it may appear that alternative responses appear successively in an unorderly fashion until the beginnings of a satisfactory response sequence appears. Thus, it is commonly assumed that an individual placed in an unfamiliar environment and stimulated to seek a particular goal exhibits a tendency to vary his responses which are made under conditions of uncertainty in an attempt to achieve a specified goal object. Once a correct or most satisfying response has been achieved, then experimentation diminishes and incremental learning proceeds. An essential component of this theory is the notion of search. Examination of aspects of search, from provisional try to stereotyped procedures, has produced a spate of geographically relevant models. Job search (Rogerson and MacKinnon

1981), the search for new housing (Smith, Clark, Huff and Shapiro, 1979), locational search (McDermott and Taylor, 1976), consumer behaviour (Rogers, 1970; Hanson, 1982), and way-finding behaviour (Golledge, et al., 1983), among others have developed from this useful and powerful learning related concept. Notions of directional and distance biases (Adams, 1969; Humphreys and Whitelaw, 1979; Brown and Holmes, 1971; and so on) have focused on spatial regularities in the search process. Almost inevitably, the traditional distance decay effect enters into discussions of search activity regardless of the search context.

5.2.5 Luce's Choice Theory
Obviously, a choice of responses is an essential part of any learning process. Many mathematical learning models are designed to predict a change in response probability as the result of the prior sequence of correct and incorrect choices. Probability of choice of some future trial, then, is a function of the sequence of correct or incorrect responses and their appropriate outcomes and/or reinforcement schedules. The question of choice in a spatial context has been of continued interest to geographers. Huff (1963), Thompson (1963), Wolpert (1964), Gould (1963), Golledge (1967), Rushton (1969) and many others initially used learning theory concepts in their attempts to understand decision processes and choice acts. For many years, for example, geographers and other researchers equated rational choice with those acts that were economically maximizing. Gould (1963) and Wolpert (1964) indicated that aversion to risk was a critical factor influencing decision processes and choice acts, while at the same time pointing to the need to identify the criterion by which choice acts were to be evaluated before being able to assess the appropriateness of choice. Thus, subsistence farmers who chose to use a mixed strategy of planting a variety of crops may have been economically irrational in the sense that a monocultural activity in any given year could have produced a higher income. But at the same time, they may have achieved a given level of aspiration concerning the long run well being of the whole subsistence group by assuring adequate (but not necessarily bountiful) food supplies in each year. Similarly, Wolpert's Swedish farmers chose their land use practices in any given year on the basis of their existing knowledge of the system, their expectations about economic fluctuations and environmental conditions, as well as with respect to their own farming habits and knowledge of farming practices and what could be observed as occurring amongst their peer groups. Thus, choice acts resulting from bounded rationality or satisficing with different levels of aspiration, became commonly used as a basis for explaining human spatial behaviour.

Much of the ability to use principles and models of choice relies on a fundamental choice axiom introduced by Luce (1959). This axiom concerns itself with the relationship between choice probabilities as the number of alternatives involved in the choice act change. The fundamental premise is that the ratio of likelihood of choosing element A to be the likelihood of choosing element B in a set of K alternatives in a constant irrespective of the number and composition of the other alternatives in the choice set.

Let:

x,y,z,t,u   be alternative elements
T   be the total set of alternatives
R   be some subset of T
Pr(x:R)   be the probability that x is chosen when the choice is restricted
        to subset R
Pr(x,y)   be the probability that x is chosen from a subset of x and y

Then

$$Pr(x{:}T) = Pr(R{:}T) \ Pr(x{:}R). \tag{2}$$

If we choose an arbitrary element of (a) of T, then the response strength of x, [v(x)] is:

$$v(x) = \frac{Pr(x,a)}{Pr(a,x)} = \frac{Pr(x{:}T)}{Pr(a{:}T)} \tag{3}$$

Response strengths of elements have the following property:

$$\frac{v(x)}{v(y)} = \frac{Pr(x,y)}{Pr(y,x)}$$

If we let

$$Pr(x,T) = \frac{1}{* \ \dfrac{Pr(y,x)}{Pr(x,y)}} \tag{4}$$

then

$$Pr(x{:}T) = \frac{1}{* \ \dfrac{V(y)}{V(x)}} = \frac{V(x)}{V(y)} \tag{5}$$

The response strength or scale values represented above, when multiplied by a positive constant retain the original relationship of scale values to choice probabilities.   To calculate probabilities of choice in pairwise choice situations or where K alternatives are ranked, it is necessary to define a ratio w_{xy}

$$W_{xy} = \frac{Pr(x,y)}{Pr(y,x)} \tag{6}$$

Thus in a pairwise choice experiment for 3 objects

$$\frac{Pr(x,y)}{Pr(y,x)} \cdot \frac{Pr(y,z)}{Pr(z,y)} = \frac{Pr(x,z)}{Pr(z,x)} \tag{7}$$

$$\frac{Pr(x,z)}{Pr(z,x)} = \frac{Pr(x,z)}{1-Pr(x,z)} = W_{xz}$$

$$= Pr(x,z) = W_{xz} - W_{xz} \quad Pr(x,z)$$

$$= \frac{W_{xz}}{1+W_{xz}} \tag{8}$$

Once estimates have been made of any given w-ratio, one can then proceed with obtaining the estimates of probability of choice of one element over another. Given a sample of potential shopping centre patrons who are presented with a list of three alternative centres, the problem related to the use of Luce's choice axiom would be to use estimates from paired comparison procedures to determine the choice ratios amongst each of the centres. For example, Table 5.1 gives the result of a paired comparison of three shopping centres.

Table 5.1

Paired Comparison of Shopping Centres

		1	2	3
	1	—	0.60	0.90
Shopping Centre	2	0.40	—	0.80
	3	0.10	0.20	—

Source: Hypothetical data

If we were arbitrarily given the results for the probability of choosing 1 over 2 and 2 over 3 (.60 and .80, respectively) in the above table we could, in the absence of other information, estimate the probability of choosing 1 over 3 from the choice axiom as follows:

$$w_{12} \cdot w_{23} = \frac{Pr(1,2)}{Pr(2,1)} \cdot \frac{Pr(2,3)}{Pr(3,2)} \tag{9}$$

$$= \frac{0.60}{0.40} \cdot \frac{0.80}{0.20} = 6 = w_{13}$$

$$\text{and} \qquad Pr(1,3) = \frac{w_{13}}{1+w_{13}} = \frac{6}{7} = 0.86 \qquad\qquad (10)$$

While the above procedure is inherently appealing, it relies on an assumption that individual choice probabilities can be meaningfully aggregated before any significant generalizable statements can be obtained from use of the axiom. Nevertheless, the axiom appears in many subjective probabilistic choice models, as will be seen in later chapters dealing with residential choice. In the context of stimulus ranking experiments, probabilities of rank orders can be obtained using the principles of Luce's choice axiom. For example, if a subject is shown K different stimuli simultaneously and told to rank them in order of preference, Luce would assume that the individual picks the most preferred object and ranks it 1, then chooses the 2nd ranked object from the remaining K-1 objects, and so on for successive decisions. Using his axiom, we would also assume that each choice depends on the ratio of the scale values computed from the stimuli remaining in the reduced set. Thus, if we have three objects A, B and C with scale value a, b, c, there would be 3 or 6 possible rankings: ABC, ACB, BAC, BCA, CAB, and CBA. With replication of this experiment, each of these will occur a certain proportion of the time. Consider the probability of the sequence BAC occurring. From Luce's choice axiom, we calculate the probability that B is chosen out of the three elements, then eliminating B, we calculate the probability that A is chosen over C in the 2 object comparisons. The joint probability of the ranking BAC, then, is the product of these two probabilities:

$$Pr(BAC) = [b/a+b+c] \ [a/a+c] \qquad\qquad (11)$$

It should be noted that the likelihood of an element of the total set receiving a rank of 1 is the same as its likelihood of being chosen from a set of K alternatives when only 1 choice is permitted. For example, the probability that B receives the rank of 1 is defined as the sum of the probability of the ranking BAC and the ranking BCA. In symbolic terms, this would be:

$$[b/a+b+c] \ [a/a+c] + [b/a+b+c] \ [c/a+c] = b/a+b+c \qquad\qquad (12)$$

5.2.6 Developmental Theory

The developmental theories of Piaget have become a critical part of the literature of environmental learning and environmental cognition. The critical stages of development, and appropriate sequences in the development of spatial knowledge according to Piaget's theories, are shown in Figure 5.1.

In brief, Piaget argues that development progresses through four stages from infancy to adolescence and beyond. The first of these is called the **sensory motor stage,** and generally covers the period from birth to two years old. Development proceeds from reflex activity to hand-mouth co-ordination to representation and sensory-motor solutions to problems. A second, **preoperational,** stage is said to exist covering the period from about 2 to 7 years. At this stage, development proceeds from sensory-motor representation to pre-logical thought and solutions to problems. Problems are solved through representation which is in part dependent on language development. Thought and language are both dominated by egocentric controls and children at this stage are not believed able to solve conservation problems. The third stage, **concrete operational**, lasts from about 7 to approximately 11 years, and at this time development proceeds from pre-logical thought to logical solution to concrete problems. Concepts such as reversibility occur, and the child is able to solve conservation problems using

Figure 5.1

Sequences in the Development of Spatial Knowledge

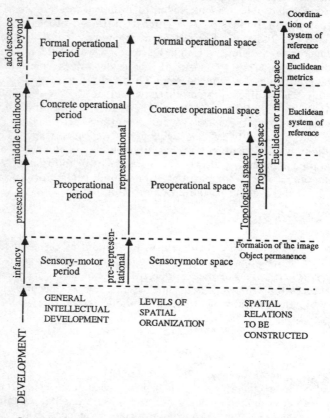

Source: After Hart & Moore, 1973:265

logical observations, but cannot solve complex verbal problems. A fourth stage, **formal operational thinking**, appears around 11 years and beyond where development proceeds from local solutions to concrete problems to logical solutions of all classes of problems. The individual appears capable of scientific thinking, can solve complex verbal problems, and all the cognitive structures mature.

In a spatial context, Piaget argues that the representation of space arises from the coordination and internalization of actions. In this view, representations of space result from manipulating and acting in an external environment rather than from a perceptual copying of it. Thus, interaction in space not perception of space, is a fundamental building block for the acquisition of spatial knowledge. It is further suggested that the initial actions of the sensory-motor child include copying or imitation of other people's actions. As imitation schemas are internalized, then responses become more symbolic. In the specific relational context, three classes are seen to conform to the general notion of spatial cognition and, along with the progression through development stages, one proceeds from an egocentric prerepresentational frame of reference, through topological, projective, to a Euclidean or general metric relational structure.

While the geographer in general is turning more and more to special populations to examine the completeness of inferences about the acquisition of spatial knowledge, it is generally agreed that most of the geographer's subjects come from the group located in the formal operational reasoning stage. This means that individuals generally are capable of removing abstract spatial operations from real action, real objects, or real space, and that any specific act can be placed in the context of the universe of spatial possibilities. However, it is also obvious that spatial understanding and knowledge is not only cumulative but comprehensive. Thus, newcomers first exposed to an area, in their efforts to learn about it, may revert to a pre-operational level of spatial comprehension. At this level, the fundamental topological properties of space (like proximity and separation, openness or closure, dispersion or clustering, and so on) will dominate in their cognitive representations. As interaction with the environment increases, then progression from pure topological to projected relations may occur such that relations are more readily expressed in terms of particular perspectives or points of view which are relatively invariant under projective or perspective transformations. In the words of Shemyakin (1962), there is a combination of pre-operational and route-type knowledge schemas which develop in the early stages of understanding or comprehending an environment. As more knowledge accumulates about the environment, a transition to knowledge of abstract relational spaces, which may or may not have coordinate frames of references, occurs. Again in Shemyakin's terminology, this represents the development of survey-type schema where abstract configurational properties of space can be understood by the subject. Perhaps the final relevant comment from the point of view of the geographer relates to the changing geometries potentially used in spatial representation as development occurs. It appears that in the pre-representational levels, set theoretic concepts of clustering, inclusion, exclusion, and intercept, may be sufficient for establishing the relevant spatial property of an environment cue or object. As development occurs and an egocentric frame of reference develops, the concepts of linearity and sequence or order appear along with some first notions of distance and direction and their various transforms. Beyond projected relations at the concrete operational stage, it becomes evident that coordinate structures are comprehended and may be developed and used, while at the formal operational level and beyond, general and mixed metrics may be much more representative of an individual's understanding and use of spatial concepts than any single formal metric space (such as Euclidean space).

5.3 THE ACQUISITION OF SPATIAL KNOWLEDGE

Up to now we have summarized a number of relevant learning theories which have use or implications for the understanding of the knowledge acquisition process. While most of these theories are much more general than we have illustrated here, each of them, or segments of them, are particularly relevant to conceptualization of knowledge acquisition in a spatial context. The conceptualization developed in the following section draws on elements from several existing theories.

At a very general level, we can conceptualize spatial knowledge as having the following components. First, a **declarative component** which includes knowledge of objects and/or places together with meanings and significances attached to them. This is sometimes referred to as **landmark** or **cue** knowledge, and it requires knowledge of existence, i.e. ability to recognize an element when it lies within a sensory field. This knowledge is the minimum required for object and pattern recognition and discrimination. A second component for spatial knowledge may be called **relational** or **configurational**. Here information about spatial relations among objects or places develops. Concepts such as proximity and sequence allow one to develop various knowledge structures which may include hierarchical networks, knowledge chunking, and an understanding of the notion of configuration in a multidimensional sense. A third component is called **procedural knowledge**. This is required for the development of locomotive ability, and consists of knowledge of how to move from one location to others along available routes. This is also frequently referred to as **way-finding knowledge**.

In the process of acquiring knowledge, a number of relevant questions come to mind. Perhaps the most obvious and important of these relate to finding features of objects and/or locations that cause them to be selected as recognizable elements of environment. In Chapter 3, when discussing the spatial relevance of perception, we emphasized that characteristics such as size or dominance, the type of visible form, perceptual clarity, symbolic function, outstanding features such as colour, contour, and design, location, proximity to other cues, and other characteristics, help us discriminate amongst elements in a total environmental set. Obviously these characteristics are important in terms of discriminating among objects at the declarative or configurational knowledge levels. At the procedural level, features such as the nonlinear relationship between subjective and objective distances, asymmetries in distance and path segmentation, directional distortions, knowledge gaps, and fuzziness (or variance in locational estimates) all contribute to the extent to which procedural knowledge develops in one context or another. Route knowledge by itself consists of a series of procedural descriptions involving a sequential record of starting point or anchor point, intermediate choice point recognition, directional selection, path segment identification and sequencing, and destination recognition. An example is given in Figure 5.2. Thus procedural knowledge involves identification of points on a path or at landmarks on or near a chosen route segment where a decision is to be made relating to successful navigation of the next segment of the path. Obviously the more detailed knowledge one has of a route, the more intermediate landmarks or junction points can be identified and hierarchically organized into secondary, tertiary,

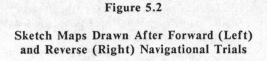

Figure 5.2

Sketch Maps Drawn After Forward (Left)
and Reverse (Right) Navigational Trials

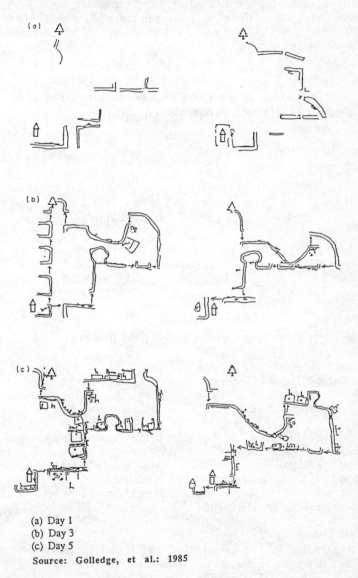

(a) Day 1
(b) Day 3
(c) Day 5
Source: Golledge, et al.: 1985

and lower order nodes and segments (see Figure 5.3). Similarly, the more one knows of a route, the more accurately one can evaluate path lengths regardless of the criteria used in this evaluation process. Route segments of equivalent lengths, for example, may require different amounts of procedural

95

segment proximity to major choice points or to environmental cues of major or minor importance. Again, route segments of equivalent length can vary in terms of degree of difficulty of navigation depending on whether they are contextually simple or complex, i.e. whether or not route segment end points are within a visual field, and whether directional change is absent, gradual, or abrupt. In a sense, therefore, route segmentation characteristics may be related to the mental effort involved in recalling and/or recognizing cues to identify where one is at in the segment.

Figure 5.3
Knowledge of Cues and Features as a Function of
Route Location and Day of Testing

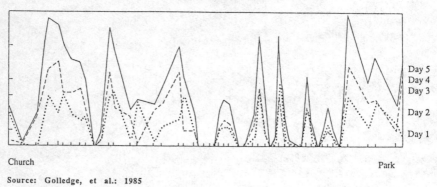

Source: Golledge, et al.: 1985

5.4 THEORIES OF THE DEVELOPMENT OF SPATIAL KNOWLEDGE

5.4.1 Route to Survey Knowledge
An embryonic theory relating to the transition from route to survey knowledge can be found in the works of Shemyakin (1962) who argues that the acquisition of spatial knowledge progresses consecutively from landmark recognition to path definition and the understanding of general relational characteristics of areas. As knowledge accumulates and interpoint information becomes more precise thus reducing notions of variance or fuzziness, precision also accrues to concepts of angularity, direction, proximity and separateness, and other fundamental spatial properties. The similarity between this conceptualization and Piaget's notions of movement through the various developmental stages is obvious.

5.4.2 Developmental Theory
One formalization of the notion of spatial knowledge development can be found in the works of Siegel and White (1975). These authors argue that individuals initially learn paths through an environment which link topologically clustered and relatively ill-defined segments of space. A transformation begins as accurate landmark knowledge anchors paths and relations within clusters become more formalized in terms of well known topological or geometrical properties. The final developmental stage is the construction of a cognitive representation with an abstract frame of

reference which can be anchored at any point in space, and suitably reflected or otherwise transposed depending on the purposes of the individual and the context of the task environment.

In Siegal and White's developmental model, the first stage in the acquisition of spatial knowledge involves some landmark recognition. Paths or routes then develop between the landmarks, with route knowledge progressing from topological to metric in terms of properties. Subsequently, sets of landmarks and paths are organized into clusters based on metric relations within a cluster and maintaining general topological relations between clusters. In the final stages, an overall coordinated frame of reference develops with metric properties being available within and across clusters (survey knowledge). This theory, along with others (e.g., Golledge 1978; Kuipers, 1978), assumes that a memory representation of a complex external environment contains hierarchically organized knowledge including landmarks or salient locations, routes, and configurations representing the integration of information about routes into coherent structures organized about the relative location of landmarks.

5.4.3 Anchor Point Theories

This characterization closely resembles the anchorpoint theory suggested by Golledge (1975, 1978), in which a hierarchical ordering of locations, paths, and areas within the general spatial environment is based on the relative significance of each to the individual. Initially locations that are critical in the interaction process such as home, work, and shopping places anchor the set of spatial information developed by an individual, and condition the search for paths through segments of space capable of connecting the primary nodes or anchorpoints. Both node and path knowledge is organized hierarchically with primary, secondary, tertiary and lower order nodes and paths forming a skeletal structure upon which additional node path and areal information is grafted. Home, work, and shopping tend to serve as the initial primary nodes and are among the major anchor points from which the rest of the hierarchy develops. Other anchor points may include commonly recognized known and used places in the environment. A total set of anchoring nodes then is a combination of those selected in common with others as part of a general pattern of recognition of critical things in an environment (i.e. the common cues that identify cities as being distinct one from another), together with the principal idiosyncratic sets of points that are relevant to any single individual's activity patterns. As interactions occur along the paths between the primary nodes, there is a spillover or spread effect and the development of the areal concepts of neighbourhood, community, region, and so on. Neighbourhoods surrounding the primary nodes sets become known first, and continued interactions along developing node-path networks strengthen the image of segments of the environment for each individual while formalizing the content and order of the basic common knowledge structure at the same time.

5.5 CHILDREN'S WAY-FINDING BEHAVIOUR

Empirical literature on the acquisition of spatial knowledge in children has typically examined what is known about a familiar environment which is the child's neighbourhood. Such studies generally focus on tasks such as the accuracy of distance judgments for pictorially presented routes, and tasks with significant spatial components such as way-finding and route reversal have for the most part been restricted to small scale spaces and short routes, generally within buildings. More recently, extensive empirical work by Golledge, et al. (1985) has focused on the process of way-finding in children acting in known and unknown neighbourhoods. The following represents a summary of their critical results to date.

5.5.1 Assumptions and Hypotheses
There are three critical assumptions underlining the empirical task set out by Golledge, et al. (1985). These are:

(a) Individuals tend to code more information at spatial decision points than nondecision points in a way-finding task.
(b) During way-finding tasks, automatic processes of perception, concatenation, pattern matching and generalization respectively extract, store, access, and reorganize information received from the environment.
(c) Any given environment consists of sets of objects or features, their properties, and values or saliences attached to each one. These vary from individual to individual.

Given the above set of assumptions, it is possible to derive sets of hypotheses such as:

(i) Environmental cues or other features of the environment have the highest probability of being perceived and recognized if they are in the immediate vicinity of choice points.
(ii) Any given route tends to become segmented with respect to choice points.
(iii) The amount, variety, and accuracy of information extracted at choice points varies according to the nature of the action required at the choice point (e.g., simple versus complex responses).
(iv) Information recalled about features of the environment is related to the significance of the choice points anchoring any particular segment in which the feature is located.
(v) Route segments and routes themselves become concatenated in long term memory and can be used in other tasks.
(vi) Generalisation and spread effects inevitably lead to hierarchical representations of environment.
(vii) Areas of recognition, action, and expectation, are likely to occur with decreasing frequency on successive way-finding trials.

5.5.2 A Case Study: Way-Finding in a Residential Neighbourhood in Goleta, California

An empirical study based on the above assumptions and designed to test the above hypotheses was undertaken in a moderate density residential neighbourhood in Goleta, California. The area was completely residential in character, thus simplifying the task of recognizing categorizing and using environmental cue information. Most of the empirical features related to housing, street, or cross street characteristics. There were no visibly dominant cues in the neighbourhood to aid in orientation, and spatial knowledge had to be acquired in a sequential manner as a specific route was followed on successive trials through the neighbourhood.

Figure 5.4
Street Map of Neighbourhood
Showing Route from Church to Park

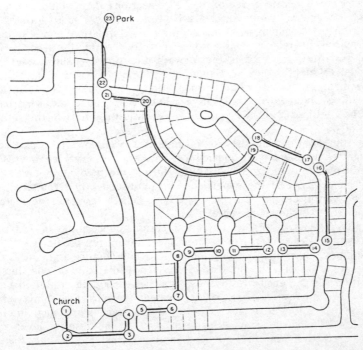

The route chosen was one where the origin and destination points were not simultaneously visible, but were identifiable only on the first and last segments of the route. Along the route were a number of choice points requiring decisions concerning left or right hand 90 degree turns, street crossings, by passing of inconsequential side streets and cul-de-sacs, navigation of long straight-aways with good visibility, and navigation along gently curving sections (Figure 5.4). Although the route length was 0.8 miles, the origin and destination were only 0.4 miles apart indicating that the route was approximately "U" shaped. Some general references provided background and possible orientation information - mountains to the north and a noisy free to the south.

The basic cue structure of the neighbourhood was obtained from cue lists and sketch maps compiled from a large sample of neighbourhood children. These were contacted through local school and scouting groups. Frequency of feature or cue mention was considered the main criteria for including cues in a common recognized neighbourhood cue set. Pilot testing of route difficulty was undertaken with male and female children from ages 9 to 11, where navigation in both a forward and reversed mode was undertaken. The pilot data indicated that information about the route was still partial and/or fragmentary even after several exposures.

Multiple trial testing was then carried out with an 11 year old male over five successive days. The boy again undertook way-finding in a forward and reversed mode, and after each way-finding task was completed, extensive debriefing occurred in a mobile laboratory at the beginning of the route. As part of this debriefing the child was asked to describe the strategy for navigation and to list salient features recalled about the route. He was also asked to generate a set of verbal directions that would allow another child to navigate the route successfully, followed by a map-drawing task on a blank sheet of paper with the origin and destination nodes indicated in their appropriate relative and absolute positions. Finally, a complete video tape of the route traversed in the forward direction was shown and the child was asked to identify any particular cues, locations, features and so on that were remembered and what actions had to be taken at specified loci. Expectations about what would appear next in sequence and what behaviour would be required were also probed. This multiple trial testing provided a wealth of data.

By the tenth trial the route appeared well-known, was segmented consistently, travelled with confidence, and was relatively error free. Little new information was produced either during the navigation task or in the debriefing period and the experiment was consequently terminated. Sketch maps and verbal descriptions matched very well in terms of the features and characteristics of the route represented.

Referring back to the first assumption concerning information and choice points, the authors constructed a composite representation of cue and feature knowledge for loci along the entire route (Figure 5.5).

Examination of this cumulative frequency diagram of cue and feature recognition for the entire route shows that whether data is plotted separately for forward and reverse trials, or aggregated, the most frequently referenced points represent loci at or near choice points - particularly near intersections or corners. There was some difference between the absolute level of cue or feature frequency in the forward and reverse mode but the critical importance of choice points is made quite obvious in such a graphic representation. It also appeared that choice points with complex operations (e.g. change in direction and cross the street) had the potential for greater cue and feature coding than a similar point where only a single simple action was required. Other locations or cue segments, where no major action or choice was mandated, were less well known, less frequently mentioned, and less accurately represented in either verbal or sketch map representation mode.

Figure 5.5
Plots and Choice Points in Goleta, California

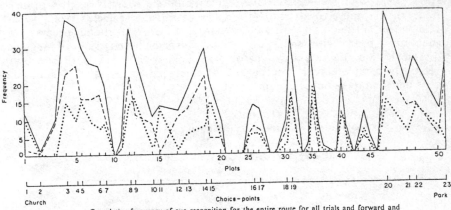

Cumulative frequency of cue recognition for the entire route for all trials and forward and reverse navigation trials by plot and choice point. ———, Total; ----, forward; ·····, reverse.

Examining data across a sequence of days shows a progressive differentiation of cues along the route, with the initial information primarily tied to the origin and destination, and with second, third, and other lower order nodes emerging on subsequent exposures. Cues devoid of any specific action other than the maintenance of the current state remain consistently low with respect to degree of knowledge.

In general, the following appear to be evident from these experiments:

(a) Origin and destination nodes anchor and define the task environment.

(b) Interstitial second, third, and lower order nodes identifying choice points emerge on successive trials, with those points mandating multiple actions providing the critical intermediate anchor points.

(c) Lower order nodes in the vicinity of higher ones help to define expectations with respect to behaviour or to potential behaviour at choice points.

(d) Some cues were trial or episode specific and were used as peripheral or supplementary reinforcing information only, and their absence or presence (e.g. a barking dog) did not substantially influence the knowledge level in their vicinity.

Examination of the verbal reports, video tape reactions, and sketch maps, throws some light on the segmentation and sequencing of components of route knowledge acquisition. For the route to be segmented appropriately and concatenated in correct sequence, the individual must have sufficient knowledge of origin, destination and major choice points along the route. This knowledge emerges over sequential trials and the lack of such knowledge in the early trials results in an inability to generate appropriate

101

sequences of route segments. Thus segment order is violated, directional changes at intersections or street crossings may be reversed, and sections curved in an inappropriate manner on these early trials (refer to Figure 5.2). The sketch map sequences shown in Figure 5.2 indicate the degree of completeness of sketches produced on both forward and reverse trials. They show some well identified route segments in the vicinity of the primary nodes on the initial trials with incomplete or missing segments typifying the remainder of the early structures. A gradual elaboration occurs over successive trials with some distortions, reversals, and lack of segment differentiation, but the final maps, after five trials in each direction, are relatively complete with respect to segments, and in terms of detail about cues and features at choice points and in their vicinity.

Table 5.2
Proportion of Features Occurring on Same Trial
and First in Video or Map Task
and Trial Lag for Different Route Segments

Choice point boundaries for segments		Same trial	Video first	Map first
1–3	Proportion	0·50	0·33	0·17
	Trial Lag	—	8·00	4·00
7–8	Proportion	0·20	0·60	0·20
	Trial Lag	—	5·00	1·00
19–20	Proportion	0·23	0·69	0·08
	Trial Lag	—	2·80	1·00
20–23	Proportion	0·50	0·50	0·00
	Trial Lag	—	3·70	—

An interesting phenomena related to the **appropriateness of the sketch mapping technique** was a marked difference in the trial sequence at which information occurred (Table 5.2). For many second and third order nodes, the subject was well into the sequence of trials before he was able to add such detailed information to his sketch maps in all segments. However, this cue and segment information regularly appeared much earlier in the verbal descriptions and discussions based on video tapes of places along the routes. Similarly, slides of cues taken at various places along the route could be identified earlier than they were found on the sketch maps. Thus while at the end of the trials the type and quantity of information on sketches, verbal reports, and video tape or slide recognition was equivalent, in the early states there were vast differences amongst results obtained from each of these methods. Obviously, one must beware if using sketch-mapping techniques in situations where subjects have little prior exposure or practice with this representational form, as a means of summarizing their existing knowledge structure.

Errors occurring during the space learning process can be classified into two types - action and expectation errors. Errors of action consisted of navigational or procedural mistakes which caused the child to deviate from the established route. Expectation errors, or errors of confusion, may not directly result in a mistake in action but indicate incomplete knowledge at a particular choice point. Confusion errors included allocating particular non-existant cues to specific locations, substituting cues from one route segment to another, nonrecognition of scene sequences, and an inability to couple cues and actions undertaken during the way-finding task. Figure 5.5 illustrates the decreasing number of errors in action or expectation, as well as total errors, as the trials proceeded. Many errors had disappeared completely after the third day.

If we examine particularly where the errors occurred (see Figure 5.5) by plotting the frequency of error at potential choice points, we see that the peak of error making occurred at a location in the middle of the route where multiple actions were mandated. Relatively few errors occurred during the beginning or end of the route and in the vicinity of other major anchor points (nodes 9 and 12). In contrast, errors at locus #10 persisted until trial 7 and are the last recorded errors. Obviously, the probability of error occurrence is related to the relative significance of a cue or route segment in the total task situation.

5.6 AN ARTIFICIAL INTELLIGENCE MODEL OF WAY-FINDING

Given the quantity of evidence from this empirical experiment, it is possible to highlight critical features of the way-finding decision process and to model it in an artificial intelligence context. A model representation of this decision making task can be constructed with two major components. The first is a representation of a **static spatial task environment** (SSTE), and the second is a representation of the cognitive structures and processing of the individual performing tasks in such a static spatial task environment. The essence of the model is to develop the possibility for a decision maker to move around this representation of the environment, obtaining information for making navigational decisions. In modelling the SSTE, a representation of a given real environment is produced in which subjects can be tested. The task area is modelled in such a way as to incorporate the salient cues that subjects employ during spatial navigation.

In constructing the representation of the SSTE, two basic units are required. The first (**PLOT**) is essentially a parcel of land from which a given dwelling and appurtenant structures are located, together with the pavement and roadside adjacent to the plot. A **decision point** represents a place at which a navigation decision must be taken. Each plot can be represented as two data structures - the PLOTFRAME contains information about the visual cues on a plot including structures, vegetation, parked vehicles and so on. The VIEWFRAME contains information characterizing other plots as they are seen by a subject standing in front of the given plot and may include context information such as curvature and slope of the street, visible intersections, and unique features such as hills, trees, mailboxes,or so on which may serve as cues during navigation.

A simple logical language is developed focusing on elements known as feature-property-values (FPV triples). Each FPV consists of: one member of a class of objects (e.g., houses, mailboxes, trees, cars), one member of a class of properties characterizing the object (e.g., shape, size, colour, orientation), and a member of the class of values that can be taken on by the property (e.g., large, blue, sculptured, untidy). Relational properties (such as the logical connectives "and", "or" and "not") are used to link object, properties, and values in order to produce complex forms (house/object–next to/property–big tree).

Along with the representation of the SSTE is required a computational process model (CPM) of the individual who interacts with the SSTE during navigation tasks. The individual modelled by the CPM obtains information from direct experience of the immediate environment. This is then employed in accessing other information stored in the individual's knowledge structure to allow the making of decisions regarding what actions must be taken to complete a given task. Actions include information processing tasks such as perception, storage, accessing and transformation of environmental information. Obviously, the modelling process at this stage gets complicated and the structures and processes that are invoked are only models of the cognitive structures and processes in human decision makers. An obvious test of the validity of any given CPM is the ability of the model to predict behaviour and error making in given experimental situations. Figure 5.6 summarizes the major components of the CPM.

Figure 5.6

Diagrammatic Representation of Knowledge Structures in the Cognitive Model

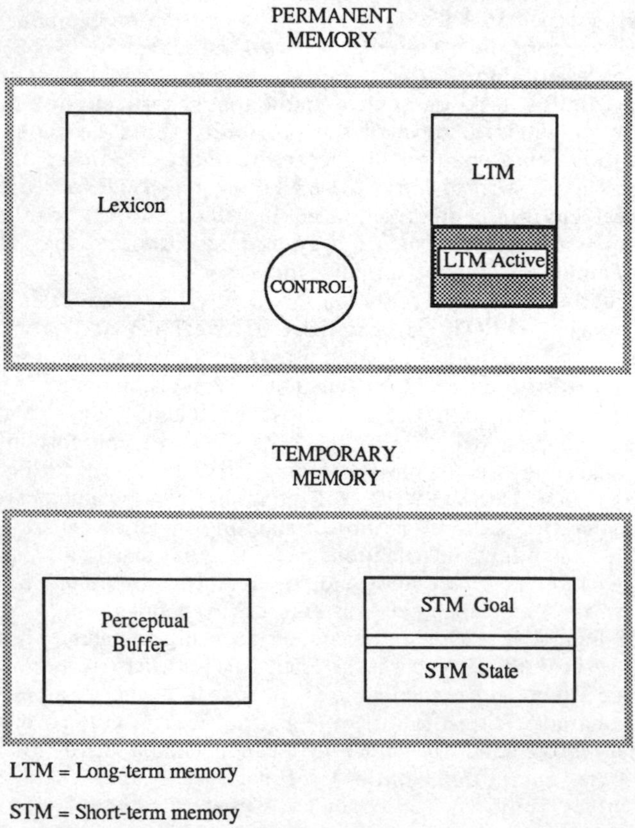

PERMANENT
MEMORY

Lexicon

CONTROL

LTM

LTM Active

TEMPORARY
MEMORY

Perceptual
Buffer

STM Goal

STM State

LTM = Long-term memory

STM = Short-term memory

The **first** **component**, a conceptual one, involves three **cognitive** **structures** - a **perceptual buffer**, a **lexicon**, and a **short term memory**. The lexicon contains each individual's lists of feature, properties, and values together with saliencies for each F, P or V, reflecting idiosyncratic and individual differences in the relative ordering or significance of environmental information. Short term memory is assumed to have two substructures, one containing FPV triples that one expects to find in the SSTE, and the second containing FPV triples that are actually found in the SSTE.

The second **component** is a **storage component**. This component focuses on actions and states, with a_i representing a particular action, and S_j representing a sequence of states of the system. An appropriate sequence is to represent a state-action-state sequence is SAS. The storage component involves a short term memory, a long term memory, and a buffer containing an activated portion of long term memory. This buffer is a temporary store for those elements of long term memory that have been recently accessed in connection with other processing. The transfer of information from STM to LTM involves a process of spreading activation in an attempt to accomplish pattern matches between elements in STM and LTM. A second process takes the most recent sequence of state-action-state from STM and places it in a buffer such that it can be concatenated with other actual or expected SAS sequences. Transfer from STM to LTM occurs when action is taken, thus admitting possible change of saliences associated with features or strings of plots represented in the states, and hence, to possible errors of knowledge acquisition.

The **third** **component** is an **action-choice component** (ACC). This accesses LTM and selects the most appropriate action to take in any given point in a way-finding task. Here for any SAS sequence in LTM, the current state and goal stored in STM are matched up, and a specific action is chosen for execution. Part of this total procedure involves action, choice, and goal setting behaviour, and a goal comparison process that compares the state achieved after taking the action with the goal state expected.

A **fourth component** of the computational process model is a **set of** **processes** restructuring LTM by allowing long **concatenations** and by generalizing over selected SAS's combinations.

The above model can be formalized as a set of interacting computer programs which allow for any given spatial task environment, e.g. selecting origin-destination pairs to be given to a decision making unit which is expected to find a route between them. The model is thus capable of predicting a given navigational task for a specific individual whose saliences have been obtained from prior experimentation. The test of the validity of the model, then, consists of a comparison of the model selected route and its appropriate segments and error components, with the actual route selected and errors made by a given subject.

Chapter Six

ACTIVITY AND ACTION SPACES

6.1 THE NATURE OF HUMAN ACTIVITIES IN TIME AND SPACE

All human activities occur coincidentally in time and space. Thus, we need to find ways to describe and explain the patterning of these activities in time and space. Traditionally, geographers have given considerable attention to the study of locational aspects of human activities. However, it has only been more recently that the location of activities in time has been given the same significance in research. It is relatively easy to study the absolute spatial locations of activities and the locational outcomes of human decision-making with reference to grid coordinates, such as are used on maps. But, the absolute locations of activities can also refer to location in time that is derived from a clock or calendar. In this context, clock time acts as a type of grid, and activities and decisions are put into it. In this way, we may consider the position of an activity in time in relation to the position of another activity in time, or relative to some other location in clock time. In their book on times, spaces and places, Parkes and Thrift (1980: 4) have emphasised the necessity of analysing human activities in a time-space framework. They have this to say:

"The separation of two items in space may be described by the distance between them and the separation of two items in time by the interval between. When spatial metrics such as meters or kilometers are used to measure distance we have a measure of absolute distance. If temporal metrics such as hours or days are used to measure interval we have a measure of absolute interval. However, when as aspatial metric is used to indicate distance and an atemporal metric is used to indicate time, for instance money, then distance and interval are being represented in relative terms, as relative distance and relative time. One of the most common relative space measures combine space with time, as distance with interval. Thus in everyday life we consider the time it takes to get somewhere. This notion of distance and interval in combination is now frequently referred to as a time-space metric... The geographer's space time is not a new physical structure, as is the four-dimensional space time of Minkowski or Einstein, instead it is a technical convenience and a more realistic way of looking at the world."

We may thus think of human activities occurring within a context of locational space coordinates, with distance being separated within a space metric and all of these occurring within a time period, thus giving an overall space time metric. In this way activities and events can be located on a time-space map.

In this chapter the nature of human activities will be investigated in a time-space context. A distinction is made between obligatory and discretionary activities.

6.2 ACTION SPACES AND ACTIVITY SPACES

The concept of **action space** has been developed to describe an individual's total interaction with and response to his/her environment. People gather information about their environment and ascribe subjective values, or utilities, to various locations. In this way places are given a **place utility**. As Wolpert (1965) has indicated, it is the nature and spatial extent of all our place utilities that comprise our action spaces. Thus, in a broad context, action space provides a framework within which individual or group spatial interaction can be viewed. Jakle, et al. (1976: 92) say of action space:

"It specifically draws attention to the individual's relationships with his surrounding social and spatial environment and allows us to examine the patterns in which individuals interact in space. We can most effectively use the concept by dividing it into meaningful components - movement and communications."

We will look at the notion of individual action spaces and their components.

6.2.1 Individual Action Spaces

Although, theoretically, the individual has access to a broad range of environmental information, usually only a limited portion of the environment is relevant to his/her spatial behaviour in any given context. Horton and Reynolds (1969: 70-71) have suggested that, even though an individual's **action space** is spatially limited, an examination of its formation leads to the consideration of a wide range of spatial behaviour, such as the journey to work, shopping, visiting neighbours and friends, and so on. One cannot ignore the individual's perception of the objective spatial structure of physical, economic and social environments within which this behaviour takes place. Because no two individuals perceive a given environment, such as a city, from exactly the same point simultaneously, and because each person bases interpretation of information obtained from the environment on past experience, action spaces vary from person to person. However, while perceptions and action spaces are, to a large degree, individualistic, there is much reason to suggest that they can be shared by groups of people. Horton and Reynolds claim this to be the case, because the formation of an individual's action space is almost certainly affected by group memberships, position in social networks, position in life cycle, and spatial location with respect to potential trip destinations. Generally, the residence is a primary node in an action space. Horton and Reynolds claim that the perception of the urban environment is an important determinant of an individual's action space. Of equal significance is the perception of time and time preferences. In this context, time preference refers to an individual's waiting of time allocations for various types of activities. They suggested that:

"It would appear appropriate to adopt a behavioural approach which examines the formation of the individual's action space as a function of his socio-economic characteristics, of his cognitive images of the urban environment and his preferences for travel."

The individual's perception of his/her environment is not static, but has been seen to change via a complex learning process, as discussed in Chapters 4 and 5. Given socio-economic constraints, and provided that the individual does not change his/her place of residence, we can expect the individual to modify his/her perception of the environment by moving within it and by communicating with his/her peers about it. The individual's behaviour thus approaches a spatial equilibrium over time. However, this presupposes that the objective urban environment itself does not change. In fact, this is far from the case, as its components, such as its retail structure, the location of employment opportunities, residential qualities, and so on, are constantly undergoing change. This results in the continuous reordering of perceived urban space structure. In addition, technological change plays an important role in extending an individual's action space and in modifying its morphology. For example, the increased use of private transportation has, without doubt, made it possible for an individual to extend the perimeter of his/her action space. At the same time, the increased use of private transportation, particularly for the journey to work, has led to spatial distortions and place disutilities within the action space by yielding penalties in the form of congestion and its concomitant psychological and physiological effects. Thus, Horton and Reynolds maintain that:

"Continuous technological change and perceptual lags would seem to preclude the possibility of the individual achieving spatial equilibrium and economically rational behaviour, although they may be approached. Herein lies at least a partial explanation why deterministic, non-behavioural models have met with little success in dealing with the problem at hand. Nevertheless, an individual's environmental perception should be in equilibrium within his action space, the one being a satisfactory predictor of the other."

The individual's **time preferences** are likely to be important in effecting the morphology of his/her action space. As is well known, time preferences vary systematically throughout an individual's life cycle. Other factors can also have direct and indirect influences, in particular, income, education, occupation, and social status.

The location and spatial structuring of urban activities are also important in understanding action spaces.

Thus, we can conceptualise the formation of individual action space in the model proposed by Horton and Reynolds reproduced in Figure 6.1.

This represents one of several ways in which household action spaces can be examined in order to isolate factors which are important to their formation, spatial structure and change.

6.2.2 Components of Action Spaces
One important part of an action space is the **collective movements of individuals**. The movement component of an action space may be termed an

activity space, which may be defined as the subset of all locations within which an individual has direct contact as a result of his/her day-to-day activities. A second part of an action space is defined as **communicating over space**: using interpersonal communication channels such as telephone, mail, or mass media such as newspapers, magazines, radio and television. Thus, activity spaces represent direct contact between individuals and their social and physical environments, whereas communication channels are indirect links with their environment.

Figure 6.1

A Conceptual Model of Action Space

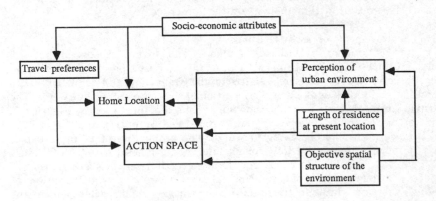

Source: After Horton & Reynolds, 1969:73

The **activity space** for a typical individual will be dominated by three things:

(a)   movement within and near the home
(b)   movement to and from regular activity locations, such as journeys to work, to shop, to socialise, and so on
(c)   movement in and around those activity sites.

Furthermore, some individuals undertake extensive travel across broad areas of their region, country, or the world as part of their work and leisure activities. Jakle, et al. (1976: 93) claim our

"activity spaces are an important manifestation of our everyday lives, and, in addition, represent an important process through which we gain information about and attach meaning to our environment."

For example, direct contact has an important influence on the way in which we define territories, both at an individual and group level. Perceived, as well as formally defined, territories act to constrain and direct our trips through space. People living in cities often avoid particular places in their spatial behaviours because of perceived hazards relating to areas of high crime rate, and so on. Formal boundaries, such as international political boundaries and other man-made boundaries, may also act as constraints to movement. In this way, two important geographic concepts, **identification of territory** and **movement in the environment**, are closely linked.

Activity spaces are also closely linked to an individual's role within society. Both the temporal and the spatial aspects of a person's activity space are the product of his/her defining a set of activities in which he/she desires to participate. The real world behaviour patterns of individuals, as defined by their activity spaces, may thus be seen in the context of an activity system. Through their experiences over time, people develop territorial familiarity varying in degree according to the locations they patronise in space, and the extent of cognitive reinforcement attached to places. This occurs within their overall action space.

6.2.3 Some Aspects of Activity Space
It is useful to identify both the temporal and spatial aspects of activity space. Concerning the **temporal aspects** of activity spaces, movement to specific activity locations are related to the frequency and regularity with which an individual will choose to participate in a specified activity. The possible forms that such regularities might take are illustrated in Figure 6.2. Part (a) of Figure 6.2 shows regularly scheduled activities, such as a club meeting, going to church, going to work. The probability of taking a trip is high at specific times, and low during intervening times. Part (b) of Figure 6.2 illustrates trips to purchase regularly needed items that are consumed regularly through time. These trips take on a probability distribution of gradual increase through time until the trip is made, after which the probability of going again is reduced to near zero. These types of trips, such as shopping trips, tend to be evenly spaced in time. Part (c) of Figure 6.2 illustrates trips to time contagious activities, such as playing golf. Here, participating in the activity increases the probability of participating again soon, a probability that gradually decreases through time. This type of activity and its associated trips tend to be clustered in time. Finally, Part (d) of Figure 6.2 illustrates trips to randomly occurring activities, such as emergency trips. Trips in response to emergencies or accidents are randomly distributed in time. Participation in this type of activity does not affect the probability of participating again.

We may also view the temporal nature of activity spaces with respect to the overall mix of activities in which people participate. For example, Chapin (1965) took a planner's perspective, in which activity spaces are viewed in terms of the time durations an individual, family or household, spends in different kinds of places. Such an approach is illustrated in Table 6.1. A simple classification for time budgeting is given in the left hand column. With each type of activity, we can associate a trip type. At both the individual and household level, the progression of people and households through the life and family cycles means that particular types of activities and associated trip types may occur and then disappear at key points. Thus, life and family cycle stages have a direct impact upon the nature of activity spaces and the spatial nature of trips that are undertaken.

Examining the **spatial** aspects of activity spaces involves both the location of activities (particularly relative to important nodes, such as

Figure 6.2

Relationships Between Time and the Probabilities
of Trips to Different Activity Locations

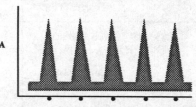

Regularly scheduled activities (club meeting, church, work)

Trips to purchase regularly needed item (groceries)

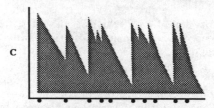

Trips to time-contagious activities (sports)

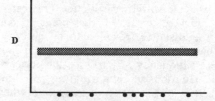

Trips to randomly occurring activities (emergency trips)

• Occurrence of an activity

Source: After Campbell, 1980

location of residents and location of work) and distance decay. Mapping trips and recording their timing are important for planning purposes, especially in forecasting transportation and other facility needs and locations. Certain spatial regularities have been noted in activity spaces. The simplest

111

Table 6.1

Classification of Activity and Trip Types

TYPES OF ACTIVITIES	TYPES OF TRIPS
Income producing (may only apply to household heads)	Journey to work
School (applies only to children)	Educational trips
Buying food and other goods	Shopping trips
Socializing with friends, relatives, etc.	Informal social trips
Community and club activities	Formal social trips
Outdoor recreation, entertainment	Recreational trips
Church, political activities	Cultural trips

Source: After Chapin, 1965

and most universal is that of **distance decay**, which is an aggregate concept that indicates a tendency for people to take trips most frequently to places nearby and less and less frequently as distances from the origin of the trip increases.   At the individual level, however, the form of movement with respect to distance is typically much more complex, being related, for example, to the specific location of a person's origin, the home, and to the location of chosen activities. Thus, significant variations between individuals can be seen.

Jakle, et al. (1976: 99) have noted linkages between the temporal and spatial dimensions of activity spaces. Activities with the greatest frequency of participation are generally located close to the home.   An inverse relationship is found between the distance travelled to an activity and the frequency of participation in that activity, owing in part to the greater time or monetary cost of longer trips. Frequency of participation in an activity is also related to the spatial distribution of opportunities surrounding an individual's home. An individual is either constrained to live where he/she does and be the victim of spatial inequalities in the distribution of activities, or he/she chooses to live where he/she does and not to participate in a certain activity. Jakle, et al. point out that it is useful to view an activity space map in two dimensions, thus introducing the idea of **directional bias**. Directional bias is often related to a partiality for a particular place over other equally distant places, owing to some perceived quality of the preferred place.

A critical factor in any bias is the **distribution of opportunities**, but certain regularities can be seen in similar environments. For example, in most urban areas, similar distributions of activity locations exist. There is a dominant centre, usually the central business district. Around that centre there tends to be decreasing population density with increasing distance, and an associated decline in the number of activity locations. This simple pattern may be modified by important radial transport lines, secondary nodes of activity, and particular physical characteristics in a given city. Nonetheless, urban areas have some common structural characteristics. Because of this commonality in regularity, activity spaces of people living in cities tend to have a common directional bias, taking the form of a sector or wedge-shaped bias. People tend to move around in, and be familiar with, that part of their metropolitan area that is on the same side of the city as their home location. It has been noted in many empirical studies that reasons for such biases include a resistance to travel through or around the centre of large cities, the tendency for individuals to select activity locations nearest them when they are duplicated elsewhere, and the radial nature of some transportation lines (see, for example, Adams, 1969; Zannaras, 1976). This bias, however, may not hold for individuals living near the centre of cities.

6.3. ACTIVITY SPACES, TRIPS AND SCALE DIFFERENCES

We may conceptualise **individual activity spaces** as being made up of a **hierarchy of movements** as illustrated in Figure 6.3. At the top of the hierarchy is the home, which is a focal point in the network of movements and from which and to which the greatest number of trips occur. Focusing on the home location are short movements which are often pedestrian, and longer trips to and from activity locations using a variety of modes of transport. Other activity locations act as centres for additional pedestrian movements.

Short distance trips involving pedestrian movement focus in and around the home and other activity locations. Many environments are arranged in anticipation of certain types of walking behaviour. For example, in large department stores, high value per volume items which are subject to impulse buying, such as women's jewellery, are placed on the ground floor near main entrances, where the greatest pedestrian traffic flows. High bulk items which are more subject to purposeful buying, such as furniture and large appliances, are placed on upper floors, where less traffic is found. In supermarkets, items with high profit margins are often placed in locations that would be encountered early in shoppers' trips through the store. Within the shopping centre as a whole, walking behaviour is an important consideration in design. For example, a typical large shopping centre will place its two or three major department stores at polar locations, with smaller specialty and comparison shops being strung out along the paths between them.

Most of the research on specific types of trips within activity spaces is focused on the journey to work. This is a segmented approach, focusing on trip type. Trips for different purposes, such as work trips, social trips, shopping trips, tend to exhibit contrasting time distributions. Work trips tend to peak at the traditional morning and evening rush hour times, whereas social trips tend to peak just after noon, around lunch time, and in the evening.

Figure 6.3

Individual Activity Space: A Hierarchy of Movements

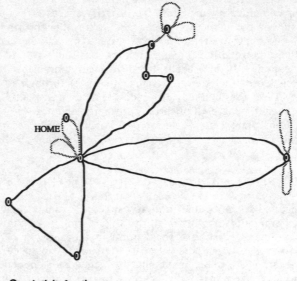

HOME

⊚   Activity locations

——   Trips by mechanized transport

········   Walking trips

Source: After Jakle, et al., 1976:101

We may further distinguish between trips made on the basis of the consistency of the activity location. Work trips usually go from home to a specific place and then back (sometimes with intermediate stops) on a regular basis, and usually five times per week. In contrast, social trips may have a regular component, such as weekly participation in formal social organisations, or an irregular component, such as visiting friends and going to parties. It has been found that in the United States people make only one stop in two-thirds to three-quarters of all of their trips. In large metropolitan cities, between 75 percent and 90 percent or all trips either begin or end at home, the remaining going between other activity locations. Thus, between 20 percent and 25 percent of trips were from one out-of-home activity to another. Apart from the home based trips, approximately 40 other out-of-home activities have been identified. These data were derived from a study by Hemmens (1970) in a major household activity pattern study in the city of Buffalo, New York. A brief look at the characteristics of particular types of trips would be worthwhile.

6.3.1 Work Trips

Work trips are the most important of trips that households and individuals undertake. The individual decisions determining the nature of the journey to work is often complicated by the decision of where to live. Thus, two separate processes are important in the journeys to work - a residential location decision and a job location decision. These two processes in combination suggest two extreme situations in which individuals find themselves selecting a journey to work.

First is one in which a family does not want to move its residence, but the head of the family seeks a job location. He/she is likely to define an outer limit beyond which he will not commute, and an inner range within which location makes no difference. These limits are perceived distances and vary with individual travel preferences and with the structure of the transport system available in the city. In between these two limits, distance may be considered as a trade-off with the attributes of the job. On the other extreme, an individual may acquire a job in a new city or state, and his/her family's selection of a residence determines the nature of the journey to work. A similar set of limits, this time around the new work place, may be set up within which distance trades off with other factors, for example the cost and size of the home, type of neighbourhood, and other site factors. As an additional complicating factor, the home location decision is often based on accessibility to other locations (such as shopping centres, schools, recreation areas and friends) in addition to the job location.

Thus, the trade-off between home and job location is not a simple one. In between these extremes many complicated situations occur. It may be that a job location is moved to a place that is still within the commuting range of an employee's home, but that has significantly increased the commuting distance. This means the activity space now includes one very long daily trip. After tolerating such a stress for a time, a decision may be made to reduce it by either moving the residential location closer to the work place, or by looking for a new job closer to the residential location.

6.3.2 Social Trips

Social trips contrast with work trips in a number of ways. In the United States, it has been found that there is a strong relationship between social trips as a percentage of all trips and family income. Also, household size has shown to be related to percentage of social trips, larger households having a lower proportion of social trips. Nearly 60 percent of social trips have a residential origin, and 20 percent have an origin at a previous social activity, 10 percent from a work or business origin, and 5 percent from a shopping or recreation origin (Wheeler and Stutz, 1971). It is also evident that different types of social trips exhibit different distance decay characteristics, the highest distance decay obviously being for trips to neighbours, with decreasing distance decay for social trips to friends and very little, if any, distance decay for social trips to relatives. However, distance decay is only part of the explanation of the spatial characteristics of social trips. Another important concept is that of social distance. There is a tendency for social trips to occur between persons, and hence neighbourhoods, of similar socio-economic status. As individuals of similar status tend to live in proximate locations within cities, this probably explains some of the distance bias that is seen in social trips. It also explains the numerous exceptions to the distance decay idea.

6.3.3 Trips to Other Activity Locations

Trips to other activity locations are many and varied, and may be taken on a regular basis (such as trips for shopping, recreation and participation in various cultural activities) or on an irregular basis. Such trips may be regarded as being scaled on a continuum from economically rational at one end to economically non-rational at the other. Shopping for groceries may reflect a genuine attempt to minimise costs (price of groceries plus transportation costs) and in such cases the distance travelled is not always the shortest, but is minimised cost-wise in conjunction with the costs of items purchased. At the other end of the continuum are those trips that minimise neither cost or distance, and instead are made for aesthetic or hedonistic purposes. These include recreation trips, where the trip itself might be part of the recreation.

6.3.4 Substitution Effect

Different trip types can be contrasted in terms of the **substitution effect**. In this case, one activity location, and its associated trip, is substituted for another, or an in-home activity is substituted for a trip. Different activities are spaced in the environment in different densities. High density activity may be subject to more substitution because of a wide range of choices, but activities with only one or two locations in a city may not allow substitution. Thus, different activities and activity locations have varying degrees of flexibility in terms of the choices that people have.

6.3.5 Multi-Purpose Trips

Not all trips are for a single purpose, and some may focus on **one location for several activities**, while others may lead to **several different locations, for one or more purposes**. A good example of the former are trips taken to major shopping centres and downtown areas for a variety of shopping purposes. Sometimes they combine social, recreation, business and other activities. It is interesting to note that the demand for multi-purpose shopping trips has led to the development, in recent decades, of higher order regional shopping centres providing a range of goods and services in one location. There has also developed a marked tendency for shoppers to bypass the nearest commercial centre and to shop at more distant ones. A study by Looman (1969) in the city of Newark, Ohio, USA, showed that 42 percent of all shopping trips were multi-purpose trips. Of the remaining 58 percent single-purpose trips, 16 percent of these involved multi-stops (Recker and Pas, 1982).

The second type of multi-purpose trip is one that includes **numerous stops at separate locations**. In a study in the city of Lansing, Michigan, USA, Wheeler (1972) collected data on multi-purpose trips which showed the correspondence of activity types and trip destinations with activities at trip origins (excluding going to and from home). The results are reproduced in Table 6.2. The data are presented in the form of a probability matrix. Thus, the first row of numbers show that 39 percent (or a probability of 0.39) of people making multi-purpose trips from a place of work went to a location for purposes of socialising or eating a meal; 12 percent went to a

Table 6.2

Probabilities of Going From One Type of Activity to Another in Multi-Purpose Trips in Lansing, Michigan

Trip Purposes	1	2	3	4	5	6	7	8	9	10
1. Work	.005	.095	.016	.003	.390	.014	.121	.024	.195	.138
2. Personal business	.043	.293	.014	.012	.177	.006	.273	.042	.056	.084
3. Medical/dental	.023	.180	.039	.023	.203	.008	.391	.031	.047	.055
4. School	.065	.082	.032	.125	.287	.090	.125	.093	.007	.093
5. Social - eat meal	.018	.049	.004	.020	.363	.005	.148	.089	.193	.111
6. Change mode	.153	.112	.000	.337	.133	.010	.102	.102	.000	.051
7. Shopping	.011	.110	.004	.006	.230	.005	.459	.005	.032	.093
8. Recreation - ride	.020	.052	.008	.023	.432	.012	.101	.208	.020	.125
9. Business	.030	.040	.006	.001	.114	.001	.049	.009	.694	.056
10. Serve passenger	.164	.103	.008	.019	.172	.002	.142	.054	.040	.296

Rows refer to origins, columns to destinations

— probability between .20 and .40

☐ probability > .40

"Change mode" trips terminate at a place where change to another form of transportation takes place.
"Serve passenger" trips terminate at a place where a passenger is being taken on or discharged (usually by car).

Source: After Wheeler, 1972:645

shopping place, 19 percent to a business location (that is, to conduct business) and 13 percent went to a location to pick up or drop off a passenger. Table 6.2 examines the linkages of trip types by focusing upon the highest percentages in each row. Thus, in the second row, personal business trips tend to be followed by other personal business trips or shopping trips. In the third row, medical and dental related trips tend to be followed by trips for socialising, shopping, or eating a meal. Wheeler was able to isolate the linkages between various types of trips in multi-purpose trip behaviour (Figure 6.4).

Wheeler made the following generalisations:

(a) Many trip types are followed by trips to social and/or meal eating destinations. These activities are quite important as part of multi-purpose trips, and are linked with a variety of other activities.

(b) The diagonal of the matrix shows that certain activities are often linked to other activities of the same type. This is particularly so for personal business, social and recreational trips, trips to serve a passenger, shopping and business trips.

(c) Work and medical/dental trips are rarely followed by a trip to a similar activity. This would be intuitively expected.

Figure 6.4

Activity Types That are Linked Together by a
Probability of at Least 20 in Lansing, Michigan

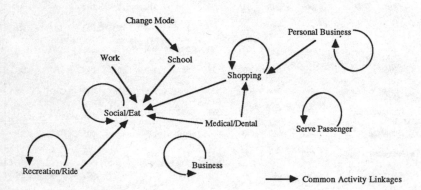

Source: After Wheeler, 1972:645

Hansen (1980) has found a number of reasons why an individual may regularly visit several establishments within one functional class in undertaking multi-purpose trips. These are:

(a) the individual's drive to reduce uncertainty by learning about available options

(b) the traveller's desire to spread risk by developing a portfolio of regularly visited destinations

(c) the variability in the spatial, temporal and modal constraints found by the individual.

(d) the individual's desire to reduce boredom by adding some variety to the travel pattern

(e) differentiation of stores, or activity sites, within a given functional class means that different stores may meet different needs at different times

(f) for employed worker the workplace is second in importance only to the home. Thus, within any given functional class, the establishments chosen in connection with a journey to work may differ from those having the greatest utility when visited directly from home. (Hansen, 1980: 247).

In a study of household travel conducted in Uppsala, Sweden, in 1971, Hansen showed how individuals spread these stops for a particular purpose over several locations. She looked at four different land types to illustrate behaviour for distinctly different purposes, namely, convenience (food store) shopping, shopping for non-convenience goods (clothes, etc.), conducting personal business (post office), and socialising/visiting (another person's home). She found that stops at food stores and other people's homes are made more frequently than are stops at clothing stores or at the post office. There was considerable interpersonal variability in the frequency with which a given land use type was visited, in the number of different (unique) locations visited per person over the 35 day study period, and in intra-personal variation in the spatial diversification of destination. It was found that only 27 percent of food shoppers confined their shopping to one store, while 60 percent of post office users went to a single location. Thus, the purpose of the travel affects number of destinations used. Furthermore, the study showed that for all land use types an average of one half of the individual stops were made at the one plan that was most frequently visited, this being 68 percent for food stops.

Hansen concluded that the results of the Uppsala study showed that although not everyone spreads stops for a particular purpose among several different outlets, for three out of the four land use types studied (post office being the exception), more people do spatially diversity by visiting more than one destination of a given type than do not; those who confine their visits to one location of a particular land use type are in the minority; thus it is "reasonable to assert that spatial diversification is an important component of spatial choice." (Hansen, 1980: 251). She showed that there are groups, or bundles, of functions that are frequently used in combination on the same multi-purpose trip. Principal components analysis was employed to show that there is a group of land uses linked to the home, the work place, while other groups are linked most strongly to other urban functions. Table 6.3 reproduces the factor loadings of activities and functions used for the first six factors which together explain 77.1 percent of the total variance among the set of destinations. While the groups of land uses are not discrete sets, it is clear that bundles of functions or purposes are frequently combined on the same trip and that the composition of the bundle that contains a certain purpose may vary from trip to trip.

Finally, Hansen showed that there was little overlap between the set of destinations individuals visited only on single purpose trips and the set of places visited only on multi-purpose trips. When all purpose travel is considered, the average per person number of different places visited only on a single purpose trip was 12, and the average number of locations contacted on a multi-purpose trip was 24. However, an average of only 4.7 places per person fell in both sets. Finally, it was found that more locations overall and within a given functional class (food stores) are contacted during multi-purpose trips than on single purpose trips, thus demonstrating the importance of the multi-purpose trip in generating spatial diversification in destination choice. The particular bundle of purposes to be combined on a multi-purpose trip is therefore important in deciding on the establishment chosen at a destination.

Table 6.3

Results of Principal Components Analysis of Matrix Travel Linkages Between Land Use Types

Factor	(Destination) Land Use	Factor Loading	(Source) Land Use	Factor Score
1	Outdoor recreation	.928	Own home	4.771
	Train, bus station	.914		
	School	.892		
	Meeting places	.887		
	Indoor recreation	.881		
	Work place	.896		
	Other person's home	.868		
	Doctor, dentist	.842		
	Cinema, theatre	.831		
	Hospital	.800		
	Church, cemetery	.793		
	Cleaner, shoe repair	.696		
	Public offices	.660		
	Barber shop	.548		
	Post office	.531		
Explained varience:		36.1%		
2	Restaurant	.884	Work place	3.945
	Kiosk	.799		
	Car repairs	.793		
	Bank	.792		
	Photography shop	.756		
	Liquor store	.603		
	Grocery store	.595		
Explained varience:		20.2%		
3	Clothing, jewellery	.910	Clothing, jewellery	2.757
	Department store	.828	Department store	2.678
	Book store	.700		
	Hardware, paints	.656		
	Library	.654		
	Home furnishings	.540		
Explained varience:		9.8%		
4	Bakery, cafe	.645	Grocery store	2.799
	Drug store	.618	Doctor, dentist	1.921
	Barber shop	.543	Drug store	1.472
	Flower shop	.495	Kiosk	1.090
Explained varience:		4.2%		
5	Insurance, other offices	.769	Bank	3.107
			Post office	1.944
	Gas station	.600	Bakery, cafe	1.306
	Post office	.523	Insurance	1.286
Explained varience:		3.9%	Parking place	1.210
6	Sports, toy stores	.762	Sports, toys	2.204
			Department store	1.840
			Hardware, paints	1.729
			Restaurant	1.310
			Other persons's home	1.060
			Post office	1.027
Explained varience:		2.9%		
Total explained varience:		77.1%		

Source: Hanson,   1980

6.4 SUMMARY OF FACTORS INFLUENCING DAILY ACTIVITY PATTERNS

A number of general conclusions can be drawn from the foregoing discussion of the nature of human activities in time and space within the context of individual action spaces and activity spaces. There appear to be three major components of daily activity patterns. These are:

(a) the time of an activity
(b) the space over which the activity takes place
(c) the type of activity.

All of these are highly interconnected. Time is taken into consideration in two ways. First, in terms of the duration of each activity, and second, in terms of the time of occurrence of the activity.

The **duration** of each activity is a basic ingredient in the account of a day's activities. But not much is known about this aspect of activity patterns. The **time of day** when activities occur is also important and may be critical in determining whether or not an activity will take place together with others that are needed during the daytime.

The distribution of facilities in space for particular activities appears to be of prime importance in determining whether or not a given activity will be performed, perhaps more so in determining the frequency with which an activity will be performed. We may hypothesise that activities will have longer duration when access is close and easy, rather than when it is difficult. Further, the distribution of potential places of activity is viewed by the individual from a certain perspective, that is, from where he/she is located in the urban area. This means there is a need to relate activity patterns to the overall cognitive map that people have of an urban environment and, in particular, to identify orientation nodes. It is well known that an individual's view of opportunities available for inter-action changes as he/she moves about an urban area. The selection of any activity can be explained in terms of motivations, needs, wants, and capabilities of individuals. The whole range of socio-economic characteristics of individuals and family units thus becomes an important aspect in any attempt to explain the structure of various activity patterns. It is also important to consider the fact that activities are a function of preferences, tastes, information habits, and financial circumstances.

6.5 AN ACTIVITY APPROACH

King and Golledge (1978) have noted that an **activity approach** to urban analysis will provide great insights into the functioning of urban areas and to their spatial structure. The urban analyst views the city as a collection of individual activities, actions, reactions, and interactions. They describe urban places in terms of what is going on instead of in terms of quantities of land use of various types. In adopting this approach, the rationale is that by knowing how people actually use an urban area, how they respond in choice situations, how they sequence their activities and the duration of their activities, and the relation of each of these things to changes in their own circumstances, then we will be in a better position to evaluate policies designed to change urban environments, and in a better position to describe the city as it is used by the people living in it. Human activity analysis, guided by theory and using time-budget records, will offer the promise of supplying some conceptual guidelines for relating behaviour patterns to the spatial organisation of the city. Cullen (1978) makes the following claim:

"To understand human spatial behaviour, rather than just monitor it, we must treat time explicitly as the path which orders events as a sequence, which separates cause from effect, which synchronises and integrates...(in fact) the lack of an explicit treatment of time in behavioural studies, apart from the odd desultory venture into the field of predictive analysis...has been truly remarkable." (Cullen 1978: 28-31)

A number of theoretical approaches have been developed and empirically tested. We will examine a number of the more important approaches of the last two decades. But first a few basic notions.

6.5.1 Activities as Routines
Basic to these approaches is the notion that **activities are discrete episodes** that occur at uniform intervals in the life of a person or household. Their motivation is derived from a set of prior values. An activity results, produced by a choice mechanism, that has a spatial manifestation. Thus, activities are viewed in terms of routines. A **routine** is a recurring set of episodes in a given unit of time. A recurrence may not apply the same length of time for each activity, because different routines require different periods of operation. Activities may be modified on consecutive trials until feedback no longer substantially alters the activity and a routine, or habit is formed. Almost all frequent routines will be daily, weekly, seasonal, or life cycle. It is the daily routine on which researchers have concentrated most. The main components, or episodes, of household activity patterns may be defined in terms of how available time is budgeted and where activities take place. Also of importance is the mode of transport between origins and destinations which separate activity episodes.

6.5.2 Activity Systems
The fundamental **activity systems** of a city will be those of its people, and these collectively generate the need for, and set in operation, other entities that develop their own activity systems. An example will help illustrate. Activities associated with shopping, commuting, and recreation may progress to the stage where business or government activities will have to be ordered to cope with them, and as a consequence, the environment in which activities take place will change. Schedules of individuals may have to be adapted to conform with schedules of institutional entities in matters such as working hours, transportation times, and so on.

6.5.3 Obligatory and Discretionary Acts
A further important general notion is that activity systems consist of **obligatory** and **discretionary** acts. Obligatory acts include sleep, work, and school. Discretionary acts include recreation, some shopping activities and leisure. Obligatory activities occur more or less in cycles with timed regularity. Identifying these cycles is the first phase in being able to predict

and plan for activities in cities. In a typical week-day, up to 18 hours may be expended on obligatory activities such as sleep, work, home-making, and shopping. Of the remaining 6 plus hours that are available for discretionary activities, most are spent at home. Thus, the importance of the home and its neighbourhood is evident. This has implications for the allocation of public resources for leisure time facilities. Discretionary acts will vary from household to household and produce some variation of behaviour within groups. Discretionary acts may be deliberately selected by people and reflect people's initiatives, or they can stem from changing external circumstances.

6.6 MODELLING APPROACHES TO HUMAN ACTIVITIES

Three basic modelling approaches will be examined. The first may be termed the **transductive** approach, in which the focus is on solving urban planning problems through a better understanding of the living patterns of city residents, the way they allocate their time to different activities in the course of a day, the rhythm of these activities around the clock, and the locus of these pursuits in city space. It is an approach pursued by Chapin and his followers at the University of North Carolina (see Chapin, 1974). Chapin suggested that there were variations in activity patterns among sub-societal segments in the population, and, when studied, we may postulate antecedent ties which these patterns may have with felt needs and preferences.

The second approach may be termed **routine and deliberated choice** approach, as proposed by Cullen and Godson (1975). They propose that for any population it is the recurrent routine activities which structure the day. Thus, an individual or household's routines will be structured around a relatively small number of deliberate choices made rather infrequently. There is little demand for deliberate choice about the majority of activities in which people engage, and, in fact, there is usually neither time nor opportunity for alterations to the schedule. They claim that a few key times and activities will act as pegs around which the day is organised.

The third approach is termed the **routine and culturally transmitted structure** approach, which was developed at the Martin Centre for Architectural and Urban Studies at Cambridge University. In this approach there is no explicit attempt to explain behaviour, as evident through activity patterns, in terms of motivations or other aspects of psychological underpinnings of behaviour. Instead, the approach postulates that time rhythms have a culturally transmitted structure. Shapcott and Steadman (1978) claim that there will be a pattern of constraints which restrict and limit social and spatial behaviour in such a way as to confer freedom and possibilities for a variable choice of patterns of personal activities. Thus, a structuralist method is adopted which implicitly includes motivations as part of a determined and determinate social structure.

A full analysis of these and other model approaches is given in Parkes and Thrift (1980, Chapter 5). What follows is an attempt to summarise the main aspects of these approaches.

6.6.1 The Transductive Approach

The approach developed by Chapin and his fellow workers at the University of North Carolina may be described as an aggregated, survey-based approach. In it, the population is categorised on the basis of socio-economic and demographic characteristics, and sub-groups are seen to interact with the processes that produce the spatial organisation of a city.

Chapin (1974: 40) describes the model as transductive because it is concerned with the individual and the household, and behaviour will be regulated primarily by biological time, coupled to learned behaviour related to social time. The model seeks explanation by assessing the relative importance of the role and personal background factors which pre-condition people from different population sub-sets to adopt particular activity patterns. In addition to looking at the relative significance of motivations and other attitudinal factors affecting predisposition to act in one way or another, predisposing factors mean most closely associated with activity routines.

The approach uses human activity patterns as the means by which people satisfy needs and wants. These are:

(a) **subsistence needs**, such as sleep, food, shelter, clothing, and health care, plus activities which supply income to help satisfy these basic needs

(b) **culturally, socially, and individually defined needs**, which are met by engaging in a wide range of social and leisure activities.

Chapin also recognised **obligatory** and **discretionary** activities. This distinction was very much related to the two types of needs outlined above. Chapin also recognised activities as learned behaviour or acts of individuals, as motivated behaviour which is on-going, initiated by an individual through want and directed to the end of satisfying that want through the use of suitable elements in the environment. This is somewhat akin to operant conditioning, in the tradition of Skinner's theory of learning. In this, "the environment not only provides the opportunity for the act but also it conditions the act through its consequences." (Chapin, 1974: 27).

In this context, Chapin's approach views activities as consisting of three components:

(a) a **motivational component** (felt need or want directed towards a goal)

(b) **choice component** (alternatives are considered)

(c) an **outcome component** (observable action).

In more recent work, Chapin (1978) developed a choice model of time allocation to daily activity patterns (reproduced in Figure 6.5). The model is in the form of a conditioned response model. Learned forms of behaviour are seen to be shaped by four influences. These are propensity, an opportunity, an appropriate situation, and an environmental context. The propensity is the motivational basis for the activity but conditioned by a person's specific constraints. A **propensity element** determines what activities are likely to fall in a person's realm of concerns, thus defining the scope of choice. The **opportunity element** refers to the availability of a

Figure 6.5

Choice Model of Time Allocations to Daily Activity

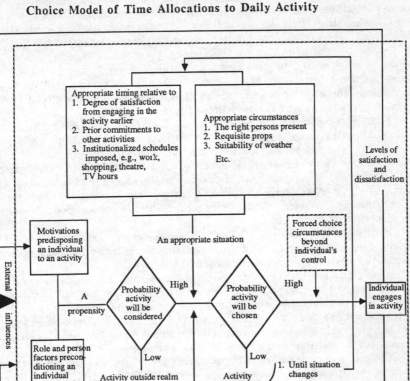

Appropriate timing relative to
1. Degree of satisfaction from engaging in the activity earlier
2. Prior commitments to other activities
3. Institutionalized schedules imposed, e.g., work, shopping, theatre, TV hours

Appropriate circumstances
1. The right persons present
2. Requisite props
3. Suitability of weather
   Etc.

Levels of satisfaction and dissatisfaction

Motivations predisposing an individual to an activity

An appropriate situation

Forced choice circumstances beyond individual's control

External influences

A propensity

Probability activity will be considered

High

Probability activity will be chosen

High

Individual engages in activity

Role and person factors preconditioning an individual for an activity

Low

Activity outside realm of individual's concerns

Low

Activity postponed

1. Until situation changes
2. Or until opportunities are available

An Opportunity

Effects on environmental context

Congeniality of surroundings for an activity

Accessible place and facility of acceptable quality for an activity

Urban environmental context

Source: After Chapin, 1978

physical place or facility suited to the activity and to the congeniality of surroundings for engaging in an activity. The **situational element** refers to the appropriateness of timing and circumstances for the activity. The environmental context is a milieu within which choices are made, and it has everything of a non-physiological nature influencing a person's behaviour, including previous behaviour. In Figure 6.5 the choice process is represented by the flows on the diagram. The urban environmental context (the dashed outermost line) envelopes and influences the whole process of behaviour choice. The motivations which predispose an individual to an activity combine with certain role and personal characteristics to pre-condition an individual for an activity. Predisposing and pre-conditioning factors are susceptible to inputs to the activity system, and they are influenced by the activities to which they give rise. Together, these will initiate a propensity to consider an activity, and if the probability of engaging in an activity is high, then two additional factors will come into play before the activity is selected: an appropriate situation needs to exist as must an opportunity to engage in the activity.

What is the part played by **situational** factors in the probability that an individual will engage in an activity? First, timing must be appropriate relative to a number of known and anticipated factors. Second, the circumstances of the act must be acceptable. For example, the right persons must be present, a suitable time, suitable weather conditions, and so on must exist. If these characteristics of a situation are considered appropriate, information is hardened, the activity probability is raised, perhaps even to the level of forced choice.

What of the **opportunity** factor? Two things are involved here. They are the congeniality of surroundings and the accessibility in space and time to facilities which have perceived acceptable quality.

When situation and opportunity combine to induce a high probability of participation, only unexpected events will prevent the activity from taking place. If postponement of the activity occurs, the urban environmental context will have been brought into the choice process. Once an activity is engaged the environmental context will impinge on the future by reinforcing existing **predispositions** and even adjusting existing **pre-conditions**.

An important aspect of Chapin's approach concerns variations in the degree of postponability of an activity - that is, its **elasticity**. Thus, there is an ordering of activities along a continuum from obligatory activities at one pole, to discretionary activities at the other. It should be noted that the elements of the transductive choice model presented in Figure 6.5 are particularly pertinent to the discretionary activity mode. As Chapin indicates

"the ordering suggests that on the average people have more latitude for choice at the discretionary end of the continuum and little or no latitude for choice at the obligatory end...What is discretionary and what is obligatory are relative concepts. An activity is discretionary if there is a greater degree of choice than constraint." (Chapin, 1974: 37-38).

Obviously, the basic physiological needs of everyday living, such as sleeping and eating, offer limited choice possibilities, are low in elasticity and will reveal little or no difference between populations drawn from different socio-economic and demographic sub-groups. In contrast, however, self-actualising or discretionary needs are continuously confronting the variabilities incorporated in the transductive choice model.

Chapin applied his model to the analysis of data sets collected in 1968 and 1971 in Washington, D.C. Two communities were sampled, an inner city black community and a central transitional white community. High and low income groups were distinguished, as were male and female, and the degree of full or part-time employment. Activity patterns according to eleven activity categories were generated for an average spring week-day. These are reproduced in Table 6.4. Data in the table shows the proportion of people engaged in each of the activity categories, based on an initial grouping of about 225 possible activities. The lower half of the table shows the average number of hours allocated to the activity by those who engaged in it. Within the table, the boxes refer to population and activity categories which were given more detailed attention in further survey work conducted in Washington in 1971. The emphasis was on discretionary pursuits which were particularly amenable to explanation by the transductive choice model. Results of the 1971 study are reproduced in Table 6.5. By distinguishing between male and female groups working full-time or part-time, the sample could be related to the causal factors of pre-condition, and pre-disposition, which the transductive choice model suggests are activity pattern determining factors. It can be assumed that situational and opportunity components of the model are satisfied because the results refer to activities which are actually current. Furthermore, because only a single day (i.e., a 24 hour period) is involved, the urban environmental context is constant, having little or no influence on activity choices which were made during that period. Thus, there is no feedback of new information to alter pre-disposition or pre-condition, and there are no changes in the timing and spacing of activities. Satisfaction of needs is based on what has been learned from the previous day and on experience of persistence over a longer period of time.

Chapin summarised the influence of motivational factors with respect to men working full-time (WFT) and men working part-time (not WFT). This was done according to rank scores from a stepwise multiple regression analysis, and the rank order of importance of factors are reproduced in Table 6.6.

To illustrate the kind of interpretation that the transductive model allows, let us look at the status component of **esteem** (that is, the need for status) represented by the declared importance of having neighbours of similar socio-economic background. To the men in the black community, apparently this was less important than for men in the white community, especially as a predisposing factor before engaging in social activities. The transitional white community was, in fact, about three miles further from the city centre than was the black community, and during the summer, in which the survey was taken, the black community had experienced considerable violence in the streets in their neighbourhood. The concern about violence in the streets became a very significant pre-disposing factor, generated by the unsettled urban environmental context in the days preceding the study. Social activities of all kinds which involved leaving home were thus affected, especially in terms of their time location. In-house activities were adjusted in consequence. Given preconditioning factors, such as stage in the life cycle or health status, then both study groups had their activity patterns determined to a similar degree. The health status factors were marginally more significant in the determination of activity choice in the white community than was the case in the black community.

From the above, it is evident that there is a considerable value in having a theoretical structure upon which to base interpretations, such as that

127

Table 6.4

Activity Patterns of Persons According to Race and Income in Washington, D.C., 1968

Activity Measure and Population Segment	Work	Eating	Shopping	Home-making	Family Activities	Church & Orgs.	Recreation & Hobbies	Social Activities	Watching Television	Resting & Relaxing	Misc. Activities	All Forms of Discr. Activity	All Out-of Home Activities
Per cent of Persons in Each Segment Engaging in Activity													
All Persons (n = 1,667)	58	96	36	76	31	6	29	36	67	57	96	99	87
Black (n = 358)	59	93	19	71	13	5	13	22	69	41	90	99	78
Nonblack (n = 1,309)	54	97	40	78	35	7	34	40	66	62	97	99	90
Low Income (n = 592)	44	92	27	73	25	5	21	31	69	50	89	97	75
Middle Income (n = 863)	64	97	40	76	33	7	31	37	65	59	97	99	91
High Income (n = 212)	64	97	42	76	33	8	40	44	58	69	97	98	94
Mean Hours Allocated Per Participant[b]													
All Persons	8·7	1·7	1·6	3·6	1·7	2·2	2·3	2·0	2·5	1·6	2·9	5·9	10·4
Black	9·1	1·5	1·7	3·7	1·6	2·2	2·7	2·2	3·5	2·4	2·9	5·8	10·6
Nonblack	7·6	1·8	1·6	3·6	1·7	2·2	1·8	2·0	2·2	1·5	2·9	5·9	10·3
Low Income	8·8	1·6	1·6	4·3	2·0	2·4	2·2	2·3	3·1	2·1	2·9	6·3	9·9
Middle Income	8·8	1·8	1·5	3·3	1·6	2·2	1·8	1·9	2·1	1·5	2·9	5·7	10·6
High Income	8·7	1·9	1·8	3·1	1·6	1·7	1·7	1·9	1·7	1·4	3·0	5·9	10·8

a Income figured on a per-member-of-household basis. For the derivation of income groups, see Chapin (1974, Figure III–3, p. 64).
b Includes time spent in travel to and from places where activity took place out-of-home.
Note: Table 2 examines the activity patterns enclosed in the boxes using results from supplemental investigations of low income persons.

Source: Chapin, 1978 in Carlstein, Parkes & Thrift, 1978 Vol. 2:21

presented within Chapin's transductive choice model. Parkes and Thrift have presented the following evaluation of the model:

"The theory guides the selection of empirically derived relations. It should be noted that by emphasising choice factors in activity participation this becomes an ideal tool for planners. When making decisions they are better able to accommodate aggregated choices assessed through a model which is initially sensitive to the motivations which pre-dispose action; to the role in person characteristics which pre-condition action and to the perceived availability and quality characteristics of facilities in time and over space." (Parkes and Thrift, 1980: 217)

Table 6.5

Discretionary Activity by Sex and Employment Status
Washington D.C., 1971

	Inner City Black Community Low Income only[a] (1969)				Close-In White Community Low Income Only[a] (1971)			
	(n)	Social Activities	Watching Television	Resting & Relaxing	(n)	Social Activities	Watching Television	Resting & Relaxing
Per cent of Persons in Each Segment Engaging in Activity								
All Persons	(223)	34	71	56	(241)	56	70	48
Women Working FT	(45)	18	67	49	(31)	81	71	39
Women Not WFT	(120)	40	71	56	(110)	59	75	50
Men Working FT	(32)	28	75	47	(50)	32	54	38
Men Not WFT	(26)	42	73	81	(41)	61	73	59
Mean Hours Allocated Per Participant[b]								
All Persons		2·0	4·2	3·2		2·4	2·9	2·3
Women Working FT		1·4	3·6	2·2		1·6	2·0	1·2
Women Not WFT		2·1	4·0	3·2		2·6	3·4	2·0
Men Working FT		1·1	3·9	2·4		2·2	2·4	2·2
Men Not WFT		2·7	6·1	4·9		2·6	2·9	3·5

a Income figured on a per-member-of-household basis. For the derivation of the 'low-income' category, see Chapin (1974, Figure III–3, p. 64).
b Includes time spent in travel to and from places where activity took place.

Source: Chapin, 1978, in Carlstein, Parkes & Thrift, 1978 Vol 2:22

6.6.2 The Routine and Deliberated Choice Approach

A second approach to modelling human activities in time and space is that proposed by Cullen and Godson (1975: 7) who ask the question: "How do we find out more about the way in which the individual's time-space (space-time) dimensions are structured?" Basic to their approach is the role of motivational and psychological factors, the proposition that activity patterns are highly structured and routinised and largely beyond the control of the

Table 6.6

Application of the Choice Model to Survey Results from Washington D.C., 1971

Rank Order Importance of Factors for Male Heads of Households[a]

Proxies of Motivational Factors	Inner City Black Community (1969)						Close-In White Community (1971)					
	Social Activities		Watching Television		Resting & Relaxing		Social Activities		Watching Television		Resting & Relaxing	
	WFT	Not WFT	WFT	Not WFT	WFT	Not WFT	WFT	Not WFT	WFT	Not WFT	WFT	Not WFT
Predisposing Factors												
Need for security: Concern for violence in neighbourhood	—	1	2	4	4	2	—	1	2	—	—	—
Need for achievement: Evaluation of chances of 'getting ahead'	1	—	—	—	—	—	1	2	1	2	—	—
Need for status: Desire for neighbours of same SES level	—	2	3	—	3	—	3	—	—	—	3	3
General social adjustment: Degree of alienation	4	4	1	2	2	—	2	3	—	1	1	4
Preconditioning Factors												
Stage in life cycle	2	—	4	3	1	1	—	—	3	3	2	2
Health status	3	3	—	1	—	4	4	4	4	4	4	1
R²	·20	·18	·08	·17	·08	·22	·12	·56	·24	·63	·10	·15

a Rank order established from step-wise regression analysis; beyond the ranks shown, the value of the multiple determination coefficient R² changes very little.

Note: WFT means 'working full time.'

Source: Chapin, 1978 in Carlstein, Parkes & Thrift, 1978 Vol 2:23

individual except in terms of a small number of significant decisions made during a lifetime, and that motivational and other psychological factors, like stress, levels of expectation and degree of commitment, combine to influence these significant, if infrequent, decisions or deliberated choices. Cullen and Godson (1972: 8) propose the following generalisation:

"Activities to which an individual is strongly committed and which are both space and time fixed (that is to say they must occur at a particular space location and at a particular time), tend to act as pegs around which the ordering of other activities is arranged and shuffled according to their flexibility ratings."

It was hypothesised that, while not consistently rational, behaviour contains **highly organised episodes** which are structured by physical patterns and needs with priorities based on considerations such as the financial importance of the activity, the presence of certain other participants, the order in which activities are planned to occur, and the likes and dislikes an individual has for specific activities. **Constraints** were seen to operate on choice, and when related to priorities, any single activity choice would be subject to a fixity rating according to the degree of commitment of a person to that activity. Cullen and his fellow workers attached great importance to the **fixity ratings of activities**, suggesting that fixity ratings enable scheduling to facilitate **synchronisation** of activities and movements, and to consume limited time.

For Cullen and Godson, the amount of time allocated to an activity is a measure of its **utility**. Time is also a linking medium, thus time becomes a path which orders events as a sequence, separating cause from effect, always synchronising and integrating activities.

In the above context, the time-budget approach is interpreted by Cullen and Godson as an accounting medium for the analysis of activities.

A basic problem relates to how activities are classified in terms of their functional characteristics, as is the case in the transductive approach discussed previously, because this makes it harder to identify motivational factors involved in activity choice. As a partial solution to this problem, Cullen and Godson suggested it was more appropriate to classify activities directly according to motivation or degree of commitment, or of **deliberated premeditation**. In this way, one enhances meaning given to human activities differentiated and classified on a functional basis. For example, if we were to take the activity shopping, various sub-categories of this classification are evident according to whether it was premeditated or impulsive, planned at some specific time in advance or forced by circumstances, and so on. Thus, we may regard activities in terms of whether they are planned or unplanned, deliberated or spontaneous, expected or unexpected, fixed in time or not fixed in time, etc.

In studying daily activity patterns of individuals and households, Cullen (1978) noted that many activities are deliberated quite carefully, yet the profile of activities in a normal day is very much swamped by a dominant pattern of repetition and routine. Thus, there are a few deliberated choices concerning only a small number of key events in life which act as pegs around which other activities become scheduled. Cullen cited key events such as marriage, the job one has, the school one is sent to, whether one has children or not, as being the primary structuring agents for the daily activity routine. When the day begins, its programme is already printed, and the stage is set for another performance much like yesterday's. Cullen (1976: 407) saw:

"Action as a response to the means which are attached to and define the social and spatial institutions against which action is set. Adaptation is a process, whereby long-term deliberated choices about where to live, what job to take, and which clubs to join are translated into a pattern of daily and weekly routines."

Figure 6.6
Routine Activity and Long Term Choice

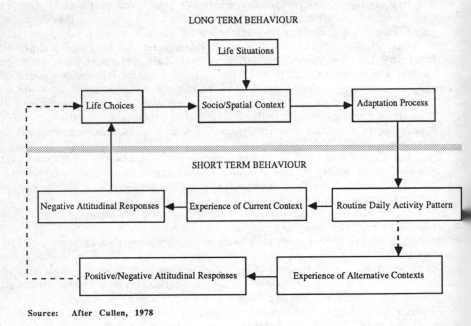

Source: After Cullen, 1978

This notion of **routine activity**, in a long-term choice context, is illustrated in Figure 6.6. In this way, Cullen suggests that each day is a product of a mixture of choices and constraints. In the long term, we seriously deliberate over limited aspects of our situation, and accept others that are simply beyond our control. In Figure 6.6 time enters the cycle in the form of the dotted line shown in the diagram, and helps overcome a paradox whereby actions which are dependent on motives and attitudes are, in turn, the initiators of motives and attitudes through experience gained in action. The cycle is broken with explicit reference to time, thus enabling us to differentiate the long-term attitude behaviour relationships from those which operate on a day-to-day basis. Cullen claims that, to a greater or lesser degree, every activity is fixed in time or space, sometimes in both. Cullen identified four categories of activities which affect the subjective

132

rating of fixity which people may ascribe to activities. They also relate to existing objective fixity factors, like the opening times and closing times for shops, locations of recreation facilities, and so on. The four subjective factors of fixity are as follows:

(a) **Arranged activities**, involving joint activities with others, which may be more or less difficult to arrange at some other time or some other place, depending on the status of those involved.

(b) **Routine activities**, which are undertaken with sufficient regularity and frequency that may become highly fixed, particularly in time.

(c) **Planned activities**, which need not involve others but will be assigned a level of subjective fixity according to commitment. Generally, the nearer in future time an activity is, the harder it is to adjust its planned space-time location.

(d) **Unexpected activities**, which may impose fixity ratings onto existing arranged, routine or planned activities.

To summarise the position reached by Cullen and his colleagues, Cullen (1978: 33) had this to say :

"What we have argued is that an understanding of long term behaviour must be based upon a logically prior understanding of everyday activity patterns for one very simple reason. Whilst the important choices which determine the way people fashion their own environments, and which obviate the need for choice in the short-term, are infrequent and oriented to distant time horizons, their implications are experienced day-to-day as discreet moments of pleasure, indifference or pain."

In empirically testing the routine and deliberated choice approach thus developed, Cullen and his colleagues focused on the **day-to-day diary technique** as the core element among their survey instruments. This is because if the aim is to explain choices in the long-term, the model described above requires monitoring not only overt behaviour, but also the way attitudes develop against the backdrop of everyday activities. This can only be achieved if we ensure that the environment, the activity and the attitude are each recorded with a device which does minimum violence to the way they were experienced. The diary approach is a device which recalls a sequence of events from the recent past. While being far from perfect, it categorises, pre-codes and punctuates everyday behaviour in a variety of more or less arbitrary ways.

Analysis of data collected from such diaries involves frequency counts using **activity episodes** as units. This allows cross-tabulations to be undertaken, for instance of pre-arrangement and subjective fixity. Time allocation analysis, involving statistical description of the time-budget, is based on computed mean durations and other statistical moments around the mean, with activities further classified according to fixity, deliberation commitment, and so on. An example from Cullen and Godson (1975), is given in Table 6.7. Once means and variances for the duration of time allocated to activities, classified by function, premeditated choice, and so on, have been computed, it is possible to calculate intercorrelations among all activity classes and then to use factor analysis to determine whether there is

Table 6.7

Allocation of Time by Degree of Pre-Arranged and Fixity
(Mean Duration Figures in Minutes)

	Mean number of episodes per day	Mean percent of episodes	Mean time in minutes/day	Mean percent of time	Mean duration of episodes
Pre-arrangement					
Arranged	2•8	8•8	133	9•2	47•0
Planned	5•4	16•8	225	15•6	41•7
Routine	9•8	30•6	301	20•9	30•6
Unexpected	6•8	21•1	196	13•6	29•0
Time-space fixity					
Not able to do anything else at that time	7•1	24•7	324	22•6	45•6
Not able to do activity at any other time	9•2	28•5	375	26•1	40•8
Not able to do activity else-where	10•1	49•8	534	37•2	52•9
Could not have been elsewhere at that time	9•1	29•7	351	24•4	38•6
Generalized fixity	3•6	11•2	203	14•1	56•3

Source: After Cullen, 1975:21

any underlying structure in the day. Furthermore, time series analysis may be used to analyse relative time location, that is when something happens in relation to some other event. Using such approaches, we are able to answer questions such as, which activities tend to lead and which tend to lag other activities? and how does one activity tend to lead or lag another activity?

The sequencing of activities is an important aspect of this approach. Computing transition probabilities and using time series analysis are two methods which clarify the degree to which there is internalised structuring of activity patterns, independent of time allocation and durations. The object here is to investigate and determine the probability of occurrence of given sequences of activities.

Cullen and Godson (1975) used time series analysis to study activities and their various attributes throughout the whole day. Taking the period of 17 hours from 07.30 hours to midnight, the period during which most people are awake, broken down into 100 equal 10 minute intervals, from survey data they were able to show, for each interval, the number of people engaged in a particular activity. Also, they determined the number of people who describe the activity in which they were engaged as being of a certain fixity or deliberated choice type, such as a routine, planned alone, fixed in space, fixed in time, and so on. In this way, they were able to develop an indication of the changing shape or structure of the activity and its perceived constraints during the day. They studied 19 activities, or attributes of activities, in detail. Three of these are discussed here to illustrate the approach. The results are presented in the graphs in Figure 6.7. It must be remembered in interpreting these graphs that the data was a 14 day diary survey collected from an institutional population, namely university students in a British university. The first graph shows the characteristics somewhat akin to a normal curve, peaking around the noon time.

There are considerable oscillations in the second graph. The two marked peaks in the third graph is probably different from what would be expected in a normal community, and reflects the institutional community on which the survey was based. Cullen and Philps (1975) also looked at stress as an explicit feature of the routine and deliberated choice approach. They studied 50 married couples (in Hackney in London). Their conclusions were that, while the structure of the normal day was highly routinised, the subjects did note the stresses of everyday life and were more prepared to talk about them than they were to talk about the unstressed highlights of the day. Stresses have to be coped with, and they form part of the adaptation process which operates to produce long-term behaviour. Stresses may be graphed in a way similar to that used in Figure 6.7.

As might be expected, the graphs showed that the number of husbands who reported feeling under stress at various times of the day showed lags of about 4 hours related to work distribution peaks. While less than 30 percent of the working day was spent at work, over 70 percent of all stress was experienced during that time. However, the cumulative effect of stress was marked; sensitivity increased as morning became afternoon, and as afternoon became evening. It would seem from the routine and deliberated choice approach that it is possible to structure the analysis of human activities in a manner allowing very positive contribution to be made towards explaining some of the basic characteristics of human activities. Parkes and Thrift (1980: 229) suggest that the possibility of coupling the transductive and the deliberated choice approaches exists, and would be a fruitful area for research, particularly in transport choice studies.

6.6.3 The Routine and Culturally Transmitted Behaviour Approach.

The aim in this approach is to estimate the distribution of aggregates of people in the three-dimensional frame of location, time and activity. Environmental contraints may be built into an elementary entropy maximising method. Sets of equations allow the prediction of the population aggregates distribution in relation to the three principal dimensions of location, time and activity. This method has been outlined in Thomlinson, et

Figure 6.7

Daily Activity Structure With Time and Space Fixity

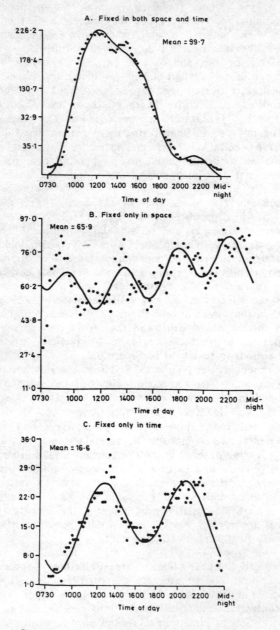

Source: Redrawn from Cullen & Goodson, 1975

al. (1969). A simple diagrammatic scheme, shown in Figure 6.8, is used to illustrate the various normal constraints operating on daily behaviour. These constraints operate through a combination of the three dimensions - time, location and activity. The sum of the cells formed by the intersection of the planes of time, location and activity, accommodate all the people engaged in various activities. The modelling problem involves allocating population groups to activities in time and space, in accordance with times allocated to similarly classified activities derived from time budgets. Parameters of the dimensions have to be estimated, subject to restrictions on the availability of locations. In Part (d) of Figure 6.8, an interrupted matrix is shown. This indicates that certain cells are not available for occupation because time, location or activity restrictions of some kind are operating. The problem to be solved is to find the most probable permutation of the permissible restrictions. The result will be the distribution of the number of people engaged in any activity for each time period in each location over the day (Bullock et al. 1974: 48).

This modelling approach is based on a number of propositions. Shapcott and Steadman (1978) have suggested that:

"a rhythmic pattern of behaviour is established, and is transmitted culturally in the form of a known timetable of activities."

This is a routine, rather than erratic conduct which is taken to be the primary factor in structuring an activity pattern for an aggregated population. No attempt is made to examine patterns of activity from the standpoint of the individual as a decision maker. Rather, the time-budget is taken as the starting point for the modelling of activity patterns in time and space, and the concern is with the overall pattern of behaviour of groups of people who are identified by similar easily-measured characteristics. Thus, the approach has similarities with the transductive approach of Chapin, discussed above. However, the approach has no underlying individual behaviour model on which it is based. It is similar to the deliberated choice model in that significance is assigned to the structuring powers of routinised behaviour, and it is hypothesised that there is stability of activity patterns over long periods of time. However, there is an absence of a motivational, premeditative component in the model.

A key to the model is the definition of **constraints** and **opportunities** which apply in a society or culture as a whole. Shapcott and Steadman (1978: 52-54) claim that:

"constraints (and the opportunities which they reveal) appear as rhythmic structures ... for example, the fixed hours of work might be imagined as a series of clusters of tubes appearing regularly between the hours of 0900 and 1700, the location of these tubes in the horizontal plane corresponding to the relevant spatial positions of the workplaces in the city or region in question ... an instantaneous time slice cut through this picture will reveal the effective map of the spatial area in question, as it is defined in activity terms at the chosen time of day."

A further interesting notion is that activity patterns have a **culturally transmitted** structure. In part, this rationale belongs to Popper's world of

Figure 6.8

A Three Dimensional Time, Location and Activity Matrix

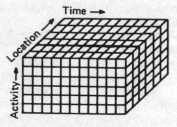

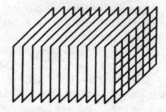

(a)   A three-dimensional array of cells representing activity, time and location

(b)   The total population in cells in each activity/location plane must obey the population constraint

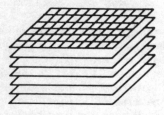

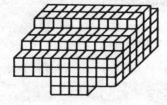

(c)   The total population in cells in each location/time plane must obey the time budget constraint for that activity

(d)   Some activity/location combinations are not available, nor are some activity/time combinations

Source: After Bullock, et al., 1974

objective knowledge (Popper, 1972). The previous approaches discussed above have placed human activity patterns in terms of interaction between the environment of the city and the subjective environment of individuals. In this approach, a third world mediates between these two environments. This is the **world of objective knowledge**, which is a cultural product. In the study of human activity it provides a perspective between that of the wholly subjective, psychological point of view, and the wholly rigid cultural and environmental deterministic point of view. At any single point in time the social structure of temporal regularities is "a given so far as the individual is concerned" (Shapcott and Steadman, 1978: 73). There have been a number of major studies which have applied this approach. We refer to one of these as an application.

A study was conducted in the city of Reading, in southeast England, involving 450 residents. It was possible to calculate the amount of time, averaged over 7 days of the week, these residents spent on various activities. The population was split into three categories: men, working women and non-working women. The study was compared with a time budget study

Figure 6.9
Comparison of Work:
Men not at Home in 1961 and 1973 in Reading

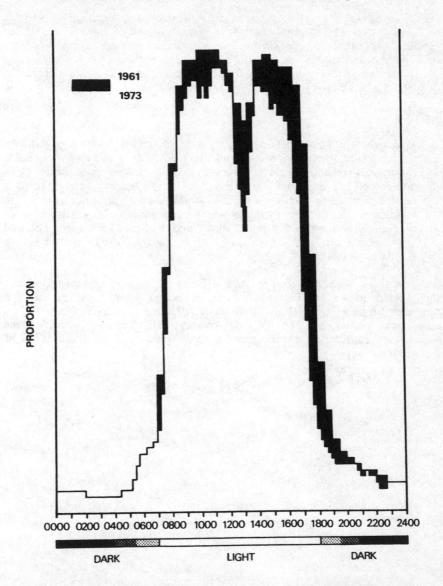

Source: Shapcott & Steadman, 1987, in Carlstein, Parkes & Thrift, 1978 Vol 2:59

that had been undertaken in Reading in 1961 by the BBC to assess the long–
term stability of population activity structure. The argument made was that
the changes in culturally transmitted structure between 1961 and 1973 would
have initiated significant differences in the structure of the daily routine.

Comparison of the 1961 and 1973 figures for the population category, 'work: men not at home', is given in Figure 6.9. Shapcott and Steadman (1978: 67) concluded that:

> "In spite of the large social changes which have occurred over this period, and which might well have been expected to have a real effect on daily activities: (for instance) an average increase in real incomes over the period of something like 30 percent, a change in the proportion of women in the work force from 30 percent in 1961 to 42 percent in 1971."

it seems:

> "...that decisions about the timing of most of the major kinds of activity are not made on a daily basis at all. Instead, individuals and households collectively commit themselves over a much longer time scale by a number of life decisions - marriage, taking particular jobs, choosing a particular place to live, sending their children to a particular school - to a series of rhythmic constraints which then govern the greater part of their daily routine and around which and within which these optional and variable activities which do occur at the day-to-day level must be fitted in."

The links with the routine and deliberated choice approach outlined above need to be emphasised. Thus, it would seem that routine and constraint enable people to cope with the complexity of an urban environment which is faced on a day-to-day basis, thereby eliminating the necessity of considering anything but a small fraction of the true variety of that environment.

Chapter Seven

TIME-PATH ANALYSIS

7.1 ACTIVITIES IN A SOCIETAL CONTEXT

While geographers have long been concerned with investigating the spatial organisation of society, man-environment relationships and the nature of processes underlying human spatial behaviour and spatial decision/choice, relatively little attention has been directed to investigating individual behaviour in a societal context. In this chapter we focus on what may be described as **time-path analytic approaches.** Here, individual behaviour is seen as interrelations between people and between people and the environment (natural and man-made) in which there is a fundamental bond between life, time and space. An integral interface between individual behaviour and the waking of society in a holistic sense is recognised.

The approach originates from research by Swedish geographers and has been incorporated in comprehensive reviews of the time-geographic framework recently published (see Pred, 1973, 1977; Thrift, 1977; and Carlstein, Parkes and Thrift, 1978, Vol. 2). The approach deals with the actions of specific individuals and groups as well as the temporal and spatial organisation of entire activity systems, thus presenting a bridge linking the micro level of the individual with the macro-level of society.

The chapter examines in detail the characteristics of time-space activity budgets and discusses a range of examples from studies conducted at different levels of analysis.

7.2 THE LUND APPROACH

An innovative and instructive approach to the study of time, space, and activities is what has become known as the **Lund time geography approach.** It is the result of attempts by geographers at Lund University in Sweden to develop a model of society in which constraints on behaviour (activity) may be formulated in the physical terms "location in space, areal extension and duration in time" (Hagerstrand, 1970: 11). Although known for more than two decades within Sweden, it was not until 1970 with publication of Hagerstrand's seminal paper, "What about People in Regional Science?" that this approach first became more widely known.

7.2.1 Constraints, Paths and Projects
At the heart of Hagerstrand's time geography, as initially formulated, is the notion that all of the actions and events that sequentially make up the individual's existence have both temporal and spatial attributes. Consequently, the biography of a person is always on the move and can be

depicted diagrammatically at daily, weekly, annual or life-long scales of observation as an unbroken, continuous path through time-space. In the time geographic approach, the first step is always to try and define a **bounded region of time and space** and treat everything in it as a time-space flow of "organisms and artifacts" (Hagerstrand, 1970). The framework thus begins with the environmental structure that surrounds every individual. It attempts to capture the complexity of interaction at the scale of the smallest indivisible unit. It permits the physical boundaries of space and time to be evaluated as they impinge on intended activity programmes. There are no direct references to motivational factors which are involved in intention. Why we do things is obviously an important factor in the understanding of human activities, but it is also important to know what stops us from doing certain things.

The approach suggests that there are a relatively smaller number of primary factors in everyday life which impinge upon all individuals and constrain their freedom to occupy certain space and time locations. When these **constraints** are identified, it is possible to deduce reasons as to why a particular individual follows one path rather than another. For Hagerstrand, the life of the individual is his foremost project, and a logical place to begin the study of human geography is thus with the individual. A **project** in time geographic terms is a set of linked tasks which are undertaken somewhere at some time within a constraining environment. Any bounded region will contain a population made up of individuals (organisms and artifacts) represented in the geographic approach as point objects. These describe trajectories or **paths** through time and over space, from the point when and where they come into being (birth) to the point where and when they cease to be (death). For the purpose of time geographic analysis, such paths are followed until they make a permanent exit from the bounded space-time region that is under study, or until they are transformed into some other entity, as in the case of many materials. We may study point object populations in two ways. One way is from a **demographic** point of view, where the concern is only with numbers and descriptive characteristics, such as age and sex. The other is **geographically**, where the concern is to develop explanations of the ways in which different individuals and populations co-exist in the same time-space frame or region.

The Lund time geographic approach may be seen as capturing the spatial and temporal sequence and co-existence of events by using a dynamic map to represent the path of an individual in motion over space and through time. This is illustrated in Figure 7.1. Each **path** shown represents a particular **trajectory** of one individual. When the line of the path is vertical, there is no movement over space. When the line is sloped, **velocity** is registered. The shallower the slope, the greater the speed or velocity of movement, and less time is consumed to cover a given distance. The opposite holds true when the line is steep. If we record the movement of a number of individuals over a period, it is easy to see that we build up a **web of interacting trajectories**. When this is repeated over the lifetime scale for each individual, we construct the geographic biography of the population within a "constrained environment" (both space and time are limited in supply).

Figure 7.1

Some Elements of the Time-Geographic Dynamic Map

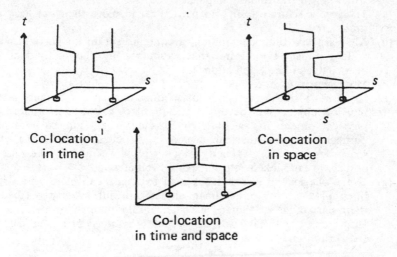

Co-location
in time

Co-location
in space

Co-location
in time and space

Source: After Parkes & Thrift, 1980:245

7.2.2 The Prism

Time and space are absolutely inseparable from the intricacies of human behaviour. Using time and space is contingent upon the constraints which operate on individuals. These constraints affect people's ability to influence their environment thus, an individual's spatial reach is limited. This physical limit sets an accessibility field within the environment which constitutes a connected and continuous set of positions in space-time, and has been called a **prism** (Lenntorp, 1976). The time geographic approach may be described as physicalist, because it is explicitly only concerned with the physical, concrete observable realism of the location and movement of individuals, and not with individual experiences and intentions. However, this does not mean that there is no awareness of the significance of factors which underlie the conduct of human behaviour. Motivations and intentions are rather seen as being elusive, and difficult to handle.

7.2.3 Physical Conditions

Hagerstrand (1975) has summarised the physical conditions of existence which we need to consider in the development of a time geography in the following terms:

(a) There is an indivisibility of human beings and of many other objects. It is always necessary to take into account the fact of the individual's corporealities, that is the constraints that a particular physical limitation of the human place upon action.

143

(b) There is a limited life span of existence of all human and other physical entities. This alone does not account for many demographically based interactions amongst individuals and upon which all life ultimately depends.

(c) There is a limited ability to participate in more than one task at a time.

(d) All tasks are time demanding; a commitment to a particular task will diminish the finite time resources of the individual and ultimately, of the population.

(e) Movement uses time.

(f) Space has a limited capacity to accommodate events because no two physical objects can occupy the same place at the same time. Any physical object has a limit to its outer size, and so limits the number of objects that can occupy a particular space. Thus, every space has a packing capacity which will be defined by the types of objects to be packed into its area or volume.

(g) Every physical object which has an existence will have a history or biography. Most non-human objects are sufficiently defined by their past alone. Humans have an ability to plan or permute the future and are sufficiently defined only by considering the past and the future.

Pred (1977) has claimed that these time geographic realities will always be true, regardless of any individual variations in the perception, conception and measurement of space and time. They are facts of life, springing from the nature of physical being and they are responsible for the local connectedness of existence with which time geography is concerned. In this way, the web formed by the connectedness of individual trajectories, or life paths, is the outcome of collateral processes within bounded regions, or, as described by Hagerstrand (1976: 332):

"...processes which cannot unfold freely as in a laboratory but have to accommodate themselves under the pressures and opportunities which follow from their common existence in terrestrial space and time."

7.2.4 The Nature of Constraints: Projects and Paths

The Lund time geographic approach is based on the premise that individuals have goals. To attain goals, projects must be formulated. **Projects** are composed of a series of tasks and act as the vehicle for goal achievement. Thus, projects will include people, resources, space and time. To complete a project, one must overcome the constraints which exist in the environment. The pursuit of projects involves events and actions that are incorporated into an individual's **path**. We have listed above the factors that are likely to limit these events and actions. The action and event sequences, or behavioural choices that accumulate along an individual's path on a day-to-day basis, also may be thought of as being constrained by three major factors. These are:

1. **Capability constraints**, which circumscribe activity participation by demanding the allocation of large portions of time to physiological necessities, such as sleeping, eating and personal care. These

constraints also limit the distance an individual can cover within a given time span by the transport technology at his command.

2. **Coupling constraints**, which influence where, when and for how long the individual must join other individuals or objects in order to form production, consumption, social and miscellaneous activity bundles. Coupling constraints largely determine the pattern of the paths which occur within an individual's daily prism.

3. **Authority constraints**, which limit access to either space locations or time locations. They subsume those general rules, laws, economic barriers and power relationships which determine who does or does not have access to specific domains at specific times for specific purposes. All environments are replete with control areas or domains of authority, the purpose for which seems to be to protect resources, according to Hagerstrand (1970: 9). There is a hierarchy of domains of authority. These range from near absolute regardless, of individual attributes, to subordinate domains, which can be entered given social power of one kind or another.

Pred (1981) has stated that:

"The composition of an individual's path will be circumscribed by the number and mix of specialised, independently existing, roles proffered up by the organisations and institutions found within any given bounded area (or by the activity system of a given area), and by the rules, competency requirements, and economic, class and other constraints that govern entrance to those roles. (The specialised roles embedded within organisations and institutions exist independently - until terminated or superseded - in the sense that when they are not filled by one person they sooner or later must be filled by another person.)"

The paths of individuals may be regarded as dynamic maps consisting of **path space-time bundles** (Parkes and Thrift, 1980: 250). Paths have different life spans or durations. They meet at different **stations** as a result of different tasks and projects. Stations have different physical extent in time and space and are represented as tubes of varying size, according to the length of time for which they are in operation. The length of time a station is open may result from an authority constraint, such as a licensing law.

Pred (1981: 236) has pointed out that the path perspective with its emphasis on behavioural restrictions can easily lead to the mistaken conclusion that the Lund time geography approach is merely a form of constraint analysis that is best suited for exercises in social engineering. This is a mistaken conclusion and is probably one of the main reasons why the time geographic framework has not gained more widespread acceptance.

A **project** needs to be seen as consisting of "the entire series of tasks necessary to the completion of any goal-oriented behaviour." (Pred, 1981: 236). A project can be something as mundane as writing a letter. On the other hand, it can involve a chain of tasks as complicated as that necessary for organising and carrying out production of goods and services. The tasks associated with either a simple or a complex project will have an internal logic of their own which requires that they be sequenced in a more or less specific order. We may view the logically sequenced component tasks in a project as synonymous with the formation of activity bundles, or with the convergence in time and space of the paths that are traced out either by two or more humans. Thus,

"when an individual's path becomes wrapped up with the activity bundle(s) of a project defined by an organisation or by some institution other than the family, there is a direct intersection between the external actions of the individual and the observable workings of society."

It does not matter whether a project has a one-time or a repetitive character, because the paths that must be synchronised will not normally be identical for every constituent activity bundle. Some paths will necessarily be tied up with all, or most of the project's activity bundles, whereas other parts will have only an abbreviated association with the project. In order to complete more complex projects, it may be required that several sub-projects are carried out temporarily parallel to one another. For complex projects it may also be necessary to develop subordinate and anticipated offshoot projects with activity bundle sequences of their own.

Participating in a project places demands on the limited daily time resources of the individual. This is so because the daily time resources of the individuals, groups and entire populations are limited to 24 hours times their number. As projects must be carried out at one or more locations in space, any time-space region will have a bounded capacity for accommodating the activity bundles that are generated by a project. During the period of time when the paths of people are committed to one activity bundle, they will not be able to simultaneously join an activity bundle belonging to another project. In this way, participating in a project will render individuals temporarily inaccessible to other individuals who might wish to join them for the purpose of doing some other thing at the same place, or at other locations. Thus, these individuals will opt to form their own project-related activity bundles at another time, and they, in turn, become inaccessible to other persons at that new time, possibly pushing aside or completely eliminating any chance that yet other project-related activity bundles can be developed. In this way, we can identify what is known as a **spread effect** in conjunction with carrying out projects, and a local connectedness is created between otherwise seemingly unrelated activities, events and processes. In this manner, we may view the whole operation of society as consisting of projects connected with economic production, consumption and social interaction, plus acts of contemplation which will be carried out in personal isolation. All these act in competition with each other as events and states for exclusive spaces and times.

Pred (1981: 237-239) states:

"Thus, whatever the scale of a project, whatever its degree of complexity, it cannot make its entrance, or become assimilated, into the time-space of a specific area unless: there already is a niche, or a series of openings, in the existing way of doing things, which will allow individuals (and any necessary natural or man-made objects) to couple their paths at required times and places to form activity bundles for required durations; or a niche is chiseled out to fit its time and space demands and path participation requirements through the elimination, modification or rescheduling of previously routinised projects and their component activity bundles."

Figure 7.2   Mutual Adjustments between Population System and Activity System

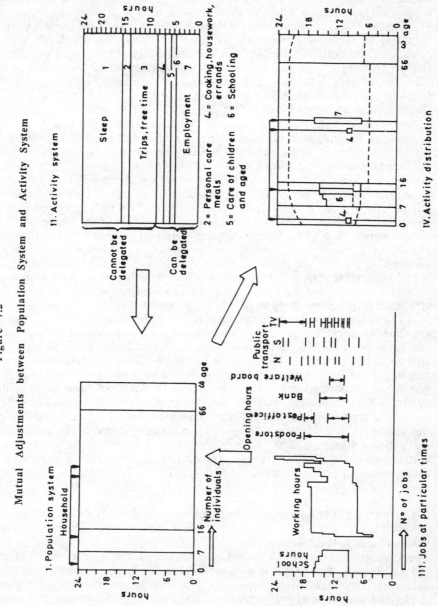

Source: Hagerstrand, 1972:147

147

7.2.5 Scales of Analysis

It is possible to discern three distinct scales of analysis in the geographic approach. These focus upon the individual, the station, and the population or activity system. We will look at these in turn.

First is the **individual scale**. At this level, the simple geographic device of the dynamic map can reveal the joint interplay of path, location and constraint. It illustrates the fact that the choice of one task by an individual implies that there will be less time available to devote to alternative tasks. This choice may lead to a blocking effect, constraining other individuals from interacting or coupling with that individual. This can lead to a displacement or a knock-on effect of those blocked activities into other activities, and possibly lead to the formation of a queue. The family may be taken as an example of a unit consisting of individuals among whom there is a high degree of interrelatedness. Decisions on the part of one member of the family can have substantial effects on the others.

Second is the **station scale**. At this level, which may include segments of the paths of individuals, the method of time geography involves mapping out the reach of each individual. In other words, we look at all the events in which an individual can participate in one way or another. These possible events, which must occur at stations, are specified by means of a **prism**, or **activity area**, which is the volume of space-time in which it is possible to carry out a particular activity, or set of activities, at a given point at which the activity must start and finish. The prism is the potential path area, and its shape is described by the individual's speed of travel, and whether the station of origin is the same as the station of destination.

Third, we have the **population or activity system scale**. At this level, the time geographic approach is built around the concepts of time supply and time demand. We need to distinguish between the population system and the activity system. This is done in Figure 7.2. The population system consists of all individuals in a bounded region of time-space. A particular population's characteristics, such as its distribution of ages and skills, determines its dynamics. In addition, there are capability constraints. The total daily supply of time for the population system is 24 hours multiplied by the number of people. Time demand is the interplay between the population and activity system, and is represented in the multitude of human projects that are conducted within various groups and organisations as part of the institutionalised activity system.

7.3 SOME APPLICATIONS OF THE LUND APPROACH

7.3.1 The Individual Scale

The Lund time geographic approach may be demonstrated very simply at the individual scale. Figure 7.3 is a dynamic map for five households and their individual members. Metric space is replaced by category or functional space, and the paths or trajectories of individuals link functional categories. The access is a 24 hour time period. The daily path of each member of the five households is thus mapped. Seven categories are recognised: place of work, place of services other than commercial, commercial services, home, recreation space, other houses and schools. In the maps, members of each household are considered by age, the oldest to the left. It is evident from

Figure 7.3

The Daily Path of members of Five Households: A Swedish Study

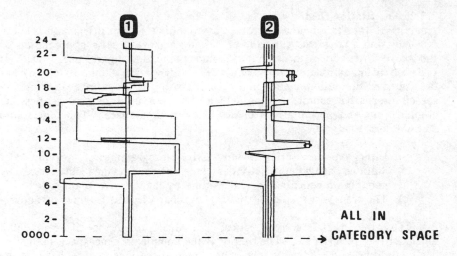

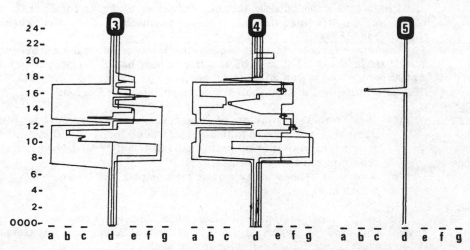

Category space as an analytical adjunct. The daily path of each member of five households. Seven categories recognized: (a) place of work (b) place of services other than commercial (c) commercial services (d) home (e) recreational space (f) other houses (g) schools. Members of each household are considered by age with the oldest to the left.

1. Man 43, car; wife 38; boy 10; boy 8
2. Man 36, car; wife 36; boy 12; girl 10; boy 3
3. Man 44, car; wife 38; car; boy 1; boy 7
4. Man 37, car; wife 34, car; boy 9; girl 7; boy 5
5. Man 81; wife 76.

Source: Martinsson, 1975

149

Figure 7.3 that there are significant contrasts between the types of households. There is a very simple map for the elderly couple, for example, and more complex maps for the larger, younger family.

7.3.2 The Station Scale
Analysis at the station level involves computation of the prism and the use of simulation analysis as a means of gaining a more precise appreciation of the possibilities open to individuals and population aggregates. Data is collected using sample survey techniques. In Sweden, Lenntorp (1976) has developed a simulation model known as PESASP (a program evaluating the set of alternative sample paths), which has been used to analyse possible combinations and permutations of activities in time-space. The inputs into PESASP are:

(a) Either one or a series of daily activity programmes of individuals
(b) Stations at which activities take place, defined in space by geographic coordinates, and in time by length of availability;
(c) The transport system of the region, characterised by lines or nodes.

Thus, the input is a hypothetical individual project, specified in detail as an activity programme. The output is the completed time-space budget of the individual. It indicates the space-time allocations which have to be made in order to achieve a project goal.

The simulation attempts to provide answers to the question - which activities would it be possible to carry out under different conditions? and which are impossibilities in a given environment for a given time period? (Martensson, 1975).

Lenntorp (1976) studied travel possibilities of public transport passengers in the Swedish city of Karlstad, which had a 1973 population of 75,000 people and occupied an area of about 35 kilometers squared. The PESASP routine was used to look at a series of questions, such as:

(a) How would alterations of timetables, a redesigned bus route network, and the addition of certain social facilities affect programme activities of individual inhabitants who have particular recurrent tasks to perform?
(b) Would the changes make certain tasks impossible?
(c) Which tasks were now impossible?

Lenntorp undertook to simulate these changes for a proposed environment, and he evaluated similarities and differences. An example shows the use of the PESASP routine in Karlstad.

The example involves an individual who leaves home 40 minutes before work begins. Five minutes of this time is involved in leaving a child at a day nursery. During the journey home after work, the child is collected. The same journey times are involved in both cases. Walking and public transport are the chosen modes of travel. This is the activity programme with which Lenntorp was concerned. The space-time environment incorporates six major workplaces in the city and the distribution of existing day nurseries. These are shown in Part A of Figure 7.4. Two proposed nurseries are shown by crosses on the map. Shaded areas represent rivers

Figure 7.4

Application of the PESAP routine in Karlitea, Sweden

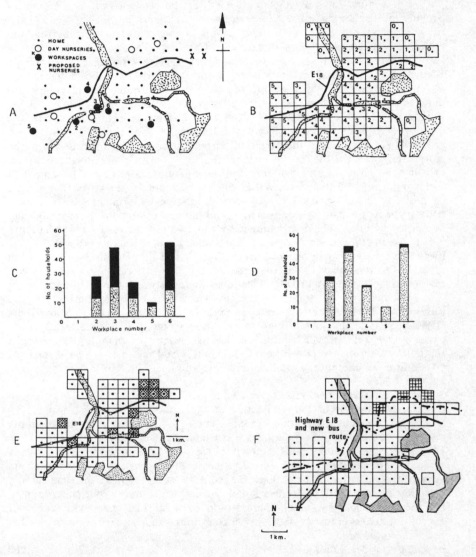

Source: Adapted from Parkes & Thrift, 1980

and other non-urban space. There are 62 residential test points which are marked as dots centred on each 500 meter grid cell they are closest to. The possibilities of performing the intended activity programme were assessed for each nursery, and in Part B of Figure 7.4 the number of workplaces accessible from each point, given the constraint that a nursery must be

151

visited are shown. The question is, if the existing environment is altered, how do the possibilities change? Change in the frequency of a bus service is made. Four departures are now made hourly instead of three. The graphs in Part C of Figure 7.4 show the number of test points from which the activity programme can be completed in relation to each workplace. The visit to the nursery is still a constraint. The graph shows the situation before the frequency of bus service is increased. The graph is Part D of Figure 7.4 shows the situation following increased bus service frequency. Part E of Figure 7.4 shows the residential test points that are now accessible to one additional workplace as a result of the new environment, and these are hatched cells in the map. The next question is, what happens to the possible individual activity programmes if the new bus route is now added to the existing network? A new transverse bus route linking the north-eastern areas of Karlstad with the western parts has been added going from the residential area in the north-east of the city through the northern areas, crossing the river on a bridge carrying the European highway, E18, and then following the motorway westward. The new route is shown as the dotted path in Part F of Figure 7.4. Another simulation experiment with the same activity program can be conducted involving increasing the number of day nurseries by two. These are shown by the two crosses on Part A of Figure 7.4 in the north-eastern corner of Karlstad. Located in the suburban areas, these new nurseries can attract custom from 9 test points, but this is only the case if the workplace is in the city centre at work point A6. For other residential test points and work locations, the constraints are too strong.

This example illustrates the use to which the PESASP routine may be put to consider alternative strategies and to test them. Parkes and Thrift (1980: 268) note that the routine can be used to test things such as adjusting existing possible travel times, increasing velocity, changing mode-split relations, altering work or nursery hours, and so on. The range of possibilities is immense, as is the range of policies.

7.3.3 Activity and Population Systems Scale

Finally, an example of the application of the Lund time geographic approach at the **activity and population systems** level. At this level, the time supply and time demand of a population are considered. The example is taken from Ellegard, Hagerstrand and Lenntorp (1976, 1978). It involves a way of assessing alternative futures for Sweden. The approach can be used to answer the question - how does the contemporary context of time supply and time demand differ from a simulation of time supply and time demand for the year 2000, by which there would be a marked change in favour of capital intensive industry, shorter working hours and an expansion of further education systems?

The model adopted by Ellegard, et al. (1975, 1977) involved investigating the future population in six stages. At the first stage, an appropriate region and time interval were chosen, in this case, a day. In stage two, a forecast of population time supply, the number of people forecast to live in an area multiplied by 24 hours, and time demanded was calculated. In stage three, the total time available was divided between activities classified into three classes, namely time devoted to production of goods, time devoted to consuming services, and time devoted to vital human activities, such as sleep.   The population was also divided into three categories corresponding with the division of these activities, and each population category was allotted a quantity of time to devote to vital needs. One group in the population was assigned to the role of production of goods, another to service consumption, and a third to a mix of production and consumption activities.   In stage four, the activities were distributed over time and within the population so that the actual time demand and time supply of the population could be evaluated.   In stage five, this distribution was related to the temporal and spatial organisation of collective activities and the age structure, household composition, and transport opportunities of the population.   In the final stage, the mix of activities in space-time given by stage five made it possible to estimate journeys generated by the need to move between these activities.   The model was run using a number of alternative formulations to try to capture general tendencies of development within a number of sectors of society so as to provide a background for more detailed future pictures by the year 2000.   Changes in the values in society, as well as trends in population development and decentralisation and the development of a self-service economy were supported by new sophisticated techniques of production.   Using this model could lead to new activity organisations by the year 2000.

7.4   TIME-SPACE ACTIVITY BUDGETS: THEIR CHARACTERISTICS

We have already noted that, in order to understand the city, we need to understand the patterns of activity in which its residents engage at an individual and a collective level.   Time budgets and time-space budgets are devices used to investigate the ways in which human activities occur coincidentally in time and space.   They furnish us with a greater understanding of the patterning of human activities.

A **time budget** is "a systematic record of a person's use of time over a given period.   It describes the sequence, timing, and duration of the person's activities, typically for a short period ranging from a single day to a week." A logical extension of this type of record is a **time-space budget** which "includes the spatial coordinates of activity location" (Anderson, 1971: 353).

Studies using these devices do not constitute a unified research field. Time budgets have been used widely in market research for the mass media and in non-spatial sociological studies of lifestyles and leisure.   During the 1960s and 1970s, considerable impetus was given to spatially-oriented research on daily activity patterns.   Travel diaries have been widely used in the past two to three decades for transport planning purposes.

It is interesting to consider the notion that time, itself, is a quantitative measure highly appropriate for studying the social organisation of society. Time is a scarce commodity, and it is feasible to suggest that it is the main rival to money in our society.   In many situations, **time is money**.   It is a quantity to be spent, saved, or wasted.   We also have to keep to time deadlines, to order our activities in particular sequences, and to take account of the amounts of time required to get from place to place, from one activity to the other.   Its main advantage (unlike money) is that everyone who remains alive within a given period has exactly the same amount of time to allocate.   The allocation of time to compete in activities involves a **trade-off**, as we have seen.

Detailed activity records will describe the whole time use pattern, or preselected types of activity such as travel, of individuals in a given area over a particular period of time. Whether data is collected in questionnaire or in diary form, activity records have been classified by Anderson (1971: 356) into four categories, namely:

(a) **Time budgets**
(b) **Space-time budgets**
(c) **Contact records**, which cover face-to-face and other preselected types of interpersonal communication
(d) **Travel records**, which typically describe origins, destinations, purposes, modes, and types of trips.

7.4.1 Time Budgets

The time budget is a means to the study of the time, location, frequency, sequence and duration of human activities. It is usually a log or diary of the sequence of duration of activities engaged in by an individual over a period of time, which is usually specified as a 24 hour day. Its function is to show how an individual's time is consumed or utilised. Typically, the data collected from individual logs and diaries is collected from a population as a whole. An important aspect of analysis is usually to search for sub-group differences in the allocation of time over a number of activities, and over a period of time. Whatever the object, the time budget should generate data which allows a summary evaluation of at least four features of activity structures:

(a) The **starting time** of an activity
(b) The **duration** of an activity
(c) The **frequency of occurrence** of an activity
(d) The **sequential ordering** of activities in a specified period of time.

In addition, there is a further requirement:

(e) The **activity location** (if the purpose is to generate a time-space budget).

In time budget surveys, as in other surveys, decisions need to be made about the size and structure of a sample. Other important questions involved relate to factors such as: should the data be collected in the presence of the subject? how much explanation of the object of the study should be given to the subject? what should be done about non-response? how is an inadequate interview or diary to be determined? These general problems associated with social survey design are often compounded in time budget surveys because of 1) the inevitable demand of very high levels of cooperation from subjects, and 2) the relatively long periods of time required to complete the survey. Furthermore, they are expensive. It is often necessary to survey individuals or households before and after a residential relocation, or before and after some important change in the operational environment, such as changes in public transport, modes and schedules.

7.4.2. Methods of Collecting Time Budget Data
There are generally four methods of time budget recording. These are:

(a) **Recall method (a)**, where the activities of some specified period in the past are recalled with as much precision, with regard to time and location, as is possible for the objectives of the study. A major problem here is the ex post facto recall problem, and it is important to limit the period of recall to as short a time period as possible.

(b) **Recall method (b)**, where the activities of some normal period are recalled. The basic problem here is the interpretation of the term 'normal' in relation to time location, duration and space location of each activity.

(c) The **diary method**, where subjects keep a diary for a specified period of time. They record activities either according to predetermined time locations, or in a free-formatted manner. This may or may not require interviewer intervention, depending on the degree of availability of money to conduct the diary survey. An ex post evaluation of a diary with the subject present is desirable as a check on reliability. The free-formatted approach is fraught with problems since the subject is given little guidance in terms of specification of activities and locations, etc. The free-formatted style of diary is also extremely difficult to code.

(d) **Game based methods**, of which there are various types. There are many reasons why this approach is used, but it is usually used in association with some other method, often in the context of a post diary or post interview situation. Game based methods are basically aimed towards investigating changes in the contingencies of the decision-making environment.

As stated by Chapin (1974: 75-85):

"A subject is asked to allocate a limited amount of time to selected free time activities according to a few simple rules, considering his present family situation and other constraints. After the subject has finished making his time allocations on the basis of initial instructions, the interviewer introduces a change in the contingencies: Now let us assume that you would have more free time during the week, a half day free on Tuesday and a half day on Thursday - but the same income you have now - please show how you would allocate these 8 additional hours."

A major problem to be solved in time budget studies concerns the **classification of activities**. There are an almost unlimited number of classification schemes which are available to the researcher conducting time budget studies. Some standardisation is essential in order to make comparative studies possible. It is also necessary to generate theory. We can use the frequency, duration, and sequence position of activities relative to some marker as a basis for activity classification. Activities can also be classified in terms of their tendency or probability to be predecessors or successors. They can also be classified according to whether they are undertaken by the individual alone or in association with other individuals. Furthermore, they may be classified in terms of whether they are obligatory or discretionary. An activity pattern is a dependent variable, dependent upon the predisposing and preconditioning attributes of the sub-population which it represents. Thus, the activities which make up an activity pattern require classification. Chapin (1974: 21) defines **activities** as:

"...classified acts or behaviour of persons or households which, used as building blocks, permit us to study the living patterns or life ways of socially cohesive segments of society."

Chapin's group at the University of North Carolina has developed a classification scheme based on a dictionary of about 230 activity codes which are grouped into activity classes at two levels of aggregation. A less complex system of classification was that used in the **multi-national time budget study** by Szalai, et al. (1972). An extract is given in Table. 7.1. Here, the full 24 hours of the day are broken down either into the original category code of 96 categories, or into a more manageable 37 activity codes obtained by collapsing certain of the detailed codes. The 37 activities are reducible to 9 sub-totals, such as work, etc. Table 7.1 gives an example of the scheme and the towns which were involved in the multi-national study. Activities are classified as primary and secondary, based on the respondent's

Table 7.1

Multinational Time Budget Classification of Activities (An Extract)

	Belgium	Kazanlik, Bulgaria	Olomouc, Czechoslovakia	Six cities, France	100 electoral districts Fed. Rep. Germany	Osnabrück, Fed. Rep. Germany	Hoyerswerda, German Dem. Rep.	Györ, Hungary	Lima-Callao, Peru	Torun, Poland	Forty-four cities, USA	Jackson, USA	Pskov, USSR	Kragujevac, Yugoslavia	Maribor, Yugoslavia
Sample size	2077	2096	2193	2805	1500	978	1650	1994	782	2759	1243	778	2891	2125	1995

00 regular work
01 work at home
02 overtime
03 travel for job
04 waiting delays
05 second job
06 meals at work
07 at work other
08 travel to break
09 travel to job

10 prepare food
11 meal cleanup
12 clean house
13 outdoor chores
14 laundry, ironing
15 clothes upkeep
16 other upkeep
17 garden, animal care
18 heat, water
19 other duties

20 baby care
21 child care
22 help on homework
23 talk to children
24 indoor playing

25 outdoor playing
26 child health
27 other, babysit
28 blank
29 travel with child

30 marketing
31 shopping
32 personal care
33 medical care
34 administrative service
35 repair service
36 waiting in line
37 other service
38 blank
39 travel, service

40 personal hygiene
41 personal medical
42 care to adults
43 meals, snacks
44 restaurant meals
45 night sleep
46 daytime sleep
47 resting
48 private, other
49 travel, personal

50 attend school
51 other classes
52 special lecture
53 political courses
54 homework
55 read to learn
56 other study

57 blank
58 blank

59 travel, study

60 union, politics
61 work as officer
62 other participation
63 civic activities
64 religious organization
65 religious practice
66 factory council
67 misc. organization
68 other organization
69 travel organization

70 sports event
71 mass culture
72 movies
73 theater
74 museums
75 visiting with friends

76 party, meals
77 cafe, pubs
78 other social
79 travel, social

80 active sports
81 fishing, hiking
82 taking a walk
83 hobbies
84 ladies hobbies
85 art work
86 making music
87 parlour games
88 other pastime
89 travel, pastime

90 radio
91 tv
92 play records
93 read book
94 read magazine
95 read paper
96 conversation
97 letters, private
98 relax, think
99 travel, leisure

Source: Adapted from Szali, et al., 1972 576-577

description given in a diary. A particular activity may, on some occasions, be described as primary and on others as secondary, thus presenting a problem. It should be noted that the classification scheme, when applied to all activities, whether primary or secondary, has a two digit code. The first digit divides activities into 10 main groups - 0 for work, 1 for housework, etc. The second digit elaborates on these main groups; for example, something coded as work may be further coded as 00 regular work, 01 work at home, 02 overtime, etc. Locational data may be coded either on a functional basis, such as using home or place of work, or by a geogrid coding system. Thus, graphs can be produced from diary data collected and classified according to this scheme to show, for instance, the proportions of people from different social or demographic sub-groups of the population that are undertaking certain activities in certain locations at different times during the day. Table 7.2 reproduces data for a number of countries showing the distribution of daily time according to different locations for two sub-groups of the population: employed husbands, and housewives.

7.4.3 Duration, Frequency, and Sequence of Activities
Duration, frequency, and sequence of activities are important aspects of time budgets which require analysis.

(a) **Duration** of an activity may be evaluated simply in terms of the amount of time spent on that activity. It may be considered either as a ratio of the total amount of time in a given period spent on that activity, or as a ratio of time spent on some other activity over a given period of time. Many simple statistical measures can be used to conduct such analyses, including calculation of the mean, variance, standard deviation, co-efficient of variation, and correlation and regression statistics in order to consider the co-variation of two or more activities within a specific population. The ratio of the standard deviation to the mean of an activity duration has been widely used in many studies as a measure of group elasticity of the activity. In this way, it is possible to compare the activity elasticities between social and demographic sub-groups of the population. The elasticity of the activity is greater as the size of the coefficient increases.

(b) **Frequency** of an activity may be considered in two ways, either as the frequency of occurrence of an activity for an individual within a specified period of time such as a day, or as the frequency of occurrence of an activity across individuals in a population or sample within a defined period. Frequency with which an activity occurs can be used as an indicator of the importance of the activity.

(c) **Sequence** of an activity is a difficult aspect of time budget analysis. Sequence may be approached by the use of time series analysis to describe sequence of activities over a period such as a day, using auto-correlation methods by determining the fixity of activities in terms of space and time locations. In this way, the structure of a period in terms of a single activity or set of activities can be determined. We may also determine the degree to which activities tend to lead or lag behind others by using cross lag correlation approaches. Use of transitional probabilities can give an indication

157

Table 7.2

Distribution of Daily Time in Various Countries According to Different Locations Among Three Sub-Groups of the Population: (Average Hours per Day)

Employed men, all days

	Belgium	Kazanlik, Bulgaria	Olomouc, Czechoslovakia	Six cities, France	100 electoral districts, Fed. rep. Germany	Osnabruck, Fed. Rep. Germany	Hoyerswerda, German Dem. Rep.	Györ, Hungary	Lima-Callao, Peru	Toruń, Poland	Forty-four cities, USA	Jackson, USA	Pskov, USSR	Kragujevac, Yugoslavia	Maribor, Yugoslavia
inside one's home	15·2	12·5	14·3	13·6	13·6	14·2	13·8	12·0	12·9	14·0	13·4	13·6	13·4	12·9	13·0
just outside one's home	0·5	0·7	0·3	0·1	1·0	0·5	0·3	0·8	1·0	0·2	0·2	0·6	0·3	0·5	1·4
at one's workplace	5·0	7·7	5·9	7·2	5·4	5·1	6·8	7·5	6·4	7·0	6·7	6·5	6·8	7·1	6·1
in transit	1·5	2·1	1·6	1·5	1·7	2·2	1·7	2·0	2·5	1·7	1·6	1·5	2·0	1·8	2·2
in other people's home	0·5	0·2	0·3	0·5	0·5	0·4	0·6	0·4	0·3	0·4	0·5	0·6	0·2	0·7	0·5
in places of business	0·7	0·6	0·6	0·5	0·4	0·4	0·1	0·2	0·7	0·0	0·7	0·7	0·4	0·5	0·5
in restaurants and bars	0·2	0·0	0·1	0·2	0·5	0·6	0·1	0·2	0·3	0·0	0·4	0·4	0·2	0·2	0·0
in all other locations	0·4	0·2	0·9	0·2	0·9	0·4	0·3	0·6	0·6	0·2	0·5	0·4	0·7	0·3	0·3
total	24·0	24·0	24·0	24·0	24·0	24·0	24·0	24·0	24·0	24·0	24·0	24·0	24·0	24·0	24·0

Housewives, all days (married only)

	Belgium	Kazanlik, Bulgaria	Olomouc, Czechoslovakia	Six cities, France	100 electoral districts, Fed. rep. Germany	Osnabruck, Fed. Rep. Germany	Hoyerswerda, German Dem. Rep.	Györ, Hungary	Lima-Callao, Peru	Toruń, Poland	Forty-four cities, USA	Jackson, USA	Pskov, USSR	Kragujevac, Yugoslavia	Maribor, Yugoslavia
inside one's home	21·6	20·4	20·9	21·7	20·4	20·5	21·3	19·7	21·0	20·9	20·5	20·9	19·6	20·5	19·7
just outside one's home	0·2	1·4	0·3	0·1	0·8	0·4	0·3	2·1	0·5	0·1	0·1	0·1	0·4	0·4	0·8
in transit	1·0	0·9	1·2	1·0	1·0	1·0	1·0	0·9	1·2	1·2	1·0	0·9	1·9	1·5	1·1
in other people's home	0·4	0·4	0·3	0·6	0·6	0·6	0·3	0·2	0·4	0·5	0·8	0·7	0·7	0·7	0·3
in places of business	0·5	0·7	1·1	0·6	0·7	1·1	0·9	0·9	0·7	1·2	1·1	1·1	1·1	0·4	0·5
in restaurants and bars	0·1	0·1	0·0	0·0	0·1	0·1	0·0	0·0	0·0	0·0	0·1	0·1	0·0	0·0	0·0
in all other locations	0·2	0·1	0·2	0·1	0·4	0·3	0·2	0·2	0·2	0·1	0·3	0·2	0·3	0·1	0·1
total	24·0	24·0	24·0	24·0	24·0	24·0	24·0	24·0	24·0	24·0	24·0	24·0	24·0	24·0	24·0

1 Data are weighted to ensure equality of the week and number of eligible respondents per household

Source: Adapted from Szali, et al., 1972:795

of the probability that an episode of a certain type will be immediately followed by one or another type in any person's sequence of behaviour.

A further approach in the study of activity structure to the identification of sequences has been proposed by Parkes and Wallis (1978) in which directed graphs or diagraphs are used. Each diagraph will show degrees of similarity and dissimilarity in individual activity structure and sequences.

7.5 EXAMPLES OF TIME-SPACE ACTIVITY BUDGET STUDIES

7.5.1 The Multi-National Time Budget Study

A total of 12 countries and 15 sites were involved in the multi-national time budget study referred to previously (Szalai, et al. 1972). One set of results from the study are reproduced and discussed here.

One of the researchers, Converse, (1972) aimed to identify the main dimensions of site differentiation in time use. The data set is reproduced in Table 7.3, and is the average time spent in 37 primary activities in 12 countries. From these data a matrix of dissimilarities was produced while calculating the absolute distance between each pair of sites. The matrix of dissimilarities was reduced to two dimensions, which together accounted for most of the variance. Converse discovered that the two dimensions retrieved from the time use profiles presented a picture that bore a substantial resemblance to a map of the western world. The first dimension was an east-west differentiation, the second dimension was a north-south axis. The plot of countries on these dimensions is given in Part (a) of Figure 7.5. The contribution of the various individual activities to the solution is dependent not so much on the absolute amounts of time allocated, but on the elasticity or variants about the mean. Thus, the magnitude of standard deviation and the degree to which an activity's inter-site variation is correlated with the dimension permitted the role of specific activities to be considered in terms of their contribution to the solution. The results for these analyses are given for both the No. 1 east-west dimension and the No. 2 north-south dimensions in Parts (b) and (c), respectively of Figure 7.5. The dimension 1, east-west axis summarises a free work time access. Activities occurring at the top of the graph in Part 1 of Figure 7.5 are reading books, trip to work, movies and radio, at work, and these imply the time spent on the activity is systematically increasing as one moves from west to east. In the lower part of this graph, various socialisation activities combine to provide a further discriminating factor between east and west so that it seems likely that as one moves from east to west, there is a significant trade-off between time release from work and gains in times spent in informal social life.

The dimension 2, north-south axis, was structured more by activities to which a climatic explanation may be attached, but other things also need to be taken into account. There is a hint of a north-south development axis, similar to the east-west dimension. Mass media, especially TV at home, seems to be a predominant factor in defining the northern pole of the axis in Part (c) of Figure 7.5.

Table 7.3

Multi-National Time Budget Study:
Average Time Spent in 37 Primary Activities in 12 Countires

	Belgium	Kazanlik, Bulgaria	Olomouc, Czechoslovakia	Six cities, France	100 electoral districts, Federal Republic Germany	Osnabruck, Federal Republic Germany	Hoyerswerda, German Democratic Republic	Gyor, Hungary	Lima-Callao, Peru	Torun, Poland	44 cities, U.S.A.	Jackson, U.S.A.	Pskov, U.S.S.R.	Kragujevac, Yugoslavia	Maribor, Yugoslavia
total N	2077	2096	2192	2805	1500	978	1650	1994	782	2754	1243	778	2891	2125	1995
total minutes*	1440	1440	1440	1440	1440	1440	1440	1440	1440	1440	1440	1440	1440	1440	1440
1. main job	255	338	297	242	225	210	254	315	200	287	225	225	324	230	254
2. second job	4	0	1	5	2	4	2	3	10	3	5	5	2	1	11
3. at work other	4	25	6	8	6	4	22	15	4	8	12	11	13	9	17
4. travel to job	24	41	33	22	18	16	32	41	37	37	25	19	33	27	29
total work	287	404	337	277	250	234	310	374	251	334	266	259	371	267	311
5. cooking	46	39	64	45	59	49	65	60	71	59	44	45	55	70	76
6. home chores	64	36	51	70	71	73	78	55	40	51	58	57	38	49	57
7. laundry	22	12	31	26	25	20	40	35	45	34	26	24	28	28	41
8. marketing	13	14	27	20	22	26	23	14	16	16	14	16	10	22	14
total housework	145	100	172	162	177	167	206	164	172	160	142	141	131	168	188
9. care to garden/pets	8	23	8	11	31	18	11	33	2	3	3	3	8	6	49
10. shopping	6	4	6	6	3	4	5	4	9	12	18	17	14	5	5
11. other household care	15	18	27	22	19	21	16	21	6	19	24	25	17	26	27
household care	29	45	41	39	53	42	32	58	17	33	45	45	39	37	81
12. basic child care	12	9	16	32	16	14	30	12	18	16	22	23	18	14	16
13. other child care	5	8	15	9	11	11	15	17	5	18	10	8	17	9	13
total child care	17	17	31	40	27	25	45	30	23	34	32	31	35	23	29
14. personal care	44	55	71	57	54	59	49	53	47	56	69	61	49	58	47
15. eating	104	86	65	106	102	103	76	73	100	72	81	78	72	79	69
16. sleep	501	418	168	498	510	503	474	473	643	467	470	480	462	472	477
personal needs	649	618	604	661	665	665	600	599	25	595	620	619	583	609	592
17. personal travel	10	24	15	16	4	7	14	15	28	21	31	31	34	24	19
18. leisure travel	14	18	12	15	13	19	11	14	52	17	19	23	21	24	18
non-work travel	30	42	27	31	17	25	26	30	36	38	50	54	55	48	36
19. study	16	11	16	13	6	12	11	16	4	21	12	9	38	14	20
20. religion	5	0	1	4	5	6	0	1	2	5	10	11	0	0	1
21. organizations	4	7	7	2	2	4	12	3	42	4	6	6	8	5	4
study-participation	25	18	24	19	13	22	23	20	8	31	28	26	46	19	24
22. radio	8	20	11	5	7	4	4	11	52	10	4	3	10	16	6
23. TV (home)	81	14	64	55	61	72	80	39	2	64	91	99	33	34	41
24. TV (away)	3	2	2	3	2	2	1	4	10	6	1	2	5	3	0
25. read newspaper	16	14	13	14	12	13	13	12	6	16	24	25	15	20	19
26. read magazine	5	1	3	4	12	13	2	1	2	3	6	5	5	1	1
27. read books	14	21	20	7	5	6	7	14	6	17	5	4	29	7	8
28. movies	4	10	4	3	3	3	1	5	87	4	3	2	15	7	6
total mass media	131	79	116	90	98	112	108	85	10	120	134	140	113	87	81
29. social (home)	15	5	7	12	13	18	10	7	19	25	25	27	4	29	13
30. social (away)	25	8	15	20	32	32	16	16	27	22	38	39	9	42	20
31. conversation	15	9	11	17	17	18	11	13	2	13	18	16	8	28	13
32. active sports	2	2	2	1	5	4	1	2	13	1	6	5	4	0	2
33. outdoors	10	24	12	11	39	32	18	17	4	10	2	5	14	13	19
34. entertainment	5	14	2	3	4	3	2	3	1	2	5	3	3	2	2
35. cultural events	3	1	3	1	1	2	1	1	63	1	1	1	3	1	0
36. resting	27	41	17	33	17	19	10	15	14	24	9	12	11	31	20
37. other leisure	27	13	18	23	14	20	20	9	152	11	20	18	13	36	10
total leisure	128	116	86	121	140	147	91	81	309	95	123	126	67	181	99
total free time	297	231	239	245	264	300	233	200	90	262	301	310	247	311	222
total travel	56	89	62	58	39	58	60	74		78	78	76	88	77	78

* Because of rounding, subtotals do not sum to exactly 1440 minutes

Source: After Robinson, Converse & Szali, 1972

7.5.2 Australian Study: Time Budgets in Albury-Wodonga and Melbourne

The second example given is the result of a study conducted in 1974 in Australia by the then Cities Commission of the Federal Government. Two cities, the large metropolitan area of Melbourne (which is the capital city of Victoria with a population of slightly under 3,000,000 people) and a

Figure 7.5

Percentage of Free Time Among Various Activities by Age Group, Albury-Wodonga and Melbourne, Australia

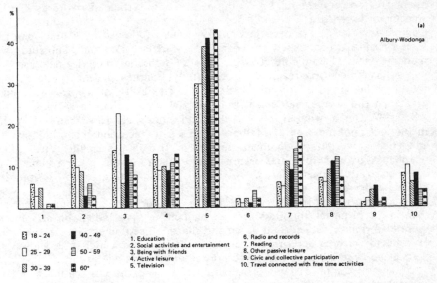

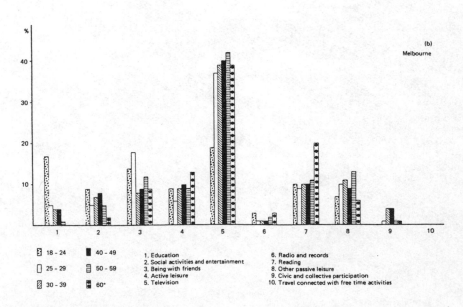

Source: Cities Commission, 1975

161

designated growth centre called Albury-Wodonga on the New South Wales/Victoria border (with a population of 50,000 people) were selected for study. The study focused on how people allocate their time in these two cities, the purpose being to develop policy-oriented answers to questions about how society should be organised and how settlement patterns may be structured to ensure a livable day-to-day existence for individuals (Cities Commission, 1975). A pre-diary interview was followed by a diary day and then a post-diary interview as the method of data collection. The study was modelled after Chapin's descriptive model of household activity patterns.

Among the many results from this study, journey to work patterns were found to be significantly different. The flexibility of choice was much greater in the smaller settlement of Albury-Wodonga than in Melbourne. In Albury-Wodonga, women felt that they had more spare time than did women in the metropolitan area of Melbourne. Face-to-face contacts with relatives and friends were a predominant feature of life in the smaller city, where telephone ownership rates were also much lower. Frequency of attendance/adult participation in socialising activities, such as picnics, attending drive-in cinemas, spectator sports, and participating sports, were all much more highly represented in the smaller city of Albury-Wodonga than in the large metropolitan area of Melbourne. An indication of some of these differences between the large and the small settlement in the allocation of time to various activities is given in Figure 7.5, which also shows the percentage time allocation to 10 activities between six age groups.

Having examined the specific notion of time-paths and the more general concept of population time budgets at various scales, we turn in the next chapter to an in-depth analysis of a particular episodic space-time use, the activities usually described as consumer spatial behaviour.

Chapter Eight

CONSUMER BEHAVIOUR

8.1 BACKGROUND TO THE BEHAVIOURAL APPROACH TO MODELLING CONSUMER BEHAVIOUR

Consumer behaviour has traditionally been a fertile area of research in geography. Because of the inherent spatial nature of consumer shopping activity - where the consumer is likely to shop directly affects the location and organisation of the retail market system, and vice versa - many researchers have been concerned with examining the relationships between consumer behaviour and the spatial structure of the retail environment.

Among the earliest approaches is that of Reilly (1931), who was concerned with defining market areas using a **law of retail gravitation**. **Central place theory**, as developed by Christaller (1933), was also relevant to understanding consumer behaviour. Concepts such as the range of a good and threshold demand requirements were particularly appropriate.

In consumer behaviour geographic research, particularly during the 1960s and early 1970s, two parallel streams developed. One was largely **non-behavioural**, having its antecedents in the standard social **gravity** model (Lakshmanen and Hansen, 1965). A second type of model, whose influence still extends throughout the discipline today, was the **entropy**-based model developed by Wilson (1969).

As opposed to these objective-oriented models, **behavioural** models of **consumer choice** and **decision-making** departed radically from the conventional format. Based on innovative articles by Thompson (1963), and Huff (1962; 1964), this alternate stream examined the importance of variables such as subjective distance and the decision-making act, or following Huff, replaced deterministic allocations of people to places with probability surfaces describing the potential for interacting with sets of places.

Although the Huff-type **probability** model was still based on objective variables (for example floor space and travel time), Huff's 1964 paper conceptualising the consumer decision process, provided an innovative schema upon which many geographers began to build. For example, Rushton (1965) developed a gravity model-type format which substituted town attractiveness and town-distance trade-off functions for conventional objective variables. These were based on actual empirical behaviours and were seen to reflect consumer **preferences** for town size-distance combinations. Thus, consumer activities were conceptualised in terms of preferences for places rather than strict objective allocation problems. Similarly, Golledge (1965) conceptualised the market decision process in a **dynamic choice** framework, and illustrated the importance of **learning** activities in the development of habitual and stereotyped behavioural activities. Golledge (1967) developed a schema from both the consumer and the producer point of view which was based on developmental processes on the one hand, and continuous behavioural change on the other. Golledge and Brown (1968) emphasised the importance of both search and learning in the market decision process. Dynamic Markov models were used in both studies as the process mechanism for showing the change of choice proportions amongst alternatives as information about the relative attractiveness of the alternatives accumulated over time.

Shortly after these preliminary attempts, Downs (1970) introduced yet another stream into behaviourally-oriented research on consumer behaviour. He emphasised that shopping centres had both an objective physical existence and a subjective or cognitive existence. He outlined procedures for defining the cognitive structure of a shopping centre and for determining the significance of a wide range of attitudinal, attributional, preference, and evaluative variables, all from the point of view of potential patrons of the centres. His paper on the cognitive structure of a shopping centre is indeed a landmark and has been one of the most influential and widely quoted papers relating to consumer spatial behaviour, consumer preference, and consumer choice.

Briggs (1969) pioneered the use of multidimensional scaling in an attempt to construct subjective-based utility measures relating to the choice of competing shopping centres by randomly selected sets of consumers. The potential use of multidimensional scaling for examining a variety of spatial problems (e.g., cognitive maps, consumer behaviour, migration behaviour, etc.) were summarised by Golledge and Rushton (1972). Shortly afterwards, an article by Burnett (1973) showed the feasibility of using multidimensional scaling procedures to explain and to predict consumer choices of shopping centres for both convenience and shopping goods.

By the early 1970s, therefore, a complete arsenal of methods, concepts, and emerging theories, were available for the geographer interested in both subjective and objective approaches to the analysis of consumer spatial behaviour. Using a variety of methods, Golledge, Rushton and Clark (1967), Clark (1969) and Clark and Rushton (1970) had attacked central place theory from the consumer and behavioural point of view, showing empirically that in many different contexts consumers did not exhibit the single-centre-least-effort syndrome required by both Christaller and Losh, and that a wide range of apparently "irrational" economic and spatial behaviours existed. This evidence, along with the emergence of a variety of new conceptual bases and methodologies, also helped to modify the existing approaches used to seek explanations of consumer spatial behaviour.

8.2 GRAVITY MODEL APPROACHES FROM DETERMINISTIC TO PROBABILISTIC ANALYSIS

8.2.1 Classic Retail Gravity Models
Early investigations of consumer behaviour in the context of market area definition were related to purpose of trip, its frequency, distance to centres at different levels in the retail centre hierarchy, and general spatial interaction principles (McCabe, 1974: 10).

In 1929 William J. Reilly made a significant application of market area analysis with his law of retail gravitation. Reilly's law states that two centres attract trade from intermediate places approximately in direct proportion to the size of the centres and in inverse proportion to the square

of the distance from these two centres to the intermediate place.
Mathematically this law was expressed as:

$$\frac{T_a}{T_b} = \left(\frac{P_a}{P_b}\right)\left(\frac{D_b}{D_a}\right)^2 \qquad (1)$$

where:

T_a = the proportion of the retail business from an intermediate town attracted by city A

T_b = the proportion of the retail business from an intermediate town attracted by city B

P_a = the population of City A

P_b = the population of city B

D_a = the distance from the intermediate town to city A

D_b = the distance from the intermediate town to city B

N,n = empirically derived constants.

This model was tested empirically, and P.D. Converse is credited with a significant modification of Reilly's original formula which made it possible to calculate the approximate point between two competing centres where the trading influence of each was equal. This was the break even-point, given by:

$$D_b = \frac{D_{ab}}{1 + \sqrt{\dfrac{P_a}{P_b}}} \qquad (2)$$

where:

D_b = the break-even point between city A and city B in km. from B

D_{ab} = the distance separating city A from city B

P_b = the population of city B

P_a = the population of city A.

These early efforts provided a basis for systematic estimating of retail trading areas. Reilly's empirical tests suggested an exponent of 2 for the mitigating effect of distance. This value was observed to have a range from 1.5 to 2.75. Some of his observations for specific goods led to power functions being derived that ranged from 0 to as high as 12.5.

There were, however, several conceptual and operational limitations associated with the use of the Reilly-type retail gravity models. Perhaps most important was the breaking-point formula which was incapable of giving graduated estimates above or below the break-even position between two competing centres. This made it impossible to calculate the actual total demand for either centre's services. In addition, when several centres were included in the analysis, invariably there was overlapping of trade areas thus derived from the break-even point geometric solution, and often some areas would not be allocated to any centre's trade area. But, more importantly, these models assumed rational economic, and invariant, individual behaviour on the part of the consumer.

8.2.2 Probabilistic Retail Gravity Models

To overcome some of the limitations of the Reilly-type retail gravity models, Huff (1962) proposed an alternative probabilistic retail gravity model. This model incorporated the realistic notion that customers do not always select one centre for exclusive shopping. Lack of consistency in choice is apparent where there is a large number of centres of varying size and functional complexity within a reasonable distance. This is the case in large urban areas. Thus, the model focuses on the customer rather than the retailer. After all, it is the customer who is the primary agent affecting the trade area of retail centres. Huff's model describes the process by which potential customers choose from among acceptable alternative retail centres to obtain specific goods and services. Huff suggested that areas of competition between shopping centres overlap, consequently shopping trips appear to be apportioned among competing accessible centres in a probabilistic manner. If the apportionment is probabilistic, then the total of all shopping probabilities must be unity.

A formal expression of Huff's probabilistic retail gravity model is:

$$P_{ij} = \frac{\dfrac{S_j}{T_{ij}^{\lambda}}}{\displaystyle\sum_{j=1}^{n} \dfrac{S_j}{T_{ij}^{\lambda}}} \tag{3}$$

where:

P_{ij} = the probability of a consumer at a given point of origin i travelling to a particular shopping centre j

S_j = the size of a shopping centre j (measured in terms of the square footage devoted to the sale of a particular class of goods)

T_{ij} = the travel time involved in getting from a consumer's travel base i to a given shopping centre j

λ = a parameter which is to be estimated empirically to reflect the effect of travel time on various kinds of shopping trips.

The expected number of consumers at a given place of origin i that shop at a particular shopping centre j equals the number of consumers at i multiplied by the probability that a consumer at i will select j for shopping. That is:

$$E_{ij} = P_{ij} \cdot C_i \tag{4}$$

where:

E_{ij} = the expected number of consumers at i that are likely to travel to shopping centre j

C_i = the number of consumers at i.

Huff (1964) refers to the way this model differs from the original Reilly-type retail gravity models:

"...the model is not merely an empirically contrived formulation. It represents a theoretical abstraction of consumer spatial behaviour. As a result, mathematical conclusions can be deduced from the model which, in turn, can be interpreted in terms of their behavioural implications."

"...the alternative model estimates the likelihood of a consumer (P_{ij}) or the number of consumers (E_{ij}) patronising a particular shopping area by taking into consideration all potential shopping areas simultaneously."

"...the parameter λ is not assumed to be to the second power. Rather, it is assumed to vary with different types of product classes. For example, in an initial pilot study was found to be 2.723 for shopping trips involving furniture and 3.191 for trips involving clothing purchases."

"The respective magnitudes of these estimates simply reflect the comparative amounts of time that consumers are willing to expend for each of these two product classes. The larger the estimated value of λ, the smaller will be the time expenditure. Similarly, the larger the estimated value of λ, the more restrictive will be the scope of the trading area.

"...equations (3) and (4) enable a retail trading area to be graduated in terms of demand gradients. These gradients are expressed as probability contours ranging from P<1 to P>0."

Huff goes on to draw these general conclusions about the nature and scope of trading areas:

(a) A trading area represents a demand surface containing potential customers for a specific product(s) or service(s) of a particular distribution centre.

(b) A distribution centre may be a single firm or an agglomeration of firms.

(c) A demand surface consists of a series of demand gradients or zones, reflecting varying customer-sales potentials. An exception of the condition of demand gradients would be in a unique geographical setting, thus representing an absolute monopoly in providing products and/or services that are of an absolute necessity. Under these conditions, no gradients would exist but rather a single homogeneous demand plane.

(d) Demand gradients are of a probabilistic nature, ranging from a probability value of less than one to a value greater than zero (except in the complete monopoly situation in which the probability value equals one).

(e) The total potential customers encompassed within a distribution centre's demand surface (trading area) is the sum of the expected number of consumers from each of the demand gradients.

(f) Demand gradients of competing firms overlap; and where gradients of like probability intersect, a spatial competitive equilibrium position is reached.

Thus a trading area may be defined as:

$$T_j = \sum_{i=1}^{n} (P_{ij} \cdot C_i)$$ (5)

where:

T_j = the trading area of a particular firm or agglomeration of firms j; that is, the total expected number of consumers within a given region who are likely to patronise j for a specific class of products or services

P_{ij} = the probability of an individual consumer residing within a given gradient i shopping at j

C_i = the number of consumers residing within a given gradient i.

A typical outcome of the application of a Huff-type probability gravity model at the intra-urban scale uses census tract centroids, weighted by households or populations for each tract, as a surrogate for demand, and investigates probability trade area surfaces for a selection of competing retail centres. The model has been widely used to investigate the potential trade area impact of a proposed shopping centre development, especially its likely effects on competing centres. Figure 8.1 gives an example from Adelaide, South Australia, for a shopping centre development at Port Adelaide in the north west sector of the city. The probability surface is shown. Figure 8.2 illustrates the potential trade area impact on competing centres, of varying size, if the proposed Port Adelaide shopping centre is increased in size, holding population constant.

8.2.3 Refinements of the Huff Model
A refinement of the Huff formulation of the probabilistic retail gravity model is the Lackshmanen and Hansen model. The main parameters of this model refer to the mass/attractive force measurement (α) and the distance or interaction decay measure (β). The α exponent may be a weighting factor reflecting centre attributes such as car parking facilities, amenity value, and range of functional units. It may be a multivariate mass weighting exponent. The exponent is simply identical to the λ distance exponent in the Huff model. Stanley and Sewall (1976) have added a retail chain image measure to the Huff probabilistic retail gravity model, which is empirically derived from survey data on store and centre image using multi-dimensional scaling techniques.

Other researchers, including Wilson and Cullen working in England, have suggested that the retail version of the general gravity model can be more rigorously formulated through processes of statistical mechanics. In this form of the model, an exponential function is used in place of the power function of and or in the Huff and the Lakhsmanen and Hanson models. Examples are given in McCabe (1974: 27-28).

8.3 DISAGGREGATE DISCRETE CHOICE MODELS

Many geographers are interested in studying how humans make spatially relevant decisions, such as where to go shopping or where to go to school. In studying this type of human, or **consumer**, decision-making, geographers

Figure 8.1

Trade Potential of Port Adelaide
With Total Retail Area of $30,000m^2$

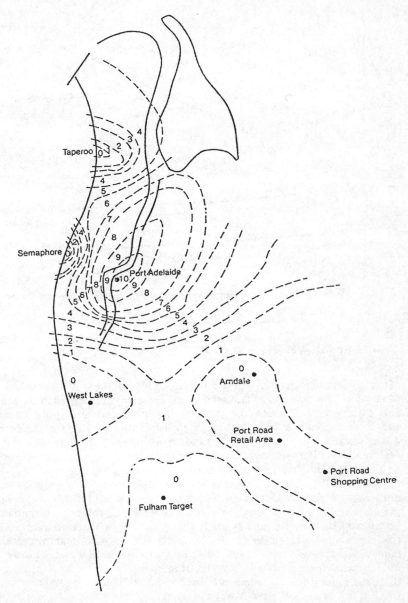

Source: Cleland, Stimson & Harris, 1977

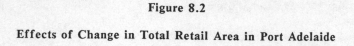

Figure 8.2

Effects of Change in Total Retail Area in Port Adelaide

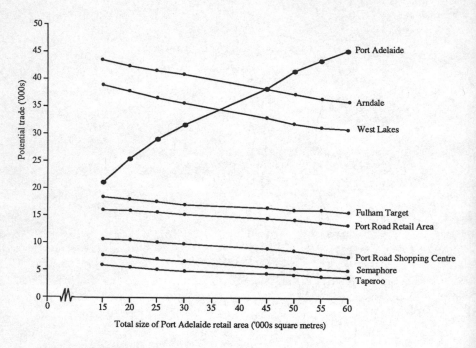

Source: After Cleland, Stimson & Harris, 1977

often use mathematically based models. Many of these mathematical models have been "borrowed" and adapted from other disciplines, such as economics and psychology. Perhaps the most widely discussed and applied models of consumer choice are those belonging to the family of **discrete choice models**. These models are also known as random utility models, and they stem from research on micro-economic theory, psychological judgment theory, and developments in statistical analysis of categorical data.

Historically, these discrete choice models have been used in studying questions relating to marketing and transportation problems. More recently, these models have been used to study and analyse problems of spatial choice behaviour, such as the choice of a grocery store, a place to shop, where to go to school, and the like. It is interesting to note that discrete choice models were developed because the previous microeconomic, or marginalist, models were inadequate for investigating spatially relevant decisions. As we shall see, marginalist models are inadequate because the assumptions upon which they are based do not accurately reflect the decisions (or the decision process) people make about consumer choices.

8.3.1 Multinomial Logit Model

The family of discrete choice models include the Multinomial Logit, the Nested Logit, the Dogit, the Generalised Extreme Value, and the Multinomial Probit. The models are ordered in terms of their complexity and comprehensiveness. The Nested Logit, Dogit, and GEV models are commonly called "halfway house" models, as they are more realistic than the Multinomial Logit model, but less general than the Multinomial Probit. Although the Multinomial Probit is the most theoretically appealing, it has rarely been applied in choice contexts with more than two alternatives.

Of all the discrete choice models the Multinomial Logit (MNL) is the simplest and most computationally tractable. It has received the widest application in the study of spatially relevant consumer choices. Here we focus on the MNL model as an example of how discrete choice models can be used to examine or model consumer spatial behaviour.

Many important decisions an individual makes in life involve selection (or choice) from a limited, constrained set of discrete alternatives (choices) such as the choice of a house, a car, an occupation, a college, a shopping destination, and so on. The assumptions upon which a model concerning these choice sets is based are therefore important.

To derive and successfully apply the MNL model, six assumptions must be satisfied:

(a) Each individual decision maker is assumed to be faced with a discrete set of choice alternatives. Proper definition of the choice set is a critical issue when applying models of the discrete choice family. It is desirable that all individuals in the sample have access to the same alternatives. For convenience, we will label these discrete choices as A_{1i} through A_{ji}, where i denotes a given person and j denotes a given choice. Thus,

$$A_i = (A_{1i},....A_{ri},....A_{ji}) \qquad (6)$$

(b) The choice rule for discrete choice models is utility maximisation. In other words, an individual will choose that alternative yielding the highest utility or (U). Therefore, mathematically speaking, alternative r will be selected **if, and only if**,

$$U_{ri} > U_{gi} \text{ for } g \neq r, g = 1,....,J \qquad (7)$$

Specifically, the utility (U) of choice r for person i is greater than choice g, where g stands for all choices other than r.

(c) The MNL is a model of probabilistic choice. In other words, an individual will have a certain likelihood of choosing different alternatives, such as a 50% chance of shopping at store (A), a 40% chance of shopping at Store (B) and a 10% change of patronising Store (C). In the event that the condition of competing alternatives holds, it will occur with the probability

$$P_{ri} = \text{prob} [U_{ri} > U_{gi} \text{ for } g \neq r, g = 1,....j] \qquad (8)$$

where:

P_{ri} is the probability of individual i choosing alternative r.

(d) An individual's utility for each alternative is divided into two components,

$$U_{ri} = V_{ri} + E_{ri} \qquad (9)$$

where:

$V_{ri} =$ the observed or systematic component of utility

$E_{ri} =$ an error or disturbance term that reflects the unobserved attribute of the choice alternative.

The systematic element is defined in terms of observed attributes of the choice alternatives and/or the decision-makers. The stochastic random component enters the utility function because certain choice-relevant attributes are unobserved and because the valuation of observed attributes varies from individual to individual.

(e) Given the above definition of utility, the probability of choosing the rth alternative can now be written as:

$$P_{ri} - \text{Prob} [V_{ri} + E_{ri} > V_{gi} + E_{gi} \text{ for } g \neq r, g=1,....J] \qquad (10)$$

which can be rearranged to express the following:

$$P_{ri} = \text{Prob} [E_{gi} - E_{ri} < V_{ri} - V_{gi} \text{ for } g \neq r, g=1,....J] \qquad (11)$$

This is known as the **random utility model**. When the partitioned expression of utility is incorporated into the probability model described above, the random utility model of choice can be derived. The equation states that the probability that individual i will choose alternative r can be defined in terms of the difference between the random utility of alternative g and alternative r being less than the difference between the observed utility levels of alternative r and alternative g. To recapitulate, the random element attempts to account for the inability of the analyst to fully represent the dimensions determining preference in the utility function.

(f) The MNL model is derived by making assumptions regarding the random component of utility. The E_{ri} is independently and identically distributed. The statistical probability distribution of E_{ri} is type 1 extreme value (double exponential). This leads to a computationally tractable form of the model:

$$\text{Pr}|i = \frac{e^{V(Z_{ri}, Si)}}{\sum_{g=1}^{J} e^{V(Z_{gi}, Si)}} \qquad (12)$$

The above equation represents the most common form of the MNL model.

8.3.2 Discrete Choice Models: An Example

Suppose that a survey of consumers has been undertaken to understand their shopping habits and to determine the percentage (i.e. the market share) of shoppers a new store might attract. Three existing stores(Stores A,B,C) and one proposed store (Store D) were rated on the following dimensions:

(a) variety of goods
(b) quality of goods
(c) parking availability
(d) value for money.

Given these variables, a MNL model can be used to estimate the relative importance of each attribute and to derive market share predictions with and without the new store.

The average attribute obtained from the sample are set out in Table 8.1. The importance weights (a_d) were estimated by fitting the shopper's choices of existing stores to their ratings using the MNL model.

Table 8.1

Attribute Ratings

Store	Variety	Quality	Parking	Value for Money
A	0.7	0.5	0.7	0.7
B	0.3	0.4	0.2	0.8
C	0.6	0.8	0.7	0.4
D	0.6	0.4	0.8	0.5
Importance Weight (a_d)	2.0	1.7	1.3	2.2

The attractiveness or utility of each store can be derived as follows:

$$U_r = \sum_{d=1}^{4} (a_d \cdot X_{rd}) \tag{13}$$

where:

U_r is the utility of store r

a_d is the importance weight for dimension d

X_{rd} is the rating for store r on dimension d

As an illustration, the utility of Store A is

U(Store A) = (2.0*0.7) + (1.7*0.5) + (1.3*0.7) + (2.2*0.7) = 4.70

The results of the logit model analysis of this simple hypothetical situation are given in Table 8.2.

Table 8.2

Sample Logit Model Analysis

Store	(a) Utility $(U_r = \sum a_d X_{rd})$	(b) U_r e	(c) Share Estimate without New Store	(d) Share Estimate with New Store	(e) Draw [(c) - (d)]
A	4.70	109.0	0.512	0.407	0.105
B	3.30	27.1	0.126	0.100	0.026
C	4.35	77.5	0.362	0.287	0.075
D	4.02	55.7		0.206	

As an illustration, the market share estimate for Store A (including Store D) can be obtained by:

$$P_r \text{(Store A)} = \frac{e^{U(\text{Store A})}}{e^{U(\text{Store A})} + e^{U(\text{Store B})} + e^{U(\text{Store C})} + e^{U(\text{Store D})}}$$

$$= \frac{109.0}{109.0 + 27.1 + 77.5 + 55.7}$$

$$= .407$$

A major drawback of the MNL model is the "independence from irrelevant alternatives" property. It implies that a new alternative entering a choice set will compete equally with each existing alternative and will obtain a share of the market by drawing from the existing alternatives in direct proportion to the original shares of the market held by these existing alternatives. This is demonstrated in column (e) of Table 8.2, where the draw is proportional to share. If it was decided to build Store (D) right next to Store (C), and each store was perceived to have the same utility, the predictions in Table 8.3 would be yielded.

These predictions indicate that Store (D) has drawn shares proportionally from each of the other stores. However, since Store (D) is perceived to be identical to Store (C), it is intuitively more plausible that the market share for Store (C) would be "cannibalised" to a much greater degree, and much less for the other stores.

Table 8.3

Sample Prediction

Store	e^{Ur}	Share Estimate
A	109.9	0.376
B	27.1	0.092
C	77.5	0.266
D	77.5	0.266

8.4 INFORMATION PROCESSING MODELS

8.4.1 From Rationality to Satisficing and Information Processing

Many of the early models of consumer behaviour required assumptions not only of economic and spatial rationality, but also a set of assumptions related to **psychological rationality**. For example, decision makers were:

(a) required to have consistent and fixed preferences
(b) assumed to be able to separate preferences and beliefs (their preferences and ultimate choices were assumed to be one and the same)
(c) assumed capable of computing optima of one sort or another.

Just as economic and spatial rationality was assaulted by both empirical evidence and theoretical probing in the 1960s and 1970s, so too did the necessity of these "psychological man" assumptions become questioned during the same period. For example, Tversky and Kahneman (1974) claimed that the majority of individuals have rather limited information processing capabilities, and because of these limitations were unlikely to be able to perform or to make decisions according to some a priori computed optimal function. This echoed the earlier thoughts of Simon (1957), who had argued strongly for the replacement of the economically rational being with assumptions more relevant to a sort of bounded rationality or **satisficing** capability.

Louviere (1974) introduced an information **processing** paradigm into geographic research on consumer behaviour. In particular, this new approach viewed choice as a process rather than a final act, it considered choices to be purposive with the decision maker being an active manipulator of information about the choice environment, and it tried to model consumers as selective information processors in which general decision-making criteria are filtered down to specific choice instances. The approach (information integration theory) also echoed earlier suggestions that consumer decision-making necessarily involved feedback from each purchase act and could therefore be considered a type of learning process. While some of these earlier approaches had decided limitations - for example, they did not cover a wide range of decision-making heuristics, they only sketchily covered the influence of task attributes, and were somewhat incomplete in their descriptions of information processing itself - their pursuit continued. While much of the work is still at a conceptual stage, it has led to the development of a major tie between consumer behaviour models and computational process models of decision-making and choice. These latter are now most commonly found in the cognitive science and artificial intelligence literature (Smith, Pellegrino and Golledge 1982).

8.4.2 Information Integration Theory

One approach which has enjoyed a considerable measure of success, despite the complexity of its task situation and general propensity to operationalise the model in laboratory rather than field settings, is **information integration theory** (sometimes also appearing in the literature under the heading of functional measurement theory).

In this type of model, individuals are assumed to be able to discern key attributes of products or situations about which they have to make choices. They are then assumed to have the capability of developing **trade-off** functions among different quantities of each of the attributes, and to combine all attribute and trade-off information or factors into a single numerical judgment, i.e., they perform an information integration task prior to making a choice (Louviere and Henley 1977).

Basically, it is assumed that individuals can supply direct numerical estimates of their degree of preference for quantities of a particular attribute or stimulus and that this degree of preference can be represented on an interval scale. Thus weight and scale parameters can be developed and insights gained into the types of combination rules that an individual appears to be using when making a choice. In general, the term **functional measurement** refers to the evaluation of what the individual sees as being "functional" in the decision-making process. This perception of different functional degrees is translated into relative weights which are then incorporated into a trade-off function that is accessed during a particular decision-making and choice process.

Information integration theory uses **factorial**, or quasi-factorial, **experimental designs**. Obviously, when the number of attributes or stimuli increases, the complexity of the task situation increases dramatically. Generally, only a limited number of factors are used (e.g., 3 to 5), and even this can present some substantial problems for a decision maker unless the factors are clearly defined and their component parts easily perceived to be different one from the other. Since geographers generally incorporate a distance variable amongst those used in the evaluation process, their problems may not be as severe as others who have to work with less concrete attributes (e.g., bitterness, chewiness, or colour intensity).

Louviere and his students have used this approach in a number of interesting geographic situations, ranging from the choice of rental housing accommodation by students new to a campus, to the selection of an appropriate stream in which to fish for trout.

As practitioners are well aware, the use of this technique has opened some serious debate as to whether individuals combine attribute levels in an additive or multiplicative manner. For example, accepting the assumption of additivity allows some inadequate or unfavourable attribute level to be compensated for or traded off for higher levels of another more favourably imaged factor. A non-additive rule might, on the other hand, suggest that a given attribute may never be satisfactory unless the level of each alternative attribute is above some minimum threshold level (Meyer, et. al., 1980). Finally, there is still controversy over whether it is possible to use additive or non-additive criteria by themselves. Norman and Louviere (1974) and Levin and Gray (1977) argue that many individuals appear to use a multiplicative rule rather than an additive one or they may use some combination of additive and multiplicative rules.

As an example of the use of the information integration approach in the study of consumer choice of shopping centre, we refer to the work of Timmermans (1982) in the Netherlands. He looked at the relationships between the physical attributes of the retail system, consumer decision-making and overt behaviour. Attributes of centres used were: choice range, distance to residence, and availability of parking facilities. Respondents were required to numerically evaluate the attributes for each of the shopping centres on a 1-9 rating scale. The average weightings were graphed against their corresponding physical measures, which showed an almost perfectly monotonic relationship. Interactive least squares procedures were used to obtain the functional relationship between the pairs of variables from Spearman rank order correlation coefficients. To validate the nature of the consumer decision-making process, a laboratory experiment was designed whereby subjects were tested over varied numbers of shops, travel time and time taken to find a parking place. The levels of the three attributes were combined to a 3x3x3 factorial design to yield the 27 hypothetical shopping centres, and subjects were required to evaluate all 27 shops plus an additional two stimulus combinations more extreme than the 27 design combinations, which they were asked to consider "best" and "worst". The data were subjected to an analysis of variance for a between-subject factorial design. Each two-way interaction effect was graphically plotted, as shown in Figure 8.3 (a,b,c).

Results revealed all main efforts and the NxT effect were statistically significant, while the NxP and TxP effect were not statistically different from zero beyond the 0.05 level. Timmermans stated that we cannot calculate firmly either for a multiplicative or an additive combination rule. A multiplicative rule would predict that each interaction effect would plot as a series of divergent-convergent lines. An additive composition rule would predict that each interaction will plot as a series of parallel lines. Figure 8.3a shows that the NxT interaction effect is plotted as a series of diverging lines, whereas the plots for the NxP and PxT interaction effects shows series of approximately parallel lines. Figure 8.3 shows consistency of the evaluations. As the number of shops increases, the average evaluation of the subjects increases, but the average evaluation decreases with increased travel time and time required to find a parking place.

Arguments about the relative usefulness of information integration approaches are still ongoing. At the same time, there is a slowly increasing amount of literature which must be described as successful applications of the approach. This is true in situations such as mode choice (Levin and Corry 1975); residential preference (Louviere and Meyer, 1976; Louviere 1979), migration choice (Lieber, 1979); and shopping destination choice (Louviere, et. al., 1977; Louviere and Meyer, 1976, 1981; and Timmermans,

Figure 8.3

The Results of Laboratory Judgment Experiments

(a) Average category value as a function of distance and number of shops

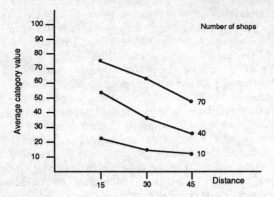

(b) Average category value as a function of parking and distance

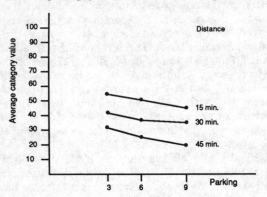

(c) Average category value as a function of number of shops and parking

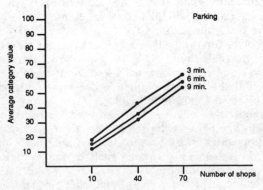

Source: After Timmermans, 1982

1982, 1983). Most reviewers agree that applications such as these provide good descriptions of the judgmental processes involved in choice situations.

8.5 STOCHASTIC CHOICE MODELS

Whereas many of the traditional consumer behaviour models are static and cross-sectional in nature, and rely for operationalisation on samples of consumers' responses taken at specific points in time, the last two decades have seen an ever increasing emphasis on **stochastic choice** models based on longitudinal (e.g., panel) survey data. Many of the developments in this area are classified into one of two categories. First there are the individually based **brand choice** models. Second there are the more market share based **purchase incidence** models (see Table 8.4 for a summary of these models). A brief explanation of the essential nature of these models, and some critical differences between them, follows.

8.5.1 A General Stochastic Model of Buying Behaviour

The critical components of a general stochastic model of buying behaviour include a state space, a choice process, a purchase or patronage event as an outcome of the choice process, and feedback.

To illustrate the format of such a model, it is necessary to:

(a) define a **state space**, e.g., for visits to two alternative grocery stores
(b) define an **event**, defined as a single outcome of the process involved in patronising a given store.

Given a market with two stores, the state space may be one of the three alternatives, namely,

$$S_0 = \text{no purchase}$$

$$S_1 = \text{patronise Store 1}$$

$$S_2 = \text{patronise Store 2}$$

The aim of a stochastic model would be to predict the probability of patronising Store i at time t, where i is selected from state space i = 0,1,2, and t is a single trip. Thus:

$$P_i = \Pr\{S_i(t)\} \qquad (14)$$

This describes a stationary multinomial process. It is stationary because, in this case, the probabilities are constant over time.

If, however, $\Pr\{S_i(t)\}$ depends on things such as the date of the last purchase, the brand last bought, size of family, level of income, exposure to advertising, and so on, then the buyer's behaviour would be **conditional** upon some set of characteristics. For example, consider the following conditional probability statement:

$$\Pr\{S_i(t)|X_t\} = f(X_t) \qquad (15)$$

where (X_t) = the set of relevant characteristics.

179

Table 8.4

Stochastic Models of Buying Behaviour

	No Time Effects		Time Effects	
	No Purchase Event Feedback (A)	Purchase Event Feedback (B)	No Purchase Event Feedback (C)	Purchase Event Feedback (D)
BRAND-CHOICE MODELS				
(1) Homogeneous Population	Bernoulli	Markov, Lipstein (1959) Linear learning, Kuehn (1958)	None	Semi-Markov, Howard (1963) Variable Markov, Tesler (1963) Dynamic Markov, Lipstein (1965)
(2) Heterogeneous Population	Household-Bernoulli, Frank (1962) Compound Bernoulli, Morrison (1965a,b)	Household-Markov, Massey (1966) Compound Markov, Morrison (1965a,b) Compound learning, Kuehn (unpublished research)	Change and response uncertainty, Coleman (1964a) Dynamic inference, Howard (1965) Probability diffusion, Montgomery (1966)	Household-variable Markov, Duhammel (1966) Variable learning, Kuehn and Rohloff (1967) Learning diffusion, Jones (1969)
PURCHASE-INCIDENCE MODELS				
(3) Homogeneous Population	Poisson Exponential Logistic	None	Variable exponential, Fourt and Woodlock (1960) Variable logistic, Massy (1960) One-element learning, Haines (1964)	Depth of repeat-penetration, MCRA (unpublished research) Penetration-repeat buyer share, Parfitt and Collins (1968)
(4) Heterogeneous Population	Negative binomial (compound Poisson), Ehrenberg (1959) Compound exponential, Anscombe (1961)	None	Compound logistic and one-element learning	Two-period negative binomial and logarithmic series distribution, Chatfield et al. (1966) Compound Wiebull, Massey (1967)

If, as in the above example, probabilities are independent of time and household characteristics, the appropriate multinomial process is stationary, i.e.:

$$\Pr \{S_i \ (t)|X_t\} = \text{constant} \tag{16}$$

Thus, to build a stochastic model of buyer behaviour we need to:

(a) determine state space
(b) determine those components of X_t which are to be included in the model
(c) determine the functional form of $f(X_t)$ - this shows how the included X's affect probabilities of purchase
(d) estimate parameters for the model.

In general, it must be possible to obtain data showing which event in the state space occurs on each trial, and what the X's values were on that trial.

Three factors affecting purchase probabilities are:

(a) **feedback** from past purchases of the product,
(b) influence of **exogenous** market forces (time effects),
(c) factors **endogenous** to the household not affected by the above (population heterogeneity).

Purchase event feedback is considered important because some models assume the act of purchasing (and using) products has a dire effect on household subsequent purchase probabilities (e.g., if Store 1 or 2 were patronised, then $\Pr \{S_0(t)\}$ would diminish for days). A first order Markov model would thus assume that the last state to be realised determines probability on next trial, i.e.:

$$\Pr\{S_j(t)\} = f[S(t-1)] \tag{17}$$

and is dependent on the outcome of the previous day.

The transition probability

$$\Pr\{S_i(t)|S_i(t-1)\} = \text{constant for all } t \tag{18}$$

Obviously households differ from each other in many ways. The model can account for population heterogeneity by:

(a) obtaining data from each customer to estimate parameters for the model - including an element of X
(b) segmenting samples on household specific bases and estimating parameters for each segment (e.g., high/low incomes, etc.)
(c) assuming parameters of the buying model have a prior distribution that estimates for populations rather than households.

We have noted earlier that the two major subdivisions of the class of stochastic models of buyer behaviour are **brand choice** and **purchase**

incidence models. Briefly, brand choice models predict which of a specified list of brands will be purchased. Purchase incidence models predict how many purchases will occur over given time intervals.

Consider the following set of events and states:

Event	State	Definition
B_1	S_1	Purchase Brand 1
B_2	S_2	Purchase Brand 2
P	S_1 or S_2	Purchase product class
P	S_0	No purchase

From the above consider:

$$Pr\{B_j \varepsilon (t, t + h)\}$$

i.e., the probability of brand i being purchased within the period $(t \rightarrow t + h)$. This statement can be elaborated in terms of a purchase event (P), i.e.

$$Pr\{B_j \varepsilon (t,t+h)\} = Pr\{B_j | P \varepsilon (t,t+h)\} \quad Pr\{P \varepsilon (t,t+h)\}$$

or the probability of brand j being purchased in time period $(t \rightarrow t+h)$ is equal to the conditional probability of brand j being purchased in time period $(t \rightarrow t+h)$ given that a purchase occurs, times the probability of a purchase taking place in this time interval.

Given the above type of formulation we can specify the critical elements of brand choice probability and purchase incidence as follows:

$$Pr\{B_j | P \varepsilon (t,t+h)\} = \text{brand choice probability,}$$

$$\text{and } Pr\{P \varepsilon (t,t+h)\} = \text{purchase incidence probability.}$$

Brand choice examples include market models and linear learning models. Purchase incidence models include exponential market penetration models, logistic market penetration models, and negative binomial market penetration models. Each has different binomial postulates and different mathematical structures. As an example of these classes of models we now turn to consider the negative binomial distribution model.

8.5.2 Negative Binomial Distribution (NBD) Model

Whereas in a previous section of this chapter we focused on the individually based information integration models, which in a real sense can be used as indicators of brand choice models, in this section we concentrate on stochastic purchase incidence models calibrated more on the decisions of sample populations. In particular, we will focus on one of the most widely applied of these models, the **negative binomial distribution** (NBD) approach.

Initially recommended by Chatfield, Ehrenberg and Goodhardt (1966) and Ehrenberg (1972), the NBD has been the basis of large and important consumer behaviour studies undertaken in recent years in England by Wrigley et al. (1984, 1985), and in the US by Halperin (1985).

The NBD is a two dimensional stochastic model that describes and predicts many major regularities in consumer purchasing patterns. It does so for a single object (e.g., a single brand) or for a single event, (e.g., patronising a single store or shopping centre). The model is based upon several key assumptions:

(a) The frequency of purchase of a particular product (or visit to a particular store) by a single consumer in successive equal time periods follows a Poisson distribution, with a parameter representing the consumer's long-run average rate of purchase or patronage.

(b) These average purchasing rates (U_1, U_2,...U_n) vary among consumers (1,2,...N) and these rates follow a gamma distribution across all consumers.

(c) The frequency of purchase or patronage across consumers in a given time period can be described by the negative binomial distribution, which itself results from compounding the Poisson and gamma distribution.

(d) The average purchases (or patronage) - the key parameters (m) - exhibit periods measured in weeks. The formal expression for the NBD, which is a two parameter discrete distribution is given by:

$$P_r = \left(1 + \frac{m}{k}\right)^{-k} \cdot \frac{\Gamma(k-r)}{\Gamma(r+1)\,\Gamma(k)} \cdot \left(\frac{m}{m+k}\right)^{r} \qquad (21)$$

where:

P_r = the probability of obtaining any non-negative number r.

. = the gamma function.

m = the mean number of purchases made by all consumers in a given time period.

k = the shape parameter of the gamma distribution which describes the average long-run purchasing rates of different consumers in a given time period (Wrigley and Dunn 1984a).

To calculate the purchase incidence probabilities (P_r), one utilises an expanded form of the binomial:

$$1 - \left(\frac{m}{m+k}\right)^{-k} \qquad \text{or} \qquad 1 - \left(\frac{a}{1+a}\right)^{-k} \qquad (22)$$

A major advantage of the NBD is that it provides some theoretical norms for wide range of indices of consumer spatial behaviour. These norms provide a series of benchmarks to which observed behaviours can be compared.

8.5.3 An Example: Fitting the NBD Model

Recently the NBD model has been used to investigate consumer behaviour in Cardiff, Wales (Golledge and Wrigley, 1985) and Goleta, California (Halperin, 1985). We refer to the latter study.

In 1984 a carefully selected panel of approximately 190 individuals began keeping a four week daily shopping diary. Subjects were selected by spatially stratified random sampling procedures. Diary instruction was carried out at the beginning of the survey and diary sheets were picked up every seven days. The purpose of the diary was to record the origins, destinations and other stops of panelists on a variety of shopping trips. Both grocery store and women's apparel functions were targeted for data collection. Within the grocery stores a specific subset of items known to be frequently purchased by most households was emphasised. Mode of transportation, trip purpose, time and duration of trip, and other useful information was recorded for each store visited on each trip. When coded, the diaries represented a mass of consumer behaviour, brand choice, and store choice (purchase incidence) information which was used to help calibrate an NBD model for the area. All possible purchase outlets, both stand alone and shopping centre locations, were included in the survey. General population characteristics such as weekly purchase frequency, product purchase, transportation mode, and time and distance travelled, and other purchase incidence characteristics were carefully recorded both for individuals and for the entire sample. The sample population was further broken down into four subregions, three of which were typically suburban neighborhoods, while the fourth was a student dominated residential area.

The NBD predictions were derived using a sample mean of observed purchasing rates and the observed number of non-shoppers (Halperin 1985). The fit of the model, in terms of a comparison between observed numbers of purchases or store visits and theoretical estimates provided by the NBD (see Figure 8.4 and Table 8.5) indicate that the predictive capacity of the model was very good. Taking a single store as an example, (e.g., Smith's in Magnolia shopping centre), the NBD model predicted that 12 shoppers would make one visit there during the four week period; the actual number of shoppers to make such a single visit was 13. It was predicted that 4 consumers would shop twice at that particular store in the four week period, while in fact 6 recorded such visits. Similar close correspondences between observed and predicted outcomes is evident for most of the other stores in the area. Over the entire bundle of shoppers, average error rate of .007 was obtained (Halperin 1985). Similar extremely low error rates were obtained by Wrigley and Dunn (1983) when using the NBD in a predictive mode on a consumer panel from the city of Cardiff in Wales. Although Halperin found a very good fit for store patronage using the entire sample population, he also recognised that some stores in the area relied primarily on local regional trade. It was suspected that the NBD would not prove as effective in estimating purchase incidence and store patronage in those cases, and in fact, when the model was reapplied using only sub-regional populations and the stores located within each sub-region, the overall fit improved. The one exception to this general rule was a store in the heavily student-dominated Isla Vista area (Isla Vista Market). In this case there was a substantial overprediction (22 predicted to 10 observed) of once only shopping and an underprediction of heavier repeat shoppers.

Figure 8.4

The Fit of the NBD Model

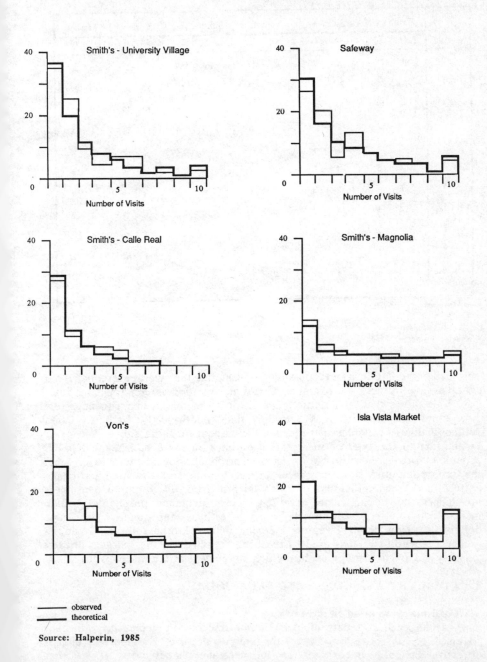

observed
theoretical

Source: Halperin, 1985

185

Table 8.5

The Fit of the NBD Model

Number of Visits	Smith's UV		Safeway		Smith's CR		Smith's Mag		Vons		IV Market	
	O	T	O	T	O	T	O	T	O	T	O	T
0	107	107	122	122	149	149	169	169	121	121	126	126
1	34	35	25	29	26	27	13	12	27	28	10	22
2	24	19	19	15	9	11	6	4	10	15	10	12
3	9	12	6	10	6	6	3	4	14	10	11	8
4	5	8	12	7	6	3	2	2	8	7	11	6
5	6	5	4	2	4	2	3	2	5	5	3	4
6	6	4	2	3	1	1	3	1	4	4	7	4
7	2	3	4	2	0	1	0	1	4	3	4	3
8	4	2	2	2	0	0	1	1	1	2	4	2
9	1	1	1	1	0	0	0	1	2	2	4	2
10+	3	4	4	5	0	0	3	2	5	6	11	12

O = Observed
T = Theoretical

Source: Halperin, 1985

Using the NBD it was possible to examine the average frequency of shopping over time. An example of this information is contained in Table 8.6. This shows that Von's customers' shopping increased in frequency from 1.6.3 times per week in week 1 to 3.61 times per week by week 4. Other similar changes in increased frequency are evident in Table 8.6.

In addition to the type of information outlined in these tables, the NBD is capable of providing information on market penetration of stores over time, the proportion and significance of repeat buying and the total patronage pattern, and some indication of the total proportion of potential consumers not tapped by a particular store (e.g., zero incidence purchases). Such information is also useful in attempting to estimate the quantity of escape dollars that flow from a region. Escape dollars in these terms would be grocery expenditures that could have been satisfied by the markets already existing in a particular region but which were spent at alternative sites.

8.6 IMAGERY AND CONSUMER BEHAVIOUR

8.6.1 Distance-Related Studies

One of the earliest tenets of behavioural research in geography was that cognised, or subjective, variables were likely to prove more important than objective variables in explanations of consumer behaviour. It was not

Table 8.6

Average Frequency of Shopping - Predicted Growth

Store	Week One		Week Two *		Week Four	
	O	T	O	T	O	T
Smith's UV	1.53	1.57	2.10	2.10	3.06	3.09
Safeway	1.48	1.62	2.19	2.19	3.38	3.24
Smith's CR	1.23	1.32	1.62	1.62	2.15	2.17
Smith's Mag	1.68	1.80	2.47	2.47	3.78	3.65
Vons	1.63	1.79	2.48	2.48	3.61	3.75
IV Market	2.08	2.22	3.26	3.26	5.43	5.14

O = Observed
T = Theoretical

* The two-week values were used in calibration

Source: Halperin, 1985

difficult to accept this reasoning for individually based models. When put in a context of population aggregates, however, important questions were raised concerning the definition and meaning of cognised variables such as shopping centre or store image, subjective distance, familiarity, preference, and so on. Attempts to define these concepts and to incorporate them into operational models of consumer behaviour have been at the forefront of much recent behavioural research.

As we have seen earlier in this chapter, Thompson (1963) introduced a notion of **subjective distance** to replace the traditional Euclidean measurement of objective distance in a range of consumer behaviour models in the early 1960s. Building on the empirical work of Golledge, Rushton and Clark (1966), Rushton and Clark further showed that concepts of **bounded rationality** (i.e., decisions made according to subjective information sets), and **preferences** for specific town size/distance combinations (Clark, 1969; Clark and Rushton, 1970) were able to build highly successful models of consumer spatial behaviour.

The notion that consumers had idiosyncratic, schematised, incomplete and highly subjective images of places such as shops and shopping centres was pursued by Downs (1969). Briggs (1969) used multidimensional scaling techniques to translate pairwise preferences for stores into a utility scale that had considerably greater success than traditional gravity model formulations in predicting consumer spatial behaviour. Demko and Briggs (1970) used similar **scaled preference** ideas to evaluate the attractive potential of places in southern Ontario for immigrants.

In essence, each of these studies looked at a different component of what is generally called an individual's **cognitive map**. This incomplete, augmented, schematised, and somewhat idiosyncratic representation of objective reality contains the keys to explaining individual behaviour. If a place is cognised as being difficult to get to or dangerous, its probability of patronage is reduced. If a shop or a shopping centre is imaged as being glamorous, attractive and exciting, there is a tendency to patronise it more frequently than any of its competitors.

Golledge, Briggs, and Demko (1969) used arguments such as these in their study of configurations of distance in intra-urban space to help explain the decline of patronage of central business districts, whose declining image encouraged patrons to turn their trade towards suburban shopping centres. In other words, the argument was advanced that if a consumer's cognitive map is incomplete, distorted, or fragmented, or has within it substantial **distance directional** or **temporal biases**, the individual may behave "irrationally" in terms of choosing possible destinations from an available opportunity set. Such behaviour might include acts such as choosing routes or time paths that were not even close to minimal path solutions, or patronising stores or centres that were much further away than more obvious, closer ones, even when the stores were from the same chain or the shopping centres had approximately the same functions in them.

One of the most fundamental components of a cognitive map is distance. Cadwallader (1975) tested a hypothesis that spatial rationality is more closely linked to cognitive than objective Euclidean distance. He found that a greater proportion of sampled shoppers believed that they patronised the nearest supermarket rather than did actually patronise the closest one. He suggested that more distant shopping centres had exaggerated attractiveness image components, and in a later study (1981) demonstrated that goodness of fit between model choice and actual choice was improved by substituting cognitive rather than objective distance in the model. In a similar vein, MacKay and Olshavsky (1975) investigated the significance of cognitive time and cognitive distance in consumer behaviour task situations. They also examined the differences that exist between **preference** (an ideal state) and **choice** (an actual state severely constrained by a host of economic, environmental, and other factors), showing there was no one-to-one mapping between the two.

8.6.2 Search and Learning

Behavioural work has emphasised the fact that consumer choice was not a repetitive invariant act. As Rogers (1970) had pointed out, consumer behaviour, even with respect to frequent purchases such as groceries, took 6 to 8 weeks to form. Prior to that, considerable **search activity** and experimentation was undertaken and the **funnelling** of behaviour took place. Funnelling simply involved successive elimination of unfavourable alternatives consequent to evaluation of a particular choice act such that over time the average number of places visited per chosen episodic interval decreased and then became relatively stable. This confirmed the theoretical suppositions made by Golledge (1967), who had developed the consumer behaviour, or market decision process, in the form of a dynamic Markov chain, which eliminated a number of alternatives after feedback had shown that reward expectancy thresholds were not reached.

Further studies by Potter (1976, 1977, 1978, 1979) have indicated that consumers undergo some type of **spatial search process** before sufficient information is accumulated about retail opportunities to begin the process of winnowing out the less favourable opportunities. He develops the notions of usage and **information fields**. His concepts paralleled the notion of action and activity space discussed in Chapters 6 and 12 on intra-urban mobility. Like those other studies, Potter found that information fields and the opportunity sets contained therein were sectoral in nature and, given the context of central business district dominated centres with which he dealt, the sectors were frequently stretched from a home location in the direction of the central business district. Potter also provided evidence that higher income groups were aware of more opportunities than lower income groups and they had a tendency to travel greater distances to a greater variety of retail outlets than did the lower income groups.

The importance of the **information** component was emphasised by Hanson (1978, 1984), whose work on households in Sweden demonstrated that the majority of spatial opportunities available to a given population subset were very poorly known. Only a subset of what might otherwise be regarded as a feasible opportunity set was recognised and there was a pronounced **distance decay effect** found with respect to familiarity with retail and other shopping opportunities. The distance effect decayed gently up to two miles from the home base but beyond tapered off quite sharply. This and other work lends strong support to the original behavioural hypotheses that assumptions of complete information (or perfect knowledge) were far too strong for most real-world situations, even when the spatial scale was extremely small.

8.6.3 Store and Centre Image
While this work on subjective distance, information, and search and learning proceeded apace in the 1970s, a gradually increasing body of parallel work focused on **store and centre image**. The largest component of this research attempted to identify the principal characteristics of store and shopping centre images. Using a variety of multivariate techniques on subjectively collected data sets, researchers tried to uncover the principal dimensions of store and shopping centre images which influenced consumer choice processes. Whereas the studies quoted in the previous section emphasised the friction effect of subjective time and distance in reducing the size of opportunity sets, the greatest emphasis on the store and shopping centre image research focused on the attractiveness component and how it conceivably influenced consumer choice.

In geography, a seminal study by Downs (1970) epitomised the concerns for recovering these **attractiveness dimensions**. Using bipolar rating scales typical of semantic differential scaling, and incorporating principal components analysis as the dominant analytical device, Downs postulated nine "cognitive categories", including visual appearance and shopping atmosphere, as representing the main components of shopping centre image. Downs attempted to unravel the degree of symbiosis in the relationship among urban form and spatial behaviour by focusing on the cognitive links.

The variety of work on store and centre image has escalated since 1970, as indicated in the selected studies set out in Table 8.7.

Table 8.7

Major Geographical Studies of Store and Centre Image

Study	Choice Context	Sample Size	Methodology	Important Attributes
Downs (1970)	Downtown shopping centre in England	202	Factor listing; rating scales; factor analysis	Service quality, prices, structure and design, shopping hours
Burnett (1973)	Apparel stores/shopping centres in Australia	40	Multidimensional scaling	Parking, product quality, distance from home, product variety
Hudson (1974)	Grocery stores in England	26	Repertory grid	Prices, distance from home, product quality, on route from University to home
Pacione (1975)	Shopping areas (towns) in Scotland	393	Rating scales	Product quality, prices, product reliability, product variety
Spencer (1978)	Grocery and green-grocery stores in England	381	Multidimensional scaling	Product variety, convenience, prices, produce freshness
Patricios (1979)	Shopping centres in South Africa	443	Rating scales, analysis of variance, correlation analysis, factor analysis	Service quality, cleanliness, convenience, product variety
Schuler (1979)	Grocery stores in Indiana	110	Rating scales, conjoint analysis (preference modelling)	Price, product quality, nearness of parking, speed of checkout, service, distance from home
Bloomstein, et al. (1980)	Shopping centre in the Netherlands	60	Multidimensional scaling	Price, product variety, service quality (non-daily goods), accessibility (daily goods)
Hudson (1981)	Apparel stores/shopping centres in Australia	20	Factor listing; rating scales; multidimensional scaling	Store variety, product variety, prices, product quality, distance from home
Timmermans, et al. (1982a, b)	Shopping centres in the Netherlands	20	Repertory grid	Number of shops, parking, distance from home, atmosphere

8.6.4 Repertory Grid Techniques

More recently, Timmermans (1981) has undertaken comprehensive studies of consumer shopping and shopping centre imagery in Eindhoven, the Netherlands, using **repertory grid** techniques. He looked at 12 shopping centres, plus the city centre in Eindhoven. The Kelly repertory grid method was employed to elicit the variables which customers use to discriminate between shopping centres. This is a flexible method, combining in-depth interviews and standard questionnaires. It elicits **personal constructs**. A subject is asked to name elements which fulfill certain roles for him. Alternately, the researcher may select these elements, and the subjects are presented with a number of triads of grid elements and asked to specify some important way in which two of these elements are alike and thereby different from a third.

In the Eindhoven study the number of personal constructs specified by 20 subjects ranged from 8 to 16, with an average value of 11.8. Table 8.8 summarises the results. In total, the subjects specified 236 constructs, and the content of the constructs shows that the number of shops were most frequently mentioned as a factor of differentiation between shopping centres. Other frequently mentioned constructs were: parking facilities, location relative to home, atmosphere, choice range and presence of non-retailing functions. Constructs like advertising, cleanliness and safety, were mentioned only occasionally. Timmermans emphasised that his findings indicated that there were clear differences both in terms of number and range of constructs people use to differentiate between shopping centres. Mainly economic-type constructs were used by most subjects, with social and marketing-type factors mentioned only occasionally.

However, greater understanding of the underlying basis of individual subject cognitive structure is obtained by checking each interview data by using principal components analysis. In this way, similar attribute rating profiles will cause strong positive associations, and will point to a single underlying basic dimension. Table 8.9 is a summary indicating the extracted components, the number of extracted components, the explained variance of each individual component, and the cumulative percentage of explained variance of subjects in the Eindhoven study. It is evident that most subjects used only a limited number of dimensions to differentiate between shopping centres. For half of them, three independent dimensions were extracted from their scoring pattern, 30% had only two basic dimensions, and 20% had four basic dimensions that were significant. The results indicate that although clear differences between subjects exist in terms of the number of personal constructs elicited, these constructs seem to be linked to a small number of underlying basic cognitive dimensions. On average, the percentage of the explained variance was 89.4%, which was a satisfactory result. Table 8.9 also indicates the construct of the extracted components. It shows that, in general, the basic underlying cognitive dimensions are those of size of shopping centre and accessibility. Often the size component was associated with atmosphere variables, indicating that for some subjects the larger shopping centres are preferred in terms of variables relating to atmosphere of the shopping centre. However, some subjects attached a different meaning to the atmosphere aspect of shopping centres, and underlying the size dimension are different verbal constructs, such as number of shops, range of choice, presence of department stores, availability

Table 8.8

Content of the Repertory Grid of Each Respondent

Description of constructs	1	2	3	4	5	6	7	8	9	10	11	12	13	14	15	16	17	18	19	20	Total per construct
1 few / many shops	x	x	x	x	x	x	x	x	x	x	x	x	x	x		x	x	x		x	19
2 poor / good parking facilities	x	x	x	x	x	x	x	x	x	x	x	x	x	x		x	x	x	x	x	17
3 far from / near to home	x	x	x	x	x	x	x	x	x	x	x	x	x	x		x		x	x	x	17
4 not cosy / cosy	x		x	x	x	x	x	x		x	x	x	x	x		x			x	x	14
5 narrow / wide range of stock	x		x		x	x	x	x	x	x	x	x	x	x		x			x	x	12
6 absence / presence of non-retailing functions	x		x			x	x	x	x	x	x	x	x							x	11
7 badly kept / well-kept environment	x	x	x			x		x		x	x	x	x		x	x				x	10
8 a / not a centre to shop around	x	x	x		x			x	x	x	x	x	x	x	x	x				x	10
9 narrow / wide range of speciality shops	x	x	x						x	x	x	x	x	x		x		x	x	x	10
10 poor / good service	x		x		x	x	x	x		x	x	x	x	x		x		x		x	9
11 poor / good choice range		x				x	x	x		x	x	x	x	x		x			x	x	7
12 quiet / busy	x	x	x					x			x	x	x		x	x				x	7
13 badly organized / well-organized	x	x	x								x	x	x	x		x		x		x	7
14 dark / light			x	x	x	x								x		x		x		x	6
15 high / low prices	x			x	x	x					x			x		x		x		x	6
16 absence / presence of especially attractive shops	x	x												x	x	x		x		x	6
17 dangerous / safe	x	x		x	x			x	x												5
18 no / plenty of non-daily goods	x	x		x				x	x										x		5
19 poor / good quality goods	x	x		x				x	x												5
20 windy / sheltered									x								x		x	x	4
21 poor / sufficient information	x	x					x													x	4
22 old/new				x			x												x	x	4
23 unattractive / attractive shopping environment	x	x												x							3
24 open / covered	x	x																	x		3
25 small / large	x	x												x							3
26 no / many boutiques											x				x			x			3
27 difficult / easy access	x															x			x		3
28 compact / extensive	x			x																	2
29 no / various department stores					x		x														2
30 small / extensive pedestrian area			x										x								2
31 impersonal / personal atmosphere												x								x	2
32 poor / excellent window displays									x											x	2
33 never / frequent special activities		x															x				2
34 difficult / easy to recognize													x						x		2
35 few / many special offers							x					x									2
36 far from / near to bicycle stand	x																				1
37 dangerous / safe to walk around																			x		—
38 a / not a centre to meet people															x						—
39 intimate / too big																	x				—
40 feeling of unsafety / safety					x																—
41 no advertisement / advertisement									x												—
42 dirty / clean								x													—
Number of constructs per respondent	11	9	13	11	10	11	11	10	16	12	12	15	13	15	10	13	13	8	10	13	Total 236

Source: Timmermans, 1982

Table 8.9

Cognitive Components of the Twenty Respondents

Components	1	2	3	4	5	6	7	8	9	10	11	12	13	14	15	16	17	18	19	20	Frequency
Size	★		□	□	□	□	□	□	★	□	★	□	□	□	○	□		□	★		20
Atmosphere		□○	□	□	□	★	□	○		□	□	□	★	□	★		□	★		□	13
Accessibility		★	★	★	○		★	★	○	★		★	★		□		★○			□	13
Physical lay-out					★		○		●	○			★		□		○		□		7
Cognitive accessibility									□												4
Character of centre								●						○			●				4
Distance	○											○		★		★				★	3
Specialization				○								●○				○					3
Price													○								1
Convenience																					1
Multifunctional																					1
% Explained variance																					
Component I (□)	48.4	57.1	60.6	59.9	51.9	77.3	61.2	38.7	49.7	67.6	57.6	50.4	52.3	63.2	49.9	46.8	29.1	64.7	71.8	80.3	
Component II (★)	30.0	17.5	29.4	22.0	27.2	12.8	18.9	23.3	16.2	12.8	29.5	18.8	24.2	13.6	28.5	26.2	23.9	27.1	14.6	11.7	
Component III (○)	10.1	13.8	—	13.1	11.4	—	14.8	13.0	14.6	10.9	—	10.0	12.5	11.5	15.2	10.5	20.0	—	—	—	
Component IV (●)								11.6	7.4			8.6					11.8				
Cumulative percentage of explained variance	88.5	88.4	90.0	95.0	90.5	90.1	94.9	86.6	87.9	91.3	87.1	87.8	89.0	88.3	93.5	83.6	84.8	91.8	86.4	92.0	
Number of components	3	3	2	3	3	2	3	4	4	3	2	4	3	3	3	3	4	2	2	2	

Source: Timmermans, 1982

of non-duty goods, presence of non-retailing functions, and the presence of specialty stores.

8.6.5 Multi-Dimensional Scaling

A more indirect method of recovering image concepts uses a technique known as **multidimensional scaling** (MDS). Here data is collected from subjects who evaluate similarity or dissimilarity among pairs of alternatives (e.g., pairs of stores or pairs of shopping centres). The similarity measures yield a set of independent dimensions that represent the structural relationships among the alternatives. The resulting MDS configuration of stimuli reveal the space of minimum dimensionality in which all the stimuli can be mapped. The number of dimension, then, represent the number of critical variables used by subjects in the reasoning process (i.e., making judgments about such stimuli).

Identification of dimensions can be undertaken in two ways. If some prior data is collected on a number of dimensions generally hypothesised to have an effect on consumer choice, then the scores of different factors can be correlated with the projections of the stimuli on each dimension in turn, thus identifying which factor is most highly related to which dimension. This property fitting procedure (Carroll and Chang 1970) can be used with either subjectively or objectively defined factors. Alternatively, once the MDS configuration has been achieved and a space of minimum dimensionality determined, a posteriori property fitting procedures can take place (in a manner similar to that used in factor analysis) in a subjective attempt to identify dimensions. In either case, however, testing is done to see whether or not the hypothesised factors relate to the discovered dimensions. This leads to interpretation of those dimensions, rather than adopting the standard scaling procedure of first identifying factors and having them rated by subjects without really identifying those latent variables that may be of most importance to any particular subject or group of subjects.

Examples of consumer behaviour studies using MDS procedures include those by Burnett (1973), who examined women's choices of both convenience stores (e.g., groceries) and shopping goods (e.g., women's apparel), Singson (1975), Lloyd and Jennings (1978), Spencer (1978, 1980), Blommestein et al. (1980) and Hudson (1981). This has, in fact, proven one of the more popular and productive areas of consumer behaviour research, and it has consistently demonstrated the benefits of recovering the latent dimensional structure underlying the choice act and using identifiable components of this structure to define store and centre image attractiveness components.

There continues, however, to be considerable advocacy of each of the techniques discussed above (e.g., semantic differential or Likert scaling, repertory grid analysis, and MDS procedures), and the relative advantages and disadvantages of the difference methods are discussed in Timmermans, et. al. (1982a,b).

8.6.6 Effects of Constraints

Whether researchers have focused on behavioural approaches, such as those discussed above, or whether they rely more on selection of standard socio-economic and demographic variables to help categorise and explain different types of choice patterns, a common feature across all studies is the recognition that consumers act with various degrees of **constraints** imposed on them. The distance and time constraints, the subjective preference and attractiveness constraints, or the latent structures recovered using MDS procedures, all admit that the wide range of constraints existing within a society frequently make it impossible for consumers to "actualise" their preference for retail choices.

The constraints may be personal, structural, societal, or institutional in nature. For example, a member of one ethnic group may not wish to venture to a nearby store located within the turf of a different ethnic group; a theoretically nearby choice alternative may be made impractical by a major freeway construction; an individual may not be able to do his banking after 3:00 pm or his office work after 5:00 pm because of institutional constraints on opening, working, or closing hours.

Constraints-oriented consumer behaviour research emphasises that many standard traditional spatial choice models are not structured to allow for these types of effects, and consequently mistakenly allocate individuals to places where it is not possible or feasible for them to become patrons. In an influential paper, Sheppard (1980) emphasised the importance of differentiating those subsets of the populations that may be characterised as having more or less free choice as opposed to those subsets that have severely constrained choices. Often the free choice subset involves higher socio-economic mobile subgroups. In contrast, the constrained choice is more typical of lower income, less mobile, or culturally or ethnically constrained groupings. For example, Burnett and Hanson (1982) and Desbarates (1983) have focused on the constrained choice problem and suggest that many of the mismatches between spatial cognitions of choice situations and objective descriptions of the same situation are the result of existing constraint situations. The specification of that particular role different types of constraints play in different choice situations needs to be investigated further, for it is undoubtedly an item of critical importance to the understanding and explanation of consumer spatial behaviour.

8.6.7 Retailer's Cognitions of Store and Shopping Centre Environments

As pointed out by Golledge (1970), the way a **producer** images his market will influence a variety of things, such as how the product is presented to the potential buying population, the location chosen for the display and sale of the product, the reaction towards competition, the dollars spent on advertising, and so on. For example, the retailer who assumes that his buying populace are Marshellian calculating machines, adopting rigid economic principles to guide their purchase acts, will focus only on getting a message to the consumer that their prices are lowest. Regardless of where they locate, they would argue that the lower prices will attract all the customers needed to surpass that threshold population required for profitable store operation. The retailer who believes clients are primarily Freudian consumers may invest heavily in advertising a product's personal appeal, and packaging becomes the dominant theme of the marketing project. Those assuming customers are basically Veblenian social animals will perhaps emphasise locations in prominent busy shopping places, such as central business districts or regional shopping centres, where purchasing the product will be part of a social interaction process.

Consumer Behaviour

The types of locational decisions made by different retailers, therefore, give some insights into how they image their potential customers and which forces drive their marketing actions.

But retailers are also influenced to a substantial degree by the quality of the local environment in which they develop their service. As pointed out by Golledge, Halperin and Hubert (1983) in a study of retailers in Melbourne, Australia, a wide range of attitudes are considered to be important (see Table 8.10).

Table 8.10

Influences Affecting Retailer Location Choice

Attributes of Retail Environments	Categories of Respondents	
	Type of Business	Response Frequency
A. Layout of shopping centre	1. Department stores	-
B. Shopping centre appearance	2. General store	1
C. Access for delivery and loading	3. Grocer, small supermarket	2
D. Number and size of shops	4. Fruit & vegetables	3
E. Business mix	5. liquor	-
F. Accessibility to main roads	6. Bread and cake	6
G. Acess within centre	7. Milk bars	5
H. Location relative to competing centre	8. Fish, take away	2
I. Customer base	9. Butcher	12
J. Turnover in types of business	10. Men's and boy's wear	8
K. Overhead costs	11. Women's and girl's wear	24
L. Property costs	12. Footwear	16
M. Labour turnover and absenteeism	13. Fabrics, household textile, carpets	18
N. Town council and planning controls	14. Furniture	9
O. Diverse activities in town helping trade	15. Hardware, builder's supplies	7
P. Future of the town	16. Household appliances/repair	12
Q. Town draw from wide area	17. Florist, nursery	8
	18. Watchmaker, jeweller	8
	19. Chemist	14
	20. Photographic	6
	21. Sports, toys, music	22
The original survey requested respondents to scale the attributes as follows:	22. Newsagents, books, stationery	15
	23. Cafe, restaurant	7
1 = Good	24. Laundries, dry cleaners	5
	25. Men's/women's hairdressers	8
2 = Satisfactory	26. Motor accesories	1
	27. New/used vehicles	1
3 = Not Applicable	28. Clothes store	11
	29. Tobacconist	3
	30. Gift shop	6
	31. Babywear	5
	32. Wool/handcraft	6
	33. Health food	6
	34. Travel agency/travel services	4
	99. Other	31
	VV No answer	26

Retailer choice as to whether to locate in an existing business district, or in a dispersed suburban location, might depend on:

196

(a) their image of the rigidity of the local board of supervisors or town planners
(b) their perception of the cleanliness, orderliness, or degree of control exerted over the shopping environment
(c) their image of how accessible their place of business is to available on-street and off-street parking facilities, or
(d) it may simply be a result of where they believe the hub of shopping activity is currently focused.

Fears of competition, not only from other retailing specialists, but from other competitive shopping centres, appear to play an important role in deciding whether to continue leasing a given location or undertaking a major move. Similarly, image of turnover rates in, say a suburban planned shopping centre environment, may be quite critical in terms of influencing retailers to retain an established business district location or vice versa.

As more and more retailers obtain access to an ever growing mass of sophisticated models for estimating consumer patronage, market penetration, and considerations such as the proportion of habituated vs. intermittent patronage patterns, the significance of adopting a behavioural approach to analyse location problems, as well as behaviour problems, becomes more obvious. Despite a surge of interest by behavioural researchers in the whole question of decision-making (largely in an industrial locational context) in the 1970s, little headway was made on this problem.

There is every reason to suspect that further research undertaken on the decision-making process of individual and chain store owners could throw considerable light on the more general decision-making process. By using an appropriate mix of standard models emphasising objective variables, and incorporating the decision maker's image of the potential locational environments in the explanatory paradigm, could substantially change our ability both to understand and to predict these complex decision-making actions.

8.7 SOME EMERGING NEW APPROACHES IN CONSUMER BEHAVIOUR RESEARCH

There has been a proliferation of different models for analysing consumer spatial behaviour within geography. Many models have been developed in the context of a spatial choice paradigm (Pipkin, 1981a; 1981b), focusing on the individual. The disaggregate orientation of this behavioural research represents a movement away from the traditional aggregate approaches, such as central place models or gravity/entropy formulations. By concentrating on humans as individual actors, the spatial choice paradigm has sought explanation, rather than simply macro-level prediction. The research has recognised that there are forces operating outside the spatial system that may influence behaviour, and that these forces are associated with an individual's decision-making process and the implications of those processes with regard to the environmental situation in which consumer behaviour takes place.

A further characteristic of spatial choice modelling has been a recent emphasis on developing approaches that can account for dynamic aspects of behaviour (Martin, Thrift and Bennett, 1978; Tardiff, 1980; Crouchley, et al., 1982). This reflects a more general concern in the social sciences with understanding the **dynamic** behaviour of social systems (Bowers, 1978a, 1978b; Arbib and Cornelis, 1981). As Wrigley (1981) has pointed out, a number of methods have recently been introduced into the geographical literature, including time-varying parameter models, recursive residual techniques, Kalman filter models, and so on, that complement and build upon the more traditional spatial time-series models (e.g., autoregressive moving-average techniques). Furthermore, the continuing work in catastrophe and bifurcation theory (e.g., Beaumont, 1980; Wilson, 1981) seems to suggest a desire among researchers to move beyond static descriptions and predictions of spatial behaviour. A whole host of new approaches are emerging which represent exciting developments in consumer behaviour research. We briefly refer to three of them below.

8.7.1 Panel Data Approach
It has been suggested that the development of a number of very promising analytical techniques has been delayed by the lack of extensive and highly disaggregated data sets concerning shopping behaviour. Concurrent with the shift towards more dynamic models has been the increased interest in collecting **longitudinal survey** or **panel data** (see Guy and Wrigley, 1982). In this form, data typically are collected on some sort of recurrent behaviour (e.g., shopping, voting, or travel) through the monitored use of **diaries** and/or **repeat interviewing**. Data is typically collected on actual choices of shops and shopping centres made over a period of time, and on the exact locations of origins and destinations for shopping trips, as it is often required to obtain fairly precise measures of distance. Implicitly, this approach also requires information about shopping places **not** visited by respondents, as they may or may not be assumed to have been preferred less than those that were visited. In addition, data is also collected describing the feasible shopping opportunities, socioeconomic and sociodemographic characteristics of the panelists, and various other types of information contingent upon specific research objectives (e.g., consumer attitudes, movement patterns, and so on). Certainly, diary surveys of this type are by no means new. They have frequently been employed in geographical and planning research, and they form one of the cornerstones of market research practice.

In a **discrete choice** context, Johnson and Hensher (1982) have suggested a number of advantages of the **panel data approach**. Perhaps the most important is the explicit recognition of the intertemporal nature of many choice outcomes, or, more specifically, the effect of experience on decisions. The use of panel data in linear models with continuous dependent variables is frequently more efficient, both statistically and behaviourally, than the estimation of separate relationships for each cross-sectional sample. Though as yet unverified in empirical research, it is probably reasonable to assume that similar conditions hold for models with categorical dependent variables (i.e., the discrete choice models used to predict choice or travel mode, shopping centre, and so on; see Heckman, 1982).

Panel data may also be used to investigate other issues related to consumer spatial behaviour. For example, a well-designed consumer diary survey can provide the calibre of information - in terms of location of purchase, socio-economic and sociodemographic characteristics of the respondents, physical and psychological (i.e. perceived or cognised) attributes of the shopping places, and so on - necessary for investigating the reliability of discrete choice models for predicting consumer spatial behaviour. Moreover, the longitudinal nature of panel data partially circumvents the problem of choice set definition, as patronage patterns are fairly well established during the monitoring period (Dunn and Wrigley, 1983a).

Another research objective using diary data might involve the assessment of a behavioural, process-oriented approach to analysing consumer spatial behaviour. More specifically, questions of whether cognitive/subjective variables are important determinants of spatial choice behaviour, and if there is a significant dynamic component associated with these variables, can be addressed. Also, panel data can be used to examine model transferability through space and over time. Finally, detailed locational information on consumers and shopping places over time enables an exploratory analysis of the influence of direction on consumer movement patterns (Hubert, et al., 1985).

8.7.2 Spatial Autocorrelation, Directional Bias and Consumer Behaviour
A methodology that has received relatively little attention from researchers of consumer spatial behaviour is **spatial autocorrelation analysis** (Cliff and Ord, 1980). Spatial autocorrelation is evaluated by assessing the degree to which the observed measurement of a phenomena (e.g., consumers' levels of expenditures) in one area corresponds to the observed measurement of that phenomena in neighbouring areas. The general evaluation strategy thus involves comparing the structure in some data defined for a set of places with the structure defined by the spatial configuration of those places, and deriving a statistic to assess the correlation between the data structure and the geographic structure (Moran, 1948; Geary, 1954; Cliff and Ord, 1981).

When examining spatial autocorrelation in the journey to shop, two basic questions can be considered. The first is concerned with autocorrelation with respect to the consumers' residences, and the second with respect to the shopping places. In the former case, the question is: Do consumers who live close to each other travel in similar directions to shop? In the later case, the question could be stated as follows: If goods are purchased at nearby locations, can this behaviour be attributed to consumers who have come from similar directions? Many analyses of consumer spatial behaviour concentrate upon distance as the fundamental spatial component. It should be emphasised, however, that direction, as well as distance, is implicit in all spatial relationships (Gaile and Burt, 1980). Indeed, recent research indicates that there are significant directional biases associated with many aspects of spatial behaviour (Cadwallader, 1977; Costanzo, Halperin and Gale, 1983).

Recently a nonparametric procedure has been developed by Hubert, et al. (1985), to assess the degree of spatial autocorrelation in directions of consumer travel.

8.7.3 Spatial and Temporal Transferability of Discrete Choice Models
While one of the early hopes and claims for discrete choice models was that a "well-specified" model, calibrated in one area and at one point in time, would be appropriate for predicting choices in other geographical locations and in other time periods. This was not so, however. It is of great importance that the parameter estimates of the model should be **spatially**

and/or temporally transferable. Obviously, the development of transferable models would allow the costs of conducting studies to be greatly reduced, and would provide a means of "validating" the discrete choice modelling approach (Wrigley, 1984).

Recently there have been a number of empirical studies that address the transferability question. The results of these analyses, however, have been somewhat contradictory. The initial studies yielded optimistic conclusions on both spatial and temporal transferability. For example, Atherton and Ben-Akiva (1976) estimated a mode choice model for Washington, D.C., and then applied the same form of model to explain travel behaviour in Los Angeles and New Bedford, Massachusetts. It was found that the parameter estimates of the model were remarkably similar in all three cities, which was regarded as empirical support for spatial transferability. They also suggested a set of possible updating procedures, including a useful Bayesian procedure, that would allow a small amount of context-specific information to be used in improving the predictive ability of a transferred model. Nevertheless, a subsequent study (Talvitie and Kirshner, 1978) was substantially less optimistic. In their analysis of work-trip data from Washington, D.C., Minneapolis-St. Paul and the San Francisco Bay Area (both before and after the introduction of the Bay Area Rapid Transit System), the authors discovered that parameter estimates could be neither successfully transferred either within an urban area or between cities, nor transferable over time.

More recent studies of transferability have attempted to achieve greater consistency across different data sets, and have been more sensitive to issues associated with variable definition, functional form, and so on. McCarthy (1982) has found evidence that supports the short-term transferability of parameter estimates in a study of work-trip mode choice in the San Francisco Bay Area. Galbraith and Hensher (1982), on the other hand, found no evidence to support the intra-urban spatial/temporal transferability of work-trip mode choice models in a study of two suburban areas in Sydney, Australia. Clearly, in view of this contradictory evidence, the scope for transferability of discrete choice models may be more limited than was previously envisioned.

It has been suggested that transferability problems arise because many of the current discrete choice model specifications do not adequately incorporate situational and contextual factors, unmeasured choice alternative attributes, and socio-economic characteristics that may influence choice (Wrigley, 1984). For example, Galbraith and Hensher (1982) note that investigations of spatial transferability have been hampered by the absence of contextual measures in many of the previously developed travel demand models. Moreover, with regard to temporal transferability, McCarthy (1982) and others stress the importance of incorporating measures that reflect interactions between longer-term locational decisions and shorter-term travel decisions. Therefore, if transferability is a primary objective, a model should be estimated in the base area (or time period) on criteria that define the new area (or time period).

Chapter Nine

SPATIAL CHOICE AND ACTIVITY PATTERNS: TRAVEL MODEL
ORIENTATIONS

9.1 THE NATURE OF BEHAVIOURAL TRAVEL MODELS

It is in the field of modelling travel behaviour and in the analysis of travel
patterns, in the context of transport planning in cities, that the behavioural
approach to the investigation of human activity patterns has found its major
applications. Time budgets and time-space budgets have been used as a
means of data collection for investigating travel choice for transport
planning. The strength of the behavioural approach to travel modelling is
that it is formulated on a set of hypotheses related to the decision making
unit, such as the individual household, and is tested with models which
adopt the decision making unit as the unit of analysis, even though most
individual choice models seek a set of parameters aimed at describing a
group of individuals and their behaviours. These approaches are concerned
with modelling recurrent travel behaviour, for it is this behaviour that is
most relevant in the transport planning context.

In this chapter, the nature of behavioural travel models is first
examined, and some of their problems are discussed. Three types of
approaches that have been proposed in studying human activity patterns in a
time-space context are then examined. These are: first, the use of
individual-oriented behaviour models in transport planning based on human
activity analysis; second, a situational approach to modelling individual travel
behaviour; and third, the analysis of repetitive travel behaviour in a
cognitive spatial choice paradigm.

9.1.1 Some Theoretical Developments
At a general level it is possible to distinguish two approaches to modelling
travel behaviour in cities. On the one hand, the economic-psychological
based model assumes utility maximisation in which travel is modelled as a
choice process in isolation from a wider set of human activities. On the
other hand, behavioural based models, while also employing a type of utility
maximising assumption, assume that travel is only one of a range of
complementary and competing activities operating in a continuous pattern or
sequence of events in time and space. In this latter context, travel is seen as
the procedure by which individuals trade time to move location in space in
order to partake in successive activities (Hensher and Stopher, 1979: 12). In
terms of the development of models, in recent years two broad approaches
have been adopted: first, those concerned with attempts to improve the
multinomial logit (MNL) models which formulate individual choice, and
second, those concerned with attempts to examine alternative model
structures of travel behaviour, in particular, Markov and semi-Markov

processes, and threshold models.

9.1.2 The Multinomial Logit Models

The multinomial logit (MNL) model is a discrete choice model in which the fundamental notion is that an individual will choose an alternative which is perceived to have the greatest utility. A functional expression of common utility is:

$$U_{ri} = V(Z_{ri}, S_i) + \xi_{ri} \tag{1}$$

where:

U_{ri} is the utility function associated with the r'th alternative for the i'th individual

$V(Z_{ri}, S_i)$ is composed of both a vector of attributes of the choice-alternative faced by individual i (Z_{ri}), and a vector of socio-economic characteristics of individual i (S_i). $V(Z_{ri}, S_i)$ is known as the representative or systematic component of the utility function. It represents that part of the utility that can be observed by the analyst.

ξ_{ri} is a random component which requests the idiosyncratic tasks of the individual and/or the unobserved attributes of the choice alternative; it is therefore that part of the utility contributed by the attributes which are observed by the analyst. (Hensher, 1979).

According to this model, an individual i will choose alternative r if

$$U_{ri} > U_{ji} \ V_j \ \epsilon A \quad \text{or}$$

$$(V_{ri} + {}_{ri}) > (V_{ji} \xi_{ij}) \quad \text{or} \tag{2}$$

$$(V_{ri} - V_{ji}) > (\xi_{ji} - \xi_{ri})$$

The MNL model assumes that the random component is independently and identically distributed as Weibull double exponential. This is equivalent to assuming there is no taste variation in the population of interest and that the effects of unobserved attributes are uncorrelated across alternatives or individuals. The MNL model assumes the form:

$$P_r |i = \frac{e^{V(Z_{ri}, S_i)}}{\sum\limits_{g=1}^{j} e^{V(Z_{gi}, S_i)}} \tag{3}$$

where $P_r|i$ is the probability that the r'th alternative will be chosen given the values of the explanatory variables.

The MNL model of choice assumes that the ratio of probabilities of choosing one alternative over another, where both alternatives have a non-zero probability of choice, is unaffected by the presence or absence of any additional alternatives in a set. This independence of irrelevant alternatives (IIA) property results in two major problems. First, a failure to recognise that all alternatives are distinct can lead to a biased estimation of model parameters. Second, prescribed market share changes may occur when any existing alternative is altered or the set of alternatives is changed by addition or deletion (Hensher and Stopher, 1979: 13). Certainly in recent years there have been many improvements to the MNL models. In particular, researchers have sought alternative formulations of individual choice models that are capable of producing information to assess the degree of similarity among choice alternatives. There has been considerable progress in eliminating problems that result from violation of the independence of irrelevant alternatives property to give a structured logit model in which similar alternatives in a choice set are modelled together initially and then redefined as a single alternative in the next stage of the structure. There has also been considerable progress in using information theory as a basis for assessing MNL models.

9.1.3 Markov Process Models

Markov process models, and particularly semi-Markov process models, have also received considerable attention in the last decade or so. In these models, it is necessary to define a set of states that an individual might occupy at various points in time. The process then defines either the probability of an individual being in a given state at time T, or, given the total number of individuals in various states at time (T-1), the model will estimate the number in each state at time T, based on a transition probability matrix (Hensher and Stopher, 1979: 18). These Markov models are very attractive because the concept is one of a dynamic model, but they do have some drawbacks. There is a problem of assumed independence of previous states occupied by the individual as being stable with time in the transition probabilities. There is also a problem of defining the state that an individual occupies at any given time.

9.1.4 Threshold Models

A further approach has been the development of threshold models. While these operate within the utility maximising assumption, an important departure from the logit model approach is that the individual is not seen as reacting in a continuous fashion to attribute change, but rather reacting only when the changes are sufficiently large to cross a threshold. This threshold could be a threshold of awareness or a threshold of acceptability. The notion of threshold is very much related to Simon's notion of man as a satisficer. An extension of the threshold approach is the elimination by aspects (EBA) model, which postulates a hierarchy of attributes or aspects, each of which must meet a threshold value in an alternative before that alternative can be considered or chosen.

9.1.5 Notion of Indifference

Inherent in the models relating to thresholds and elimination by aspects, is the notion of indifference, which relates to the way a traveller trades off between the generalised costs of alternative modes of travel. The notion of what is the just noticeable difference on a traveller's choice of mode of travel will depend upon his/her indifference surface which comprises probability bands of indifference around levels of utility for alternative modes. This approach incorporates a classic economics indifference surface analysis proposed by Quandt (1956). The action that is required to move from a lower to a higher utility level involves a utility cost that is not compensated by the gain in utility. This effect is analogous to the threshold concept, suggesting a net utility band of indifferences.

The 1970s saw the evolution of the second broad framework of theoretical developments: models with a broader behavioural base and with the aim to isolate the mechanisms by which actual and optional interaction of individuals in time and space occurred. These approaches focused on the nature of choice and constraints, the sequential courses of events at both an individual and an aggregate level, and how events are distributed in coherent blocks of space-time. This time-space approach to the study of human activities as spatial behaviours within a choice framework is an appropriate focus for the remainder of this chapter. The unit of analysis in this approach is the individual or household carrying out typical daily activities. The daily programmes, or sets of activities, are defined by performance time for an individual on an origin destination point basis, the spatial locations in which activities occur are mapped in time and space, and trips taken on a multi-modal transport system are analysed on a model basis. To a large degree, the approach is exemplified by the PESASP simulation model developed by Lenntorp (1978) which was discussed in Chapter 8. This procedure evaluates alternative paths to show the number of possible ways in which a given activity programme can be carried out in a given environment.

These recently developed disaggregated behavioural approaches to travel modelling are important. Hensher and Stopher (1979: 23) have this to say:

"An immediate implication of the research into the arrangement of human activities in time and space for individual-choice modelling is that arrangement of activities (origins and destinations) by modifying time and space constraints, can work conjunctively with the linkage of trips to increase accessibility to opportunities and conserve energy (both human and non-human)."

9.1.6 The Human Activity Approach
The human activity approach to modelling travel behaviour is conducted within the time space activity pattern context which was discussed in detail in Chapter 6. What were the reasons for its development in this context? Brog and Erl (1981: 1) explain:

"By the mid 1970s, an international discontent had arisen with models generally used for transportation planning. New, behaviourally-oriented approaches started to dominate the discussion among people involved in transport research. While the standard four-stage transportation demand models had depicted the locational change of the individual as the basic transport situation, and statistically combined these into trip patterns, the new approach focused on the individual as being embedded in a complex social and material environment. The notion that out-of-house mobility is not an end in itself, but rather serves as a means for individuals to participate in activities which cannot or should not take place in their direct neighbourhoods, was of far reaching consequence for further research. It made it necessary to change from a mobility or trip survey to a method of determining out-of-house activity patterns. Since the analysis of activity patterns quickly showed that an individual's activity pattern is not only influenced by his own autonomous decisions, but also by the other members of the household within which an individual lives, it became necessary to include entire households in empirical surveys."

In discussing the need for the development of models based on the human activity approach, and in identifying the problems inherent in the choice-based models used in the 1960s and 1970s in transport planning, Burnett and Thrift (1979: 116-119) list the following:

(a) A major defect of choice-based models was that they paid lip service to the notion of travel as derived demand. While it is widely recognised that travel is rarely desired for its own sake, few models related the demand for travel to the biological and social needs it fulfills. For example, activities generated by the biological needs of people, as identified by Hagerstrand's capability constraints, include eating, sleeping, and so on. Other activities were seen to arise from the individual's social role and location in the physical environment, and in Hagerstrand's scheme, these activities were circumscribed by authority and coupling constraints, and are regarded as socially produced. Thus, the choice-based models did not identify the basic forces which generate travel, and the linkages of these fundamentals with trip timing, length, frequency, mode, destination and route choices were not understood.

(b) The majority of models were based on the assumption of two stop-single purpose journeys. This represents only 60%-70% of individual journeys within cities, multi-stop journey sequences constituting the remainder. Thus, there was a need to develop a framework which would help describe, explain and forecast the allocation of trips by individuals over a daily sequence of stops. In this way, additional insights would be provided into the spatial and temporal variations in, and levels of, demand for urban transport facilities.

(c) Many of the models assumed static equilibrium conditions. The MNL model of mode or destination choice assumed that there was a single allocation of trips between choice alternatives by a given population group, and this allocation presumably arose from stable individual utility functions. The allocation of trips reaches a new equilibrium following a shift in the socio-economic characteristics of travellers or a change in mode or destination attributes. While it is true that several recent models incorporate the notion of constantly changing utility functions, these have generally been left aside, especially daily, weekly, monthly and other cycles in the combinations of activities which individuals pursue. These cycles affect the choice of activity sets over the short run and thus affect choices of the frequency and timing of single and multi-purpose trips of different kinds.

(d) There are important long-run changes in utility functions which many models do not allow for. Long-run alternatives in travel needs or constraints can generate alternations in the individual's daily activity set, and, hence, in purpose, type of frequency, timing, destination and route choice. For example, as leisure time or needs increase, or as work places and shopping areas increasingly decentralise, there could be complex changes in multi-purpose combinations and resultant mode and destination choices. Few models can handle this. Thus, there was the need to develop a theoretical framework which would help relate short and long-run variations in travel behaviour to variables other than population characteristics and transport systems.

(e) Choice models derived from economics and psychology and which are presented in a utility maximising framework do not really explain individual travel behaviour per se. Although they were often mathematically specified for the individual, in practice, these models were commonly used to describe, explain and forecast the travel behaviour of homogeneous population groups. This means that the individual is considered atomistically, that is, out of the context of the individual's household of which he is a member.

The human activity approach is one theoretical framework that does not suffer from these limitations. Why is this so? Burnett and Thrift say:

"Each individual in a household at the start of each time period (usually a day) selects an activity set (e.g., working, shopping, eating, sleeping). Activities are the outcome of the biological needs, social role requirements and the physical realities of the environment. Thus, some activities are obligatory, some are discretionary. Realisation of the activity set during a time period involves the selection of a time schedule for each, together with trip purposes, frequency, destinations, modes and routes. The travel choice which are normally modelled and are therefore viewed as the outcome of the need of individuals to undertake a sequence of activities within the constraints of time space. Other constraints, such as income and travel costs, operate through their effects on the time availability for activities and/or the distances over which travel can occur."

This approach links urban travel behaviour to the fulfillment of needs through the formation and accomplishment of activity sets. **Travel** is handled as a **derived demand**. Daily allocation of trips can be described and explained. Single and multi-purpose journey generations can be understood. Short run variations in demand for public transport facilities can be related to factors such as diurnal, weekly or monthly changes in activity sets, as well as to changes in learning about destinations, modes or routes. Long-run variations in demand can be associated with changes in socially determined needs, with changes in time and space constraints through alterations, and with changes in socio-economic status, technology or characteristics of the physical environment. Travel is seen as the outcome of all of these elements. Figure 9.1 presents a representation of how urban travel may be viewed within this broad context.

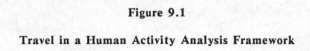

Figure 9.1

Travel in a Human Activity Analysis Framework

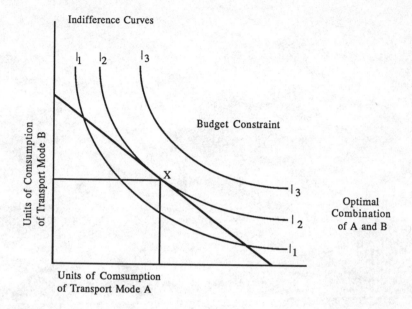

9.2 USING INDIVIDUAL ORIENTED BEHAVIOURAL MODELS IN TRANSPORT PLANNING

9.2.1 The Activity Concept

In using the human activity approach as a basis for modelling in transport planning, three time-space related concepts are used to transform the general theoretical approach into a rigorous and precise framework with many potential applications. These are:

(a) Travel choice options constrained in space-time
(b) Trip generation as an outcome of activity choices
(c) Constant time budgets.

Because transport planning ultimately is concerned with traffic flows, it is necessary to use the individual trip as the basis for an activity-oriented study. However, the trip should not be viewed in isolation. Rather, the manner in which an activity is related to a specific trip, how this activity fits into the overall activity programme of the individual and the household, and which out-of-house activities result, must be considered. Brog and Erl (1981) have presented this highly complex set of interrelationships in diagrammatic form which is redrawn in Figure 9.2. In this diagram the **activity patterns** of the individuals in the household are shown. The husband is seen to drive his car to work. The wife goes shopping twice; once she walks and once she uses a bicycle. Later in the day, she uses

Figure 9.2

The Activity Concept

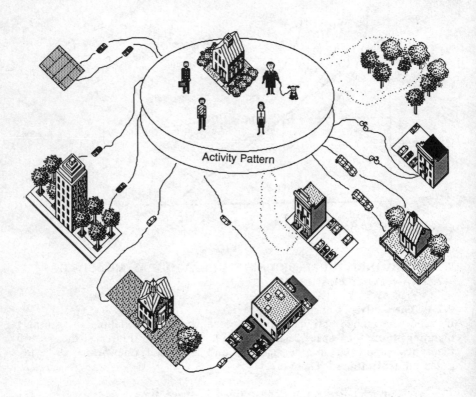

Source: After Brog & Erl, 1981

public transport to go and meet her friend. The son uses his own car to drive to the university, and on the way home, he stops at a supermarket to do some shopping for the family. The grandmother takes the dog for a walk. The household members have undertaken eight out-of-house activities during the day. These activities may be classified as work, education, shopping, and recreation trips. The household members actualise their activity patterns differently. In total, members of the household have left the house seven times in order to achieve their activity patterns, and they make a total of 15 trips using three modes of transport, individual modes (7), public modes (2), and non-motorised modes (6).

Another way in which travel and activities may be envisaged is presented in Figure 9.3. Part A of Figure 9.3 illustrates how we may represent, on a time axis, duration of travel between activities. In Part B of Figure 9.3, the activity time perspective is added to the travel perspective. Note that, at some locations, multiple activities take place, and travel itself is an activity, classified as A3. In Part C of Figure 9.3, a further concept is illustrated. Since it takes time to travel through space, there is a limit to the range of destinations which may be visited in a given period of time. Travel by a faster mode of transport will increase the distance range, and therefore the number of practical opportunities. This concept has been formalised by Hagerstrand (1970) in terms of **space-time prisms**, which are discussed in detail in Chapter 7. In Figure 9.3 Part C, an individual is committed to take part in Activity A, at location l_0 (say home), from t_0 -t_1, and to engage in activity A_2, at l_1 from t_2 -t_3. He/she has uncommitted time from t_2 to t_1, but the use that can be made of it depends on the speed with which travel from 2 to 1 can be undertaken. On foot, it might take (t_2 -t_1), leaving no time for an alternative primary activity. Faster modes of travel will enable the person to reach an enlarged area of space, and within this envelope some trade-off distance between intermediate destinations can take place. Public transport waiting times effectively shrink the prism and reduce the range of destination choice and the time which may be spent there. Space-time prisms will thus define a potential range of choice.

In the transport planning context, trip generation may be regarded as a trip/no trip travel option, and this will be a function of a number of elements, including socio-economic characteristics of the potential traveller, the level of service offered by public transport systems, and so on. Within the activity framework, Jones (1979: 65) says that the trip/no trip dichotomy can be replaced by an examination of activity choices which lie between participating in activities at the decision-maker's current location, involving no trip, or in other activities which make use of facilities elsewhere, hence requiring travel. This decision has three components:

(a) the range of possible activities
(b) the set of destinations offering suitable facilities for activity participation
(c) the characteristics of the available transport system.

Individual choice is a function of the attributes of these three factors and is be constrained in space-time by the appropriate prism. In this way, travel can be handled as a derived demand.

Figure 9.3

Travel, Activity Travel and the Space Time Prism

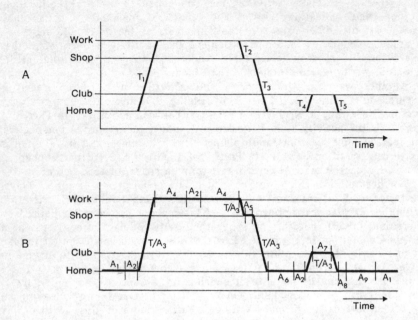

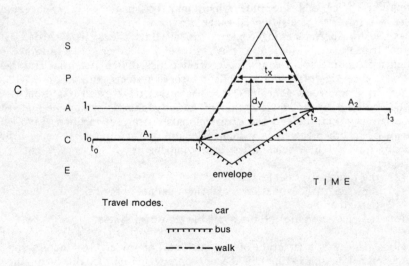

Travel modes.

—————— car

⊥⊥⊥⊥⊥⊥⊥ bus

—·—·—· walk

Source: After Jones, 1979:63-64

Activities utilise a finite limit of daily time budgets (24 hours). They also require facilities to be available at a limited number of locations in space (often only at home). Further, locations operate at fixed times or between certain hours of the day. Other activities are fixed in timing and/or location to a varying degree, and they provide fixed points in space-time around which more optimal or flexible activities have to be analysed. The degree of freedom of choice at such times is limited absolutely by the appropriate space-time prism, and often by financial constraints, which are determined by the overall availability of transportation modes. Choices lie between combinations of activities and locations within the prism which are perceived as options by the individual. At an aggregate level, factors operate which tend to control overall time allocations to activity and travel time, placing a further limitation on activity and travel patterns (Jones, 1979: 66). The role of travel is particularly important within this activity approach, because it can both be diminished and enhanced through the role of time. Travel takes time and thus diminishes the number of activities that can be undertaken. At the same time, travel is an enhancing agent because it smooths the operation of daily activity patterns in space and time.

9.2.2 A Model of Individual Travel Behaviour

During the 1970s numerous studies were conducted into the nature of activity patterns. An example of attempts to model individual travel behaviour was proposed by Kutter (1973), who sought to explain **cause-effect relationships** in person movements in urban areas.

Kutter proposed that people determine the individual structure of role behaviour. In turn, this implies certain time sequences of place-related activities and the sequence of spatially distributed activities as the basis for seeking explanation of cause-effect relationships in individual travel behaviour. He focused on the day's schedule of activities for one individual. The individual, (P_i), has at his/her disposal an urban system composed of communication facilities (G_k) and the communication means and paths (W_k). In the course of one day, the individual (P_i) carries out activities (A_{ij}), corresponding to the individual structure of role behaviour, with the parameters of the communication facilities (G_k) and the parameters of time and duration of the activity itself. The spatial distribution of facilities induces changes of place (F_{ij}) (for $j = 2,n$) with the parameters of the activities related to these changes of place. These relationships are illustrated in Part A of Figure 9.4.

Kutter defined the **individual activity pattern** as the sum of all activities carried out by one person in the course of one day, plus the movements required for these activities. This can be expressed as

$$T_i = \sum_{j=1}^{n} A_{ij} + \sum_{j=2}^{n} F_{ij} \qquad (4)$$

The individual movement pattern only includes movements within the scope of an activity. This is represented by

$$O_i = \sum_{j=2}^{n} F_{ij} \qquad (5)$$

211

Figure 9.4

Kutter's Activity Pattern Individual Travel Behaviour Model

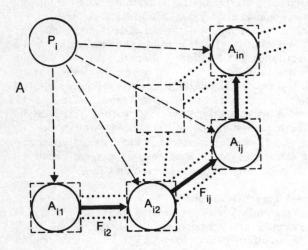

A

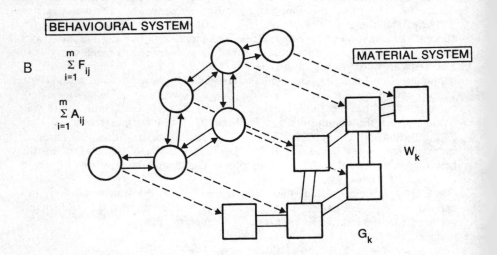

B

$$\sum_{i=1}^{m} F_{ij}$$

$$\sum_{i=1}^{m} A_{ij}$$

BEHAVIOURAL SYSTEM

MATERIAL SYSTEM

A = An individual activity pattern
B = Superimposition of a behavioural system on a material system

Source: After Kutter, 1973:241

The **activity system** of an urban area is defined as the sum of all individual activity patterns for persons within that urban area. As such, activities are elements and the movements are relations in a behavioural system expressed as

$$\text{Activity System} = \sum_{i=1}^{n} T_i = \sum_{i=1}^{n} \quad \sum_{j=1}^{n} A_{ij} + \sum_{j=2}^{n} F_{ij} \tag{6}$$

Total urban person movements (person movements, as used by Kutter include all changes of place, even walks to a shop or rides on a bicycle) is the sum of the individual movement patterns caused by the superimposition of the activity system as a behavioural system on the urban environment as the material system. This is represented in Part B of Figure 9.4. Thus, the individual characteristics of people in the behavioural system and the characteristics of the existing material system will influence the nature of regularities of urban person movements in an urban area. Kutter limited his analysis to what actually exists in terms of structures in the urban environment, and hypothesised that spatial and temporal structures of urban person movements would be determined by the concurrence of individual activity patterns. In this way, he was able to assign typical behaviour categories to these individual behavioural patterns. Figure 9.5 conceptualises this approach. The empirical data necessary to conduct such an analysis is time budgets of out of home activities, and requires

(a) a priori grouping of individual populations according to individual characteristics of persons
(b) detection of components of both activity patterns and movement patterns for these defined groups of people;
(c) examination of a priori grouping with regard to its significance for activity patterns and movement patterns. (Kutter, 1973: 237-238).

The a priori grouping of urban populations according to individual characteristics of people is achieved on the basis of the social status and stage in the life cycle. Data on car ownership is also an important factor. In addition, duration and time of work is taken into account.

The description of activity patterns and movement patterns was approached by categorising activities into classes, such as work, school, shopping, personal, business, social, and recreation activities. An activity index was defined as the quotient of persons being out of home and of all persons in a given population. In this way, Kutter was able to divide the activity profile of a population into activity profiles of single activities, as represented in Figure 9.6.

The main activities depicted therein account for about 80% of all activities in the sense of trips, and account for 93% of the duration of all activities in the activity pattern. Kutter proposed that the duration of activities was a determining factor for the requirement of an individual time potential, and an activity model was defined as the matrix of duration of the five main activities applied to a number of urban zones and to a number of time intervals in the day. In this way, the movement indices for any population or any group in a population could be specified according to the definition of activity indices. For any group of the population, it is possible

Figure 9.5

Relationships Between the Assignment of the Population to Homogenous
Behaviour Categories and the Structure of an Urban Activity System

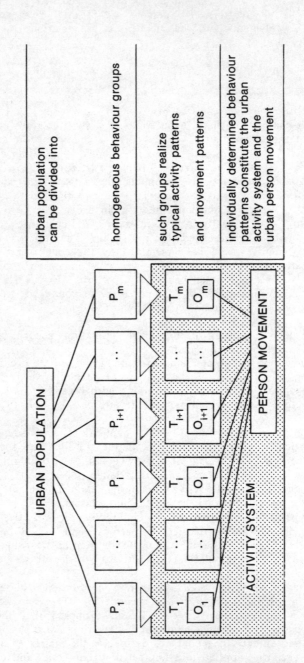

Source: After Kutter, 1973:238

214

Figure 9.6

**Activity Profile of an Urban Population Divided
into the Activity Profiles of Mean Activities**

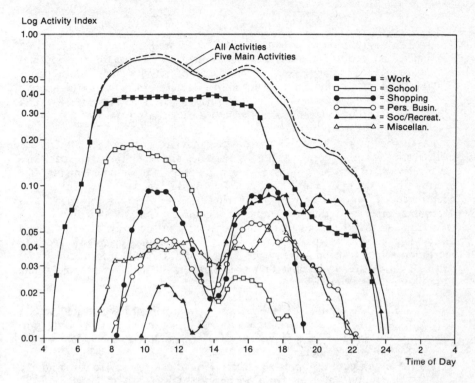

Source: After Cutter, 1973:241

to show the distribution of specified time period trip generations that are influenced by the duration of main activities, such as work, school, and shopping.

A criticism may be levelled at the approach adopted by Kutter in regard to the a priori definition of groups in the population. He addressed this problem by using factor analysis on the correlation matrix between the individual person movement indices. As a result, he was able to confirm that the occurrence and temporal distribution of certain activities over the period of a day did constitute a determining factor for the activity profiles of well-known archetypes in the population. For example, for pupils and students the determining activity was school; for housewives and retired persons the determining activities were shopping and personal business. For employed persons the determining activity was work. His analysis uncovered the following temporal and spatial extent of these activities:

(a) work activities at long duration and an urban area location
(b) school activities at middle duration and dwelling area locations
(c) shopping and personal business activities at short duration and dwelling area and CBD locations.

Kutter (1973: 246) was able to conclude that:

"A priori grouping of urban population is based on the hypothesis that individual activity systems are determined by criteria of persons and household. Typology based on the matrix of activity model substantiates this hypothesis and, over and above, results in a more distinctive grouping of population: only person related criteria such as age, sex and employment are relevant to the structure of activity patterns."

A further aspect of individual travel behaviour analysed by Kutter was to determine whether certain activity categories and their time and space ties were relevant to certain groups of the population. It would seem that the determining factor in the structure of individual activity patterns is the occurrence of work over a day's period. The time ties of work also determine other activities of employed persons. Considerable importance was attached to the fact that car ownership in no way affected these individual movement patterns. While car ownership might increase recreation trips, such an increase in trips is of little relevance to the travel patterns which are of interest to travel planners. Three broad conclusions were drawn by Kutter from his study:

(a) The total number of daily trips is, to some degree, related to the age of a person and role behaviour. It is evident that trip reduction is an insignificant value to differentiate human behaviour in an urban environment.
(b) A significant grouping of urban populations results from the hourly distribution of trips from home and back (first and last leg of the journey). According to these home base trips, urban populations can be divided into pupils, employed persons, and housewives.
(c) The hourly distribution of changes of place is determined by the temporal distribution of activities over the period of a day. As individual activity patterns are constituted by simple journeys, activity profiles are indeed a significant criterion of the resulting movement models. (Kutter, 1973: 252-253).

In testing his **individual factor model** using empirical data from three study areas in Germany, Kutter found that, using the matrix of the first and last legs of journeys, his model was able to predict total daily traffic values to within 5 percent accuracy. Mean root square errors computed for the deviation of predicted hourly values came to less than 50 percent. In forecasting changes of place according to activities in the dwelling area and other places, the root mean square errors were respectively 11 percent and 9 percent.

9.2.3 A Demand Model for Travel: A Queueing Theory Approach

An interesting study using a queueing model approach to investigate demand for travel in an activity framework has been proposed by Kobayashi (1976; 1979). Using the analogy of transportation systems on queueing models, a representation of transportation and activity systems by **serial queues** is investigated in an urban area of Japan. The model assumes that time required for transportation and various activities are key factors to determine the number of trips for users within the study area. A cost effectiveness function is used to obtain the optimal trip patterns of users. In this way, an optimal visiting rate may be calculated for any specification of transportation and activity time.

Kobayashi takes the Chapin (1968) definition of an activity in an urban area as an interaction between human behaviour and the environment. This is an evolutionary process of motivation-choice-activity in which both fundamental and supplemental needs are optimised. In this process, the three components of time, space and activities are the key factors. The likelihood of multiple journeys, the number of trips per journey, and the duration of trips are analysed.

Kobayashi developed his serial queueing model as follows: (refer to Figure 9.7). A route from an origin area A to a destination area B is given in Part A of Figure 9.7 to show the structure of the activity model. Starting from the origin (I), an individual travels using a commuting transport system (1) to the first destination (II) in the B area. After spending some time at (II), he/she leaves for the next destination (III), using one of the area's transportation systems (2) in B. The same approach is applied to the rest of the journeys within the area's transport system. An objective for the model is to predict the number of visits to the destination places in area B and the number of journeys to the area B from the origin area A. These numbers of trips are usually considered to be a function of effectiveness of both the transportation system within the area B, and between A and B areas. Area B may be regarded as the destination cluster of similar functions such as shops, leisure facilities, office blocks, and so on. Its probability characteristics are postulated as being equal. The most random case is when the probability distribution function of the required times to be consumed at destinations is expressed in an exponential form. Part A of Figure 9.7 can then be simplified as Part B of Fig. 9.7, and the destination places (II), (III), (IV) and (V) are combined into one queueing stage 3. The area trips 2, 3, and 4 are also combined into one stage 4. In Part B of Fig. 9.7, five queueing stages are shown to represent both the activity and the transportation systems. Queues 1 and 3 are doubly circled to show the activities at the origin and destination areas respectively, and singly circled 2, 4, and 5 show the transport activities within and between areas A and B. Kobayashi makes a number of assumptions about the queueing process. These are:

(a) the service times of each queue stage are exponentially distributed
(b) the inter-arrival times at queue 2 are also exponentially distributed
(c) the number of servers for each queue is infinite.

The interdependence of each queueing stage is finite and waiting time of users may be calculated. A transition probability matrix is calculated between origins and destinations, and a specifically conceptualised cost-

Figure 9.7

An Activity Model for the Analysis of Trips

(a)

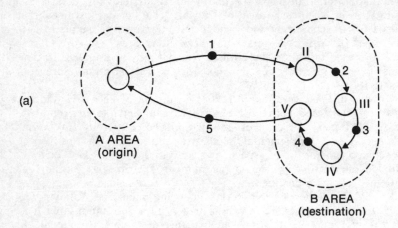

A AREA
(origin)

B AREA
(destination)

Original activity model

(b)

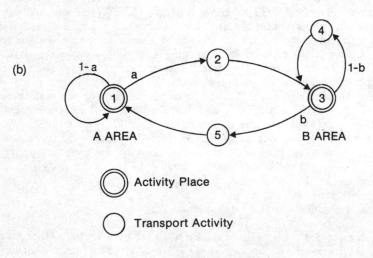

A AREA

B AREA

Activity Place

Transport Activity

Simplified activity model

Source: After Kobayashi, 1979:111

effectiveness function was developed to calculate optional visiting rates at activity locations. Optional trip patterns under various transport circumstances were calculated.

Kobayashi empirically tested the model using data collected in October 1976 in the Japanese cities of Osaka and Takatsuki. He collected data to identify the utilisation time for various mixes of journey purposes. The categories of journey purposes were daily shopping, non-daily shopping, and business. The data was collected on a Sunday because most non-daily shopping journeys in Japan occur on this day of the week. A Thursday was selected to survey daily shopping journeys. A Friday was taken to survey business journeys. Interviews were conducted in all cases at the time of the trip making. The most important data to be collected was allocation of time, but in addition, socio-economic characteristics of the interviewees were noted. The time associated with each trip and activity and a record of all trips undertaken was collected from respondents. Samples in excess of 1,000 were taken in each city. Activity place codes were used in coding the sequence of activities of journeys. Thus, a place trace code of 51345 would represent a journey from home (5) to office (1), to leisure (3), to private business (4) and home (5). The time trace for each activity and travel phase could also be recorded, for example, 30(150)20(50)15(40)30. This represents 30 minutes travel time from home (5) to office (1), 150 minutes spent at the office, followed by 20 minutes travel from the office to a place of leisure activity (3) where the person stayed for 50 minutes. This was followed by a 15 minute trip to complete private business which took 40 minutes, and finally the individual travelled to the final destination, home (5) which took 30 minutes.

In performing a validation test, actual visiting rates (b'act) and the calculated visiting rate (b'cal) were compared using the activity data t_2, t_3, t_4, and t_5. Here, t_2 and t_5 were the times associated with the use of the commuting transport system, t_3 is the time associated with activity places, and t_4 is the time spent using the area transport system. Actual visiting rates for the ith segment can be calculated using

$$b'act = \sum_{j=1}^{n} v_j / n_i \qquad (7)$$

where

n_i = the number of individuals in the ith segment.
v_j = the number of places visited by jth individual in the ith segment.

The calculated number of visits is given by:

$$b'cal = \frac{(\bar{t}_{2i} + \bar{t}_{5i} - \bar{t}_{4i})}{(\bar{t}_{3i} + \bar{t}_{4i} - \bar{t}_{4i})} \quad \text{and b'cal} \geq 1 \qquad (8)$$

where t_{ki} is the average required time at the kth activity place for the ith segment. The variance associated with the mean number of visits can be calculated from equation (8), and if we assume that the variance of (t_3/t_4) is relatively small to its mean value, and that the variance (b') is dependent only on the variance of $(t_2 + t_5 /t_4)$, and that $(t_2 + t_5)$ and t_4 are independent, then the variance b(b') may be written as:

$$\text{var (b')} = \frac{1}{1 + \bar{t}_3 \, \bar{t}_4} \left\{ \frac{\text{var}(\bar{t}_2 + \bar{t}_5)}{} + \frac{\text{var}(\bar{t}_4)}{E(\bar{t}_2) + E(\bar{t}_5)^2} \right\} \tag{9}$$

The relationship between the average number of visits (b') predicted from the model, and that present in the population may thus be calculated for various values of (b'act - b'cal). Kobayashi found that about 75 percent of the individual observations were predicted by the model to within 20 percent of the actual value of b'. He found that the best agreement occurred with non-student shopping journeys on a Sunday and home-based daily shopping journeys. Commuter and office-to-home journeys produced good levels of agreement. Home based daily shopping journeys and office-based non-compulsory journeys showed lesser levels of agreement. The correlation between the actual number of visits and the calculated number of visits for each segment, and for the total sample, overall was 0.84. This suggests that the calculated optimal visiting rate (b'cal) is strongly related in a positive way to the actual visiting rate (b'act). Kobayashi concludes that the model has been validated by real world data, at least for non-compulsory journeys (Kobayashi, 1979: 107-110). The configuration of model agreement from Kobayashi's study is given in Fig. 9.8.

Figure 9.8
**Configuration of Model Agreement (b'cal vs. b'act)
for predicting Number of Trips in Japanese Cities**

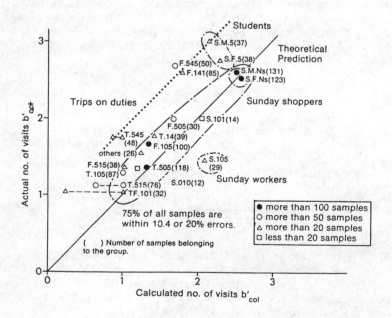

Source: After Kobayashi, 1979:111

9.2.4 The Household Activity-Travel Simulator (HATS) Model

A final example illustrates the human activity approach in developing individual-oriented behavioural models in transport planning. This draws on the work conducted at the Transport Studies Unit at Oxford University in England. The research team at Oxford developed what is known as HATS (Household Activity-Travel Simulator). This is an interactive gaming device. It is used in a household interview context and enables members of the household to create a physical representation of their daily activity-travel patterns, which can then be modified under guidance from the interviewer to explore responses to different hypothetical external changes, such as revised public transport schedules, or the introduction of staggered working hours. Each member of the household is provided with a board on which they set out their activity-travel patterns. The lower part of the board comprises three horizontal parallel grooved sections marked with 15 minute time periods relating to away from home, travelling, or in-home activities. The upper part of the board is in the form of a map display for the environment in which the person lives. On it are marked the locations at which activities take place, and the travel routes can be indicated. Coloured blocks of different sizes are provided which fit into grooved sections on the board to represent the time periods spent on different types of activity. Up to 10 activity groups are distinguished by colour, and up to six different modes of travel can be represented.

In explaining how the HATS game works, Jones (1979: 7) relates how once each member of the household has set the board to show their activity locations, the duration of those activities, and the route and mode of travel used, then it is possible to look at changes that will be made by each individual member of the household in response to some given external space-time modification. The household member that is directly affected first by the external modification will alter his board, and then consider the likely secondary effects that will result throughout the day. Other members of the household then consider any indirect impacts they might experience. In this way, an interactive procedure is used to arrive at a solution which is acceptable to all. The game encourages discussion among all individuals in the household at all stages of the procedure, and a tape record is kept for subsequent analysis. The use of the gaming board provides a clear visual display of daily behaviour, and draws attention to the structure of the individual activity patterns among household members, and it enables the identification of any anomalies which may arise from any tentative adjustment, such as being in two places at once, or having unaccounted periods of time.

Jones goes on to describe how HATS has been used to study the impact of a proposed school hours change in West Oxfordshire in England. In this study, the model identified three forms of repercussion:

(a) changes in the school journey
(b) changes in other travel patterns and associated out-of-home activities
(c) changes in in-home activity patterns.

The experiment worked very well, and household response was generally favourable. The use of the HATS game was able to considerably improve on intuitive forecasts about the impact of the proposed change in school hours.

9.3 A SITUATIONAL APPROACH TO MODELLING INDIVIDUAL TRAVEL BEHAVIOUR

An interesting extension of the individual-oriented behavioural models used in transport planning derived from the human activity approach is what Brog and Erl (1981) have described as the **situational approach**. This approach assumes that the individual is given a certain number of options by his environment, and that these form an objective situation. The options which an individual has are determined by the material supply of the transport infrastructure; the constraints and options of the individual and his household (which can be socio-demographically deduced), and the social values, norms and opinions relevant to transport behaviour (Brog and Erl, 1981: 2). The situational approach assumes that individuals and their behavioural situations determine individual options, and that decisions concerning spatial behaviour are made using a subjective logic which is very different from that of the transport planner or politician. This does not necessarily mean that individuals act in a totally irrational way, only that rationality would be subjective.

9.3.1 Conceptualising the Situational Approach
The situational approach has as its basis the activity concept illustrated earlier in Fig. 9.2., which showed a highly complex set of interrelationships among members of a household. The activity and travel patterns can be considerably altered when, for example, a new transportation policy is instituted. As Brog and Erl (1981: 5) state:

"This can lead to a reorganisation of individual activity patterns, substitutions in destinations, persons and/or times. These substitutions can go hand in hand with a mode switch or they can take place using the same modes which were previously used."

Let us assume that there is a change in the activity patterns of the household depicted earlier in Figure 9.2. Assume further that there has been an improvement in the public transport system in the city in which the household lives, which permits easy access to the husband's place of work. He thus switches from using the family car to using public transport to get to work. He continues to participate in his recreational activities, but now these can take place elsewhere, such as at a location within walking distance from his office. In the evening after school, the son picks up his father from his recreational activity and they drive home together in the son's car. The wife now has use of the family car and she uses it to do the shopping which her son had previously done on his way home from the university. The wife no longer uses public transport to meet her friend, and now can take her friend along when driving to the store. Shopping is done by the wife as previously, but the grandmother now also does some shopping, since the wife is now occupied elsewhere with the car. She stops at a store which she passes each day while walking the dog. Figure 9.9 illustrates the change

Figure 9.9

The Activity Concept: Changes in Individual Activity Patterns in a Famly
as a Result of Introduction of a New Public Transport Route

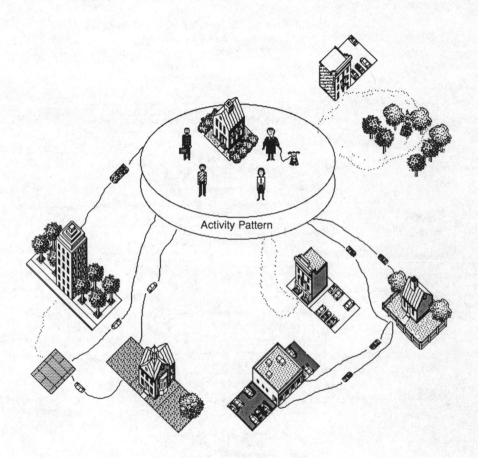

Source: After Brog & Erl, 1981

in the activity patterns of members of the household as a result of this single change whereby the introduction of a new public transport route enables the husband to switch from the use of the family car to public transport in order to travel to work. Brog and Erl depict the entire range of these reactions in terms of the diagram reproduced as Figure 9.10.

Figure 9.10

Conceptualizing the Effects of Planned Policies
on Individual Activity Patterns

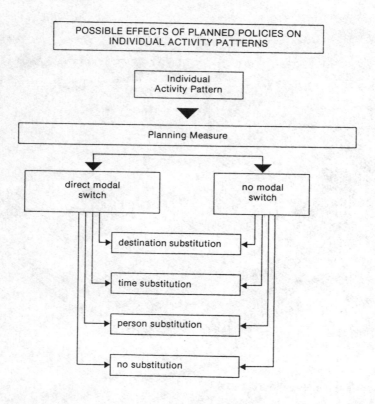

Source: After Borg & Erl, 1981:7

They note that the transport planner who is only interested in the number of trips made by public transport is overlooking an important consideration, namely, the number of additional passengers either being attracted to or being lost from public transport. In the example above, after the introduction of the new public transport route, we note the following changes in trip modes by members of the household before and after this change. After the change, eight individual modes of transport are used rather than seven. However, after the change only one trip is made on public transport, whereas before two trips were made. There has been no change in the number of non-motorised trips being made, these being six. Actual use of public transport decreased while the use of individual modes increased.

It is interesting to compare the before and after activity patterns and number of trips and modes of trips by individuals in the household. These are given in Table 9.1.

Table 9.1

**Activity Patterns for a Four-Member Household
Before and After a Change in Public Transport**

(a)

		ACTIVITY PATTERN
Husband	before	W - A - W - F_1 - W
	after	W - A - F_1 - W
Son	before	W - B - F_3 - W
	after	W - B - S *) - W
Wife	before	W - E_1 - W - E_2 - W - E_2 - W
	after	W - E_1 - W - F_2 - E_3 - S*) - W
Grandmother	before	W - F_3 - W
	after	W - F_3 - E_2 - W
*) S = Service (picking up and dropping off others)		

(b)

		Number of times home is left	NUMBER OF TRIPS			
			Total	Individual Mode	Public Transport	NM *)
Husband	before	2	4	4	-	-
	after	1	3	1	1	1
Son	before	1	3	3	-	-
	after	1	3	3	-	-
Wife	before	3	6	-	2	4
	after	3	6	4	-	2
Grandmother	before	1	2	-	-	2
	after	1	3	-	-	3
TOTAL	before	7	15	7	2	6
	after	6	15	8	1	6
*) NM = Non motorized trips						

The activity patterns of all household members have been affected, even though the activity programme of the household remains the same. Brog and Erl refer to a major West Berlin study which showed that the effect of lengthening an already existing subway line led to changes in 11 percent of all trips, but these changes affected 19 percent of the activity patterns, 28 percent of the households and 35 percent of the mobile persons included in the study. The effect that the new stretch of subway had on out-of-house activity patterns could not have been identified if one had simply looked at the number of trips made.

9.3.2 An Application of the Model

An example of an individual-oriented behavioural model in transport planning based on situational ideas can be found in the West German city of Hannover, a city of approximately 1.1 million inhabitants. The aim was to forecast the likely impact of an urban rapid train system. The planning authority was interested in ascertaining how the number of passengers using public transport would increase if public transport time was decreased by 10 percent, 20 percent, and 40 percent. In addition, the authority wished to forecast the likely impact of increases in gasoline prices by 50 percent, 100 percent and 150 percent. The study looked only at trips made on weekdays. Thus, long distance travel was not taken into account. Some interesting results came from an analysis of car drivers' trips. These are reported in full in Brog and Erl (1981: 18-24). The study was a large one, with over 10,000 persons participating.

It was found that, in aggregate terms, for each driver, almost every second car trip could have been made on public transport. However, when one looked at the individualisation of actual options (that is, when one identified those persons who were actually oriented towards, or amenable to, the use of public transport in their choice decision making), the proportion of trips that could have been made with public transport was very much smaller. This is illustrated in Fig. 9.11. The study identified eight situational groups which are represented by the roman numerals in the figure. Situational groups relate to trip categories, not persons. They are deterministic in nature. Most of the decisions of different situational groups will be determined either by objective reasons, such as no alternative, by personal reasons (car needed at work), or by subjective reasons (persons insufficiently informed, or people disliking a specific mode). Groups (i) through (vii) have a deterministic character in the general status quo. But, every twentieth car trip can usually be made with public transport, as demonstrated by group (viii), the group with options. Brog and Erl show that in this way one can determine the maximum potential for change and estimate the equivalent responsiveness in making changes in public transport in a city. They were able to show that reducing travel time resulted in a much greater potential for change than increasing the price of gasoline. They calculated elasticity coefficients and showed that the proportionate increase indicated that when using the car becomes increasingly difficult, the number of trips made by public transport will increase considerably. However, when the impact of increased cost of gasoline was further examined, it was shown that many adjustments could be made to given activity patterns for all situational groups, and changing to public transport was only one, albeit a major way of reacting. Table 9.2 shows the maximum potential for changes to public transport use from current car driver trips in the Hannover study. The increase in the maximum potential which results when persons are better informed, for example, shows the scope of possible

Figure 9.11

**A Situation Approach to Identifying Persons Who Have the Option of Using
Public Transport for Trips: Hannover Study**

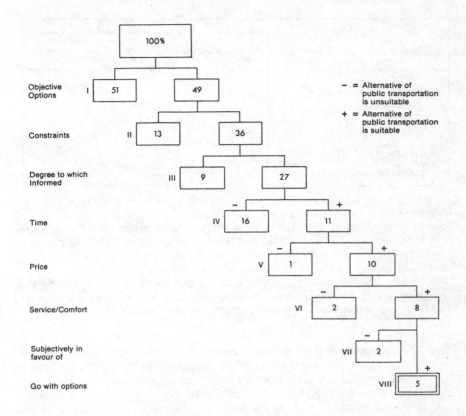

Source: After Brog & Erl, 1981:20

adaptability of persons in the learning process which always results when a
planned policy is introduced. It is shown how from the status quo, where
the maximum potential gain is 5 percent conversion to public transport, this
may be increased by maximum of 35 percent with improved information and
long-term attitude changes resulting through equalising the perceived values
of the time dimensions, cost, and level of service.

9.4 THE ANALYSIS OF REPETITIVE TRAVEL BEHAVIOUR IN A COGNITIVE SPATIAL CHOICE PARADIGM

The foregoing discussion of various approaches to modelling activities and
trips leads finally to a discussion of how one may view **repetitive travel**

Table 9.2

Potential for Change in Public Transport Use for
Current Car Driver-Mode Trips: Hannover Study

Potentials for Change in Public Transport	Car Driver		
	Maximum Potential	Maximim Potemtial with Improved Information	Maximum Potential with Improved Information and Long Term Attitudinal Changes
	%	%	%
- Status quo	5		
- When travel time with public transport is decreased 40%	12	14	
- By equalizing the perceived values of the dimensions time, cost, and level of service	16	19	35

behaviour in a **cognitive spatial choice** paradigm. Indeed, within urban and economic geography, repetitive travel behaviour (which focuses on work, shopping, recreation and social trips) has been a central theme, and geographers have contributed significantly to the development of predictive models of travel (see, for example, Wilson, 1972, 1973). It has also been conceded in the humanistic and phenomenological writings in geography that repetitive travel behaviour has an important role in moulding perceptions, values and meanings (see Ley and Samuels, 1978). Pipkin (1981: 143) claims that

"The explanation of repetitive travel as conventionally defined, remains a principal test of the success of the cognitive-behavioural paradigm in geography. Cognitive-behavioural approaches must produce accounts of travel that are incisive and also distinctive, in that they rest on specifically cognitive or behavioural assumptions. That the paradigm should be judged in these terms is implied by the theoretical and applied context from which it emerged, by programmatic statements of its practitioners, and by the view of unsympathetic critics."

He goes on to state that while the traditional theories of urban and economic geography and their assumptions about repetitive travel behaviour yielded uniform accounts of the behaviour of consumers and producers, no cognitive-behavioural equivalents of those theories have so far been produced. To assess the impact of cognitive ideas in the analysis of repetitive travel behaviour, we need to look to two strands of work in behavioural geography, these being paradigms of **spatial choice** and of **cognitive maps**.

These two paradigms have quite different approaches. In the **spatial choice paradigm**, the structure of trips as revealed behaviour is accepted, as is the dichotomy of dependence of choice and independent attribute variables. Explanation of trips hinges on inferred choices, subjective utilities and preferences. Empirical studies have furnished a considerable increase in the knowledge of cognitive dimensions of trip destinations, and have established statistical relationships between attitudes to sites and trip frequencies to them. In the area of discretionary travel behaviour, the choice paradigm has had a pervasive effect, especially in studies of shopping and recreational trip behaviour. The second paradigm concerns **cognitive maps**, or mental constructs. These have been discussed in detail in Chapter 4, and it has been stated how travel patterns, within the notion of activity patterns, provide considerable insight into the way people develop cognitive images of their environment. However, this cognitive mapping approach has had little impact in overt travel behaviour studies. A synthesis of the choice and cognitive paradigms is seen by Pipkin (1981: 171) as essential if there is to be a significant development in the analysis of repetitive travel behaviour in a cognitive spatial choice paradigm. We will briefly review the problems involved in the analysis of repetitive travel behaviour within this paradigm.

9.4.1 Destination Choice in Trip Behaviour in a Cognitive Framework

From the foregoing discussion of individual-oriented behavioural models in transport planning and the analysis of travel patterns, a central factor was the notion of choice by individuals, especially relating to mode, and particularly within discretionary travel. Discretionary travel such as shopping and recreation trips has tended to receive disproportionate emphasis in studies by behavioural geographers, whereas the work trip, which is an obligatory trip, has been the dominant concern in disaggregate travel demand modelling. This emphasis in cognitive studies on choice in discretionary travel, such as shopping and recreation has had the features of:

(a) a priori segmentation of trips from individual behaviour
(b) separation of point destinations from their objective context in real space and from their associative context in cognitive schemata
(c) a choice base model of explanation that, at best, drastically simplifies the account of behaviour provided in cognitive psychology.

The approaches followed have sought explanation from cognitive, attitudinal and other psychological transformations of traditional predictors of travel behaviour, such as attributes of sites, distance and locational variables and relevant individual characteristics (Pipkin, 1981: 148). In particular, emphasis has been focused on destination choice, and on perceptions of sites, rather than on size or price, as being salient in preferences in destination choice in shopping behaviour. As was discussed in detail in Chapter 8, there is a high degree of cognitive complexity of destinations in discretionary travel. A problem is that attributes cited as being important in preference and choice are often incompatible across different types of goods and services which are used in shopping as an example of discretionary travel. Furthermore, there is a major problem disentangling store attributes from attributes of shopping centres of retail clusters in which they are found. There is further compounding of problems relating to prevalence of multi-purpose trips.

We saw in Chapter 4 how important the study of distance perception is within behavioural geography. However, it is relatively rare for these distance perception studies to be conducted specifically in terms of destination choice. It has been explicitly recognised by Schuler (1979) that cognitive transformations of distance are uniformly implicated as important variables in destination choice. Spencer (1980) has given evidence that accessibility is confounded with site attributes in a single cognitive dimension. The mode choice literature seems to indicate that time spent waiting is perceived as more costly than time in motion (Stopher, 1977).

In both the conventional and the cognitive models of destination choice, it has been common practice to control individual characteristics, usually on the basis of socio-economic and demographic characteristics of respondents, car ownership, length of residence, location of residence and so on.

There is considerable empirical evidence concerning how groups of individuals relate to socio-economic phenomena that shows differences in the way mean distance travelled to shopping places correlates with socio-economic status. This literature also shows that cognitive rating models predict lower income consumer behaviour more accurately than high income group behaviour. But these attempts at stratification do not furnish a psychological based behavioural explanation for such differences. This problem of segmentation on the basis of socio-economic and demographic groups and of location is a particularly pressing problem. The importance of attitudes, preferences, intentions and perceived constraints is now well recognised in travel demand models as being just as, if not more, important in segmentation (see Dobson et al., 1978).

9.4.2 Problems in the Spatial Choice Paradigm

Two major problems in the use of destination choice models for studying repetitive travel behaviour involve the divergence of recorded and revealed preferences. Possibly this divergence is due to the inconsistencies in individual behaviour plus the inability of questionnaire techniques to elicit respondents' true attitudes. Furthermore, predictors which have been identified as being related to preference formation and choice behaviour may well differ in their salience for different individuals, even within homogeneous groups on the basis of socio-economic and demographic characteristics. Furthermore, it is probably incorrect to assume that choice actually exists except for very few groups differentiated on the basis of socio-economic criteria. Spencer (1980) says that while attitudinal and preference scaling procedures might elicit an individual's true preferences, because of the constraints on income and mobility, they cannot be accurately attained. Thus, desired but unattainable choices will never be observed in actual behaviour. Hensher and Louviere (1979) and Dobson, et al. (1978) further suggest that observed discrepancies between actual behaviour and attitude may represent a lack of adjustment between structures that evolve at different rates, and that there will be different behavioural intentions between people towards specific alternatives in the choice set. According to Pipkin (1981: 158):

"These perspectives on the relationship between attitudes and behaviour indicate clearly that an understanding of the cognitive transformation of site and location attributes, no matter how detailed, is insufficient in explaining repetitive travel."

There has been considerable literature developed which criticises the choice paradigm approach to the study of repetitive travel behaviour. This is due to a number of factors. First, conventional choice models are not really behavioural at all. The findings from the time-space based approaches to human activity discussed in Chapters 6 and 7, have shown that the spatial structure of activity patterns in the behavioural context of travel may be explained to a high degree through the notion of constraints that people face in their day-to-day activities. Second, there is the problem of multi-purpose travel, and it is probably more appropriate to focus on studying the structure of trips in their own right, particularly placing emphasis on the strength of linkages between various types of trips, activities and their locations. Within the context of multi-purpose travel, decision making needs to be seen as an extremely complex phenomena, in which potential stops acquire opportunistic utility by virtue of their proximity to other sites. Hanson (1980) has provided some interesting insight into modifications that need to be made to choice models in order to address this problem. She suggests that visit frequencies and inferred preferences for sites within a function category do not vary on single and multi-purpose trips, with some functions actually possessing stronger trip linkages to the workplace than to the home or to other establishments. Traditional categories of data, and modes of collection have tended to minimise the importance of such trips. She makes a strong case for the collection of detailed longitudinal information that will distinguish stages of journeys that are required to study the time and space aspects of multi-purpose trips. Third, in most geographic studies of trip choice destination, choice sites are characterised by their location relative to the respondent's home. Proximity to other sites, such as banks, drug stores, and discount stores may be equally important components in the attractiveness of grocery shopping (Schuler, 1979). Furthermore, multi-purpose trips need to be studied in both the temporal and behavioural context. We have seen in Chapters 6 and 7 the need to study human activities in a space and time framework, and how the Lund time geography approach can achieve considerable advances towards explanation of choice in travel behaviour.

9.4.3 The Cognitive Paradigm and Repetitive Travel

Pipkin (1981: 162) claims that there is a fundamental discontinuity between the cognitive approach seeking psychological transformations in predictor variables with respect to trips and the goals originally formulated for cognitive behavioural geography. A distinctive feature of the cognitive paradigm is the structuring of behaviour, not by observable, spatial or topological properties, but by inferred motives and intents. Behaviour is seen from the viewpoint of the primacy of inferred cognitive structures, as represented through cognitive maps. The approach aims to develop postulates of behaviour that are general and cognitive and, in some sense, spatial (Cox and Golledge, 1969). It is difficult to reconcile this cognitive paradigm with work on repetitive travel behaviour. As Pipkin (1981: 164) states:

"A simple dichotomy of 'habitual' or routinised and genuine or innovative choices is inadequate to understand the behavioural context of repetitive travel, since even habitual trips are likely to be linked to stress eliciting choices concerning timing, car availability, income constraints and the like. Thus, in the specific context of decision making, and in the more general task of showing relationships between ongoing mental activity and relevant behaviours, geography has failed to satisfy the requirements of cognitive explanation."

Inferred cognitive schemata, or cognitive maps, their formation and characteristics, have been the central focus of concern within the cognitive paradigm in behavioural geography. The constructs of cognitive maps have not been properly integrated into behavioural studies of repetitive travel destination choice studies, nor for that matter, into studies of overt travel behaviour in general. One of the problems is that studies of destination choice, particularly in discretionary travel behaviour, such as shopping trips, have emphasised the affective aspects of urban image, particularly those relating to attitudes towards price, convenience, travel time, and so on. Destination choice studies are concerned with point or specific location site characteristics, which may be characterised in only a few geometric measures such as distance from home or distance from origin of the trip, and by some contextual measures relating to the locational setting of retail clusters and shopping centres, whereas cognitive maps are represented by configurations in more holistic form. In travel studies, attitudinal and other cognitive variables are usually applied as independent or explanatory variables in relation to dependent choices or preference rankings. In studies of cognitive maps, the contents of images are usually treated as dependant variables in relation to socio-economic status, length of residence, mobility characteristics, and activity patterns of people (Pipkin, 1981: 164-165).

On the basis of the above, it is reasonable to conclude that there is little evidence that a general axiomatic system for travel behaviours can be developed that is strictly cognitive and distinctively geographic. Even the approach used by Burnett and Hanson (1979) in which single or multi-purpose trips are studied in a space-time context, are basically non-cognitive (in the sense that the cognitive paradigm is concerned with viewing behaviour as a continuum of motivated acts in which various goals may be pursued simultaneously). Perhaps the only way to bring together the choice and the cognitive paradigms is to concentrate on the cognitive processes of decision making rather than on the structure of schemata as such. Yet it is on the latter where most of the emphasis has been directed in modelling in individual travel behaviour.

Chapter Ten

MIGRATION IN A BEHAVIOURAL CONTEXT

10.1 THE NATURE OF MIGRATION

Migration is a fundamental process that redistributes people over the surface of the earth. It influences many types of spatial behaviour, since the choice of a residential location directly affects the accessibility of a person to all other locations within his living environment. Migration can thus be regarded as a decision process whereby a household unit chooses a specific residential location from a range of feasible alternatives. It is the process whereby people 'sort themselves out' in space. It can be studied at various levels of scale, but there are two general criteria that must be met for a movement to be regarded as migration. The first is that the household unit (or individual) moves from one residential location to another. The second is the intention of setting up a permanent or semi-permanent residence at the new location. The residential location choice that is the end product of a migration process is one of the most important spatial decisions people have to make. Most people make such decisions several times during their lives.

10.1.1 Absolute and Rate Measures
Migration phenomena are very diverse and it is necessary to conceptualise alternative types of migration at different levels of scale. Migration is measured at an aggregate level in either absolute terms or as a rate. **Absolute measures** usually describe migrations in terms of distributions by age, sex, occupation, and so on, and may be used in analysing population attributes of migration flows. **Rate measures** are used to examine the rate at which areas gain and lose migrants with respect to their socio-economic characteristics. However, it is the reasons and processes underlying migration flows and residential location choice that are of major concerns to us.

10.1.2 Approaches to the Study of Migration
Various lines of enquiry are evident in migration research. Six of these may be identified in geographical studies. These can be summarised as follows (after Shaw 1975):

(a) **Migration level** activity and differential studies, in which the principal explanatory variables are age, sex, marital status, education, occupation, career and lifestyle.
(b) **Economic aspects of migration**, in which the principal explanatory variables are wages and salaries and employment opportunities, and in which cost benefit and factor allocation techniques are used.

(c) **Studies of spatial aspects of migration**, in which the explanatory variables are distance, directional bias and information flows, and in which intervening opportunities and gravity models are used.

(d) **Studies of behavioural aspects of the decision to migrate**, in which migration is related to place utilities, preferences, stressors, and residential complaints.

(e) **Migration probability studies and mover/stayer continuum studies**, in which migration expectancy in the analysis of intra- and inter-regional flows.

(f) **Stochastic process studies**, in which migration histories and cumulative inertia are investigated

These approaches may be further classified into macro studies, which are concerned with flows at the aggregate level between origins and destinations, and micro studies, which seek explanations of the residential location decision process. But, these approaches are properly viewed as complementary for, as Clark (1981: 187) states:

"Knowing why an individual decides to move, and the impact on the system of his decision to change residences, can lead us to a better understanding of why some districts are areas of high in and out migration and why some areas are more stable. While the microanalytic or behavioural approach focuses on the decision to move, on the role of differential access to sources of information in shaping that decision, and on the spatial patterns of search, the macro analytic is still largely concerned with the spatial regularities in migration streams and the interrelationship between areas of in and out migration."

Each mode of analysis is important and can provide information that is relevant to the other. Both yield insights into residential mobility.

10.1.3 Migration and Mobility

It is important to distinguish between **migration** and **mobility** in the context of migration studies. The term **migration** refers to the relocation process which involves an individual or household shifting geographic location from an origin to a destination. The term is also used in a wider sense to refer to aggregate levels of migration flows from county to county, city to city, and so on. The term **mobility** is used in the content of migration studies to refer to the propensity of an individual or household to change residential location in a given period of time. It sometimes refers to the actual number of moves, relative to some benchwork, by an individual or household over a given period of time, regardless of scale. In rate form, it is also used to represent the proportion of households in a given geographic area (e.g., nation, state, city, or suburb) that change their residential location in a given period of time.

A further distinction can be drawn between migration and mobility depending on the nature and scale of moves. In some of the literature, mobility refers to residential shifts within the same general geographic area (e.g., within a city), whereas migration refers to residential shifts involving movement across or between geographic areas, such as cities or states.

Yet a further meaning is often attached to the term mobility when it is used to describe the movement of individuals or households up or down some type of socio-economic status scale.

10.1.4 The Behavioural Approaches

The **behavioural approach** focuses on the migration decision and residential location choice process. Before migration, an individual or household must decide whether to move and where to move. These decisions are not easily separated. Different households have different propensities to move and different degrees of freedom in their migration and residential location decisions. For example, in the USA many wealthy households are virtually free to move or stay as they wish. Many poor and ethnic minority groups are frequently forced to move because of government imposed urban renewal projects, freeways and other land use change programmes. Ecological invasion and succession and **residential segregation** theories have clearly shown that some groups are often forced to move for a wide variety of reasons. In making their residential decisions, higher income groups may exercise choice over a wide spectrum of the housing market. In contrast, underprivileged minority and poverty groups are severely constrained by economic, social, and discrimination factors. Differences in the **relative freedom to exercise choice** in these two basic migration decisions has been observed at various levels of scale, ranging from black poverty groups living in ghettos in the USA to the totally enforced migration of refugees and persons displaced as a result of war or political takeover.

The majority of migration decisions appear to be voluntary, however, and occur in the context of **place utility** and **place preference choice** frameworks and cognitive maps. A person's place utility surface forms the framework within which he/she makes a decision to move and where to choose a residential location. The evolution of alternative locations within his/her space preference surface evolves over time, and the choice made reflects relative abilities to satisfy needs and fulfil aspirations at both the large area scale (such as the city) and the site scale (such as the area of a chosen city and the dwelling within that area)

10.2 TYPES OF MIGRATION

It is convenient to distinguish between various types of migration and to point to the nature of spatial segregation and assimilation that often characterises larger migration flows from a specific origin to a destination city.

10.2.1 Partial Displacement Migration

The vast majority of migrations are of a **partial displacement** nature in which the moving unit stays within the same general area, such as a city, but relocates to a new residence. This type of movement thus takes place within the household's action space, and the area searched will be determined by the combined effects of the activity space, the location of friends, and the hierarchical structure of information sources. Sometimes it is referred to as mobility. It is typically biased to those areas that are more accurately defined in the individual's cognitive map of the city, and also influenced by the spatial biases of the media and agent information sources consulted. The current residential location is the base from which search occurs. The reasons underlying this type of migration are discussed in Chapter 11.

10.2.2 Total Displacement Migration

These migrations are to a new general area, such as from one city to another and one country to another. But, they do not occur within a directly searchable action space, and they are thus related to different information-gathering and evaluation processes. It is usual for the search phase at the **total displacement** level to be influenced by a **distance decay of general information flow**. However, the **urban hierarchy** strongly influences the directions and volumes of such flows. Also, interpersonal communication ties between particular areas tends to cut across this distance decay prediction. With respect to the latter, a good example is that of World War II immigration of southern European settlers to Australia, where flows from countries such as Italy and Greece were typified by so-called chain migration, in which people from a specific region of, say, Calabria in Italy tended all to concentrate within Melbourne and in a well-defined section of that city (in the inner suburbs). The factors underlying total displacement migrations are usually less complex than is the case for partial displacement migration, and they tend to relate to things such as job opportunities (both perceived and enforced transfers), and retirement resettlement (in the sun belt areas such as Florida, Arizona and southern California in the USA). Total displacement migrations are often made by migrants moving back to areas with which they had previous ties (reverse migration), but over time and sequences of moves the place utility surface of high preference for previously experienced locations tends to decrease.

It is not unusual for total displacement migration to match household types with places, so that within the USA, for example, white and black populations and rich and poor groups do not get clearly sorted out at a regional level of scale. However, in the past many overseas migrants tended to develop regional concentrations, such as Scandinavians in the upper Mid West, Italians in some larger north-eastern cities, and so on. Retirement settlement in the sun belt areas is an example of the former general rule.

It is significant to note that there is commonly marked spatial segregation demonstrated in the choice of new residential locations.

10.2.3 Relating Geographic, Social and Occupational Mobility

It is interesting to conceptualise mobility in social and occupational terms, as well as spatially. Figure 10.1 shows how social and occupational mobility can occur or not occur in association with residential mobility. Thus, social space moves can occur without migration. However, it is common for partial displacements to be related to changes in reference groups. Total displacements, however, are strongly linked to occupational mobility and by definition they involve substitution of old social contacts for new ones.

10.2.4 Necessary or Obligatory Moves vs. Moves Caused by Needs

It is instructive to consider the **motives** behind migration. In this context we can consider the influence of push-pull factors. At an international level, we can think of migrations as moves caused by necessity

Figure 10.1

Relationship Among Geographic, Social and Occupational Mobility

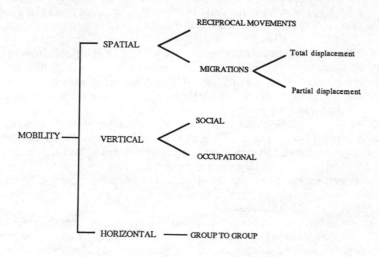

Source: After Jakle, Brunn & Roseman, 1976:155

or obligations versus moves caused by needs. **Necessary** or **obligatory** moves are related to push factors, such as **forced or semi-forced moves** from an area of origin due to political, religious, or other push factors. In contrast, moves caused by **needs** are a result of both push and pull factors, usually due to economic forces pushing people from areas of origin accompanied by economic pull factors at the destination. For example, Gould and Prothero (1975) have documented these factors as important in migration moves within African populations.

Peterson (1958) proposed that migration is either a decision by individuals and groups to improve things at a destination over their condition at the origin, or an attempt to retain what they have in response to changing conditions. Peterson classified migrations into four categories:

(a) **primitive migrations**, where innovating and conservative movements are largely attributable to man's inability to cope with natural forces
(b) **forced or impelled migrations**, where the primary cause is some state or some functionally equivalent social institution
(c) **free migration**, where the will of the migrant to either achieve the new or retain what they have is the decisive factor in the decision to move
(d) **mass migration**, where innovating or conservative movements become a style or an established or semi-automatic behaviour.

10.2.5 Circulatory Migration
In this type of migration it is typical for members of a household, usually the husband or grown sons, to move from one place (e.g., a rural village) to

another (e.g., the rapidly expanding city) to seek work in the service or manufacturing sector of the economy, that member returns on a periodic or seasonal basis to the permanent place of residence (e.g., the rural village). Thus, a **circulatory** pattern is established which is repeated in a time framework. Examples are present in the rapidly changing third world countries such as Indonesia, where circulatory movement takes place between rural villages and big cities like Jakarta.

A similar type of circulatory migration pattern, but at a different level of scale, is evident in the movement of unskilled and semi-skilled workers from southern and south-eastern Asian countries on a seasonal or annual basis to the oil countries of the Middle East. In developed countries circulatory migration also occurs for reasons of regional labour shortage. For example, in the USA there has been considerable movement of workers on a short term basis from regions like Kentucky to the auto plants of Detroit, Michigan. In Western Europe, unskilled labour from Turkey and other Eastern Mediterranean countries come seasonally and on a contract basis to West Germany to meet its shortages of unskilled labour in specific industries.

10.2.6 Migration and Assimilation

For migrants who are members of minority, ethnic, or racial groups who enter an area dominated by a larger homogeneous group an important problem faced is that of **assimilation**. By this we mean the process whereby the minority group is gradually absorbed by the host population.

Assimilation has both **social** and **spatial** implications. From the social perspective, members of the minority migrant group gradually assimilate into the host society, and numerous changes take place during this process. Hanson and Simmons (1968) have suggested that individuals gradually change their roles with respect to individuals in the host society, as well as with respect to people within their minority group. In this way, they adopt a role path which is a movement through social space that may correspond to some types of movement through geographic space. Gordon (1964) refers to these changes as **acculturation**. In this process, the minority group accepts certain cultural patterns of the host population, such as language, cultural norms, religious beliefs and practices. As they enter the host society's groups and institutions, the minority group begins to lose some of its ethnic character. During this process there is both an elimination of prejudicial attitudes on the part of the host society and an elimination of over-discriminatory behaviour. The two groups must eliminate power and value conflicts that are due to ethnic differences between the migrant and the host population. This process is clearly evident in the North American city, particularly in the north east, which from the late 19th century to the early 20th century received wave after wave of eastern and southern European migrant minority groups who, over time, became acculturated within the American urban society. However, more recent urban migrant groups, such as the blacks and Puerto Ricans, have made less progress towards assimilation in these terms.

Assimilation also has a spatial dimension. We have noted earlier in this chapter that minority racial and ethnic migrant groups moving into a city tend to exhibit a high degree of residential segregation from the remainder of the population by settling in well-defined residential areas of a city, often leading to the development of ghettos. Over time, as acculturation occurs with the assimilation of the migrant minority group through a gradual movement in social space, spatial assimilation is likely to occur through the **residential diffusion** of the migrant group households out of the ghetto into the suburbs. This spatial assimilation process is illustrated in the model in Figure 10.2.

Figure 10.2

Spatial Assimilation Model Showing Spatial Behaviour at Different Levels of Assimilation

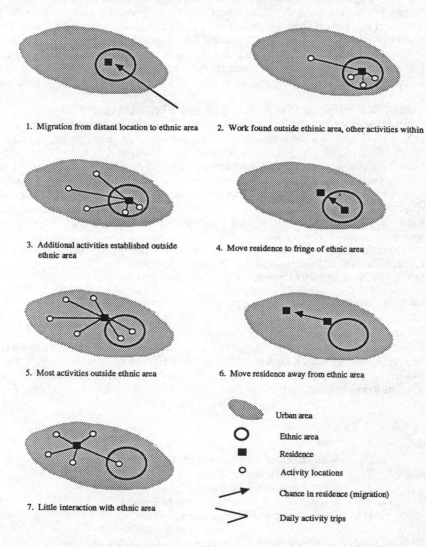

1. Migration from distant location to ethnic area

2. Work found outside ethinic area, other activities within

3. Additional activities established outside ethnic area

4. Move residence to fringe of ethnic area

5. Most activities outside ethnic area

6. Move residence away from ethnic area

7. Little interaction with ethnic area

	Urban area
○	Ethnic area
■	Residence
○	Activity locations
→	Chance in residence (migration)
>	Daily activity trips

Source: After Jakle, Brunn & Roseman, 1976:161

239

This model considers spatial behaviour involving partial displacement migration. Here, migration is seen as choosing a residential location from which activity space behaviours develop. The migrant moving into the city tends to choose a residential location in or near the centre of the ethnic area. At this stage, activity space behaviours are confined predominantly to members of the ethnic group. As the assimilation process begins, there is a gradual extension of the activity space to locations outside the ethnic area. In this way, an action space develops and expands to incorporate members of the host population. This may be followed by a residential relocation to the fringe of the ethnic area. From here, there is increased activity outside the ethnic area, which may be followed by a residential relocation away from the ethnic area into the host population. From here, the activity space is mainly related to the host population, and decreasingly with the ethnic population centre. The end result may be complete assimilation through both residential separation and activity space separation from the ethnic area.

10.2.7 Summary: Migration is a Complex Phenomenon

We may summarise the nature and types of migrations discussed thus far as follows. Migration is a complex phenomenon. In area terms, it may be short or long distant, it may involve the crossing of boundaries within countries and across international boundaries. It may involve areal units that are communities, counties, states, nations and cultures. It involves individuals, households and groups. The motivating factors underlying migration are complex, based on the social organisation of the migrants, their family clan and the role of individuals. Migration may be voluntary and involuntary. It may be a result of predominantly socio-economic factors that manifest themselves in a push-pull manner. It has psychological underpinnings. Furthermore, it can involve the acculturation and assimilation of minority groups into a host population.

10.3 MODELLING AGGREGATE FLOWS

At the aggregate level, geographers and other social scientists have studied migrations and flows of phenomena between origins and destinations using analogue models which go under the general title of **gravity models**. Gravity models have been used to investigate all types of spatial interactions. The general gravity model takes the form:

$$I_{ij} = f \left(\frac{P_i P_j}{d_{ij}{}^n} \right)^N \qquad (1)$$

where:

I_{ij} = an index of interaction between places i and j
P_i = the population of place i
P_j = the population of place j
d_{ij} = the distance separating places i and j
N,n are empirically determined exponents.

This general gravity model is so termed because of its obvious similarity to Newton's law of gravity. It attempts to predict or estimate the aggregate amount of interaction between two places in a given period of time based directly upon the product of the population (or a mass measure) of those two places and inversely on the intervening or separating distance raised to some exponent between those places. It is worth noting that this model has been used with considerable success to predict interactions such as migrations between cities, traffic flows, telephone traffic calls between cities, and flows of goods between states. In this section we will look at the use of gravity and related models to the study of human migration.

10.3.1 Ravenstein's Laws of Migration

It is now about 100 years since the geographer, Ravenstein, reported his laws of migration to the statisticians of London (Ravenstein, 1876, 1885, 1889). He was the first social scientist to make a detailed analysis of the massive population movements of the industrial revolution of Europe in the 19th century. He formulated a number of **laws of migration**, relating to distance of migration and the volume of flows between places of varying size. Ravenstein's laws may be paraphrased in the following terms:

(a) The majority of migrants travel only short distances. Long distance migrations are directed to the major centres of commerce and industry.

(b) The process of dispersion is the inverse of that of absorption of migrants, and it exhibits similar features.

(c) In estimating the displacement of people, we need to take into account the number of natives in each country which furnishes migrants, and also the population of the districts which absorb them.

(d) Countries having extended boundaries in proportion to their area naturally offer greater facilities for an inflow of migrants than countries with restricted boundaries.

(e) Migrant currents across countries sweep along with them many of the natives of the countries through which they pass and deposit, in their progress, many of the migrants which have joined them at their origin.

(f) Even in the case of countries of dispersion, which have a population to spare for other countries, an inflow of migrants takes place across the border which lies furthest away from the great centres of absorption.

(g) Migratory currents flow along certain well-defined geographic channels. The more distance from the fountainhead which feeds them, the less swiftly do these currents flow.

Studies in many parts of the world have confirmed Ravenstein's laws of migration. In fact, the apparent dependence of migration volume on distance has appeared so striking that social scientists have tried to express the association in a mathematical form. Two broad approaches have emerged. First, the **empirical approach**, the aim of which is to refine the description of migration distance by fitting a suitable curve to data on migration volume by distance. Such a formula simply represents the migration field in a more concentrated and convenient form than does the original map or table. The second is the **deductive approach**, in which researchers begin with a set of plausible basic assumptions and then elaborate hypotheses of migration from them. These hypotheses may be given mathematical formulation and then tested using empirical data.

10.3.2 The Empirical Approach: Migration Fields

Analysis of the migrations to or from a certain place looks at the volumes of movements that come from specified distance zones. Thus, for a given destination, such as a city receiving migrants, we may plot the number of migrants coming from all points of origin according to the distance of those points from the destination. In this way, we may fit a Pareto-type curve to such data. This will take the form:

$$y = ax^{-b} \qquad (2)$$

where:

     $y =$ the number of migrants coming to a destination from an origin
     $x =$ the distance of an origin from the destination
     $a =$ the distance up the y axis (i.e., y intercept)
     $b =$ slope of the distance decay curve.

The migration field of the city receiving migrants is thus plotted, as demonstrated in Figure 10.3. Note that in the above equation the distance decay variable, which is the exponent b, is negative. This negative b exponent will become smaller as the distance from which volumes of migrants are attracted to the city increases.

Figure 10.3

The Migration Field for a City

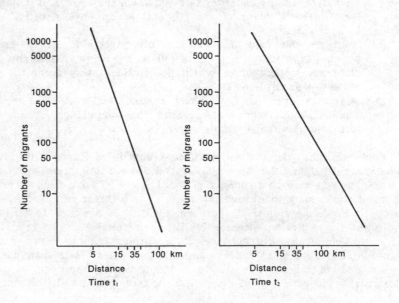

Using this approach, we may define the **migration field** of a city. This may be defined as the area which sends major migration flows to a given place. Conversely, it may be the area that receives major flows from a place. Thus, we may have an **in**-migration field and an **out**-migration field for a given place.

An important study of migration field of places was undertaken in Sweden by Hagerstrand (1957). In studying the migration fields of various communes, he found that over the period 1860-1930 there was a decrease in the negative b exponent, which defined the migration field of a typical commune, of from -3.0 to -2.4. Thus, he concluded that there was an increase over time in the distance from which communes attracted migrants, with an increasing proportion of total migrants coming from increasingly distant places. Clearly, this coincided with improvements in transport methods and reduction in the relative cost of transport. We may regard an in-migration field as a type of nodal region created by migrants who are attracted to a place from an area.

It is possible to draw a number of general conclusions about the migration fields of cities in the USA. Most cities have a significant level of in-migration from all nearby metropolitan areas and from larger metropolitan areas at greater distances. Jakle, et al. (1976: 168-171) have commented on the importance of the urban hierarchy in influencing migration flows that make up the in-migration field of any city. The urban hierarchy structures the flow of information through the media, thus having an important impact on people's mental map of the United States. As major cities play a predominant role in the media, these are likely to be prominent areas in people's mental maps. In addition, there is a greater probability of obtaining specific information about jobs and amenities in a given metropolitan area, than similar information about a small city. Thus, hierarchical migration occurs, i.e., larger places are likely to provide larger numbers of migrants than smaller places.

Most cities have significant in-migration from non-metropolitan areas in their own state and adjacent states. This is called **hinterland migration**. Much of the origin area is a region that is influenced, to a considerable degree, by the metropolitan functions of that city. However, the spatial pattern of hinterland migration is usually characterised by a distance decay effect. It is also influenced by the flow of information patterns that relate to the structure of the lower levels of the urban system, and thus the lower levels of the media hierarchy. Also, it is influenced by the degree to which the city is within the activity spaces of people within the hinterland, thus influencing the degree to which the place figures prominently in the mental maps of people in the hinterland.

A final form of migration may be termed **channelised migration**. This refers to the fact that many cities have at least one significant source of migrants from a non-metropolitan area at some distance from the hinterland. Interpersonal contacts are important here. This can lead to a form of **chain** migration developing.

10.3.3 The Gravity Approaches: Interaction and Intervening Opportunities

The majority of attempts to model migration have been conducted within the framework of the **general gravity** or **interaction model** presented earlier in equation (1). The basis of the gravity model is that it attempts to estimate interaction or flows between places on the basis of potential interaction between them. Thus, the greater the population masses, or attractive pull between two places, the greater will be the amount of movement between them. However, this will be affected inversely by the effort involved in moving between the two places, that is, the intervening distance, which represents a barrier through time and cost, as well as distance.

A considerable advance was made in the use of gravity interaction models during the 1940s when Stewart, an astronomer turned social scientist, observed that there were regularities in terms of the distances from Princeton University of its students' home towns. This interested him, as it seemed to conform to Newton's law of gravitation. Consequently, Stewart develop the idea of **social gravitation**, which was the amount of interaction between two places expressed directly proportional to the number of people living in the two places and inversely proportional to the distance separating them. A little later another social scientist, Zipf, formulated his principles of least effort. Both Stewart and Zipf tested the gravity model on a great mass of material of different social interactions, including migrations, traffic flows, and exchanges of information between places. The results they obtained supported the basic gravity equation's predictions. However, they found that there was a tendency to over-estimate short distance interactions. Both Stewart and Zipf had used exponents of -1 for the distance variable. Other social scientists, particularly those working in Scandinavia, experimented with different distance exponents, finding in general that the exponent of -1 was suitable for large urban populations, but exponents of between -2 and -2.5 were appropriate for rural populations. They also found that an exponent of -1 to -2 tended to represent a later stage of transport technology developments than an exponent of -2 to -3. It may well be that the United States, with its more advanced transport technology than western Europe, had during the 1930s and 1940s less steeply sloping gradients of migration and communication fields than was the case in Europe.

A number of criticisms can be made of these early, rather simplistic, applications of the basic gravity model in the investigation of migration. A commonly voiced objection is that it depicts an empirical regularity for which no theoretical explanation is furnished. This has led to difficulties in using the model for prediction or projection. Furthermore, the application of the rigid Newtonian formula tends to hinder the development of gravity models as empirical research tools. There are further problems relating to both the mass and the distance variables. Concerning the mass measures, it was suggested that it was necessary to weight the $(P_i \, P_j)$ mass measures of origins and destinations on the basis of consideration of sociological variables, such as age, income, occupation, and educational characteristics of the populations at those places. This made it possible to weight populations or places according to the desirability of those places as centres for in-migration and as places of likely out-migration. It was suggested that the most appropriate population weighing was the income potential of each place. Regarding the distance variable, there was a need for more flexible treatment of the distance exponent. The use of physical distance also presents some difficulties. For example, it might be appropriate to use social and economic distance and to developed measures which incorporate travel time, travel costs, transfer or hire costs instead of straight physical distance.

A final criticism of the basic gravity model is that it gives a static picture of a dynamic process.

One important variation on the gravity model was the **intervening opportunity model** proposed by Stouffer (1940). This model used a similar idea to the gravity model, except that the distance component was replaced with a measure of opportunities for interaction that exist between places. It took the form:

$$I_{ij} = \frac{P_i P_j}{Q} \tag{3}$$

where:

$\quad I_{ij} \quad$ = some index of interaction between places i and j
$\quad P_i \quad$ = the population of place i
$\quad P_j \quad$ = the population of place j
$\quad Q \quad$ = some measure of intervening opportunities between i and j.

Stouffer's hypothesis was that the number of persons moving a given distance is directly proportional to the number of opportunities at that distance, and inversely proportional to the number of intervening opportunities. It is thus not the intervening distances between places per se, but the amount of intervening opportunities for interaction that retards interaction. As an example, take the case of the north-eastern United States cities of Philadelphia and Boston, and the Texas cities of Dallas and Houston. Boston and Philadelphia are similar in size to Dallas and Houston. However, there is a considerably greater amount of movement between Dallas and Houston and Houston and Dallas, than is the case between Boston and Philadelphia and Philadelphia and Boston. This should not be surprising, because there are many more opportunities for migrants between Boston and Philadelphia (e.g., cities in New York and New Jersey) than is the case between Dallas and Houston. The conclusion is that because there are fewer intervening opportunities between Dallas and Houston, there is a greater degree of migration both ways between those cities than is the case between Boston and Philadelphia.

The intervening opportunities model proposed by Stouffer thus appears to have a high degree of validity according to empirical tests. However, the hypothesis has only been tested against a complete set of migration data by Hagerstrand in Sweden. In Hagerstrand's study, detailed small area migration data was available over a long period of time. Hagerstrand set out to test the model using in and out migration data for every parish in Sweden between the period 1946 to 1950. He drew 10 kilometre distance zones around each parish. Using the Stouffer model, he was able to calculate expected migration against observed levels of migration. Using six randomly selected parishes, Hagerstrand found that the agreement between observed and expected frequencies of migration was poor. Hagerstrand thought that one of the problems might lay in the fact that he had treated every member of a migratory group, such as a family, equally. This presented some flaws, since two identical opportunities at a given place can be filled in one case by a single person, and in another by a large family. Thus, Hagerstrand conducted a second test using groups of migrants instead of individuals. He found, however, that agreement between expected and observed migrations was no better. It is also worth noting that a study by Anderson (1955) in the United States found that nothing is gained by substituting geographical distance with intervening opportunities in investigating migration flows.

Perhaps it is best to sum up the general gravity model and intervening opportunities models in Hagerstrand's words (1955):

"Each formula which in some way makes the frequency of migrations directly proportionate to the population and at the same time introduces a reverse proportion to distance, is somehow able to be brought into line with actual observations, yet the ultimate conformity is missing."

10.3.4 Push-Pull Migration Gravity Models

A more fruitful approach to the study of migration is to regard it as a response to **push** and **pull** factors. The push factors are those situations which give rise to dissatisfaction with one's present location. On the other hand, the pull factors are those attributes of distance places which make them appealing to the potential migrant. Investigations of migration in the context of push and pull factors take two basic approaches. The first uses a **regression** format in which migration distance is an independent or explanatory variable, while migration volume is dependent upon a range of push and pull factors relating to the place of origin and the place of destination. The second approach is to take a **structural** view of push and pull factors. In this way, both distance and push-pull factors are incorporated with a gravity-type model. Two examples illustrate these approaches.

The first is a study by Olsson (1965) on migration in Sweden. On the basis of an exhaustive analysis of many empirical migration studies, Olsson selected a number of independent variables which he considered relevant in explaining variations in migration distances. These are listed in Table 10.1. Note that the variables related to measures of income and unemployment at the place of origin and destination, age and income of the intended migrant, plus the traditional variables relating to size of origin and destination that were included in the gravity model.

Olsson tested the relevance of these variables in explaining variations in the migration distances in a randomly selected group of Swedish population. This was done using a **stepwise multiple regression** technique. This method of analysis is designed to include one variable at a time, and at each step, the variable which accounts for most of the non-explained variation in the dependant variable is entered. This means that the variable with the highest correlation coefficient with respect to the dependant variable is the first one to be included in the model. Partial correlation coefficients are then derived for the remaining variations in the dependant variable. The variable explaining most of the remaining variation is included next. Subsequent steps are taken, by adding new variables and repeating the process.

We may summarise Olsson's findings, as reflected in the data in Table 10.1, as follows:

(a) length of migration is positively related to level of income at the place of origin

(b) length of migration is positively related to the degree of unemployment, both in the place of origin and the place of

destination
(c) length of migration is positively related to the population size of both the place of origin and the place of destination
(d) length of migration is negatively related to the age of the migrant
(e) length of migration is positively related to the migrant family's income.

Table 10.1

Multi-Variate Stepwise Regression Analysis of Migration in Sweden

1. Level of income in place of origin	(1) 0.8656	
2. Level of unemployment in place of origin	(4) 0.8853	intercorrelated 0.975
3. Number of inhabitants in place of origin	(3) 0.8826	
4. Level of income in place of destination	(5) 0.8856	
5. Level of Unemployment in place of destination	(5) 0.8855	
6. Number of inhabitants in place of destination	(2) 0.8792	
7. Age of migrant	(7) 0.8856	
8. Income of migrant	(6) 0.8856	

Source: After Olsson, 1965

The test which Olsson conducted was quite encouraging, with a multiple correlation coefficient exceeding 0.885, which indicates that the model would explain 78% of the variance in migration distance. Individual migration distances were found to be positively related to increases in the level of income of the migrant, the degree of unemployment and the population size in both the places of origin and destination. On the other hand, the variables representing personal characteristics of the migrant did not significantly contribute to the power of the model.

Tobler has been critical of this regression approach to the study of migration. He advocates the use of push-pull factors in a structural model. This approach includes distance discounting, thus it is a gravity-type model. But it also is an optimising model with shadow prices and with a well-known simple objective function, which place it in the category of mathematical programming problems. A formal model has been presented by Dorigo and Tobler (1983). It consists of one elementary equation for each directed exchange of migrants between pairs of places. Migration is modelled as:

$$M_{ij} = P_i P_j (R_i + E_j)/d_{ij} \qquad (4)$$

where:

M_{ij} = magnitude of movement from place i to place j (of r places)

d_{ij} = the distance between those places measured in appropriate units (e.g., km of road distance, dollar costs, travel time, employment opportunities)

R = "rejecting", "repelling", "repulsing" variables

E = "enticing" variables

R_i = the **push** away from place i

E_j = the **pull** toward place j.

By combining the R and E variables, migration is seen as the sum of the push and pull variables, discounted for distance effects. The distance effects may be interpreted as an attenuation of information or as intervening obstacles to be overcome. Note that the model does not include self-migration, i.e. M_{ii}. By aggregating the basic equation (4), we obtain the out sums and the in sums as shown in equation (5):

$$\sum_{\substack{j=1 \\ j=i}}^{r} M_{ij} = R_i \sum_{\substack{j=1 \\ j=i}}^{r} \frac{1}{d_{ij}} + \sum_{\substack{j=1 \\ j=i}}^{r} \frac{E_j}{d_{ij}} = O_i$$

(5)

$$\sum_{\substack{i=1 \\ i=j}}^{r} M_{ij} = \sum_{\substack{i=1 \\ i=j}}^{r} \frac{R_i}{d_{ij}} + E_j \sum_{\substack{i=1 \\ i=j}}^{r} \frac{1}{d_{ij}} = I_j$$

Thus, one can determine the value of all the push factors (R) and all the pull factors (E) if one knows the out sums and in sums for all of the places. Push factors might incorporate such things as high unemployment rates, but this would need to be reduced by the cost of leaving friends and a familiar environment. Conversely, pull factors might be large cities with lots of employment opportunities and an attractive, exciting environment. Typically, one may use unemployment rates, wage rates, and the number of people in respective labour markets, thus getting a magnitude of movement measure presented in equation (6):

$$M_{ij} = k \frac{U_i}{U_j} \frac{W_j}{W_i} \frac{L_i L_j}{d_{ij}}$$

(6)

where:

U = unemployment rates

W = wage rates

L = number of people in their respective labour markets.

By substituting in equation (5) and cancelling the distance terms, we obtain:

$$R_i + E_j = k \frac{U_i}{U_j} \frac{W_j}{W_i} L_i L_j$$

(7)

248

A problem with the above is that we do not get good estimates of the push/pull factors. However, Dorigo and Tobler (1983) point that it is possible to run a regression on either R or E, or both. Once the Es and the Rs are calculated, it is possible to estimate gross migrations. In this way, the model predictions may be compared with observed values.

For a place k with a given pull E_k and a hinterland containing places i and j of equal push (R_i) and pull (R_j), and with d_{ik} less than d_{jk}, then M_{ik} is greater than M_{jk}. This shows that migration diminishes in strength with distance. If we let $A_k = E_k - R_k$, then we can show that net migration flows are:

$$M_{ij} - M_{ji} = (A_j - A_i)/d_{ij} \qquad (8)$$

This shows that the attractability (A) of a place is the difference between the pull factor and the push factor at that place, and that net movement between the two places will be equal to the difference between their attractabilities, discounted by distance as a gradient.

If we call $T_k = E_k + R_k$, then the total two way movement between the two places will be equal to

$$M_{ij} + M_{ij} = (T_i + T_j)/d_{ij} \qquad (9)$$

Thus, the "T factor" measures the total turnover or exchange at a place, with both in and out movements involved. High values of T will imply an active migration market, with a lot of movement in both directions, whereas low values of T imply a passive place, and intermediate values can mean high in-migration with low out-migration, and so on.

It is possible to rewrite the above in the following terms:

$$R_k = \left\{ O_k - \sum_{\substack{i=1 \\ i=k}}^{r} \frac{E_i}{d_{ik}} \right\} \bigg/ \sum_{\substack{i=1 \\ i=k}}^{r} \frac{1}{d_{ik}} \qquad (10)$$

$$E_k = \left\{ I_k - \sum_{\substack{i=1 \\ i=k}}^{r} \frac{R_i}{d_{ij}} \right\} \bigg/ \sum_{\substack{i=1 \\ i=k}}^{r} \frac{1}{d_{ik}}$$

In this form the equations show that the push factors at any place depend on the pull factors at all other places plus the number of people leaving the place. The pull at a place depends on the push factors at all other places plus the number of people entering the place. In both cases, the dependence is that of distance decay. All places are related to every other place, but new places are more related, and the push and pull factors are thus structurally intertwined. Dorigo and Tobler conclude that the model describes an important property of actual behaviour, with identifiable impacts of observed or proposed changes at places on the total migration system, thus making it an extremely useful policy tool. It is possible to indicate where one should make a unit change in out- or in-migrants at a place, without changing the push or pull factors so as to have greatest or least impact on the total migration pattern. It is also possible to differentiate between different migrant groups, (e.g., sex and age differences) and incorporate these within the model. One problem that exists is the assumption that distances are perceived similarly for each thus differentiated group. This may not be the case. However, this type of problem is one that is symptomatic of the gravity model approach, which assumes constant aggregate behaviours across groups.

Dorigo and Tobler (1983) have applied the model, in its various modifications, to US census migration estimates for 1965-1970, between the nine regions of the USA. Table 10.2 shows the results for the model

$$M_{ij} = P_i P_j (R_i + E_j)/d_{ij},$$ (11)

as given in equation (4). The fit of the model to the inflow and outflow migration data was about the same as is usual for gravity models ($R^2 > 80\%$). The resulting push, pull, turnover and attractivity values in a geographic context showed the Pacific Region as the most "repulsive", high housing costs and metropolitan air pollution being possible reasons. Conversely, the same area was shown to be the most "enticing", perhaps because of the attractive scenery, climate and lifestyles afforded. Dorigo and Tobler do not consider the outcomes as contradictory, because their model, through summation, turns these two into a larger turnover, and it also assigns a high net activity to the region. One may compare those regions known to be losing population, such as the mid-Atlantic, in the same way. This is an area that still has strong drawing power, but it is overrun by the push effect. It is possible to examine each region in this manner.

10.4 SIMULATING MIGRATION: A DISAGGREGATED BEHAVIOURAL APPROACH

10.4.1 The Hagerstrand Model

While gravity based models may be calibrated to give reliable aggregate predictions, it is not possible to explain individual migration behaviour using the type of approaches discussed above. An alternative approach emanated during the 1950s from the Lund School of Geography in Sweden. This was led by Torsten Hagerstrand and colleagues, who studied migration in the context of spatial diffusion.

However, in the context of migration studies, Hagerstrand's stochastic process modelling approach was a major innovation.

In his earlier work on migration in Sweden, Hagerstrand had noted that there were irregularities in migration fields because of changes in transport conditions over time, and because of other historical factors that have created a network of social contacts. Both of these factors tend to conserve

Table 10.2

US Interregional Migration Model, $M_{ij} = (R_i + E_j)/d_{ij}$ for 1965-1979

(a)

			Model Input		
Region	Insum	Outsum	I + O	I − O	Population (1970)
New England	675,408	679,180	1,354,588	−3,772	11,848,000
Mid Atlantic	1,155,811	1,874,320	3,030,131	−718,509	37,056,000
East North Central	1,789,112	2,134,267	3,923,379	−345,155	40,266,000
West North Central	942,162	1,212,105	2,154,267	−269,943	16,327,000
South Atlantic	2,484,387	1,765,650	4,250,007	718,737	29,920,000
East South Central	819,222	986,050	1,805,272	−166,828	13,096,000
West South Central	1,237,079	1,146,498	2,383,577	90,581	19,025,000
Mountain	1,067,069	987,331	2,054,400	79,738	8,289,000
Pacific	2,143,172	1,528,021	3,671,193	615,151	25,476,000

Source: U.S. Bureau of the Census (1973).

(b)

		Model Inputs*							
	1	2	3	4	5	6	7	8	9
1 NE: Boston	—	301	0	0	0	0	0	0	0
2 MA: New York	219	—	91	0	350	0	0	0	0
3 ENC: Chicago	1,009	831	—	972	264	703	0	0	0
4 WNC: Omaha	1,514	1,336	505	—	0	166	755	937	0
5 SA: Charleston	974	755	1,019	1,370	—	1,295	0	0	0
6 ESC: Birmingham	1,268	1,049	662	888	482	—	1,140	0	0
7 WSC: Dallas	1,795	1,576	933	654	1,144	662	—	637	0
8 MTN: Salt Lake City	2,420	2,242	1,451	946	2,278	1,795	1,287	—	1,542
9 PAC: San Francisco	3,174	2,996	2,205	1,700	2,862	2,380	1,779	754	—

* Distance between cities below the diagonal; length of border between regions above the diagonal. All in miles.

(c)

	Model Estimates.* Estimated by Minimization of the Functional (4) with $M_{ij} \geq 0$			
Region	Push (R)	Pull (E)	Turnover (T = E + R)	Attractivity (A = E − R)
New England	−9,150	0	−9,150	9,150
Mid Atlantic	8,010	12,885	20,895	4,875
East North Central	11,410	19,825	31,235	8,415
West North Central	−2,420	7,085	4,665	9,505
South Atlantic	11,905	31,875	43,780	19,970
East South Central	−8,415	3,255	−5,160	11,670
West South Central	555	14,355	14,910	13,800
Mountain	−4,000	12,385	8,385	16,385
Pacific	22,615	49,475	72,090	26,860

* All values to be multiplied by 10^4.

Source: Darigo & Tobler, 1983:9-10

a bias in migration frequency, even when changed conditions no longer limit travel. Thus it seemed that once they arise, irregularities in the shape of migration fields have a tendency to perpetuate themselves, because migration at any given time is dependent on preceding migrations. Hagerstrand called this a **feedback** process. He supported this hypothesis with reference to a number of empirical studies showing one migrant drawing another in his wake. This fact that one migrant often follows the path of an earlier migrant is important. Hagerstrand thus identified that there were two types of migrants,

(a) **active migrants**, being those who seek methodically for a suitable destination guaranteeing prosperity;

(b) **passive migrants**, being those who follow impulses emanating from persons of their acquaintance, perhaps mainly from those who have made fortunate moves.

Using Swedish population register data, Hagerstrand tried to develop a simulated migration field using a Monte Carlo method. Such an approach allowed migrations to occur at random, but within the framework of a probability distribution. Hagerstrand determined the probability of different migration events occurring from his empirical studies. These probabilities were fixed as the rules of the game. Then the individual events, within the frames of the probability distribution, are taken from tables of random numbers. The advantage of this simulated migration model is that all the factors are under control; there are no exogenous factors. It was also possible to examine what the results would be if conditions were changed, that is if the rules of the game are modified. In principle, one could develop such a stochastic model to be as complex as reality itself, but since this involves so much work, Hagerstrand limited the number of migrants considered and the space in which they moved. The assumptions of Hagerstrand's **Monte Carlo simulation migration model** may be summarised as follows:

(a) Migrations are assumed to occur within an area of evenly distributed population and evenly distributed vacancies which are of equal value, that is within an isolated state situation. Hagerstrand divided his study area in Sweden into square cells of equal size. These were called parishes. Each parish was denoted by a pair of geographic coordinates.

(b) From the central or origin parish (coordinates 0/0) each year 50 individuals were able to undertake their first migration.

(c) Hagerstrand constructed a table of probabilities for the number of moves which a migrant will make in his lifetime. For example, the probability that a person would move once was $p = 0.25$; the probability that a person would move five times was $p = 0.09$. These probabilities were derived empirically.

(d) Probabilities were established for the time interval between two migrations undertaken by the same individual. These were also empirically derived. For example, the probability of the time interval being under one year was $p = 0.2$; for eight years it was $p = 0.02$; for seventeen years it was $p = 0.006$.

(e) There were two kinds of migrants, active and passive. An active migrant could choose a destination in an adjacent parish only, again according to a set of probabilities. These probabilities were evenly distributed in all directions. For all cells the probability was p = 0.125. A passive migrant could select a new parish dependant upon his acquaintances, that is a parish in which a person who earlier migrated from the origin (0/0) is living at the time. All earlier migrants up to a given time (25 years) are assumed to have the same chance of enticing passive migrations, if they haven't returned to the parish of origin.

(f) The probability that a first migration from the origin (0/0) is active is p = 0.4, while the possibility that a first migration from there is passive was p = 0.6.

(g) All migrations after the first one were assumed to be active.

Clearly, there were several faults with these assumptions. However, simulation of the model over time enables one to generate migration flow patterns and test them against reality. Hagerstrand (1957) has shown the sequential development of a migration field over time, using 50 migrations initiated in one year. In year one these were distributed with a bias towards the north. Over five years, through the combined effects of continued migration of passive movements, the migration field has been extended. By ten years, the model has developed connections in all directions, yet still with a centre of gravity to the north. During the second and third decades of the model, the changes proceeded more slowly. There was a general smoothing out of the migration field, giving the neighbouring parishes lower relative shares and pushing single migrants still further outward. However, the bias to the north was still maintained. Three important aspects to the patterns are generated by the model:

(a) The general shape of the migration field was one with a steep inclination of migration frequencies with increasing distance.

(b) There was a declining steepness of the gradient with the passage of time.

(c) There was persistence of regularities created at an early stage.

Following Hagerstrand's pioneering work, there has been a proliferation of studies using stochastic modelling approaches to migration. However, most applications of stochastic models have been essentially descriptive rather than explanatory. There is the apparently insurmountable problem of the imprecise nature and great number of variables involved in actual migration behaviour, which has been over-simplified in most models. Furthermore, it may be argued that simulation methods have been used to cover up for inadequacies in theory. In general, two stochastic modelling approaches have been used, the Monte Carlo simulation and the Markov chain models.

10.5 SELECTIVITY AND DIFFERENTIALS IN MIGRATION

The gravity model and stochastic process modelling approaches to migration discussed in the preceding two sections of this chapter represent a large portion of the total migration literature. Basically, the approaches have been directed towards predicting patterns of aggregate population flows, sometimes differentiated by sex and age groups, occupation groups, income groups, and so on. Emphasis has been on migration flows between geographic areas. Explanation has been based on the relative pull-push factors on the one hand, and distance decay on the other. While migration differentials for areas may point to potentially important locational effects which must be considered in testing alternative hypotheses of migration decision making, these studies have provided no real systematic explanation or provided detailed evidence on the motivational basis of the decision to move.

An important early exception was a study by Beshers and Nishiura (1961) who argued that occupational differentials in migration represent territorial social and cultural constraints which discourage migration among persons who have a localised versus a territorially extended mode of orientation. In this context, occupational differentials have been seen as largely attributable to the modes of orientation towards goal attainment. Work by Brown and Belcher (1966) hypothesised that the basis of migration selectivity could be understood on the basis of cosmopolitan versus local social roles. Somewhat later, Ritchey (1976) argued that career mobility and individual career choice decision making underlie socio-economic differentials in migration.

In general, there has not been a clearly defined theoretical link between migration differentials and selectivity and motivations for migration. Even the aggregate life cycle and cohort approaches have given emphasis to a deterministic view in which migration is seen as a response to social and environmental pressures. Similarly, the human ecologists' approach to migration, as illustrated in Hawley (1968), have viewed it as a dynamic process for changing areas but through which an equilibrium is maintained. The causes for movement are seen in the physical and social environment without reference to individual motives and values. However, they have recognised income based differentials as a major explanatory factor in migration. It is also evident that the various economic theory approaches to migration have failed to focus on factors other than aggregate explanations, basically related to labour force migration within a pull-push framework, in which the place of migration is seen as a mechanism for the effective allocation of an economy's labour force, and the role of migration is seen within an overall economic change context at places of origin and destination.

10.6 MOTIVATION UNDERLYING MIGRATION

Where, then, do we stand with respect to the motivation underlying migration? De Jong and Fawcett (1979) have suggested that we need to take into consideration two salient points concerning motivations for migration. These are:

(a) Motivations for migration have roots or counterparts in environmental or structural factors which help explain aggregate mobility patterns.

(b) The key to an integration is the identification of linkage processes through which macro stimuli are translated into relevant considerations for individual decision making.

They have identified a number of major motive categories which are reproduced in Table 10.3. The motives - economic, social mobility/social status, residential satisfaction, motive to maintain community based social and economic ties, family and friend affiliation, attaining personal preferences - may all be seen in terms of positive direction or negative direction to the decision to move. The strength of motive to move may be estimated, and it is seen that these differ between developed and developing nations and **within** developed nations **between** long distance and short distance moves. Furthermore, we are able to identify potential migrant groups that will be most affected by the specific motives for migration category. In this way, selectivity and differentials in migration may be better understood.

Table 10.3

Summary of Major Motive Categories for Migration

		Estimated Strength of Motive		
			Developed Nations	
Major Motive for Migration	Direction of Relationship with Decision to Move	Developing Nations	Long Distance Moves	Short Distance Moves
Economic motive	positive	strong	strong	weak
Social mobility/ social status	positive	moderate	moderate to weak	weak
Residential satisfaction	positive (with level of dissatisfaction at area of origin)	weak	moderate	strong
Desire to maintain community-based social and economic ties	negative	strong	moderate	moderate
Family and friend affiliation	positive	strong	moderate	moderate to weak
Attaining personal preferences	positive	weak	weak, but increasing	moderate to weak

Source: After De Jong and Fawcett, 1979:37

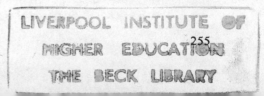

255

De Jong and Fawcett (1979) draw several conclusions from the schema presented in Table 10.3:

(a) Major motives for migration are the maximisation of actual or expected economic returns, social mobility and social status attainment, residential satisfaction, affiliations with family and friends, and attainment of personal preferences.

(b) The major motive for not moving is the desire to maintain community based social and economic ties.

(c) There is a clear difference between developing and developed countries. In developing countries, micro level migration is not sufficiently detailed to give an analysis of motives for move by distance categories.

(d) The dominant motive for rural to urban migration in developing countries is actual or expected economic returns. Also important are the facilitating influence of family and friends at urban areas of destination. In contrast, migration is constrained by the motive of maintaining community based economic ties.

(e) In developed countries, short distance mobility is strongly motivated by housing and neighbourhood residential satisfaction, with the economic motive being relatively unimportant, as job change may not be involved. In contrast, long distance migration is strongly related to the economic motive. The maintenance for community based social and economic ties appears to be relatively unimportant for both short and long distance moves.

(f) There seems to be a general proposition that individuals will choose an area that will permit the maximisation of their goals based on a hierarchy of economic values, and to minimise socio-cultural and language adjustment problems. If economic goals are assumed to be dominant, then it will follow that the choice of where to move would maximise the likelihood of income or job related values. Further, the non-local choice of destination is largely based on where family or friends are located, particularly in developing countries. Thus, family and friends are important sources of information. We also need to identify the role of prior experiences and formal and informal information flows as figuring in the development of awareness space.

(g) Another set of factors relates to structural facilitators and constraints, such as the housing stock, distance, transport flows, subsidy schemes, and so on, which may modify the feasibility of some alternative location choices.

(h) There is a further set of salient factors, such as forced moves brought on by wars, political pressures, housing evictions, urban renewal projects, occupational transfers, or the impact of environmental catastrophes, such as drought, flood and famine.

10.8 MIGRATION AS A DECISION CHOICE PROCESS

The general review of migration undertaken in the preceding sections of this chapter has highlighted the degree to which research has focused on both aggregate and generally deterministic approaches to the analysis of migration.

It is thus appropriate to conclude this Chapter by focusing attention on the **micro level decision making approach to migration**. In this context, we are concerned with the **decision choice process**. This involves a consideration of both why people move and why people do **not** move.

It needs to be emphasised that there are considerable difficulties in investigating this complex question of decision or choice making in the context of migration. An obvious problem is that of post facto rationalisation that dominates responses to questions concerning why people moved or why people did not move. It is now well recognised by researchers that the motives adduced by migrants for moves in the past may hide, rather than reveal, underlying causes for movement. People's memories get blurred with the progression of time. Important objectives and dramatic events can stand out in a person's memory, and influence recall rather than the cumulative effects of hopes and aspirations and fears, which are probably the real causes leading to a person's decision to leave one place and move to another. It is difficult to overcome these biases in survey data, which is the typical mode of data collection in micro level decision choice process studies of migration.

It has been suggested by some writers that the micro level approach to migration studies is of lesser importance than the aggregate approaches previously discussed. This view is usually put in the context that macro level studies are more useful for policies since they deal with the broad processes that public policies seek to influence, that may identify the volumes and directions of migration flows. However, it may be just as convincingly argued that an understanding at the micro level of the decision process in migration provides improved guidance for public policies that are intended to influence population distribution. As De Jong and Fawcett (1979: 45) have argued:

"to put it another way, traditional migration studies tell more about places than they do about people, with corresponding implications for applications of the findings. Migration streams to large cities can of course be deflected by making lucrative employment and attractive amenities available elsewhere, but what else can be done in a shorter term perspective and at a lower, more feasible cost? Studies that illuminate the process of migration decision making we would argue, will suggest alternative means by which such decisions can be influenced through public policies and programs. Knowledge about the range and importance of relevant motivations can be used to advantage in programs to exert direct influence on migration through educational persuasion, and can also be of value for the design of policies that would change the structure of incentives and disincentives for migration."

10.8.1 A Value Expectancy Model
When migration is viewed within the decision choice framework, it may be analysed within a general behavioural or psychological framework. One particular approach is the value expectancy model. This is based on the work of the psychologist, Crawford (1973: 54) who wrote that:

"Despite differences in terminology, the expectancy value behaviour theorists all propose that the strength of the tendency to act in a certain way depends on the **expectancy** that the act will be followed by a given consequence (or goal) and the **value** of that consequence (or goal) to the individual."

The value expectancy model assumes that people will usually behave in a forward looking, positive way, making choices that they believe will maximise their well-being. Thus, we need to specify personally valued goals that might be met by moving (or staying) and assess perceived linkage in terms of expectancy between migration behaviour and the outcome. This is a **cognitive model**, as it deals with mental events, and it is cast in essentially a cost-benefit framework. Thus, migration is an instrument of behaviour, and decision making is based on a cognitive assessment that involves subjective anticipation and weighting of the factors involved in achieving specified goals.

The basic components of the value expectancy model are **goals** (values and objectives) and **expectancies** (subjective probabilities). Pairs of value expectancy components may be assumed to have multiplicative, rather than additive, relationships. We may express the model in the context of migration as follows:

$$M = \quad V_i E_i \quad\quad\quad (12)$$

where:

V = the value of the outcome, i.e. migration.
E = the expectancy that migration will have to the desired outcome.
M = the strength of the motivation for migration, i.e., the sum of the VE products.

The multiplicative assumption means that if either the importance of a particular value is low or the expectancy concerning it is weak, then that component will contribute little to total motivation. In using this approach in analysing migration, it is first necessary to identify the goals or the values people hold that are likely to be associated with spatial mobility. De Jong and Fawcett (1979) have identified the seven broad values or goals listed in Table 10.4. These are wealth, status, comfort, stimulation, autonomy, affiliation, and morality. It is possible to link each category to a list of potential indicators of the value. They suggest that in constructing a questionnaire one would be able to measure the personal importance of each item to the respondent. He describes each of the categories in the following terms:

(a) **Wealth**, including a wide range of factors related to individual economic reward. Factors contributing to wealth can take various forms and would include things such as high wages, good income, low cost of living, low taxes, good fringe benefits, good welfare provisions, stability of employment, availability of jobs, ownership of property. It is possible to view wealth as an end in itself, but it may also be a means by which other goals may be satisfied.

Table 10.4

Values and Goals Related to Migration, With Selected Indicators and Parallel Aspects of Personal Motives and Socio-Structural Characteristics

EXPECTED VALUES/GOALS	SELECTED INDICATORS	PERSONAL MOTIVES		SOCIAL-STRUCTURAL CHARACTERISTICS	
		ATTRACTION	AVOIDANCE	PULL	PUSH
MEALTH	- having a high income; stable income - having economic security in old age - being able to afford basic needs; some luxuries - having access to welfare payments and other economic benefits	To increase income and wealth, economic security	To escape from (relative) poverty, insecurity	Economic opportunities, availability of high-paying jobs, economy expanding	Shortage of jobs, low-paying jobs, economically depressed area
STATUS	- having a prestigious job - being looked up to in the community - obtaining a good education - having power and influence	To improve social status	To free self, from low-status situation, seek new role	Social mobility by achievement, opportunities for change	Social status by ascription, lack of flexibility
COMFORT	- having an "easy" job - living in a pleasant community - having ample leisure time - having comfortable housing	To have easier, more comfortable life	To avoid harsh environment, physical labor, long work hours	Urban amenities, white collar and service jobs with regular hours and wages	Poor rural setting, labor intensive agricultural production
STIMULATION	- having fun and excitement - doing new things - being able to meet a variety of people - keeping active and busy	To seek stimulation fun, variety	To avoid boredom	Public entertainment, diversity of activities "bright city lights"	Uniformity & simplicity of village life, no night life
AUTONOMY	- being economically independent - being free to say and do what you want - having privacy - being on your own	To have freedom of choice, personal autonomy	To be relieved of traditional role constraints, free from influence of others	Impersonal social structure, urban anonymity	Tight social controls, close surveillance by family/community
AFFILIATION	- living near family, friends - being part of a group/community - having a lot of friends - being with spouse/prospective spouse	To be with friends, family or spouse, join particular community	To avoid loneliness, social isolation	Availability of certain persons or groups	Non-availability of certain persons or groups
MORALITY	- leading a virtuous life - being able to practice religion - exposing children to good influences - living in a community with a favorable moral climate				

Source: After De Jong & Fawcett, 1979

(b) **Status**, encompassing a number of factors connected with social standing or prestige. Occupation and education are important aspects of status, and they are related to income. Status itself, however, can also be an important factor in migration. For example, high status can be achieved by living a more sophisticated life, having a white collar job, having a degree, and so on. A move from a rural area to a city may be regarded as a form of social mobility with status, regardless of economic consequences.

(c) **Comfort**, meaning a goal to achieve better living or working conditions. This may include improved housing, more pleasant residential environment, easier work, shorter or more regular working hours, a healthier or less stressful setting, etc. Comfort here means essentially physical and psychological comforts.

(d) **Stimulation**, meaning exposure to pleasurable activities, in contrast to relief from an unpleasant situation. It includes such valued activities as entertainment and recreation, and may be described in terms of variety, change, fun, excitement, adventure, and so on. Stimulation can also been seen as a relief from boredom and a benefit frequently cited for rural urban migration.

(e) **Autonomy**, having many dimensions, but generally referring to personal freedom and the ability to live one's own life. The weakening and absence of traditional family obligations may be important here, and in some settings autonomy may also imply political freedom.

(f) **Affiliation**, refers to the value of being with other persons, in connection with or as a result of migration. It can include joining friends or family as a reason for migration. It may disguise other motives for migration, as affiliation with others may be a facilitating factor in migration to satisfy different personal goals. Sometimes affiliation is the main motive for migration, such as to get married, to accompany a spouse, to join close friends or relatives who had migrated earlier.

(g) **Morality**, being related to values and belief systems (such as religious beliefs systems) that proscribe good and bad ways of living. If strongly held, moral values may have a pervasive influence on behaviour, and the morality dimension connected with migration is often negatively expressed, such as the 'corrupting' or 'sinful' influence of city life.

Testing people's values by having respondents rate selected indicators listed in Table 10.4 makes it possible to compute value expectancy peer scores. The total score is considered as an index of behavioural intention. De Jong and Fawcett (1979) states that in the migration context, there can be several scores for each individual, one for the place of current residence, and one for each of several alternative destinations. The highest score would represent a propensity to move or to stay. The migration intention score is expected to be predictive of future mobility behaviour. Obviously, if migration behaviour is seen to be directed towards the goal of improving or maintaining the quality of life, expected values of migration, their strength, salience, degree of certainty about outcomes, values for oneself and for others, and short and long term perspectives on the part of individuals, may

Figure 10.4

A Value Expectancy Model of Migration Decision Making

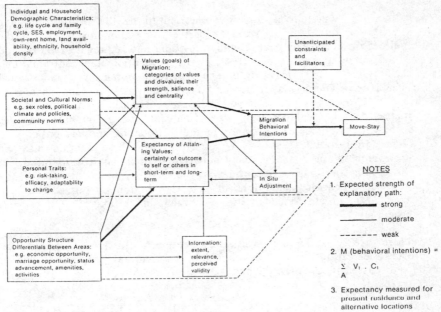

Source: After De Jong & Fawcett, 1979

be ascertained. If intervening factors, such as barriers and facilitators, are taken into account, it should be possible to achieve the stated aim of the model. In essence, the value expectancy approach provides a method for measuring at a subjective level many of the factors that are likely to enter into the decision to migrate. We have an instrument for measuring behaviour and decision-making based on what De Jong Fawcett have called a "cognitive calculus" that involves anticipatory weighting of the elements involved in attaining certain goals.

De Jong and Fawcett (1979) present the value expectancy model of migration decision-making in the form shown in Figure 10.4. It is worth noting, as shown in Table 10.4, that for each of the expected values (except morality) personal motives for migration have counterparts in social structural factors, although the correspondence is not exact. For the first six values, four distinctions are shown, attraction and avoidance in relation to personal motives, and pull and push in relation to social structural characteristics. Individual and household demographic characteristics, societal and cultural norms, personal traits, opportunity structure, and information all operate on the expectancy of attaining values; while individual and household demographic characteristics, societal and cultural norms, personal traits, and opportunity structure differentials between areas operate to effect values or the goals of migration. The **values** and **goals** of migration and the expectancy of attaining values interlink to form migration behavioural intentions, which can lead to either a decision to stay or an in situ adjustment.

In summarising their model, De Jong and Fawcett (1979: 59-60) have this to say:

"Migration behaviour is thus hypothesised to be the result of 1) the strength of the value expectancy derived intentions to move, 2) the indirect influences of background individual and aggregate factors, and 3) the potential modifying effects of often unanticipated contraints and facilitators which may intervene between intentions and actual behaviour. These constraints and facilitators may include change in family structure (for example, marriage, divorce, separation, death, increased or decreased family size), financial costs of moving, changes in health, distance, and changes in the location of support anticipated from family and friends. We suggest that these factors may be unanticipated and that they may not have been salient considerations in the original migration intentions, as derived from value expectancy based cost benefit calculations of potential migrants. Forced mobility may also create incongruities between migration intention and behaviour."

There are considerable similarities between this value expectancy approach and various models developed by behavioural geographers which will be discussed in Chapters 11 and 12.

Chapter Eleven

THE RESIDENTIAL LOCATION DECISION PROCESS
AT THE INTRA-URBAN SCALE

11.1 A CONCEPTUAL FRAMEWORK

Residential location decisions at the intra-urban scale take place within the
constraints of time and enabling factors. This framework incorporates
behavioural processes related to the satisfaction of perceived dwelling needs
and location preferences of households, and their knowledge of the subset of
the housing market in which the decision is to be made. The mosaic of
residential areas in a city, which may be differentiated on the basis of social
space characteristics and housing sub-markets, reflect the outcome over time
of the aggregate residential decisions of households. Urban, social and
behavioural geographers have proposed various theoretical explanations for
the emergence of typologies of residential areas in cities and the nature of
the residential location decision process.

This chapter outlines the nature of residential location processes. A
framework for the discussion is presented in Figure 11.1. The **mosaic of
residential areas** within which residential location choice decisions are made
in the city may be studied in terms of their **social space** characteristics using
factorial ecology and **residential typology classification** methods based on
small area census data to give a territorial expression of urban space. This is
indicated in the left-hand panel of Figure 11.1. Individual and household
residential location decisions are made in response to stress, to seek the
satisfaction of needs and to meet aspirations. Search behaviour is involved,
as is choice between alternative opportunities. This is indicated in the right-
hand panel in Figure 11.1. All these take place within the action spaces of
individuals and households, and are related to cognitive maps of the city.
Choice of residential location is made with respect to the residential space
preferences of people, as indicated in the middle panel of Figure 11.1.

We will first consider the notion of **urban social space** as it reflects the
outcome of collective residential location decisions. We will then look at the
use of **behavioural models** for analysing **residential and location decision
process**. Specific aspects of this process - such as the nature of **residential
space preferences** and aspirations, what constitute **stressors** or the factors
that trigger the desire to change residential location, and the characteristics
of intra-urban **residential search** - are discussed in detail in Chapter 12.
Finally, we will look at a more recent approach which investigates decision-
making and search in a probability modelling framework.

Figure 11.1

Framework for Analysing the Residential Typology of Cities and the Residential Location Decision Process

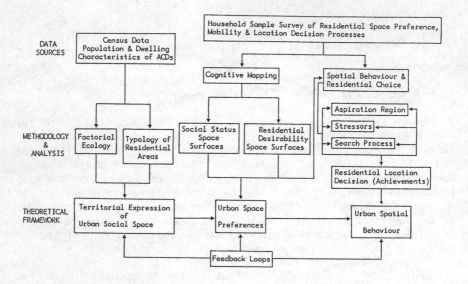

11.2 URBAN SOCIAL SPACE AND THE MOSAIC OF RESIDENTIAL AREAS

11.2.1 The Notion of Social Space

An important question confronting geographers as social scientists is "how do people sort themselves out in space?" Jakle, et al. (1976: 185) have noted the following characteristics of groups of individuals in space:

> "The individual gains knowledge about places from his own perception and by his interaction with others. When this information is processed into behaviour, it will affect his views about particular groups of the population, preferred places to live, and acceptable modes of personal communication. The groupings of like-minded individuals in a specific area, whether a distinct social area of a city or a social region of a nation, will lead to various patterns of clusterings. These are clusters of people who have decided to occupy similar spaces for economic, social, or political reasons."

The consequences of these processes may be regarded as people's aggregate location decisions. At the **intra-urban scale** one may differentiate residential areas according to the social and economic characteristics of their inhabitants and the characteristics of the dwelling stock that occur therein. In other words, the **social space** characteristics of cities and their **territorial expression** must be determined. Much of the research by urban geographers and urban sociologists during the twentieth century has been directed towards studying spatial variations in the social characteristics of urban populations. In particular, geographers have been concerned with investigating the spatial patterns of the characteristics of populations, the patterns and movements of people within urban areas, and the evolution of form and growth of cities. Sociologists have been more concerned with analysing the nature of behaviour within urban neighbourhoods and with studying the processes that give rise to social stratification in urban society. Economists have been concerned with the economic base of cities, the ability of users of space to compete for land, and the relationship between costs of travel and the cost of land (rent). Central to all approaches is the notion that certain groups of the population will be able to out-bid other groups for residential land that is most accessible and which has the highest amenity value. Those groups with greatest economic resources and with greatest access to power in the city will thus be able to exercise a wider range of choices in selecting both the location and the type of dwelling in which they will live than is the case for less fortunate groups of the population. The outcome is one of inequality of opportunity and differential abilities to exercise choice as to where to live in the city. Analyses of the social structure of urban society clearly indicate a high degree of spatial concentration and segregation in the distribution of population sub-groups over the residential areas of cities.

The French sociologist, Chombart deLauwe (1952) referred to **objective social space**, which he defined as "the spatial framework within which groups live; groups whose social structure and organisation have been conditioned by ecological and cultural factors". **Territorial space** may be stratified by the social dimensions of the population that inhabits it. Anne Buttimer (1969; 1972) discussed at length the notions of social space and its applications in urban geography. She suggested that geographers' basic contribution would seem to consist of mapping the distribution of various social groups. However, there was considerable semantic confusion over the notion of social space.

The term **social space** identifies man's relations to other men or other social phenomena chosen as points of reference. This has been defined by sociologists in the 1920s, such as Sorokin, in terms of a system of coordinates whose horizontal axes referred to group participation and whose vertical axes referred to statuses and roles within groups. In this way, the social position of any person in society could be defined. The sociologist Park (1925) stressed the subjective dimensions of social space. Somewhat later social space became defined in terms of psychological variables, as typified by Theodorson and Theodorson (1969, 394) who contended that "social space is determined by the individual's perception of his world and not by the objective description of his social relationship by the observer". This interpretation has its roots in Durkheim's (1893) concept of sociological space and says nothing of physical or territorial space. Sorre (1955, 1957, 1958) attempted to link these, as did Chombart deLauwe (1952, 1965). Basically, their proposition was that the patterns of organisation were techniques of social life, and political, economic and kinship spaces were dimensions of social space. Sorre (1957: 114) envisaged social space as:

"a mosaic of areas, each homogeneous in terms of the space perceptions of its inhabitants. Within each of these areas a network of points and lines radiating from certain points could be identified. Each group tended to have its own specific social space, which reflected its particular values, preferences, and aspirations. The density of social space reflected the complementarity, and consequently the degree of interaction between groups".

Thus it was logical for Chombart deLauwe (1952) to identify **objective social space**. Techniques such as **social area analysis** and **factorial ecology** have allowed identification, description and objective mapping of social space. While theoretical and philosophical considerations of social space were being pursued largely by French geographers and sociologists, it was not until the late 1960s and the early 1970s that Anglo-American geographers began to understand the complexity of the concept and the processes underlying social space in cities. At the same time, many urban and social geographers in America were beginning to disaggregate the normative economic models developed by the locational analysts in an attempt to investigate, and hopefully explain, human spatial behaviour.

During the 1950s and 1960s the pioneers of social area analysis and factorial ecology had looked at the isomorphism of social participation patterns and social spaces in cities and had matched activity patterns with the spatial morphology of social characteristics. However, they made little attempt to examine the isomorphism of place identification with so-called social spaces. **Factorial ecology studies**, such as those by Murdie (1969) and Berry and Horton (1970), identified dimensions of urban social space and mapped their spatial distributions, but no consideration was given to whether or not the populations resident in those social spaces were satisfied with their lot or how they came to be there. Later, the behavioural movement in geography became concerned with studying, among other things, relationships between social space and individual and household action spaces (Horton and Reynolds 1969), and the time space budgets and patterns of people (Chapin and Brail, 1969; Anderson, 1971; Parkes and Thrift, 1975), as we have seen in Chapters 6 and 7.

It is interesting to see the relationship between the study of spatial behaviour of man in urban areas and Chombart deLauwe's concept of **urban social space** which had proposed a hierarchy of spaces, within which groups and individuals live, move, and interact (Chombart deLauwe, 1960: 403-425). He had identified four spaces, namely:

(a) **familial space**, or the network of relationships characteristic of the domestic level of social interaction
(b) **neighbourhood space**, or the network that encompasses daily and local movement
(c) **economic space**, which embraces certain employment centres
(d) urban sector, or **regional social space**.

These are progressively larger and overlapping dimensions of space that constitute the nominal spatial framework within which the group or individual acts. We may relate these to:

(a) **personal space** (Sommer, 1969)
(b) **neighbourhood space** (Lee, 1964; 1968)
(c) **activity space** (Horton and Reynolds, 1969)
(d) **action space** (Horton and Reynolds, 1969).

Obviously, migration and residential location decision processes of individuals and households will have an effect on shaping the territorial social space characteristics of urban areas. As indicated by Buttimer (1969: 423) in investigating residential mobility and the residential location decision process, geographers have approached the study of social space on the three levels identified by Chombart deLauwe, namely:

(a) the **behavioural level**, which relates to where and how people live and move
(b) the **level of knowledge**, which relates to where people know what alternative opportunities are available
(c) the **aspirational level**, which relates to where people would like to go if they had the opportunity.

Where, then, does all this leave us with respect to the notion of **social space** in urban areas? We may investigate the characteristics of urban social space and their territorial expression (the traditional concern of the geographer through studies such as **social area analysis** and **factorial ecology**) and sociological and psychological processes that give rise to behaviour that may manifest itself spatially. Until recently geographers had recognised, but rarely explicitly examined, the influences of lifestyle, social stratification, stage in the family life cycle, status, role, tradition, symbolism and values in studying the relationships between the behaviour of individuals and groups and the elements of the structures that comprise the spatial environment. Buttimer (1972: 285) identified five distinct levels of analysis which attempt to integrate objective and subjective social space in urban analysis. These were:

(a) A **social psychological** level investigating a person's position within society - that is, **sociological space**.
(b) A **behavioural** level investigating activity and circulation patterns - that is, **interaction space**.
(c) A **symbolic** level investigating images, cognitions and **mental maps**.
(d) An **affective level** investigating patterns of identification of **territory**.
(e) A purely **morphological** level in which population characteristics are factor-analysed to yield **homogeneous social areas**.

This provides a useful framework for analysis. It is possible to take a number of the aspects of Chombart deLauwe's social spaces modified by the terminology developed by Buttimer.

First, **social space** can be taken to refer to Chombart deLauwe's objective social space, or Buttimer's social areas. It is the territorial expression of descriptive dimensions extracted from a factor analysis of a set of population census variables for small areas. Such variables are surrogate measures or constructs such as socio-economic status, family/life cycle

267

status, and ethnic status. These are used to classify or describe the position of people within society. The approach incorporates in a territorial framework Buttimer's sociological space.

Second, **preference space** is taken to be comprised of Buttimer's **symbolic level** of investigating images, cognitions and mental maps. It will relate to the residential aspirations of sub-groups of the population, and will be influenced by constraints such as economic factors and institutional barriers.

Third, Buttimer's **affective level** and **interaction space** are taken to be related to that form of spatial behaviour called **migration and the residential location decision process.** This incorporates the identification and description of things such as spatial search and the accumulation of knowledge, and levels of satisfaction and dissatisfaction. The process involves both spatial and non-spatial considerations which relate to those elements which constitute and shape urban social space and space preferences of people in urban areas.

11.2.2 The Constructs of Territorial Social Space

The analysis of the social structure of urban society and the spatial ramifications of the interaction of socially differentiated population sub-groups within it has been enhanced by the use of statistical techniques such as ecological correlation and residential segregation indices, by the recognition of processes of ecological competition and succession, and by the formulation of theories of urban structure such as Burgess' **concentric zone model** (1925), Hoyt's **sector model** (1939), and Harris and Ullman's **multiple nuclei model** (1945). These models related to the structure and form of cities, and the way they evolved over time. Figure 11.2 gives diagrammatic representation of such structures and forms.

A major advance in the study of social structure of the city came in the 1950s with the development of the **social area analysis.** Its development is attributed to two west coast USA sociologists, Shevky and Bell (1955). It provides a theoretical and methodological framework by which we can describe and analyse urban social space.

Social area analysis, as originally proposed by Shevky and his various associates, provided a systematic classification of residential areas in cities. A social area schema attempted to specify the nature and effects of structural change in modern urban industrial society in which the metropolis emerged as the major living space of people. It was hypothesised that social differentiation in residential areas could be viewed from the basis of three broad trends in urban society. Briefly, these trends and constructs may be described in terms of

(a) **Changes in the distributions of skills,** and subsequently the arrangement of occupations based on function, which give a **socio-economic status (social rank) construct.**

(b) **Changes in the way of life,** involving the movement of women into urban occupations, and the diversification of family patterns, which give a **family status (urbanisation/ familism/ household structure) construct.**

Figure 11.2

Models of the City Structure

(a) The Burgess Zonal Model

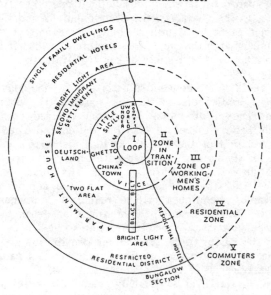

(b) The Hoyt Sector Model

(c) The Harris and Ulman Multiple-Nuclei Model

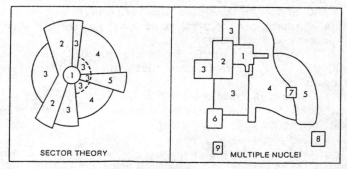

1 = Central business district
2 = Wholesaling & light manufacturing
3 = Low class residential
4 = Middle class residential
5 = High class residential
6 = Heavy manufacturing
7 = Outlying business district
8 = Dormitory suburb
9 = Industrial suburb

(c) **Changing composition of the population** through the redistribution of space of ethnic and religious groups, due to both internal and international migration, giving an **ethnic status (ethnicity/segregation) construct**.

Shevky and Bell maintained that these three constructs could be identified and described by means of selected indices taken from the census tract data relating to the characteristics of populations and dwellings. The use of census tract as an areal unit of analysis meant that the social area **typology** for enquiring into the changing structure of urban industrial society was made synonymous with the study of social differentiation in residential areas of cities.

Despite criticisms of the conceptual basis and methodology of social area analysis, empirical studies of the schema particularly when modified to permit the identification of social dimensions derived from multivariate analysis of a wide battery of census tract population and dwelling data, have led to general validation of the hypothesis that the three constructs, **socio-economic** status, **family** status and **ethnic** status, are necessary to describe the social differentiation that occurs in urban ecologial systems.

By the early 1960s, the increasing availability of computer facilities led researchers to employ techniques such as principal components and factor analysis to identify and describe the dimensions of urban social structure. These used a large battery of variables relating to sex, occupation, income and education of the labour force; sex and age distribution and marital status of the population; ethnic structure of the population; and nature of tenancy and dwelling characteristics of residential areas.

Typically, **a factorial ecology study** identifies a set of descriptive dimensions relating to the social structure of a city. Between four and ten component factors explain up to about 80% of the total variance in the data matrix. Invariably, these factors are described in terms of the three social area constructs proposed by Shevky and Bell. It has become common to compute component or factor scores for residential areas on these dimensions, and to analyse the spatial distribution of the scores, often with the intention of testing for the presence of zonal and sectoral variations in the spatial patterns of dimensions.

Thus, it is possible to identify dimensions that describe the nature of urban social space and to map the territorial patterns of these spaces using small area census data.

Figure 11.3 shows the relationships between social space and geographic space in cities. In the light of reported empirical studies, this relationship may be described in the following manner:

(a) **Territorial (or geographic) space** provides a living space within the city within which, or over which, its inhabitants reside and behave. The space contains elements that are point located and area located and that form paths along which movements take place. For example, there is a network of transportation routes (often sectoral in arrangement) that converge on locations at which urban functions are concentrated, such as the central business district, regional shopping centres, and industrial nodes. These movement paths criss-cross the city. The spaces between are functional, and contain varying mixtures of commercial, retail, residential and recreational land uses. At some focal or nodal points, and along some movement paths, there are areas of concentration of specialised functions, but the major part of these spaces particularly at locations away from those focal points and paths, have a residential function.

(b) Overlying this geographical space is the **social space** of the city, which is multi-dimensional and comprises three basic constructs, social status, family status and ethnic status. Typically, the territorial space expression of these components of social space vary, e.g.:

  (i)   **Family status space** is zonal in its geographic space occurrence, with the older inner city areas being characterised by older populations and many non-primary family unit households. With movement out of the inner city areas, there is a concentric or zonal progression through increasingly more youthful populations and areas characterised by higher fertility and mostly primary family units.

  (ii) **Social status space** is seen to vary in a sectoral pattern, the hypothesis being that once established, high and low status residential areas tend to extend along sectors defined by movement paths (transport routes) as the city grows.

  (iii) **Ethnic status space** is theoretically ghettoed or enclaved geographically, with the population sub-groups that have specific ethnic status tending to be residentially segregated in these enclaves, which have a tendency to move through time. Thus, social status spaces are sectoral cutting across zonally arranged family status spaces, while ethnic status space are enclaves usually within low social status space.

A well-known application of this approach was Murdie's (1969) study of Toronto, Canada. Here, major urban social space dimensions and their physical space occurrences were used to identify a number of communities or social areas, which were arranged in both sector and concentric patterns, and which had enclaves and areas of dominant ethnic groupings of the population. Such patterns are common in North American cities and they remain evident over time despite changes in preference and mobility of the various social groups within metropolitan areas. In this way **typologies** of residential areas of cities based on their social space characteristics may be formed. An example of such an approach is given in Figure 11.4 for metropolitan Adelaide, the capital city of South Australia, which was derived from a hierarchical grouping procedure based on the analysis of a set of 1971 census data variables. The accompanying legend shows that such procedures may initially identify broad territorial urban social spaces with increasingly detailed classification of territorial spaces on the basis of more subtle social space characteristics.

Figure 11.3

Urban Social Space Constructs and Their Territorial Relationships to Physical Space

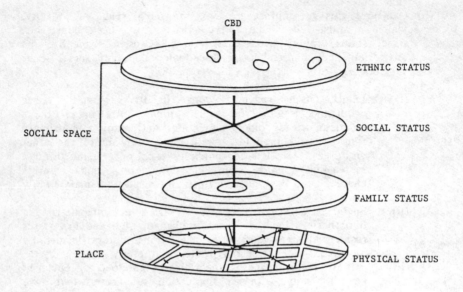

Source: After Murdie, 1969:9

11.3 MODELLING APPROACHES IN RESIDENTIAL LOCATION CHOICE RESEARCH

Models of household behaviour in the choice of residential location may be classified into two basic categories:

(a) The first assumes that residential location choice may be described in terms of a **trade-off** between **transport costs** and the **price of housing.** If we know the shape of the rent and transport gradients in the city, then a household is seen to choose a location by equating the savings on housing costs with increments to transport costs. These are basically normative micro-economic models (see Alonso, 1964; Muth, 1969; and Wingo, 1961). Such approaches are limiting in that they do not include neighbourhood effects and they assume constant income and continuous rent and transport gradients. Casetti and Papageorgiou (1971) attempted to extend this trade-off approach by incorporating some of these variables.

(b) The second approach is **micro-behavioural** modelling which argues that accessibility is not the primary determinant of residential location choice, but that amenity and environmental, socio-

Figure 11.4

A Typology of Residential Areas in Adelaide, South Australia:
Social Space Characteristics of Territorial Spaces

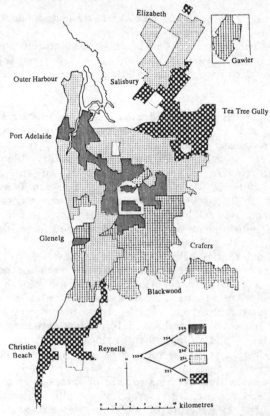

I. Group 239 (N=16): Outer suburban areas in the southern, northeastern
and northern sectors. Areas of rapid growth; very high
levels of familism; low to medium socio-economic status;
low levels of urbanization; and high concentrations of
British migrants.

II. Group 251 (N=50): Industrial suburbs of the northern, northeastern,
western and southern sectors, plus the new town of Elizabeth.
Generally low socio-economic status; high incidence of
Housing Trust housing; variable levels of familism, but
generally above average; about average levels of ethnicity,
both British and southern European; below average growth.

III. Group 250 (N=32): The eastern, southern, hills and southwestern coastal
sectors. Areas of high socio-economic status; variable
levels of familism; low ethnicity; variable growth.

IV. Group 252 (N=30): The old inner-city suburbs and the northwestern
sector. Generally low to medium socio-economic status,
with some pockets of above average levels; high ethnicity;
high urbanization; low familism; low growth.

Source: Stimson & Cleland, 1975

economic, psychological, and time factors operate together to produce a multi-variate explanation of decision-making. This behavioural approach emphasises the process by which location decisions are made.

11.3.2 Behavioural Approaches: From Aggregate to Individual Decision Choice Models

In discussing the behavioural models of residential location choice process in cities, Smith, et al. (1979:3-5) have identified the following broad approaches. The first two are empirical and the next three theoretical in nature:

(a) **Spatial aspects of the residential relocation process at an aggregate level.** These have looked at population flows at an aggregate level between census tracts and neighbourhoods, such as Brown and Longbrake's (1970) study of the degree to which people move between similar socio-economic districts of the city; Simmon's (1974) study of the flow of people between census tracts; and Clark's (1970) study of income and house value constraints on how people choose neighbourhoods in the city. Such studies give a general indication of search procedures used in residential decision-making.

(b) **Household spatial behaviour at the micro-level.** These studies are concerned with either **search behaviour,** such as those by Hempel (1969) and Barrett (1973), in which the search behaviour of households, using questionnaires administered after the search and relocation process was completed, is investigated to analyse the spatial pattern of search; or **information gathering about housing vacancies** by individuals, such as studies by Baresi (1968) and Palm (1976), which focus on the use of such information in reaching a decision.

(c) **Markov modelling of the structure of intra-urban migration.** This is the most comprehensive group of modelling strategies and is used to specify the structure of mobility rates and analyse longitudinal characteristics of migration. The focus is on when migration will be likely to occur rather than on where it will go, and is largely based on life-cycle determinants. Typical of such studies are those by McGinnis (1968) on social mobility, and Ginnsberg (1971; 1973) on mobility for heterogeneous populations. There is no concern with the decision-making of individual households.

(d) **Migration in relation to the housing stock or neighbourhood characteristics.** These are aggregate models of neighbourhood change, such as studies by Quigley (1976) and Moore (1977), and are concerned with housing characteristics in small areas, the movement of people through these housing stocks, and the impacts on communities and housing characteristics.

(e) **Issues of the decision process in residential relocation.** This approach is epitomised by the Brown and Moore (1970) model, in which the process is separated into two stages - the decision to move and the actual relocation process. They also refined Wolpert's concepts of action space, search behaviour and place utility.

To those need to be added:

(f) **Decision-making and search models.** These seek to predict the mobility pattern within a city by incorporating spatial and temporal aspects of residential choice in a probability framework (Smith, et al. 1979), and to suggest that the probability to move will be influenced by both cumulative resistancy (inertia) and dissatisfaction (stress), with the probability of moving being a function of the resultant of these two conflicting forces (Huff and Clark, 1978).

We will look in detail at two of these modelling approaches - the residential location decision process model, and the decision-making and search probability models.

11.3.3 The Residential Location Decision Process: A Behavioural Model

Behavioural theories and models of the residential location decision process emphasise the existence of multiple goals among subgroups of the population seeking a residential location, imperfect information, non-optimal decision logic, and the recognition of constraints (economic and institutional) within which choice is made. The decision maker can be viewed as having a goal of satisfaction, and behaviour is seen as inherently rational. As Wolpert (1965: 161) has stated:

"man is limited to a finite ability to perceive, calculate and predict and to an otherwise imperfect knowledge of the environment", but "he still differentiates between alternative courses of action according to their relative utility or expected utility."

The decision maker realises the limitations of his knowledge, and alternatives which minimise uncertainty will be preferred, so that there is a tendency to postpone decisions and rely on feedback information. This incorporates what Simon (1957) referred to as "intentionally rational behaviour".

The decision maker may be viewed as being satisfied when there is some measure of concordance between what may be termed **achievements** and **aspirations.** Aspirations are effective (i.e., they do not include wild dreams) and they relate only to what the decision maker perceives as being possible (i.e., feasible). Thus, if a decision maker pursues a goal of satisfaction in an intendedly rational manner, it is valid to assume that the state of equilibrium between achievement level and aspiration level is predictive of future behaviour. Brown and Moore (1970: 1) operationalized the concept of place utility, which essentially measures an individual's level of satisfaction or dissatisfaction with respect to a given residential location.

Figure 11.5 is a model encompassing the above postulates, and incorporates the phases that Brown and Moore describe as the **intra-urban migration process.**

Figure 11.5

The Residential Location Decision Process: A Behavioural Model

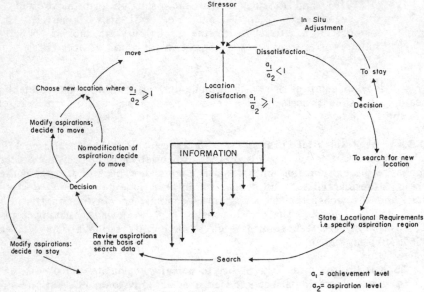

Source: After Brown & Moore, 1970

Initially the decision maker is at a satisfactory location because the current dwelling location combination tolerably meets needs, i.e., there is congruence between achievement level and aspirations. This satisfactory state turns to one of dissatisfaction through the appearance of a **stressor** which, in Wolpert's words (1966: 93), is:

"any influence, whether it arises from the internal environment or the external environment which interferes with the satisfaction of basic needs or which disrupts or threatens to disrupt the stable equilibrium".

Stressors may be **internal**, such as change in family size, or **external**, such as expiry of a lease on a dwelling. Furthermore, they may be **dwelling specific**, such as the need for an extra bedroom, or **location specific**, such as a change in job leading to an increased length of journey to work. A stressor may act upon either the achievement level or aspirations, i.e., it may alter what the decision maker already has (i.e., achievement), or it can alter aspiration.

Once it appears, a **stressor** will considerably alter the relationship between achievement and aspiration. Naturally, the degree to which a particular stressor upsets the relationship will vary between decision makers according to such factors as socio-economic status, stage in the life/family cycle, experience, and personality. Also, each individual will have a threshold of aspiration level that adjusts on the basis of these factors, thus

276

giving rise to different levels of tolerance to stress. If a stressor leads to perception of dissatisfaction, then the first decision response will have been made, and this may take one of three forms, namely

(a) to modify aspirations and adjust in situ leading to a decision to stay
(b) to modify achievement in situ leading to a decision to stay
(c) to start looking for a new location because of a feeling that only by moving will the decision maker restore equilibrium between achievement and aspirations.

If alternative (c) above is followed, a tentative decision to relocate is taken; dwelling and location specific requirements (i.e., aspirations) are formulated; and the **search process** begins. The **search process** involves information gathering during which time the achievement region is conceptualised. Brown and Moore (1970: 6) refer to a number of crucial elements which may be identified in a search situation, namely:

(a) information available to the searcher which will be biased because of selectivity
(b) information possessed initially by the searcher which will foster more awareness of space in some locations than others
(c) the manner in which a searcher utilises information which determines the way aspirations are built up, perception of the degree of congruence between achievement and aspirations, and will affect the probability of success in finding a suitable locations
(d) time is a stress factor encouraging search behaviour and exists as a variable in the learning process.

Following the gathering of information, there occurs a review of aspirations based on what has been learned. At this stage, the decision maker has one of three choices:

(a) stay put
(b) modify his aspirations but decide to move
(c) move without modifying his aspirations.

A **mover** will be distinguished from a stayer by the congruence of a greater overlap between achievements and aspirations, whereas a stayer needs to review his aspirations to bring them into congruence with his achievements.

Those who decide to move choose a new location on the basis of their search data and with reference to their aspirations. The move is made and the cycle is completed, i.e. achievements are back in congruence with aspirations.

It is evident from the above that this approach to studying the residential migration decision process identifies three important phenomena:

(a) the aspirations of people, including consumer preferences for housing and urban locational environments and achievement levels
(b) the nature of stressors
(c) search behaviour.

The characteristics of these phenomena are discussed at length in Chapter 12. Intra-urban migration is thus seen as being dependent upon the ways in which the decision maker uses environmental information and how he/she reacts to stressors in searching space to choose between locational alternatives that have place utility. Thus, the process is linked in an important way to the cognitive mapping process and the cognitive maps of individuals. As Brown and Moore (1970: 1) explain,

"If the place utility of the present residential site diverges sufficiently from his immediate needs, the individual will consider seeking a new location. The resulting search for and evaluation of dwelling opportunities takes place within the confines of the intended migrant's action space."

In this context, **place utility** is a measure of the overall attractiveness or unattractiveness of the location, relative to alternative locations, as perceived by the decision-maker.

11.4 DECISION-MAKING AND SEARCH PROBABILITY MODELING APPROACHES: RECENT DEVELOPMENTS

Much of the research on intra-urban migration has been conducted within the general framework of the behavioural model discussed above. While seeking to throw light on the processes involved in the residential location decision, the actual decision-making aspects of mobility and the spatial implications of these decisions are not as well specified as the reasons for the move and the characteristics of the search. Thus, Smith et al. (1979: 5) claim that:

"an adequate formal analysis of the decision-making process that both relates to individual behaviour and is operational is not available. In fact, a fairly thorough literative search has revealed no papers relating actual household search behaviour to an expected utility/Bayesian theoretical framework, in which the importance of uncertainty and attitudes to risk enter in significant components".

In a series of papers, Smith, et al. (1979), and Clark and Smith (1979; 1980) attempted to redress this deficiency. The housing market is a good example of a decision-making situation where there are several quite distinct channels of information and where a great deal of resources are spent on the acquisition of information, much of it spatial. Thus, the residential choice process involves three sets of factors (Smith, et al. 1979: 5):

"the characteristics of the prospective migrant that affect the evaluation and choice of a new residence; the structure of the housing market; and the interaction between the migrant and the market."

The decisions about the use of information sources available about the housing market depend on the individual's cognitive model of the environment which will be modified during the search process. The search takes place within the constraints of time, resources available for obtaining information, the individual's ability to perceive and process information, and economic enabling factors (Smith and Clark, 1980: 100-101). So far, this is no real departure from the variables identified in the process modelling approaches discussed previously. However, the divergence is that the emphasis is on the individual's perceptions of the decision-making environment and the temporal-spatial distribution of vacancies by type and price, the types of information sources available and used, and the perceived costs of using these information sources on the spatial and temporal efficiencies of search and on the sequential structure of the search process.

Before going on to describe the model thus proposed, a word on information sources.

11.4.1 Information Source

The **information** that may modify the space preference and the cognitive map of an individual during the residential search process may come from a variety of sources, such as newspaper listings, multiple listing services (MLS), estate agents, friends and relatives, driving, walking around, and encountering vacancies. These are in addition to existing knowledge of the market. Information obtained from such sources needs to be "integrated into the individual's cognitive model" and this will "depend on the cost and reliability of messages from these sources" (Smith and Clark, 1980: 103). Generally, the empirical studies conducted in North American cities have shown that information sources used include newspapers, walking or driving around, friends and relatives, and estate agents. However, there is a high degree of variability in the **usage rate** (percentage of searches using each source) and the **location rate** (percentage of searches locating an acceptable vacancy with the source). Clark and Smith (1979) have demonstrated that, using simulation techniques, cost variations led to distinct patterns of information channel use, while search was dominated by the cost of obtaining general market information.

The role of estate agents as information channels in search behaviour is particularly interesting because of their widespread use. Palm (1976) demonstrated in studies of realtors as information mediators in San Francisco and Minneapolis that:

(a) "companies cover limited portions of the housing market in both price and area, and no single company can claim to cover the entire market in either city"

(b) "the overall evaluations of real estate salesmen in both areas are generally in accord with the distribution of houses listed for sale, or concentrations of persons in corresponding income and occupational class"

(c) "individual salesmen show great variation in their evaluations of communities most 'appropriate' for certain types of home buyers. There is a spatial regularity in this pattern: salesmen tend to over-recommend areas in which they work, in which they list houses, and with which they are particularly familiar." (Palm, 1976: 38)

Palm concludes categorically that searchers who depend heavily on estate companies and agents are thus making use of a highly structured information source.

The Residential Location Decision Process

11.4.2 A Decision and Search Model

The decision-making and search model proposed by Smith, et al., is presented in the schematic diagram in Figure 11.6.

Figure 11.6

Schematic Diagram of a Decision-Making and Search Model

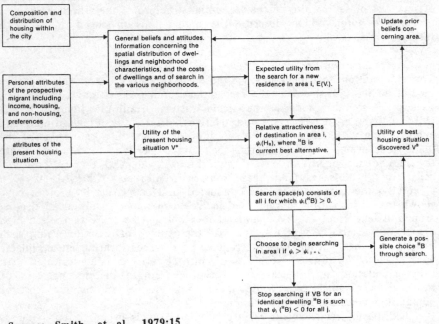

Source: Smith, et al., 1979:15

It has been described by these authors as follows (Smith, et. al, 1979: 6-8):

(a) A **household has a set of preferences** for housing and non-housing commodities. There is an **income constraint**. The household has certain **beliefs** about the housing market. These affect attitude to risk and restrict the increase of choice between alternatives generated in the search for housing.

(b) The **housing market consists of sets of vacancies**, each with a cost and a complex set of housing and neighbourhood characteristics. There are, however, distinct sub-markets.

(c) The household makes decisions under very **uncertain conditions** and **imperfect knowledge**, and this may be modelled in terms of information probability distributions. The **search process** generates **potential choices** and provides **additional information** about the housing market which is used to update the household's assessment of the housing opportunities relative to the vacancy set in each location. In this way a decision can be made whether to continue looking in an area, whether to look elsewhere, or whether to stop searching and choose the best alternative seen thus far.

(d) Spatial choice of area(s) in which to search is on the basis of first **known**, and later **acquired**, information about an area's spatial characteristics, its relationship to the household's activity space, and its preference surfaces. It will also be influenced by the role of **information mediators**.

(e) Rules are specified for interaction between the potential migrant household and the market. We assume that:

    (i) **Preference and risk aversion can be represented as a cardinal utility function**; in facing certain outcomes, the household will maximise expected utility subject to constraints; and expected utility is taken with respect to the probability distribution representing the household's beliefs.

    (ii) **The household is able to compare the expected utility of a situation involving search with the utility of a situation without search.** The expected utility attached to the search for a dwelling is based on the household's prior estimates for housing characteristics in the area (e.g., price, lot size, number of bedrooms, etc.) and the expected costs of search in that area. On the positive side, there is the chance of finding a better dwelling and/or improving information about the market; on the negative side, there is the cost of search, both in time lost and the possibility of losing a vacancy to another bidder. The difference between the expected utility of an area and the present utility is taken as a measure of locational stress. An operational form of the stress criterion can be taken from the position of a household on no-utility lines with respect to quantity of housing and cost of housing.

(f) If a set of neighbourhoods is formed with positive locational stress, **a decision must be made as to the best allocation among the various areas.** This is done by comparing expected utility with actual utility of the present situation within every neighbourhood, and the choice is made on the basis of highest degree of positive stress.

(g) **If a search is commenced, the information obtained from any neighbourhood is used to reverse prior beliefs concerning the market,** since the household may or may not find a house giving rise to higher utility, and may or may not lose a previously considered prospect to another bidder in the market. Such factors will influence the **expected utility** of future search, both in the last area searched and in other areas of the search space. Households may desire to search again, either in the area or another area(s), and as a result may bid on a vacancy, may end search and remain in situ, or it may search even further.

(h) **The manner in which vacancies are selected is important for inspection in the area giving rise to the highest stress.** It may be chosen at random from the total list of vacancies known. The usual case, however, is that the selection of a vacancy to inspect precedes the journey to view the vacancy, and the choice of vacancies to be inspected is taken from a filtered set via the aid of a estate agent.

Figure 11.7

**An Iso-Utility Indifference Approach to Satisfactory Selection of a
Residential House Site and Type**

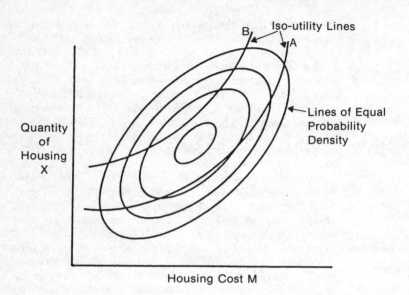

Smith, et al. (1979) have given a formal mathematical presentation of
this **sequential choice model** and have been able to derive estimates of the
parameters that can now be tested in an empirical setting. Certainly, this
modelling approach has considerable potential in predicting household
residential choice and search behaviour. It is based on satisficing behaviour.
It incorporates the concept of stress, or relative attractiveness, with positive
stress leading to search; search can be terminated at any time; bidding may
occur at any time; thus, the decision to search and the search process are not
separated. The model is based on search at any time; search and stress being
related to the relative position of specific neighbourhoods in the location
preference set of households. Because the model defines further search as a
conditional probability, stress and further search can be related (Figure 11.7).
Because the stress criterion is derived from the household utility function,
housing characteristics such as quantity (X) and cost (M) are the axes in the
graph. The satisficing level of utility is the curve in the plane X-M. A and
B are **iso-utility lines,** or household indifference curves. The graph further
shows lines of equal probability density. Any vacancy to the right of the X-
M plane area is satisfactory. If stress increases, then the indifference curve
representing the set of "reservation" houses shifts in the space of housing
properties (X and M), but the actual distinction of houses does not change.
Thus, according to Smith, et al. (1979: 20), the probability of finding a
better house than the reservation house changes, and the probability of

further search increases if the stress increases. Thus anything that increases stress increases the probability of further search.

Search probabilities may be related to all the household attributes and market forces. Such a model should enable planners to find out where certain types of households will be likely to search for housing and where they are likely to relocate. In this way, it may be possible to predict the nature of population redistributions in a city and the spatial requirements for supply of different housing sub-market dwelling stocks.

Chapter Twelve

RESIDENTIAL ASPIRATIONS, STRESSORS AND SEARCH BEHAVIOUR

In this chapter attention is focused on those phenomena that form compounds of the behavioural process model of residential location that was outlined in Chapter 11. This involves considering residential aspirations, preferences and achievement levels; the nature of stressors and level of residential satisfaction; and residential relocation and search behaviour. All are aspects of the **residential location decision process** that have been widely researched by behavioural geographers. Details of empirical studies in the USA and Australia are presented to illustrate the characteristics of these phenomena.

12.1. ASPIRATIONS, PREFERENCES AND ACHIEVEMENT LEVEL

Research on **residential aspirations** is fragmented, but results seem to suggest that social variables in the urban environment are important. For example, Beshers (1962) noted social rank or status as important; Bell (1965) referred to lifestyle factors; stage in the life and family cycle were emphasised by Pickvance (1973); and Selye, et al. (1956) highlighted value orientation. Figure 12.1 illustrates the factors that seem to be relevant in a **causal model of residential mobility**. It has been a difficult task to quantify attributes that measure preferences for housing types and residential locations. As Brown and Moore have indicated,

> "the urban population is differentiated on social, economic, and locational dimensions according to different sets of environmental needs. This differentiation is also directly applicable to the definition of systematic differences between the aspiration regions of intended migrants. In applying such differentiation to the search and evaluation phase, however, a comparable vector describing vacancy characteristics is needed, together with an understanding of the way in which the subjective aspiration levels of the intended migrant relate to objective measures of vacancy characteristics. Systematic distortions in migrant perceptions may be identified by establishing functional relationships between migrant aspirations and vacancy characteristics needed for each of the basis dimensions or the aspiration region or the variables basic to the migrant's evaluation procedures". (Brown and Moore, 1970: 10)

Despite considerable empirical investigation, relatively little progress has been made towards the development of a comprehensive explanatory model of residential mobility.

Figure 12.1

A Causal Model of Residential Mobility

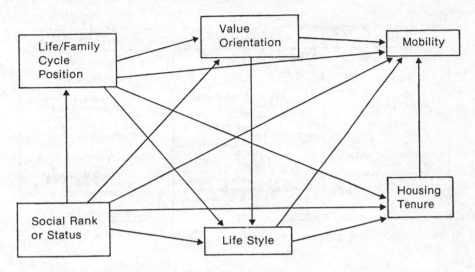

Source: After Pickvance, 1973:281

While residential mobility is seen to be triggered by discontent with the present residential location or dwelling, it is, as Boyce (1969: 2) notes, highly voluntary. Researchers tended to look for push and pull factors. Ermuth (1974: 3-4) asked these questions:

"Are social factors of the environment more important than physical or aesthetic factors? Do households in different subareas of the metropolitan area view housing quality and the social life of a community differently? How important are spatial factors, such as accessibility considerations and relative location of the subareas within the whole urban area? Also, to what extent do households trade off and substitute one factor for another?"

12.1.1 Why Families Move: Rossi's Classic Study

The classic work in this area is Rossi's book *Why Families Move* (1955). He investigated the high rate of residential mobility in the United States because it was one of the most important forces underlying change in urban areas. He posed questions on the mobility of different types of families and on the motivations underlying residential shifts. It was the first noteworthy major use of the social survey, employing modern social research methods in the study of residential mobility and choice. The focus was on residential relocation and the study provided important insights into and empirical evidence on housing preferences in terms of the characteristics of the dwelling type and its immediate social and economic environment. Rossi compiled a mobility potential index and a complaints index and proposed the accounting schema for moving decisions shown in Table 12.1. It was shown

Table 12.1

Rossi's Accounting Schema for Moving Decisions

Stage I	Stage II	Stage III

The decision to move
 	
REASONS FOR LEAVING
 	
A. Decision forced by outside circumstances (2/5 households)
  - reasons e.g. job
  - change in marital status
  - home destruction
 	
B. Decision made voluntarily (3/5 households)
  - because of dissatisfaction with old place
  - space complaints generally
	The search for a new place
	
	A. Channels of information employed
	
	a) formal - papers
	          - real estate agents
	b) informal- friends
	          - on actual and prospective vacancies
	
	B. Specifications (features desired in new home)
	  - most families looking for particualr kinds of dwellings, i.e., particular size and features
		The choice among alternatives
		
		REASONS FOR CHOICE
		
		A. Only 1 opportunity offered
		  - reasons presumed to be identical with specificatons (1/2 households)
		  - clinching factors
		
		B. Several opportunities offered
		  - choice made because of comparative attractions of alternatives
		  - generally took lower cost place

Source: After Rossi, 1955:174

how the position of the household in the family life cycle and its members' attitudes towards the home and residential neighbourhood were important predictors of the household's current desires for moving. Rossi (1955: 9) concluded that his findings

"indicate the major function of mobility to be the process by which families adjust their housing to the housing needs that are generated by shifts in family composition that accompany life cycle changes".

12.1.2 Preference and Desirability Studies
Other important works followed, but not until the 1960s. Various approaches were adopted. For example, Wilson (1962) studied livability factors in cities. Hoinville (1971) attempted to derive measures of value of residential amenity loss or gain arising from planning decisions in a trade-off situation. The Highway Research Board in the United States (H.R.B., 1969) provided data for 43 cities across the country on national housing and environmental preferences. Michelson (1966) looked at value orientation of people and the nature and extent of social interactions. A further study by Peterson (1967) employed colour photographs of neighbourhoods to stimulate visual appearance, hypothesising that residential desirability is a multidimensional phenomena that could be simplied by an orthogonal model of preferences. He found that the most significant dimensions were general physical quality and cultural conditions.

A typical study incorporating more specific locational variables in the analysis of residential environmental preferences and choice is that by Menchik (1972). He employed a regression model to look at first and second order preference choice for individuals and groups using sets of variables relating to the beauty of the natural and built environments, accessibility, characteristics of house and lot, and familiarity attributes of the residential environment. Table 12.2 lists the variables and the percentage of respondents. He suggested that preferences represented trade-offs among these attributes and that comparable measures could be derived for people's present residences, which reflects their actual choices. He found that preferences do express themselves to some extent through market choice and that different people prefer different residential characteristics.

Table 12.2
Selected Considerations in Choice of a Place to Live

Preference Variable		Number of Respondents	Percentage of Respondents
	Natural environmental beauty		
P_n	1 Ruralness, woodsiness, country-like character of the area	103	22.9
	2 Other specific considerations referring to natural environment: climate, weather, topography, etc.	46	10.2
	Man-made or non-natural environment		
	Density: presence and number of persons in the vicinity, in general, without reference to any of their characteristics		
	4 Good: wanted to be near people	6	1.3
P_c	5 Bad: did not want to be near (too many) other people	44	9.8
	Characteristics of people nearby		
	6 Good: wanted to be near a particular kind of person, near my kind of person, etc.	78	17.4
	7 Bad: do not want to live near some stated kind of person, disrespectful, unfriendly, etc.	16	3.6
	Presence of traffic and other non-residential land use		
	8 Good: wanted to live near a store, etc.	4	0.9
	9 Bad: did not want stores, factories, etc., wanted purely residential area, little traffic	21	4.7
	10 Other considerations referring to the non-natural environment: nice neighbourhood, good section of town, quiet, noise, privacy, well-paved streets, etc.	87	19.4
	Accessibility		
P_w	11 To work	63	14.0
	12 To schools	73	16.3
	13 To churches	46	10.2
	14 To transportation facilities	45	10.0
	15 To shopping	69	15.4
	16 To other specified activity or convenience	70	15.6
	Characteristics of house and lot		
	17 House size, number of rooms, size of rooms	112	24.9
	18 Price of house and land, purchasing or renting arrangements, mortgage, etc.	54	12.0
	19 House design characteristics, room layout, heating, plumbing, etc.	189	42.1
P_l	20 Lot size	94	20.9
	21 Other natural environment lot characteristics: stream in backyard, soil, landscaping, etc., lot itself, not vicinity	39	8.7
	22 Other non-natural environment lot characteristics: distance from road, sewage facilities, orientation, etc.	30	6.7

Source: After Menchik, 1972

In a detailed study of residential satisfaction and environmental preferences in the American city of Des Moines, Iowa, Ermuth (1974) set out to test the premise that the satisfaction of a household with the housing it chose and currently occupied, could be used to make statements about housing preferences, and that

"the ex post facto housing choice behaviour of the household therefore is conceptualised as being based on a revealed subjective preference scaling of all possible housing and residential environment opportunities. Given a particular housing choice of a household, these preferences are assumed to be a function of his perception and evaluation of relevant urban and environmental characteristics" (Ermuth, 1974: 15).

He found that people react to environmental stimuli on the basis of their internalised organisation of events, (their cognitive map) and that a variety of judgmental phenomena can be related to how cognitive maps are used. Preference judgments, therefore, can be meaningfully represented as transformations of the respondent's cognitive maps.

A selection of case studies will illustrate the specific nature of residential space preference and aspirations.

12.1.3 A Case Study of Residential Space Preferences and Aspirations in Adelaide, Australia

The nature of residential space preferences in the Australian city of Adelaide were studied by Stimson (1978), using a questionnaire survey over a sample of 727 individuals at a 130 locations. A cluster probability sample design was used. Respondents were asked to rate on a 5-point scale the level of residential desirability of 100 suburbs scattered throughout the metropolitan area. Figure 12.2 shows the aggregate residential desirability surface of Adelaide suburbs. It is evident that the most highly desirable suburbs are located mainly to the east of the city around Beaumont, in the south, around the foothills and the coastal areas and those inner city areas around North Adelaide and Walkerville. In contrast, the old industrial suburbs in the inner city, particularly in the west, the north-western and south-western sectors, and the northern and north-eastern fringe areas, had the lowest ranking residential space preferences.

It is interesting to note that there was a high correlation (Kendall's tau = +.895) between the rank order of average scores of suburbs on this residential desirability scale and the scores respondents gave to the same suburbs on a residential social status or social standing scale. Thus, there appears to be a high degree of relationship between people's perceptions of social status of suburbs and their expressed residential space preferences. However, the strength of this relationship varied considerably between different sub-groups of the population. Similarly, there were variations in the residential space preferences various population sub-groups exhibited for Adelaide suburbs. For example, higher status occupation groups and higher income groups had above average degrees of congruence on their social status and residential desirability space preferences. This was considerably less for the lower status occupation groups and low income groups which had below average degrees of congruence. There was little relative variation from the average degree of congruence for birthplace groups, except that

Figure 12.2

Residential Space Preference Surface of Residents of Adelaide

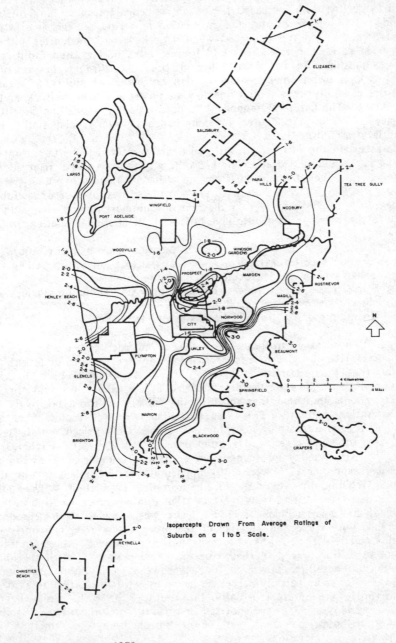

Isopercepts Drawn From Average Ratings of
Suburbs on a 1 to 5 Scale.

Source: Stimson, 1978

southern European migrants showed a very low degree of congruence. Those born outside Adelaide but within Australia, and European-born had highest degrees of congruence between their social status and residential desirability space preferences. The degree of congruence between these two scales tended to decline with increased period of residence for those born outside Adelaide. This was true and also in relation to period of residence in the present dwelling, but this occurred when a peak was reached after a three year period of residence. This could be indicative of increased familiarity with locations due to the progression of time and through the learning process, which means that people develop an increased ability to clearly depict the generally known high and low status areas within their expanded action space. The nature of tenancy of a person's current dwelling had little influence at all on the degree of congruence between social status and residential desirability scales.

To ascertain the factors Adelaide residents perceived to be important in selecting a residential location and dwelling, Stimson asked respondents whether or not they thought 20 items in a list of factors hypothesised as affecting residential location choice were considered desirable or undesirable. The degree to which they were important or unimportant was also gauged. The 20 factors were grouped into five broad sets of attributes relating to:

(a) location specific attributes related to action space and proximity
(b) location specific attributes related to the location of an area in the urban system and its residential environment
(c) location specific attributes related to provision of public services
(d) socio-economic status attributes
(e) dwelling specific attributes and site characteristics.

Respondents were asked to indicate whether or not each of the 20 attributes within these five broad sets appeared negatively (i.e. it was undesirable), positively (i.e. it was desirable) or not at all (i.e. it was indifferent) in their aspiration regions. The results are given in Figure 12.3. It would appear that respondents indicated that most of the factors appeared positively in their aspiration regions. This was particularly so for factors such as provision of public transport, sewerage, dwelling being priced within their means, low rates and taxes, and a quiet location with privacy. High resale value, well established area, an elevated or hills location, and proximity to schools and supermarkets were also important positive attributes in the aspiration regions of over 60% of the sampled population. The only attributes that figured negatively were location in a new area, location near a main road, and a large block of land. There was relatively high degree of indifference with respect to prestige of the area, a new area, proximity to recreational activities, and proximity to friends and relatives. These findings were not surprising, except perhaps for the location specific attributes that deal with public service provision, namely sewerage and public transport, which were almost universally perceived as being extreme positive attributes. The proximity attributes, especially the journey to work, while being important and positive, were not an overriding consideration. Socio-economic attributes, particularly those of an enabling-type, emerged as strong positive considerations.

Figure 12.3

Rating of Attributes in the Residential Aspiration Region
of Adelaide Residents

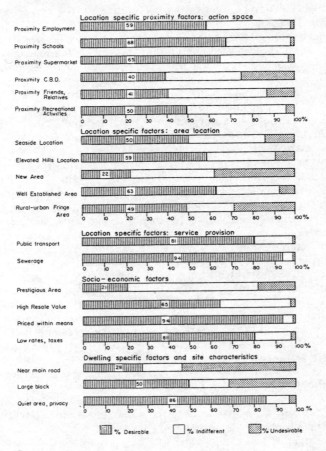

Source: Stimson, 1978

Respondents were then asked to give importance ratings to each of the attributes, depending on whether they figured positively or negatively in the aspiration region. Thus, it was possible to compile a composite 9 point scale with the midpoint represening the indifference position the 4 points to the left represented the degree of negative or undesirable occurrence, and the 4 points to the right representing the degree of positive or desirable occurrence of each attribute. The most important positive considerations in the aspiration regions of Adelaide people were mains sewerage, the dwelling being priced within means, quiet area and privacy, public transport, low rates and taxes, high resale value, proximity to supermarket, proximity to schools, well established area, and proximity to employment. The only attribute that was seen as being a negative consideration in the aspiration region was nearness to a main road. However, a number of other factors emerged as playing no apparent positive or negative role in the aspiration region These were prestige of an area, proximity to friends and relatives, newness of the area, proximity to recreational facilities, and a seaside location.

There were major between-group differences in the perceived directions and degree of importance of these 20 factors in the aspiration region. It was found that there were significant differences between sub-groups differentiated on the basis of relationship to head of household with respect to proximity to schools and supermarket, elevated and hills location, new areas, well established areas, sewered areas, high resale value, nearness to main road, large block, quiet and privacy. There were significant differences between people who had been resident various periods of time at their present location with respect to seaside location, rural urban fringe area, public transport, sewered area, high resale value, low rates and taxes, nearness to main road, and a large block of land. There were significant differences between various birthplace groups with respect to seaside location, rural urban fringe area, high resale value and large block. Significant differences between tenancy of present dwelling type occurred with respect to proximity to schools, supermarkets, seaside location, new area, well-established area, sewered area, prestige area, high resale value, dwelling price within means, large block and quiet area and privacy. Occupational status groups displayed significant differences for proximity to employment, schools and supermarkets, seaside location, elevated and hills area, new area, well-established area, rural urban fringe area, sewered areas, high resale value, nearness to main roads and large block. Sub-groups differentiated on the basis of the occupation category of their present jobs displayed significant differences for proximity to supermarkets and friends and relatives, sewered areas, prestige area, and low rates and taxes. The two sexes had differences with respect to proximity to supermarkets, well-established areas, rural urban fringe areas, public transport provision, prestigious areas, high resale value, low rates and taxes, nearness to main roads, large block, quiet and privacy.

From this study of residential aspirations of Adelaide residents it was concluded that it is a particularly complex phenomena, that the most important considerations are:

(a) proximity to convenient shopping and transport
(b) the newness of a residential area
(c) access to the CBD
(d) prestige and status of a residential area
(e) convenience and facilities for children
(f) the price of an area and the provision of sewerage.

Thus, proximity to elements in household activity spaces, community facilities, socio-economic status, life/family cycle stage, and environmental factors are shown to be important attributes in the aspiration region of Adelaide residents. This is similar to findings of other empirical studies. Also, sub-groups of the population differentiated on the basis of factors related to socio-economic status, stage in life/family cycle, and social area type of present residential location displayed differences in their assessments of the direction and degree of importance of the 20 specific attributes. Furthermore, it was clearly demonstrated that there were differences in the occurrence of many of these attributes and the aspirations of people differentiated on the basis of the socio-economic quintile group in which their present residences were located and in the search field that was covered during the last residential location decision process.

It would seem that residential preferences are strongly influenced by factors such as socio-economic status and stage in the life/family cycle. It also appears that people are constrained by economic considerations such as income and likelihood of gaining access to housing finance, plus individual taste and preferences, when forming their aspiration regions and in assessing the residential desirability of specific locations in a city.

12.1.4 Evaluative Dimensions Used to Rate Neighbourhoods in Madison, Wisconsin

In a rather different study, Cadwallader (1979) sought to investigate the dimensions used by a sample of 148 residents in Madison, Wisconsin, to rate eight neighbourhoods (containing about 10 city blocks of single family dwelling units) on eleven semantic differential scales (see Table 12.4). The hypothesis was that households rate neighbourhoods on the basis of three evaluative dimensions:

(a) the impersonal environment, comprised mainly of physical attributes of the neighbourhood
(b) the interpersonal environment, comprised mainly of the social attributes of the neighbourhood
(c) the locational attributes of the neighbourhood.

An earlier study of Christchurch, New Zealand, by Johnston (1973) had suggested that neighbourhood preferences could be understood by these evaluative dimensions.

Data derived from a 148 x 11 data matrix for each of the eight Madison neighbourhoods was examined using principal components analysis. Results showed that in almost every case the percentage of total variance explained by these three components was fairly low, suggesting that the eleven scales were not easily collapsed into underlying dimensions. In analysing the structure of these components for each of the eight neighbourhoods, it was found that for four of the neighbourhoods, the highest loadings for quiet and privacy were on the same component, and for four of the eight neighbourhoods, the highest loadings for quiet and spaciousness were on the same component. Elementary linkage analysis was used to uncover the major groupings among the variables. The two major groupings to emerge were:

(1) scales representing spaciousness, housing quality, distinctiveness, quiet and privacy
(2) scales representing neighbourhood reputation, yard upkeep, safety, type of people and park facilities.

The location variable was not indicated in either of these typical structures. Cadwallader (1979:379) noted that:

"in general, then, these variable, or scale, groupings are of great interest, as they can be conveniently categorised as representing physical characteristics, social characteristics, and location. As such they are encouragingly similar to the three evaluative dimensions postulated by Johnston." (in his study of Christchurch)

However, the factor structures associated with each of the eight Madison neighbourhoods was far from identical, (see Table 12.3a). Thus, further analysis was conducted to test for perceived similarity between the neighbourhoods, as measured by a similarity rating in which respondents were asked to identify, for each neighbourhood, three others they regarded as being most similar. It was shown that neighbourhoods perceived to be similar were cognised in terms of similar dimensions (see Table 12.3b). Thus, while evaluative dimensions are not the same for all neighbourhoods, people tend to use similar dimensions when evaluating similar neighbourhoods. Cadwallader went on to examine the relative importance of the neighbourhood attributes. People were asked to rate attributes on a 7 point scale from unimportant to important, and the mean values and standard deviations are given in Table 12.3c. Attributes of location and housing quality were considered very important, while type of people living in the neighbourhood was less important (note that Madison does not have marked racial segregation areas). The spaciousness scale was also relatively important.

Finally, Cadwallader used stepwise regression analysis to determine whether the attribute ratings remained constant across neighbourhoods. The dependent variable was the overall rating of the neighbourhood and the eleven attribute scale ratings were the independent variables. The results are given in Table 12.3d in terms of standardised regression coefficients. These reflect the relative importance of the variables in terms of determining the preference ratings. The distinctiveness attribute is more common in the regression equations than all other attributes, which was not an attribute that obtained a high ranking previously. Thus, it would seem that the weights associated with the attributes responsible for determining neighbourhood preference patterns are not invariant across different neighbourhoods.

12.1.5 Summarising the Findings

In summarising the findings of studies concerning residential space preferences and aspirations, recurrent themes occur. Determining the selection of a new residential location and choice of dwelling involves attributes that are surrogates for accessibility factors with respect to:

(a) locations of functions that are important in household activity spaces
(b) physical environmental and aesthetic qualities of the neighbourhood
(c) community services and facilities
(d) social environment factors such as prestige, socio-economic status and ethnicity
(e) stage in the life/family cycle as it relates to housing needs

Table 12.3

Neighbourhood Evaluation in Madison, Wisconsin

A. Associations between neighbourhood attitudes

		1	2	3	4	5	6	7	8	9	10	11
1	Spaciousness	-										
2	Yard upkeep	4	-									
3	Privacy	3	2	-								
4	Reputation	2	6	3	-							
5	Housing	8	4	3	2	-						
6	Quiet	5	3	4	3	5	-					
7	People	0	3	0	4	0	0	-				
8	Safety	4	5	2	4	4	4	2	-			
9	Location	0	1	3	2	0	2	2	1	-		
10	Park facilities	1	2	3	4	1	1	4	1	3	-	
11	Distinctiveness	5	2	2	1	5	4	0	3	3	0	-

B. Matrix of similarity ratings (above diagonal)
and congruency coefficients (below diagonal)

		1	2	3	4	5	6	7	8
1	Middleton	-	0•01	0•18	0•19	0•02	0•03	0•02	0•22
2	Maple Bluff	0•77	-	0•06	0•02	0•41	0•05	0•35	0•02
3	Indian Hills	0•91	0•88	-	0•16	0•09	0•20	0•07	0•23
4	Hilldale	0•74	0•87	0•82	-	0•06	0•15	0•09	0•29
5	Shorewood	0•86	0•91	0•92	0•85	-	0•04	0•38	0•04
6	Monona	0•88	0•89	0•86	0•84	0•84	-	0•05	0•20
7	Nakoma	0•83	0•94	0•94	0•78	0•90	0•92	-	0•10
8	Odana	0•68	0•55	0•67	0•76	0•59	0•53	0•58	-

C. Relative importance of neighbourhood attitudes

		Mean	Standard Deviation
1	Location	6•12	1•31
2	Housing	6•06	1•21
3	Safety	6•02	1•45
4	Noise	5•94	1•41
5	Privacy	5•67	1•54
6	People	5•55	1•45
7	Spaciousness	5•53	1•44
8	Yard upkeep	5•49	1•45
9	Park facilities	4•87	1•54
10	Reputation	4•82	1•72
11	Distinctiveness	4•41	1•66

D. A step-wise regression model

1 Middleton	$Y = 1•32 + 0•31X_1 - 0•17X_6 + 0•32X_9 + 0•16X_{11}$	$R = 0•51$
2 Maple Bluff	$Y = 1•25 - 0•17X_1 + 0•18X_4 + 0•24X_7 + 0•20X_{11}$	$R = 0•40$
3 Indian Hills	$Y = 0•96 + 0•37X_4 + 0•40X_{10} + 0•19X_{11}$	$R = 0•52$
4 Hilldale	$Y = 0.45 + 0.29X_5 + 0•27X_6 - 0•14X_8 + 0•32X_{11}$	$R = 0•66$
5 Shorewood	$Y = 1.56 + 0•15X_1 + 0.15X_2 + 0•28X_7$	$R = 0•40$
6 Monona	$Y = 2.76 - 0•18X_2 - 0•27X_3 + 0•24X_4 + 0•36X_{11}$	$R = 0•45$
7 Nakoma	$Y = 2.65 - 0•32X_2 + 0•39X_4 + 0•30X_7 + 0•17X_{11}$	$R = 0•52$
8 Odana	$Y = 0•14 + 0•28X_1 - 0•18X_2 + 0•28X_7 + 0•17X_8 + 0•17X_{10} + 0•15X_{11}$	$R = 0•51$

Source: After Cadwallader, 1979:397-399

295

    (f)   familiarity with the residential area and individual site and dwelling characteristics.

Newton (1978) has summarised aspirations and locational choice by advancing these four propositions:

    (a)   When changing residence in a city a mover household may choose, or be forced, to live among households with similar social and demographic characteristics to its own.

    (b)   When changing residence with a city a mover household will select an area which contains housing and amenities with the necessary attributes to satisfy its residential needs.

    (c)   When changing residence with a city a mover household will relocate in that part of the city which meets its accessibility requirements to nodes with which there is frequent, routinised, contact.

    (d)   When changing residence within a city a mover household will be constrained in its residential choice by:
        (i) the availability and/or
        (ii) the cost,
        of various housing bundles located at different points within the city". (Newton, 1978: 33-34)

12.2 STRESSORS AND LEVEL OF RESIDENTIAL SATISFACTION

12.2.1 Stressors Upsetting the Achievement-Aspiration Equilibrium

Residential satisfaction occurs when there is **congruence** between (or greater overlap of) achievement and aspiration (Brown and Moore, 1970). **Residential search** is a decision, be it tentative or otherwise, to relocate, and occurs in response to some stressor which upsets this equilibrium. It was shown in Chapter 11 that stressors may be **internal** or **external** to the household and that they may be **dwelling specific** or **location specific**.

Appley and Trumbell (1967: 10) have suggested that there are **differing thresholds of tolerance to stress**, depending on the kinds of threats that are encountered, and that individuals are differentially vulnerable to different types of stressors. Stress manifests itself as a **stressor** in the behavioural model of residential location decision processes. Rossi (1955) indicated that urban structure itself (manifest through things such as commercial neighbourhood blight, industrial sites, and a change in racial and ethnic composition of a neighbourhood) is an important factor that may influence an individual to seek a new residential location. Rossi, Butler et al. (1969), and Clark (1970) have shown that the evolution of households through the life and family cycle can give rise to stress. Lansing and Hendricks (1967) wrote on the effects of changes in transport technology on accessibility between neighbourhoods as a factor acting as a stressor. Finally, upward socio-economic mobility through change in income and/or job level can lead to change in aspirations that give rise to stressors. It is also likely that overt pressures of advertising may have a similar effect.

Much has been written on the nature of stress in city life, and there is a distinct possibility that some urban social dysfunction and pathologies are spatially correlated with stress indices. Urban stresses have been used to

Table 12.4

Stressors, Stress and Stress Reactions in Los Angeles

Stressor	Processes Stress Measurement	Stress Response

1. Size-facilities of dwelling
2. Access to work
3. Access to friends
4. Kind of people in
   neighbourhood
5. Air pollution (smog)
	Derived from stress model,
	using individual household
	attitude scale on stressors.
	N.B. subjectively
	evaluated by households
		a. Desire to move
		b. Actual movement
		c. Modification of dwelling
		d. Public action, e.g.,
		   petition for more services

Source: After Clark and Cadwallader, 1973:35

encompass factors such as noise, pollution, traffic density, crowding, high rise living, and the general complexity of scale of urbanisation. Stress may be seen to manifest itself in the form of detrimental effects to physical and mental health, crime, fear, breakdown of community interaction and cohesiveness, and alienation. However, it is difficult to furnish proof for cause and effect relationships. In general, there is little detailed empirical data available on the nature of stressors as they give rise to residential dissatisfaction and play a role in the residential relocation decision process in cities. Two studies will illustrate the general nature of stressors.

12.2.2 Stressors, Stress and Stress Reactions: A Los Angeles Case Study
If the decision to move is an adjustment to stressors, then it is important to be able to specify their nature. Clark and Cadwallader (1973) looked at five specific stress producing factors which are surrogates for the types of stressor sets that have been discussed and identified by various researchers. Five stressors were identified in relation to stress processes and stress response, as given in Table 12.4 in a study of Santa Monica residents, Los Angeles. The five groupings of stressor factors are interesting, as they relate to the characteristics of the dwelling and life/family cycle stage requirements, social space affinity characteristics of the neighbourhood, proximity factors and environmental factors. If the stress level is high for a household, then there would be a high degree of desired, if not actual, movement to adjust to the stress level. In the Santa Monica study, Clark and Cadwallader found a significant correlation between the desire to move and locational stress. The greater the household level of stress, the greater the potential mobility exhibited by the household. They claim that:

"there is a need to specifically introduce elements of the urban spatial structure, such as the nature of the local neighbourhood, and to analyse these elements with reference to their stress-producing potential. It is possible that this kind of approach will more directly allow the development of a model in which mobility can be fitted into the context of neighbourhood and community change."

and that:

> "the decision to move can be viewed as being a function both of the household's present level of satisfaction and of the level of satisfaction it believes may be attained elsewhere. The differences between these levels can be viewed as a measure of "stress" created by the present residential location." (Clark and Cadwallader, 1973: 30-31)

While the findings of this study need to be replicated and extended to incorporate a wider range of stressors, and while it is necessary to test the independence of a particular spatial system, the implications are important for planners, in that it may be possible to identify areas of high stress within a city that produces a high degree of desired mobility. Such identification could help show show stress may be overcome to avoid problems such as urban decay.

12.2.3 Stressors and Residential Satisfaction in Two Australian Cities: Adelaide and Sydney

Little empirical data is available for Australian cities on the level of satisfaction or dissatisfaction of people with their residential achievements. This is particularly so for the various sub-sets of the housing market. Some indication as to why people buy or rent a dwelling may be gleaned from an Australian Bureau of Statistics survey of housing occupancy, dwelling characteristics, and residential movement in Sydney, 1976-78. For example, of those who were owner-occupiers, nearly 53% said it gave them a feeling of security, 18% saw ownership as an investment, and 9% thought that it was cheaper to buy than rent. It is interesting, however, to note that of those who had purchased their dwelling before 1960, only 7% saw it as an investment, whereas 61% saw it as giving them a feeling of security. This contrasts with those who had purchased since 1971, of whom 22% saw such a move as an investment and only 48% saw it as giving them a feeling of security. For household heads who were renting their present dwelling, 58% were doing so because they could not afford to buy a house. A further 13% were renting while saving to buy, 7% thought that a renter had greater ease of mobility, about 3% did not want the responsibility of owning, and a further 3% saw renting as being cheaper in the long run. The ABS Sydney survey data does not indicate the degree of satisfaction or dissatisfaction felt by renters and owners.

In the study of Adelaide by Stimson (1978) referred to previously in this chapter, it was found that general levels of satisfaction/dissatisfaction of residents with their residential achievement were such that 38% of people were completely satisfied, 5% were dissatisfied, and 2% were completely dissatisfied with their present residential achievement. Thus, it would seem that a little less than one-third of the people are suffering from, or are highly vulnerable to, a stressor. When the sample was broken down into population sub-groups, significant differences in level of satisfaction/dissatisfaction emerged. For example, multiple head households tended to have high levels of dissatisfaction. The number of years people had been resident at their present location tended to influence level of residential satisfation, the latter increasing with increased period of residence. In general, migrant groups tended to be less satisfied than

Residential Aspirations, Stressors and Search Behaviour

Australian born with their levels of residential satisfaction. Owner-occupiers had considerably greater levels of residential satisfaction than did both private rental tenants and tenants of the Housing Trust, but all groups still had relatively high levels of satisfaction. The higher status occupation groups and the higher income groups had greater levels of satisfacton with residential attainment than did the lower status occupation and lower income groups, although the differences were not statistically significant. There were large and highly significant differences between the various age groups with level of satisfaction tending to increase up to about 40 years of age, after which it declined somewhat to increase again with the older age groups.

It would also be expected that the degree of satisfaction with residential location relates to the spatial and temporal aspects of the search process. For recent movers there is no statistical difference in levels of satisfaction with respect to the number of months spent in the search process and the mean intensity of the search, but there is a statistically significant difference in the level of satisfaction with respect to the mean number of suburbs searched. This tended to peak at around the six suburb level.

Where there is dissatisfaction with present residential location and where there has been residential relocation, a stressor has been at work. The Sydney and Adelaide surveys gave the results listed in Table 12.5 a and b. There is a considerable degree of similarity in the results of the surveys in both cities. For example, the most important single reason to emerge was the desire for people to move into their own home after being a renter (25.5% for Adelaide and 22.1% for Sydney). In Adelaide a change in the location of employment or the increasing difficulty of access to place of work was an important stressor (15.1%), whereas factors relating to inconvenience of work place and job transfer amounted to only 9.6% in Sydney. Marriage was a greater factor in Adelaide (13.5%) than it was in Sydney (6.0%), but the difference in the time of the surveys needs to be taken into account, the Adelaide study having been conducted at the earlier date of 1972. Desire to leave the parental home for greater independence was a more important factor in Sydney (6.8%) compared to Adelaide (4.4%). Dwelling specific factors, particularly relating to the dwelling being too small, were important stressors in both Sydney (10.4%) and Adelaide (10.2%). Expiry of lease or eviction from rental accommodation was more impor.ant in Sydney (9.1%) than it was in Adelaide (4.6%). High cost of rent or mortgage was a more important factor in Sydney (5.9%) than it was in Adelaide (4.4%). However, it would appear from these two detailed studies that in the Australian city common stressors are:

(a) the desire to own one's own home
(b) dwelling specific characteristics such as lack of space
(c) changes in life/family cycle and the related demands for dwelling space and different types of dwelling
(d) expiry of lease of rental accommodation.

Work transfer and problems concerning proximity to place of work seem to be more important in the smaller city than in the larger one. It is interesting to note that environmental factors and amenity factors do not seem to be particularly important as stressors per se.

Table 12.5

Stressors Causing Decision to Relocate Residence in Australian Cities

(a) Sydney

Main reason for move	Household heads who have moved between 1976 and 1978	
	Number ('000)	Proportion (%)
Dwelling		
Too large	6.8	2.0
Too small	35.0	10.4
Poor internal or external conditions	9.6	2.9
Rent or mortgage repayments too high	19.9	5.9
Other aspects associated with dwelling	5.9	1.8
Location of dwelling inconvenient		
To work	16.8	5.0
To relatives and/or friends	3.4	1.0
To schools and/or shops	1.7	0.5
Neighbourhood		
Too much traffic noise	1.7	0.5
Disliked neighbours	7.4	2.2
Other aspects associated with neighbourhood	12.3	3.7
Work		
Job transfer	15.6	4.6
Retirement	3.3	1.0
Family		
To be with relatives	3.8	1.1
To get married	20.3	6.0
To be more independent/leave home	22.9	6.8
Other		
To move into own place	74.5	22.1
Expiration of lease	8.5	2.5
Eviction	22.1	6.6

(b) Adelaide

Stressor	Number	%
1. Desire to own permanent residence	155	25.5
2. Change in location of employment	92	15.1
3. Marriage	82	13.5
4. Place of residence only temporary while looking for permanent dwelling	62	10.2
5. Desire for more room or larger house; desire for less room or smaller house	58	9.5
6. Change in size of family	37	6.1
7. Rental lease expired; evicted	28	4.6
8. Rent/rates too high	27	4.4
9. Left parental home	26	4.3
10. Residence too old	15	2.5

Source: After A.B.S., 1980, Stimson, 1978

The high importance attached to home ownership, and the fact that approximately one-fifth to one-quarter of residential relocations are persons moving from rental accommodation to an owner-occupancy situation, are of particular significance, especially in view of the fact that in recent times (and as far as one can tell, for the foreseeable future) an increasing proportion of young families are finding it difficult to raise the finance to become home owners. Thus, it is possible to infer that rental accommodation per se as a stressor will become one which is increasingly difficult for people to surmount.

12.3 RESIDENTIAL RELOCATION AND SEARCH BEHAVIOUR

12.3.1 Patterns and Biases in Search Behaviour

Residential relocation necessitates the mover searching space to choose between alternative sites and dwellings. Of importance in this process are the information available to the searcher, the initial state of information possessed, and the way information is utilised. Time, too, is an important factor which may act as a constraint. Implicit here is the learning process, which means that search takes place within the action space of households. This again gets us back to the importance of cognitive maps.

Adams (1969) made an important contribution to the literature on residential search by claiming that intra-urban migrations display marked sectoral bias because movers possess a restricted sectoral image of their city. This bias is based on the location of the home sector. He concluded that people interact less often with areas outside this wedge as compared to areas within it (see Figure 12.4). Thus, households would be less likely to choose a residential site outside this home based wedge. Adams further claimed that there would be directional bias in intra-urban migration, because people tend to perceive the quality and/or desirability of housing to upgrade from the centre of the city outwards.

Research by Brown and Holmes (1971) has questioned some of these proposals. They have shown that it is unrealistically restrictive to impose a spatial structure in which the housing market is zonally arranged. Further, perception of the totality of the larger city is difficult, if not impossible, and more friction is likely to exist in cross-town trips than in radial travel. For inner city residents, a more compact familiarity space exhibiting distance bias is likely to exist. Also, there exists among some sub-groups of population high desirability for inner city housing, particularly rental housing. They proposed various types of spatial biases that are typically found in intra-urban migration, with respect to the orientation of the sectors (Figure 12.5).

There is considerable empirical support for the notion of sectoral search and movement. It is, however, important to take into account the internal structure of the city. Poulson (1975: 4) has argued that "the shape of the city or the internal structure of the vacancy set within the city could have resulted in random movements being viewed as sectoral movements". Barrett (1973: 8) similarly suggests that the shape of an urban place will have a marked effect on spatial search behaviour. In an historical study of intra-urban migration in Liverpool, Taylor (1971: 51) found that 60% of move directions could be accounted for by the shape of the city.

Figure 12.4

Sectoral Bias in Residential Relocation

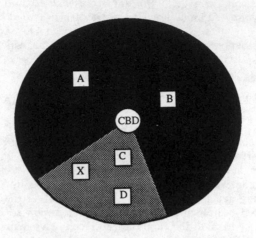

A-D = Shopping centres
X = Home residence
▓▓▓ = Area of greatest familiarity

An individual at point X is more likely to be acquainted with a shopping centre at point D or C than at point A or B.

Source: After Adams, 1969

Various techniques have been put forward whereby spatial search and residential relocation can be measured with respect to directional and **distance biases**.   Barrett (1973) developed a series of indices of search behaviour to investigate residential relocation in Toronto in a spatio-temporal framework. He derived **indices of search intensity, search cluster** and **search concentration**. He found that the behaviour of the majority was to buy a house after a very short search which covered a few houses in a small area. Barrett claimed that data suggests that search behaviour is not a process. He argued that since most people consider buying a home as a major decision, their behaviour is not consistent with the obligations of the decision.   Clearly, house searchers investigate only an incredibly small segment of the vacancy list. This fits in with the finding by Brown and Holmes (1972: 323) that initially **space converging search** occurs, to be followed by **space organising search** when **information feedback** indicates some potential has been found, and when this happens, search becomes highly spatially concentrated such that general probing ceases. This is seen by Brown and Holmes to indicate that men have a tendency to concentrate on found potential to the detriment of discovering or even thinking about remaining untapped potential.

Figure 12.5

Spatial Biases in Intra-Urban Migration

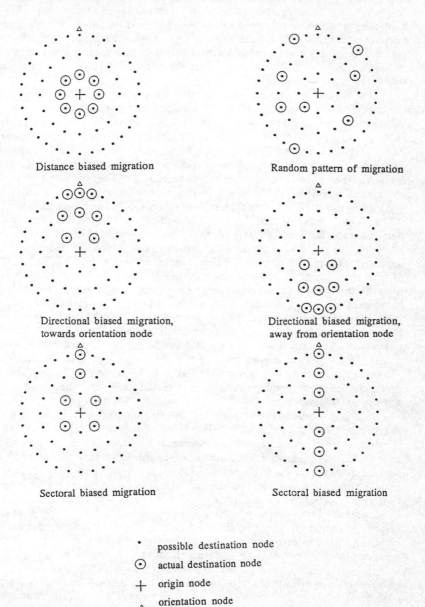

Distance biased migration

Random pattern of migration

Directional biased migration,
towards orientation node

Directional biased migration,
away from orientation node

Sectoral biased migration

Sectoral biased migration

- •   possible destination node
- ⊙   actual destination node
- +   origin node
- △   orientation node

Source: After Brown and Holmes, 1971

12.3.2 Residential Relocation and Search Behaviour in Australian Cities

Much of the work done in Australia reflects the general emphasis on residential structure and the search process. In his study on intra-urban migration and residential structure of Melbourne, Humphreys (1973) found that the predominant pattern of movement was radial from the inner-city suburbs outwards. For people with high socio-economic status, movement tended to occur within well-defined sectors, reinforcing what Hoyt (1937) and Johnston (1966) asserted as a sectoral pattern of residential structure and mobility.

The Australian Bureau of Statistics' survey of residential relocations in Sydney for the period 1976-78 demonstrated that, within the broad subdivisions of Sydney used in the study, there was a tendency for the majority of moves to occur within the same subdivision. For example, in central Sydney nearly 67% of relocations occurred within that subdivision. For inner western Sydney, 47% of relocations were internal. For southern Sydney, 65% of relocations occurred within it. For south-western Sydney the figure was 38%. 53% of relocations occurred within the subdivision for western Sydney, 63% for northern Sydney and 47% for Gosford Wyong.

In his study of residential relocations in Adelaide, Stimson (1978) demonstrated that one-quarter of the total sequences of moves were spatially compact, being confined in and around the place of initial residential location. There was a considerable degree of movement within each sector of the city, mainly outwards towards the fringe (13%), rather than inwards towards the central business district (5%), but it was more common for the movement to be outwards across sectors (17%). However, one-quarter of total relocation sequences were across sectors in the outer zones of the metropolitan area. It should be remembered that metropolitan Adelaide does not possess a spatial form that strictly conforms to either a zonal or a sector model, but is characterised by a spread of settlement from multiple nuclei. However, one can still generalise with a high degree of validity about sectoral biases in total sequences of residential relocations displayed by movers in Adelaide.

If the proposition put forward by Broom and Lancaster (1976) (that there has been a considerable degree of upward social mobility between socio-economic status groups in Australia in recent decades) is valid, then one could expect residential relocations to demonstrate movement from one social status area to a higher one. However, it must be remembered that a significant proportion of residential relocations involve the change from renter to owner status. In addition, it may be related to change in employment, often bringing with it increase in income. Very often it is related to change in stage in life and family cycle. Whatever the cause, it is reasonable to expect that a specific relocation or total sequence of relocations may display a movement of individuals or households through social space, and in particular, show upward socio-economic mobility. It was found that there is only a minute shift in the distribution of people among the quintile categories which depict the socio-economic status of their present suburb of residence in Adelaide. Concerning the total sequence of residential relocations, in only 13% of the cases was it evident that there was a substantial upward socio-economic status shift, and only a further 14% of cases showed any upward socio-economic shift. It was even more likely for some downward socio-economic shift to occur (35% in all), while 38%

displayed no apparent socio-economic status shift. Thus, while these data do not support the contention of upward socio-economic status mobility, expressed in social status space of residential location, the qualification must be made concerning the difficulties involved in accurately describing the socio-economic status rating of each residential location where the time gap involved is quite considerable. Nevertheless, there has not been an apparent large variation over time in the socio-economic status rating of Adelaide suburbs, at least in the last 20 years, except for some gentrification of inner-city suburbs.

A further important aspect of residential relocation is the actual search process, involving both **searching of space**, and **time for search**. For Adelaide residents it was found that for the last residential relocation, a total mean search time was 8.4 months. The distribution is extremely positively skewed, as 10% searched for over 2 years. The modal time (for 29% of cases) was between one and three months, but in fact just over half took less than three months. The search field was quite restricted, with 22% of households searching only one suburb, 19% two suburbs, 25% three suburbs, and 11% four suburbs. Only 3% searched ten or more suburbs. The mean number of suburbs searched was 3.4. Using Barrett's (1976) **index of search intensity**, a mean of 1.45 and a standard deviation of 1.91 revealed a considerable degree of variation between individuals. However, the data are not sufficiently reliable to be conclusive on this point because of the ex post facto problem. Furthermore, an attempt was made to arrive at a general description of the spatial dimensions of the search field and the degree of directional bias involved in relocation. There would appear to be two predominant search fields. Two-fifths of households restricted their search to the suburb in which their present dwelling was located, or to those suburbs adjacent to it, thus indicating a very compact search field. One-third of households had **search fields** not readily definable or tightly biased in a directional sense. Marked sectoral bias occurred in the search field of a further one-fifth of households, and in only 6% of cases was it linear or elongated across sectors. It is also evident that the relocation was either one that involved a small spatial shift within the same suburb (10%) or to an adjacent suburb (24%). In one-quarter of moves there was a directional bias within the same sector, with 16% of cases being outwards towards the fringe, compared to 9% of cases being inwards towards the central business district. In a further one-fifth of cases there was cross sectorial bias, but on the same side of the central business district. Moves across sectors and from one side of the inner-city to the other occurred in only 13% of cases. The other types of moves reflect the relatively small number of sampling clusters in the inner-city and the coastal and hills sectors that occur in a metropolitan-wide sample. Spatio-temporal aspects of residential search could be expected to vary between different tenancy groups.

When Stimson focused on recent movers (within the last five years), it was found that 26% were owner-occupancy to owner-occupancy moves, 20% were renter to owner-occupancy moves, 22% were renter to renter moves, and 4% were owner to renter moves. The remainder were a variety of moves between owner, renter, public rental, and parental home moves. The actual movement patterns for the 126 households thus classified as recent movers in Adelaide are shown in Figure 12.6. The patterns display a considerable **degree of directional bias** when broken down into owner-

Figure 12.6

Spatial Patterns of Recent Movers in Adelaide

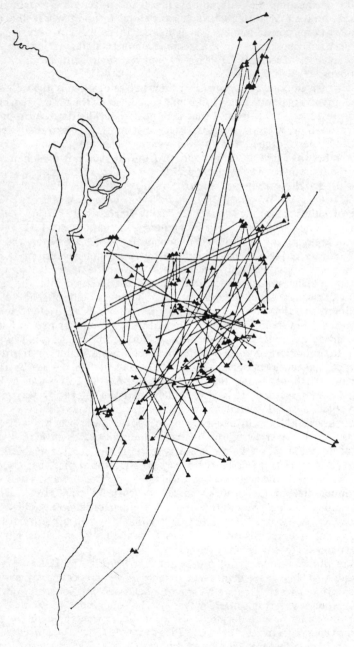

Source: Stimson, 1978

occupier to owner-occupier moves, private rental to owner-occupier moves, and private rental to private rental moves. There were also considerable differences with respect to the various spatial and temporal search statistics obtained. For example, mean search time was 38 weeks for owner-owner moves, 25 weeks for renter-owner moves, and 11.6 weeks for renter-renter moves. The median figures were 12.8 weeks, 4.5 weeks, and 2.3 weeks, respectively. Mean number of suburbs searched was 4.1 for owner-owners, 3.8 for renter-owners, and 2.1 for renter-renters. The approximate median figures were 2.9, 3.6 and 1.4. Various measures of the spatial characteristic of the search field, such as search perimeter, mean search radius, search area shape, and spatio-temporal search index, showed considerable differences between these sub-groups of movers. In particular, the search perimeter was much greater for renter-owner and owner-owner mover groups than it was for renter-renter groups, indicating that those purchasing a dwelling will search an area that is less compact than those searched by renters. To some extent, this is indicative of the high degree of spatial concentration of rental housing stock, particularly flats. Finally, with respect to direction and distance bias, renter-owner mover groups were more likely to move longer distances and across sectors than were the owner-owner and renter-renter groups.

12.3.3 Summary of Findings
On the basis of the many empirical studies referred to above, it would appear that most intra-urban relocations are:

(a) of relatively short distance
(b) they exhibit directional biases
(c) the spatio-temporal characteristics of search will vary among the different tenure subgroups of the housing market.

Poulson (1975: 12) suggests that if it is desirable for both the mover and for urban society as a whole for residential movement to take place within the home sector or close to the previous dwelling, then it is important that there are sufficient vacancy opportunities available within the various residential sectors or areas of the city. Where these vacancies do not exist, then is it desirable to set aside a portion of the vacancy set for intra-urban movers who come from that sector or area, or is it desirable to set aside new housing areas for movers from set sectors and areas of the city? Like many other problems examined in this chapter, this poses a planning problem of interest for applied behavioural geographers.

Chapter Thirteen

BEHAVIOURAL APPROACHES: ALTERNATIVES AND FUTURE
RESEARCH

13.1 INTRODUCTION

Throughout this book we have argued that, among the various approaches to behavioural research in geography, the analytical approach continues to yield the most rewards. We do not deny the existence of other means of conducting behavioural research, we simply prefer to emphasise the **analytical** approach because of the insights and advances it continues to offer.

We have not exhausted the behavioural problems that can be approached analytically. Rather, we have focused on areas that have a relatively substantial literature already in existence and which encourage continuing probing of research frontiers, both in geography and other disciplines. In this final chapter, therefore, some attention will be paid to other approaches, other types of reasoning, and other problem areas.

13.2 ALTERNATIVE EPISTEMOLOGIES AND PROBLEM CONTEXTS

13.2.1 Interactionalist Ideas
The acceptance of an **interactionalist** basis for behavioural research allows the investigation of situations mediating direct relations between person and environment. In other words, while an individual may have a preferred behavioural response to a given situation, the response may be inhibited by the presence of other people or societal or cultural constraints and taboos. Nowhere has this been found more evident than in the growing literature indicating substantial differences between the concepts of preference and choice (Smith, Huff and Shapiro, 1979). Interactional models of person/environment relationships posit that individuals differentially interpret and perceive their environment, and in fact, it may be impossible to separate the environment from the person perceiving it (Bowers, 1978). It also argues that individuals by their overt behaviours create, select, and maintain environments with properties congenial to their own cognitive motivational and behavioural states (Altman, 1975). Thus in some respects, the information filtered from the environment is consistent with an individual's purposes and intentions.

13.2.2 Humanist Ideas
Evidence of the increasingly wide epistemological bases for research in environmental cognition can be seen in a recent paper by Seamon (1982) who considers the value of **phenomenology** for environmental psychology generally (and indirectly for much behavioural research in geography). In

this paper he discusses three separate substantive themes: the phenomenology of human experience; the phenomenology of the physical environment; and the phenomenology of the person-world relationship. In particular, Seamon takes to task the existing large volume of work in environmental psychology that has accepted a positivist stance to develop conceptual and methodological devices which try to empirically represent images, attitudes, preferences, territories, and other spatial environmental concepts in mathematical or symbolic form. Although pointing out that a major aim of positivist environmental research is explanation, he argues that attempts at explanation in this mode of discourse fall short because of a potential reliance on a priori theories, laws and concepts used to organise and direct the empirical research. He then points out that phenomenological generalisation does **not** seek **explanation**, nor does it establish a guiding theoretical framework beforehand, but rather allows general patterns to appear in their own time and fashion through various instances or occurrences. This, it is claimed, strips away the screen of separation between researcher and environment established by positivist researchers and allows the full richness and integrity of the phenomenon investigated to register and be revealed.

Seamon also points out that, to date, much of the phenomenological work in human environment relations has taken place in the field of geography (e.g., Buttimer, 1974, 1976; Seamon, 1982; Ley, 1977, 1981, 1982; Ley and Samuels, 1978; Relph, 1976).

Seamon further lists comparisons between phenomenology and conventional scientific methodologies. However, throughout this paper there is an emphasis primarily on **logical positivism** as the conventional scientific procedure. As we have pointed out in Chapter 1, however, although much of the research on behavioural geography and man-environment relations was born in a strongly **positivist** tradition, it has outgrown and discarded many of the original positivist tenets. In doing so, it has retained what is truly positive in positivist thought, including the importance of public verifiability of results, the use of **logico-mathematical** languages to ensure undistorted communication, the significance of hypotheses testing, and the search for generalisation.

While continued debate between phenomenological and analytical researchers is primarily of limited academic interest, the fact the debate occurs in the literature at all is evidence of the growing concern for a wider epistemological base for continued behavioural research. Although there is some sentiment that the world of affect and the world of cognition should be kept separate, with different theories, methods and matters of concern clearly focused in each area of behavioural geography, such distinctions and differences appear increasingly irrelevant. Thus, **interactional, transactional**, and **constructivist** views appear to merge aspects of phenomenism and positivism, literature and science, human feelings and emotions and objective measurement, to a degree that is not apparent in other epistemologies. As more and more researchers bring their interests to bear on behavioural problems, the turmoil, however, appears to grow. There is increased uncertainty as to whether or not a priori theories and a consequent search for generalisation is a necessary component of research in this area. The opposite question, of course, is whether or not the uniqueness component of individual environment relations and their phenomenological interpretation is useful, or indeed, if activities of this type can legitimately be regarded as part of the ongoing research in this area.

Questions such as these reflect the relative newness of the field, the uncertainty with respect to its concepts and contexts, and the general lack of theory, concepts, core, and periphery for ongoing research. Certainly, it may be hard to argue with Seamon's conclusion that the phenomenological perspective may suggest new aspects of environment, behaviour, and experience which can then become the subject of "conventional analytical research." Certainly, this perspective is more palatable than his second alternative in which phenomenologists would work to reorient behavioural research away from its current analytic, explanatory orientation.

13.3 AFFECTIVE COMPONENTS AND CONCEPTS

Most researchers agree that environmental meaning is a complex mix of affective and denotative components. Many **denotative** aspects of meaning, however, have been explored through the use of factor analytic studies where the limitations of arbitrarily defined terms to describe dimensions (whether orthogonal or not) somewhat constrains the usefulness and generalisability of the outcome of such studies.

Much of the work relating to **affective** response to the environment and the importance of affect in spatial behaviour research builds on the work of Osgood, et al. (1957), which indicates the three significant dimensions – **evaluation**, **activity** and **potency** are the critical structural elements. Some researchers have questioned the relevance of these factors in environmental assessment (Canter, 1970); others (Russell, et. al., 1981) suggest that these three dimensions are relevant to affective meaning and not to the perceptual or cognitive processing of the environment.

Factors such as **organisation**, **coherence** and **order** appear to be important parts of the structure of some behavioural responses. In general, examination of affective dimensions of the environment are focused on concepts such as diversity, organisation, upkeep, noise, traffic, openness, presence of people, and naturalness. Obviously, the affective response to environment is a multidimensional phenomena. For example, using the principal axis factor analysis with Varimax rotation, Nasar, et. al. (1983) found three factors – evaluation, arousal and safety – appeared to be dominant in individual evaluations of scenes in downtown Columbus, Ohio. In assessing the physical attributes of environments, Nasar calculated rank correlation coefficients between scores on affect factors and scores on individual and environmental attributes scales. The results appear to indicate that affect and cognition are linked, and despite the fact that the proportion of variation in the affective responses explained by the attributes of the environment were small, the presence of significant cross-correlations was interpreted as evidence that the relationships were powerful and generalisable. The overall results of their research was to confirm for environmental affect the three-dimensional structure posited by Osgood, et. al.

Nasar, et. al. (1983) have also investigated the question of whether or not an urban landscape can influence the **feelings** for those people experiencing it. They point out that the last two decades have seen considerable uproar arise over projected changes in the aesthetic quality of urban environments, which implies that the aesthetic quality itself is an important aspect of such environments. This question then becomes of interest to those who take on the task of planning, regulating, and designing urban landscapes. The lack of adequate empirical information about the likely affective quality of a segment of the environment and the effects of change or redesign on the behaviour of people experiencing those environments, therefore, appears to be a matter of considerable practical concern.

Obviously, there is some opportunity for behavioural geographers interested in affective components and concepts to undertake a wide range of potentially useful research activity. Since this research quoted above has both planning and policy implications, it appears to be a potentially fruitful area of concentration.

13.4 ALTERNATE IDEOLOGIES

A considerable volume of criticism of analytical and phenomenological behavioural research has emerged from the camp of the **social theorists**. Largely dominated by **radical Marxist thought**, this criticism expounds the importance of societal and institutional constraints on individual behaviour, arguing thereafter that research on things such as individually based decision, choice and preference situations is thus inconsequential. We, of course, dispute such criticism. In turn, we suggest that a good deal of Marxist literature dehumanises the individual, replacing him with a social animal that is basically devoid of free will. Most probably an appropriate perspective will emerge somewhere between these extremes. For example, Pred's work on activity patterns and time paths (1981) suggests an avenue for aggregating the unique individual into groups whose members make similar decisions and undertake similar behaviour within the acknowledged constraints of a given culture or society. Whether these constraints are obvious and publicly articulated (as may be the case in Marxist societies) or whether they are subtly concealed beneath a fabric of apparent freedom of choice (as may be the case in capitalist societies) is immaterial. The critical problem is that of identifying feasible behaviours whatever the constraints, and then discovering the decision and choice rules that help select types of behaviours from a feasible opportunity set.

For some time, analytical behavioural researchers were lukewarm towards Marxist ideas because of an apparent difficulty in operationalising such ideas. How could one determine the extent to which nebulous things such as societal and institutional controls are measured or objectified? A recent paper by Webber and Fincher (1985) examines the problem of using a Marxist approach in a highly analytical manner, using either a statistical or mathematical basis. What still is missing, however, is a set of suggestions for operationalising subjective evaluations of Marxist concepts in an analytical framework such that effects on individual behaviour may be examined.

If criticism based on social theory can be developed in a constructive rather than a destructive mode (is that possible?), then the behavioural researcher can benefit and the search for explanation will be advanced. If adopting an alternate ideological base serves only to provide another set of assumptions on which research is based, then there should be no hurry to accept such alternate assumptions until they are shown to have potential use and value greater than existing ones. Given the individual base of much behavioural research, this does not seem likely to happen in the near future.

13.5 SOME PROMISING RESEARCH AREAS

The stereotyped phrase "more work needs to be done", hardly does justice to the constantly expanding research frontier of spatial behavioural research. As geographers, we pride ourselves on being able to bring to bear a unique outlook, a synthesising capability, and an unmatched set of spatial skills, on any problem concerned with spatial aspects of human behaviour. Ever the optimists, we believe this is so. Therefore, whether we urge the reworking of previously developed ideas (e.g., the Bayesian formulation of hazard perception problem) or an attack on new avenues of investigation (e.g., artificial intelligence modelling of human decision systems) we do so with the confidence that the particular insights the geographer brings will materially and positively effect the nature and quality of research in the area.

13.5.1 Reworking Previously Developed Ideas
Perhaps our first message is not to dismiss things because they appear to have "been done" already. Much earlier behavioural research was conceptually rich but operationally poor.

For example, Golledge in 1967 recommended that many spatial decisions should be conceptualised and modelled as a learning process, and suggested a dynamic Markov model framework for such analyses. At that stage, neither the survey nor the stochastic modelling technology of today was generally available to test the usefulness of such recommendations. Subsequent research has operationalised many facets of the general market decision process and empirical observation, and model development has far outstripped those earlier suggestions.

Similarly, while the notion of a cognitive map was common to the discipline for many years, it was only after a decade of experiments that confidence developed that meaningful cognitive maps could be reconstructed from individual proximity statements. Even now, the full range of meaning of the information contained in such maps is not well understood. Are they useful only in an individual context? Can they be meaningfully aggregated? Can types of cognitive transformations be defined? Or is every map a peculiar idiosyncratic representation of a common external system? How are beliefs and values incorporated into such maps? The questions go on and on; each one requires the rigorous experimental control and analytical investigation of a major research activity such as a Ph.D. dissertation.

This section could stand alone simply as a list of questions that could be asked about the various areas covered in this book. If knowledge is to be furthered, such questions will have to be asked and answered fully - reliably and with validity. There must be an opportunity for a disinterested, objective researcher to duplicate findings, to be able to ratify theoretical and empirical conclusions. This is the heart of an analytical approach. Little substantive developments can take place if we, as a discipline, prefer to take the unconfirmed word of a so-called "expert" rather than an objective evaluation of a research result.

13.5.2 New Avenues of Investigation

There are so many burning questions awaiting an answer from geographic researchers that it would be criminal not to mention some of them here.

Few geographers, for example, have paid attention to the severe **problems of disadvantaged populations** - the infirm, the physically disabled, the extreme elderly, the mentally retarded, the visually handicapped. Neither have we spent much time on the **growth and development of spatial knowledge**. Such an emphasis would require paying attention to specific populations such as pre-school and teenage children; or examining how that peculiar transfer from route to general configurational knowledge takes place. We know little of how best to teach spatial concepts to children, for as a discipline we have not paid much attention to it. That is not to say that much has not been done in how to teach spatial concepts; quite the contrary. But we don't really know if the right concepts are being taught to the right age group! Only a sound theory of the development of spatial cognition can make us aware of that. For the most part we rely on Piagetian developmental theory to help guide us - but ever more geographically based empirical research is shedding some doubts on this. The question this raises, of course, is why geographers do not have a sound and widely accepted theory of the development of spatial knowledge. This question is paralleled by hundreds of others, all of which could spawn a great deal of pure spatial behavioural research.

For many years arguments were made in geography courses that geographers tried to lump too many things together - to aggregate too much. This, of course, is necessary to get the "big picture" on which macro level theory and models are based. But when attention was switched to the micro level, geographers continued doing the same things, even though they were not sure of their meaning. In many sections in this book we have implicitly directed attention to the **aggregation problem**. On what basis does the behavioural geographer validly aggregate? Surely on the basis of similarity of behaviours! But **what** behaviour? Overt behaviour (such as distance travelled) or covert behaviour (such as similar decision rules)? It is not too strong to say that we know virtually nothing about how aggregation on the basis of covert behaviour affects results of a study. And how can we ever examine this question until we can identify behavioural characteristics and empirically and theoretically test the consequences of different aggregation schemes? Surely this is perhaps the most pressing problem of behavioural researchers. Until that problem is solved, there can be little done in the way of empirical validation of generalisations - and without these, how can theory develop?

During the last decade, research based on **social theory** has greatly expanded in geography. At this stage, there appears to be little opportunity for the behavioural researcher to interface with his social theory-oriented colleagues. The individually based, disaggregate approach of the behavioural researcher is dismissed by many social theorists as requiring an assumption of freedom of choice - an assumption which their socially constrained ideology will not accept. The consequences of this criticism, however, has been to make behavioural researchers more aware of the constraint systems which enclose them, forcing the addition of multidimensional explanatory schema in place of the more simplistic behaviourally dominated one to which they have become accustomed. The question arises about the need to interface behavioural and social theoretic work, or even if it is desirable to try. Again significant research questions arise.

13.5.3 Need for Confirmed Methodological Experimentation
The behavioural researcher has as much, if not more, need for confirmed methodological experimentation as other members of the discipline. Even now investigations concerning the amount of spatial autocorrelation (the geographer's bugbear) have appeared in their results. More immediate questions of **model transferability**, **parameter invariance**, and **cross-cultural validation** of theories and concepts are beginning to snowball. These are questions that the analytically inclined behavioural researcher cannot escape for long. There is, then, a major potential research area in terms of investigating the significance of all manner of constraints on analytical procedures. And what of the many unanswered questions relating to data collection by survey research methods and the appropriate matching of data to models.

Well, who said that behavioural geography was dead? Perhaps it could die from overwork! The critical thing is not to let our interests and expertise be subsumed by workers in cognitive science, environmental psychology, marketing, artificial intelligence, or any other area that has jumped on the spatial bandwagon. We do need more research and more researchers. We hope this book encourages many readers to venture into this exciting, growing research activity.

REFERENCES

Acredolo, L.P. (1976) Frames of Reference Used by Children for Orientation in Unfamiliar Spaces. In G.T. Moore and R.G. Golledge (eds): Environmental Knowing. Stroudsburg: Dowden, Hutchinson and Ross, pp. 165-172.

Adams, J.S. (1969) Directional Bias in Intra-Urban Migration. Economic Geography 45: 302-323.

Alonso, W. (1960) A Theory of the Urban Land Market. Papers and Proceedings of the Regional Science Association 6: 149-158.

Alonso, W. (1964) The Historic and the Structural Theories of Urban Form: Their Implications for Urban Renewal. Land Economics 49: 227-231.

Altman, I. (1975) The Environment and Social Behavior: Privacy, Personal Space, Territory and Crowding. Monterey, Ca.: Brooks and Cole.

Amedeo, D., and R.G. Golledge (1975) An Introduction To Scientific Reasoning in Geography. New York: John Wiley and Sons.

Anderson, J. (1971) Space-Time Budgets, and Activity Studies in Urban Geography and Planning. Environment and Planning 3: 353-368.

Anderson, T.R. (1955) Intermetropolitan Migration: A Comparison of the Hypotheses of Zipf and Stouffer. American Sociological Review 20: 287-291.

Appley, M.H., and R. Trumbell (1967) Psychological Stress. New York: Appleton-Century-Crofts.

Appleyard, D. (1969) Why Buildings Are Known. Environment and Behavior 1: 131-159.

Arbib, M.A., and A. Cornelis (1981) The Role of Systems Theory in Social Sciences: An Interview. Journal of Social and Biological Structures 4: 375-386.

Atherton, T.H., and M. Ben-Akiva (1976) Transferability and Updating of Disaggregate Travel Demand Models. Transportation Research Record 610: 12-18.

Baird, J., M. Wagner, and E. Noma (1982) Imposssible Cognitive Spaces. Geographical Analysis 14(3): 204-226.

Baresi, C. (1968) The Role of the Real Estate Agent in Residential Location. Sociological Focus 1: 59-71.

Barrett, F.A. (1973) Residential Search Behavior: A Study of Intraurban Relocation in Toronto. Geographical Monographs No. 1, Department of Geography, York University, Toronto :.

Beaumont, J.R. (1982) Towards a Conceptualization of Evolution in Environmental Systems. International Journal of Man-Machine Studies 16: 113-145.

Belcher, D.M. (1973) Giving Psychology Away. San Francisco: Canfield.

Bell, W. (1958) Social Choices, Life Styles and Suburban Residence. In W.M. Dobriner (ed): The Suburban Community. New York: Putman, pp. 225-247.

Berry, B.J.L., and F.E. Horton (1970) Geographic Perspectives On Urban Systems. Englewood Cliffs,N.J: Prentice-Hall.

References

Beshers, J.M. (1962) Urban Social Structure. New York: Free Press.

Beshers, J.M., and E.N. Nishiura (1961) A Theory of Internal Migration Differentials. Social Forces 39(3): 214-218.

Blommestein, H., P. Nijkamp, and W. van Veenendaal (1980) Shopping Perceptions and Preferences: A Multidimensional Attractiveness Analysis of Consumer and Entrepreneurial Attitudes. Economic Geography 56(2): 155-174.

Boulding, K.E. (1956) The Image: Knowledge in Life and Society. Ann Arbor,Mich.: University of Michigan Press.

Bowden, M.J. (1975) The Great American Desert in the American Mind, 1890-1972: The Historiography of a Geographical Notion. In M.J. Bowden and D. Lowenthal (eds): Geographies of the Mind: Essays in Historical Geography in Honor of John K. Wright. New York: Oxford University Press, pp. 119-147.

Bowers, R.G. (1981a) Statistical Dynamic Models of Social Systems I: The General Theory. Behavioral Science 23: 109-119.

Bowers, R.G. (1981b) Statistical Dynamic Models of Social Systems II: Discontinuity and Conflict. Behavioral Science 23: 120-129.

Boyce, R.R. (1969) Residential Mobility and Its Implication for Urban Spatial Change. Proceedings of Association Of American Geographers 1: 22-26.

Bracy, H.E. (1964) Neighbors: Subdivision of Life in England and the United States. Baton Rouge, La.: Louisiana State University Press.

Briggs, R. (1969) Scaling of Preferences For Spatial Location: An Example Using Shopping Centers Unpublished MA Thesis, Department of Geography. Columbus,Ohio: Ohio State University.

Briggs, R. (1972) Cognitive Distance in Urban Space, Ph.D Dissertation, Department of Geography. Columbus,Ohio: The Ohio State University.

Brog, W., and E. Erl (1981) Application of a Model of Individual Behavior(situational approach) to Explain Household Activity Patterns in an Urban Area to Forecast Behavioral Changes. In (ed): International Conference on Travel Demand Analysis: Activity Based and Other New Approaches. London: Oxford University Press.

Broom, L., and J.F. Lancaster (1976) Opportunity and Attainment in Australia. : Australian University Press, pp. 90-95.

Brown, L.A., and J.C. Belcher (1966) Residential Mobility of Physicians in Georgia. Rural Sociology 31(Dec): 439-457.

Brown, L.A., and J. Holmes (1971) Search Behavior in an Intraurban Migration Context: A Spatial Perspective. Environment and Planning 3: 307-326.

Brown, L.A., and D.G. Longbrake (1970) Migration Flows in Intra-Urban Space: Place Utility Considerations. Annals of the Association of American Geographers 60: 368-384.

Brown, L.A., and E.A. Moore (1970) The Intra-urban Migration Process: A Perspective. Geografiska Annaler 52B: 1-13.

Bullock, N., P. Dickens, M. Shapcott, and P. Steadman (1974) Time Budgets and Models of Urban Activity Patterns. Social Trends 5: 45-63.

References

Burgess, E.W. (1925) The Growth of the City. In R.E. Park, E.W. Burgess, and R.D. McKenzie (eds): The City. Chicago: University of Chicago Press.

Burnett, K.P. (1973) The Dimensions of Alternatives in Spatial Choice Processes. Geographical Analysis 5: 181-204.

Burnett, K.P. (1974) A Three-State Markov Model of Spatial Choice. Geographical Analysis 6: 53-68.

Burnett, K.P. (1976) Behavioral Geography and the Philosophy of Mind. In R.G. Golledge and G. Rushton (eds): Spatial Choice and Spatial Behavior. Columbus: Ohio State University Press, pp. 23-50.

Burnett, K.P., and S. Hanson (1979) Rationale for an Alternative Mathematical Approach to Movement as Complex Human Behavior. Transportation Research Record 723: 11-24.

Burnett, K.P., and S. Hanson (1982) The Analysis of Travel as an Example of Complex Human Behavior in Spatially-Constrained Situations: Definition and Measurement Issues. Transportation Research, A 16: 87-102.

Burnett, K.P., and N.J. Thrift (1979) New Approaches to Travel Behavior. In D. Hensher and P. Stopher (eds): Behavioral Travel Demand Modelling. London: Croom Helm.

Burroughs, W.J., and E.K. Sadalla (1979) Asymmetries in Distance Cognition. Geographical Analysis 11(4): 414-421.

Burton, I. (1972) Cultural and Personality Variables in the Perception of Natural Hazards. In J.F. Wohlwill and D.H. Carson (eds): Environment and Social Sciences: Perspectives and Applications. Washington, D.C.: APA, pp. 184-197.

Burton, I., and R.W. Kates (1963) The Perception of Natural Hazards in Resource Management. Natural Resources Journal 3: 412-441.

Butler, E.W., F.S. Chapin, G.C. Hemmens, E.J. Kaiser, M.A. Stegman, and S.F. Weiss (1969) Moving Behavior and Residential Choice : A National Survey. National Cooperative Highway Research Program, Highway Research Board, Report No. 81 :.

Buttimer, A. (1969) Social Space in an Interdiciplinary Perspective. Geographical Review 59: 417-426.

Buttimer, A. (1972) Social Space and the Planning of Residential Areas. Environment and Behavior 4: 279-318.

Buttimer, A. (1974) Values in Geography. AAG Commission on College Geography, Resource Paper 24 :.

Buttimer, A. (1976) Grasping the Dynamism of Lifeworld. Annals of the Association of American Geographers 66: 277-292.

Cadwallader, M. (1975) A Behavioral Model of Consumer Spatial Decision-Making. Economic Geography 51: 339-349.

Cadwallader, M. (1977) Frame Dependence in Cognitive Maps: An Analysis Using Directional Statistics. Geographical Analysis 9(3): 284-291.

Cadwallader, M. (1978) Urban Information and Preference Surfaces: Their Patterns, Structures and Interrelationships. Geografiska Annaler 60B(2): 97-106.

References

Cadwallader, M. (1979) Problems in Cognitive Distance: Implications for Cognitive Mapping. Environment and Behavior 11(4): 559-576.

Cadwallader, M. (1981) Towards a Cognitive Gravity model: The Case of Consumer Spatial Behavior. Regional Studies 15: 275-284.

Cannell, C.F., S.A. Lawson, and D.L. Hausser (1975) A Technique for Evaluating Interview Performance. Ann Arbor, Mich.: SRC, University of Michigan.

Cannell, C.F., P.V. Miller, and L. Oksenberg (1981) Research and Interviewing Techniques. In S. Leinhardt (ed): Sociological Methodology. San Francisco, Ca.: Joney-Bass, pp. 389-437.

Canter, D.V. (1970) Architectural Psychology. London: RIBA.

Carlstein, T., D.N. Parkes, and N.J. Thrift (1978a) Timing Space and Spacing Time I: Making Sense of Time. London: Arnold.

Carlstein, T., D.N. Parkes, and N.J. Thrift (1978b) Timing Space and Spacing Time II: Human Activity and Time Geography. London: Edward Arnold.

Carlstein, T., D.N. Parkes, and N.J. Thrift (1978c) Timing Space and Spacing Time III: Time and Regional Dynamics. London: Edward Arnold.

Carr, S., and D. Schissler (1969) The City as a Trip: Perceptual Selection and Memory in the View From the Road. Environment and Behavior 1: 7-35.

Carroll, J.D., and J.J. Chang (1970) Analysis of Individual Differences in Multidimensional Scaling via an N-way Generalization of 'Eckart-Young' Decomposition. Psychometrika 35: 283-319.

Casetti, E., and G. Papageorgiou (1971) A Spatial Equilibrium Model of Urban Structure. Canadian Geographer 15(1): 30-37.

Chapin, F.S. (1965) Urban Landuse Planning, Second Edition. Urbana,Ill.: University of Illinois Press.

Chapin, F.S. (1968) Activity Systems and Urban Structures: A Working Schema. Journal of American Institute of Planners 34(1): 11-18.

Chapin, F.S. (1974) Human Activity Patterns in the City: What People do in Time and Space. New York: John Wiley.

Chapin, F.S. (1978) Human Time Allocation in the City. In T. Carlstein, D.N. Parker, and N.J. Thrift (eds): Human Activity and Time Geography. London: Edward Arnold, pp. 13-26.

Chapin, F.S., and R.K. Brail (1969) Human Activity Systems in the Metropolitan United States. Environment and Behavior 1: 107-130.

Chatfield, C., A.S.C. Eherenberg, and G.J. Goodhardt (1966) Progress on a Simplified Model of Stationary Purchasing Behavior. Journal of the Royal Statistical Society (Series A) 129(3): 317-367.

Chombart de Lauwe, P.-.H. (1952) Introductory Statement. In P.-.H. Chombart de Lauwe (ed): Paris et l'Agglomeration Parisienne: l'Espace Social dans une Grande Ville. Paris: P.U.F..

Chombart de Lauwe, P.-.H. (1960) L'Evolution des Besoins et al Conception Dynamiques de la Famille. Rev. Francoise de Sociologie 1: 403-425.

Chombart de Lauwe, P.-.H. (1965) Essais de Sociologie, 1952-1964. Paris: Universitaires de France.

References

Christaller, W. (1933) Die Zentralen Orte in Suddeutschland (trans. Baskin,C.W.,1963, as Central Places in Southern Germany). Englewood Cliffs,N.J: Prentice-Hall.

Clark, W.A.V. (1968) Consumer Travel Patterns and the Concept of Range. Annals of the Association of American Geographers 58: 386-396.

Clark, W.A.V. (1969) Information Flows and Intra-Urban Migration: An Empirical Analysis. Annals of the Association of American Geographers 1: 38-42.

Clark, W.A.V. (1970) Measurement and Explanation in Intra-Urban Mobility. Tijdschrift voor Economische en Social Geografie 61: 49-57.

Clark, W.A.V. (1981) Residential Mobility and Behavioral Geography: Parallelism or Independence?. In K.R. Cox and R.G. Golledge (eds): Behavioral Problems In Geography Revisited. : Methuen, pp. 182-208.

Clark, W.A.V., and M. Cadwallader (1973) Locational Stress and Residential Mobility. Environment and Behavior 5: 29-41.

Clark, W.A.V., and E.G. Moore (1980) Residential Mobility and Public Policy. Beverly Hills,Ca.: Sage Publications.

Clark, W.A.V., and G. Rushton (1970) Models of Intra-Urban Consumer Behavior and Their Applications For Central Place Theory. Economic Geography 46: 486-497.

Clark, W.A.V., and T.R. Smith (1979) Modeling Information Use in a Spatial Context. Annals of the Association of American Geographers 69: 574-588.

Cliff, A.D., and J.K. Ord (1980) Spatial Autocorrelation. London: Pion.

Converse, P.E. (1972) Country Differences in the Use of Time. In A. Szalai, P.E. Converse, P. Feldheim, and E.K. Scheuch (eds): The Use of Time: Daily Activities Of Urban and Suburban Populations in Twelve Countries. The Hague: Mouton, pp. 145-177.

Costanzo, C.M., W.C. Halperin, N. Gale, and G.D.R. Richardson (1982) An Alternative Method for Assessing Goodness-of-Fit for Logit Models. Environment and Planning,A 14: 963-971.

Couclelis, H., and R.G. Golledge (1983) Analytic Research, Positivism, and Behavioral Geography. Annals of the Association of American Geographers 73(3): 331-339.

Cox, K.R., and R.G. Golledge (1969) Behavioral Problems in Geography: A Symposium, Studies in Geography No.17. Evanston,Ill.: Northwestern Univerity Press.

Craik, K.H. (1968) The Comprehension of the Everyday Physical Environment. Journal of the American Institute of Planners 34(1): 29-36.

Craik, K.H. (1970) Environmental Psychology. In K.H. Craik and T.M. Newcombe (eds): New Directions in Psychology,4. New York: Holt, Rinehart and Winston, pp. 1-12.

Crawford, T. (1973) Beliefs About Birth Control: A Consistency Theory Analysis. Representative Research in Social Psychology 4: 53-65.

Crouchley, R., A. Pickles, and R. Davies (1982) Dynamic Models of Shopping Behavior: Testing the Linear Learning Model and Some Alternatives. Geografiska Annaler B 63: 27-33.

References

Cullen, I.G. (1976) Human Geography, Regional Science, and the Study of Individual Behavior. Environment and Plannning A 8: 397-409.

Cullen, I.G. (1978) The Treatment of Time in the Explanation of Spatial Behavior. In T. Carlstein, D.N. Parkes, and N.J. Thrift (eds): Human Activity and Time Geography. London: Edward Arnold, pp. 27-38.

Cullen, I.G., and V. Godson (1975) Urban Networks: The Structure of Activity Patterns. In D. Diamond and J.B. MacLaughlin (eds): Progress in Planning: Part I. Oxford: Pergamon, pp. 1-96.

Cullen, I.G., and E. Philps (1975) Diary Techniques and the Problems of Urban Life. Wahington,D.C.: Social Science Research Council.

Day, R.A. (1976) Urban Distance Cognition: Review and Contribution. Australian Geographer 13(3): 193-200.

De Jong, G.F., and J.T. Fawcett (1979) Motivations and Migration: An Assessment and Value-Expectancy Research Model. In (ed): Workshop in Microlevel Approaches to Migration Decisions, Tenth Summer Seminar in Population. Hawaii: East-West Center.

Demko, D., and R. Briggs (1970) An Initial Conceptualization and Operationalization of Spatial Choice Behavior: A Migration Example Using Multidimensional Unfolding. Proceedings, Canadian Association of Geographers 1: 79-86.

Desbarates, J. (1983) Spatial Choice and Constraints on Behavior. Annals of the Association of American Geographers 73: 340-357.

Dobson, R., F. Dunbar, C.J. Smith, D. Reibstein, and C. Lovelock (1978) Structural Models for the Analysis of Traveller Attitude-Behavior Relationships. Transportation 7(4): 351-364.

Dorigo, G., and W. Tobler (1983) Push-Pull Migration Laws. Annals of the Association of American Geographers 73(1): 1-18.

Downs, R.M. (1970a) The Cognitive Structure of an Urban Shopping Center. Environment and Behavior 2: 13-39.

Downs, R.M. (1970b) Geographic Space Perception: Past Approaches and Future Prospects. In C. Board, R.J. Chorley, P. Haggett, and D.R. Stoddart (eds): Progress in Geography, Vol. 2. London: Edward Arnold, pp. 65-108.

Downs, R.M. (1981a) Maps and Metaphors. The Professional Geographer 33(3): 287-301.

Downs, R.M. (1981b) Maps and Mappings as Metaphors for Spatial Representation. In L. Liben, A. Patterson, and N. Newcombe (eds): Spatial Representation and Behavior Across Life Span: Theory and Applications. New York: Academic Press, pp. 143-166.

Downs, R.M., and D. Stea (1973) Image and Environment: Cognitive Mapping and Spatial Behavior. Chicago: Aldine.

Dunn, R., S. Reader, and N. Wrigley (1983) An Investigation of the Assumptions of the NBD Model as Applied to Purchasing at Individual Stores. Applied Statistics 32: 249-259.

Durkheim, E. (1893) De la Division du Travail Social. Paris: Felix Alcan.

Ehrenberg, A.S.C. (1972) Repeat Buying: Theory and Application. Amsterdam: North Holland Publishing.

References

Ellegard, A., T. Hagerstrand, and B. Lenntorp (1975) Activity
  Organization and the Generation of Daily Travel: Two Further
  Alternatives. Rapporter och Notiser, Lund 23:.
Ellegard, K., T. Hagerstand, and B. Lenntorp (1977) Activity
  Organization and the Generation of Daily Travel: Two Future
  Alternatives. Economic Geography 53(2): 126-152.
Ermuth, F. (1974) Residential Satisfaction and Urban Environmental
  References. Geographical Monographs, York University,Ontario 3:.
Evans, P. (1976) Motivation. London: Methuen.
Fishbein, M., and I. Ajzen (1975) Belief,Attitude, Intention and
  Behavior: An Introduction to Theory and Research. Reading,Ma.:
  Addison-Wesley.
Gaile, G.L., and J.E. Burt (1980) Directional Statistics. Concepts and
  Techniques in Modern Geography, No. 25, University of East Anglia :.
Galbraith, R., and D. Hensher (1982) Intra-Metropolitan Transferability
  of Mode Choice Models. Journal of Transport Economics and Policy 16:
  7-29.
Gale, N. (1980) An Analysis of the Distortion and Fuzziness of
  Cognitive Maps by Location, Unpublished MA Thesis, Department of
  Geography. Santa Barbara,Ca.: University of California.
Garling, T., A. Book, and N. Ergezen (1982) Memory for the Spatial
  Layout of the Everyday Physical Environment: Differential Rates of
  Acquisition of Different Types of Information. Scandinavian Journal
  of Psychology 23: 23-55.
Garling, T., A. Book, and E. Lindberg (1979) The Acquisition and Use of
  an Internal Representation of the Spatial Layout of the Environment
  During Locomotion. Man-Environment Systems 9: 200-208.
Geary, R. (1954) The Contiguity Ratio and Statistical Mapping. The
  Incorporated Statistician 5: 115-145.
Gibson, J.J. (1966) The Senses Considered as Perceptual Systems. Boston:
  Houghton-Mifflin.
Gibson, J.J. (1968) The Senses Considered as Perceptual Systems. London:
  Allen and Unwin.
Ginnsberg, R.B. (1971) Semi-Markov Processes and Mobility. Journal of
  Mathematical Sociology 1: 233-262.
Ginnsberg, R.B. (1973) Stochastic Models of Residential and Geographic
  Mobility for Heterogenous Populations. Environment and Planning 5:
  113-124.
Gold, J.R. (1980) An Introduction to Behavioral Geography. New York:
  Oxford University Press.
Golledge, R.G. (1965) The Future of Manufacturing in New Zealand. In C.
  Blythe (ed): Manufacturing In New Zealand. Christchurch: Pegasus
  Press.
Golledge, R.G. (1967) Conceptualizing the Market Decision Process.
  Journal of Regional Science 7: 239-258.
Golledge, R.G. (1970a) Process Approaches to the Analysis of Human
  Spatial Behavior, Department of Geography, No. 17. Columbus,Ohio:
  The Ohio State University.

References

Golledge, R.G. (1970b) Some Equilibrium Models of Consumer Behavior. Economic Geography 46: 417-424.

Golledge, R.G. (1976a) Cognitive Configurations of a City: Vol. I, Department of Geography. Columbus, Ohio: OSU Research Foundation.

Golledge, R.G. (1976b) Cognitive Configurations of a City: Vol.II, Department of Geography. Columbus, Ohio.: OSU Research Foundation.

Golledge, R.G. (1976c) Methods and Methodological Issues in Environmental Cognition Research. In G.T. Moore and R.G. Golledge (eds): Environmental Knowing. Stroudsburg,Pa.: Dowden, Hutchinson and Ross, pp. 300-315.

Golledge, R.G. (1978a) Representing, Interpreting and Using Cognized Environments. Papers and Proceedings of the Regional Science Association 41: 169-204.

Golledge, R.G. (1978b) Learning About Urban Environments. In T. Carlstein, D. Parkes, and N. Thrift (eds): Timing Space and Spacing Time: Making Sense of Time. London: Edward Arnold, pp. 76-98.

Golledge, R.G. (1980) A Behavioral View of Mobility and Migration Research. Professional Geographer 32: 14-21.

Golledge, R.G., R. Briggs, and D. Demko (1969) The Configurations of Distances in Intra-Urban Space. Proceedings of the Association of American Geographers 1: 60-65.

Golledge, R.G., and L.A. Brown (1967) Search, Learning and the Market Decision Process. Geografiska Annaler 49B: 116-124.

Golledge, R.G., W.C. Halperin, N. Gale, and L. Hubert (1983) Exploring Entrepreneurial Cognitions of Retail Environments. Economic Geography 59(1): 3-15.

Golledge, R.G., and L.J. Hubert (1981) Matrix Reorganization and Dynamic Programming: Applications to Paired Comparisons and Unidimensional Seriation. Psychometrika 46(4): 429-441.

Golledge, R.G., and L.J. Hubert (1982) Some Comments on Non-Euclidean Mental Maps. Environment and Plannning 14: 107-118.

Golledge, R.G., J.N. Rayner, and V.L. Rivizzigno (1982) Comparing Objective and Cognitive Representations of Environmental Cues. In R. G. Golledge and J.N. Rayner (eds): Proximity and Preference: Problems in the Multidimensional Analysis of Large Data Sets. Minneapolis,Mn.: University of Minnesota press, pp. 233-266.

Golledge, R.G., G.D. Richardson, J.N. Rayner, and J.J. Parnicky (1983) The Spatial Competence of Selected Mentally Retarded Populations. In H.L. Pick and L.P. Acredolo (eds): Spatial Orientation and Spatial Representation. New York: Plenum Press, pp. 79-100.

Golledge, R.G., V.L. Rivizzigno, and A. Spector (1975) Learning About a City: Analysis by Multidimensional Scaling. In R.G. Golledge and G. Rushton (eds): Spatial Choice and Spatial Preference. Columbus,Ohio: Ohio State University Press, pp. 95-118.

Golledge, R.G., and G. Rushton (1972) Multidimensional Scaling: Review and Geographical Applications. AAG Commission on College Geography, Technical Paper 10:.

References

Golledge, R.G., G. Rushton, and W.A.V. Clark (1966) Some Spatial Characteristics of Iowa's Farm Population and their Implications for the Grouping of Central Place Functions. Economic Geography 43(2): 261-272.

Golledge, R.G., and K. Semple (1975) An Analysis of Entropy Changes in Settlement Patterns Over Time. In R.L. Singh and K.N. Singh (eds): Readings in Rural Settlement Geography. Varnasi,India: National Geographical Society, pp. 247-251.

Golledge, R.G., and A.N. Spector (1978) Comprehending the Urban Environment: Theory and Practice. Geographical Analysis 10: 403-426.

Golledge, R.G., and N. Wrigley (1985) Cross-Cultural Components of Consumer Behavior: An Approach Using Panel Data, Final Report,NSF Grant# SES83-20602, Department of Geography. Santa Barbara, Ca.: University of California.

Golledge, R.G., and G. Zannaras (1973) Cognitive Approaches to the Analysis of Human Spatial Behavior. In W.H. Ittelson (ed): Environmental Cognition. New York: Seminar Press, pp. 59-94.

Gordon, M.M. (1964) Assimilation in American Life. New York: Oxford University Press.

Gould, P.R. (1963) Man Against his Environment: A Game-Theoretic Framework. Annals of the Association of American Geographers 53: 290-297.

Gould, P.R. (1966) On Mental Maps. Michigan Inter-University Community of Mathematical Geographers, Discusssion Paper No. 9, Ann Arbor, Mich. :.

Gould, W.T.S., and R.M. Prothero (1975) Space and Time in African Population Mobility. In L.A. Kosinski and R.M. Prothero (eds): People on the Move. London: Methuen, pp. 39-49.

Groves, R.M., and R.L. Kahn (1979) Surveys by Telephones: A National Comparison with Personal Interviews. New York: Academic Press.

Gulick, J. (1966) Images of an Arab City. Journal of American Institute of Planners 29(3): 179-197.

Gulliver, F.P. (1908) Orientation of Maps. Journal of Geography 7: 55-58.

Guy, C.M., and N. Wrigley (1982) A Long-Term Grocery Shopping Survey in Cardiff. SSRC Research Project HR 8037:.

Hagerstrand, T. (1952) The Propagation of Innovation Waves. Lund Studies in Geography, Series B, Human Geography, 4, Gleerup, Lund :.

Hagerstrand, T. (1953) Innovation Diffusion as a Spatial Process (translated by Pred,A.1967). Chicago: University of Chicago.

Hagerstrand, T. (1955) Statistiska Primaruppgifter Flygkartering Och' Dat-Processing - Maskiner. Ett Kombinerings Projekt. Svensk Geografisk Arsbok 31:.

Hagerstrand, T. (1957) Migration and Area. In D. Hannerberg, T. Hagerstrand, and B. Odeving (eds): Migration in Sweden: A Symposium Series B, Human Geography No.13. Gleerup,Sweden: Lund Studies in Geography, pp. 27-158.

References

Hagerstrand, T. (1963) Geographic Measurement of Migration: Swedish
Data. In J. Sutter (ed): Human Displacement Measurement:
Methodological Aspects. Monaco:, pp. 64-83.

Hagerstrand, T. (1965) A Monte-Carlo Approach to Diffusion. Archives
Europenees de Sociologie 6: 43-67.

Hagerstrand, T. (1970) What About People in Regional Science?. Papers
of the Regional Science Association 24: 7-21.

Hagerstrand, T. (1973) The Domain of Human Geography. In R.J. Chorley
(ed): Directions in Geography. London: Methuen, pp. 67-87.

Hagerstrand, T. (1975) Space, Time and Human Conditions. In A.
Karlqvist, L. Lundqvist, and F. Snickars (eds): Dynamic Allocation
of Urban Space. Farnborough: Saxon House, pp. 3-12.

Hagerstrand, T. (1976) The Space-Time Trajectory Model and its Use in
the Evaluation of Systems of Transportation. Paper Presented at an
International Conference on Transportation Research, Vienna :.

Hagerstrand, T. (1978) A Note on the Quality of Life-Times. In T.
Carlstein, D. Parkes, and N. Thrift (eds): Timing Space and Spacing
Time: Human Activity and Time Geography. London: Edward Arnold, pp.
214-224.

Halperin, W.C. (1985) The Analysis of Panel Data for Discrete Choices.
In P. Nijkamp, H. Leitner, and N. Wrigley (eds): Measuring the
Unmeasurable. The Hague: Martinus Nijhofff Publishers, pp. 561-586.

Hanson, S. (1978) Measuring the Cognitive Levels of Urban Residents.
Geografiska Annaler,B 59: 67-81.

Hanson, S. (1980) Spatial Diversification and Multipurpose Travel:
Implications for Choice theory. Geographical Analysis 12: 245-257.

Hanson, S. (1982) The Determinants of Daily Travel Activity Patterns:
Relative Location and Sociodemographic Factors. Urban Geography 3(3):
179-203.

Hanson, S. (1984) Environmental Cognition and Travel Behavior. In D.T.
Herbert and R.J. Johnston (eds): Geography and the Urban Environment:
Progress in Research and Application, Vol. 6. London: John Wiley,
pp. 95-126.

Hanson, S., and D.F. Marble (1971) A Preliminary Typology of Urban
Travel Linkages. East Lakes Geographer 7: 49-59.

Harris, G.D., and E.E. Ullman (1945) The Nature of Cities. Annals of
the American Academy of Political and Social Science 242: 7-17.

Harrison, J., and P. Sarre (1976) Personal Construct Theory, the
Repertory Grid, and Environmental Cognition. In G.T. Moore and R.G.
Golledge (eds): Environmental Knowing. Stroudsberg,Pa.: Dowden,
Hutchinson and Ross, pp. 375-385.

Hart, R.A. (1974) The Genesis of Landscaping: Two Years of Discovery in
a Vermont Town. Landscape Architecture 65: 356-363.

Hart, R.A., and G.T. Moore (1973) The Development of Spatial Cognition:
A Review. In R.M. Downs and D. Stea (eds): Image and Environment.
Chicago: Aldine, pp. 246-288.

References

Hawley, A. (1968) Ecology: Human Ecology. In D. Sills (ed):
International Encyclopedia of the Social Sciences. New York: Crowell,
Collier and Mc Millan, pp. 328-332.

Heckman, J.J. (1982) Statistical Models for Discrete Panel Data. In C.
F. Manski and D.M. McFadden (eds): Structural Analysis of Discrete
Data: With Econometric Applications. Cambridge,Ma.: MIT Press.

Hemmens, G.C. (1970) Analysis and Simulation of Urban Activity Patterns.
Socio-Economic Planning Sciences 4: 53-66.

Hempel, D.M. (1969) Search Behavior and Information Utilization in the
Home Buying Process. Proceedings of the American Marketing
Association 30: 241-249.

Hensher, D. (1979) Individual Choice Modelling with Discrete
Commodities: Theory and Application to the Tasman Bridge Reopening.
Economic Record 55: 243-260.

Hensher, D., and J. Louviere (1979) Behavioral Intentions as Predictors
of very Specific Behavior. Transportation 8(2): 167-182.

Hensher, D., and P. Stopher (1979) Behavioural Travel Demand Modelling.
London: Croom Helm.

Hoinville, G. (1971) Evaluating Community Preferences. Environment and
Planning 3: 33-50.

Horton, F.E., and D.R. Reynolds (1969) An Investigation of Individual
Action Spaces: A Progress Report. Proceedings of Association of
American Geographers 1: 70-75.

Horton, F.E., and D.R. Reynolds (1970) Action Space Formation: A
Behavioral Approach to Predicting Urban Travel Behavior. Washington,
D.C.: Highway Research Record.

Hoyt, H. (1939) The Structure and Growth of Residential Neighborhoods
in American Cities. Washington,D.C.: Federal Housing Administration.

HRB (1969) Moving behavior and Residential Choice: A National Survey,
National Cooperative Highway Research Program Report No.81.
Washington,D.C.: Highway Research Board.

Hubert, L., R.G. Golledge, C.M. Costanzo, and N. Gale (1985) Order-
Dependent Measures of Correspondence for Comparing Proximity
Matrices and Related Structures. In P. Nijkamp, H. Leitner, and N.
Wrigley (eds): Measuring the Unmeasurable. Dordrecht: Martinus
Nijhoff Publishers, pp. 399-424.

Hudson, L.M. (1981) Image: A Theoretical and Operational Framework,
Unpublished Ph.D. Dissertation, School of Earth Sciences. Australia:
Macquarie University.

Huff, D.L. (1962) Determination of Intra-Urban Retail Trade Areas, Real
Estate Research Program. Los Angeles,Ca.: University of California.

Huff, D.L. (1963) A Probabilistic Analysis of Shopping Center Trade
Areas. Land Economics 39: 81-90.

Huff, D.L. (1964) Defining and Estimating a Trade Area. Journal of
Marketing 28: 34-38.

Huff, J.O., and W.A.V. Clark (1978) Cumulative Stress and Cumulative
Inertia: A Behavioral Model of the Decision to Move. Environment and
Planning A 10: 1101-1119.

References

Hull, C.L. (1964) A Behavior System: An Introduction to Behavior Theory Concerning the Individual Organism. New York: John Wiley and Sons.
Humphreys, J.S. (1973) Intra-Urban Migration and Residential Structure. Monash Publication in Geography 6: 35.
Humphreys, J.S., and J.S. Whitelaw (1979) Immigrants in an Unfamiliar Environment : Locational Decision-Making Under Constrained Circumstances. Geografiska Annaler 61B: 8-18.
Isard, W., and M.F. Dacey (1962) On the Projection of Individual Behavior in Regional Analysis. Journal of Regional Science 4: 1-32, 51-83.
Ittelson, W.H. (1951) The Constancies in Perceptual Theory. Psychological Review 58: 285-294.
Ittelson, W.H. (1960) Visual Space Perception. New York: Springer.
Jacobs, J. (1961) The Death and Life of American Cities. New York: Random House.
Jakle, J.A., S. Brunn, and C.C. Roseman (1976) Human Spatial Behavior. North Scituate,Ma.: Duxbury Press.
Johnson, L., and D. Hensher (1982) Application of Multinomial Probit to a Two-Period Panel Data Set. Transportation Research A 16: 457-464.
Johnston, R.J. (1966) The Location of High Status Residential Areas. Geografiska Annaler 48B(1): 23-35.
Johnston, R.J. (1973) Social Area Change in Melbourne, 1961-66: A Sample Exploration. Australian Geographical Studies 11: 79-98.
Jones, P.M. (1979) HATS: A Technique for Investigating Household Decisions. Environment and Planning A 11: 59-70.
Kalton, G. (1983) Introduction to Survey Sampling. Beverly Hills, Ca.: Sage Publications.
Kaluger, G., and M.F. Kaluger (1974) Human Development: The Span of Life (second Edition). St.Louis,Mo.: C.V.Mosby Company.
Kaplan, R. (1976) Way-Finding in the Natural Environment. In G.T. Moore and R.G. Golledge (eds): Environmental Knowing. Stroudsburg,Pa. : Dowden, Hutchinson and Ross, pp. 46-58.
Kaplan, S. (1976) Adaption, Structure and Knowledge. In G.T. Moore and R.G. Golledge (eds): Environmental Knowing. Stroudsburg,Pa.: Dowden, Hutchinson and Ross, pp. 32-45.
Kaplan, S., and R. Kaplan (1982) Cognition and Environment. New York: Praeger.
Keller, S. (1965) Neighbors, Neighboring and Neighborhoods in Sociological Perspective. Athens: Athens Technological Institute.
Keller, S. (1968) The Urban Neighborhood: A Sociological Perspective. New York: Random House.
Kelly, G.A. (1955) The Psychology Of Personal Constructs (2 Vols.). New York: Norton.
Kemeny, J.G., and G.L. Thompson (1957) Attitudes and Game Outcomes. In A.W. Tucker and P. Wolfe (eds): Contributions to the Theory of Games, Annals of Mathematical Studies. : Princeton University Press.
King, L.J., and R.G. Golledge (1978) Cities, Space and Behavior. Englewood Cliffs,N.J: Prentice-Hall.

References

Kirk, W. (1951) Historical Geography and the Concept of the Behavioral Environment. In G. Kuriyan (ed): Indian Geographical Journal, Silver Jubliee Edition. Madras: Indian Geographical Society, pp. 152-160.

Kish, L. (1965) Survey Sampling. New York: Wiley.

Kobayashi, K. (1976) An Activity model: A Demand Model for Transportation. Transportation Research 10: 67-79.

Kobayashi, K. (1979) An Activity Model: A Validation. In D.H. Hensher and P.R. Stopher (eds): Behavioural Travel Modelling. London: Croom Helm, pp. 101-115.

Kotler, P. (1965) Behavioral Models for Analyzing Buyers. Journal of Marketing 29(4): 37-45.

Kuipers, B. (1978) Modeling Spatial Knowledge. Cognitive Science 2: 129-153.

Kuipers, B. (1982) The Map in the Head Metaphor. Environment and Behavior 4(2): 202-220.

Kutter, E. (1973) A Model for Individual Travel Behavior. Urban Studies 10: 238-258.

Ladd, F. (1970) Black Youths View their Environment: Neighborhood Maps. Environment and Behavior 2: 74-99.

Lakshmanan, T., and W.G. Hansen (1965) A Retail Market Potential Model. Journal of the American Institute of Planners 31: 134-143.

Lansing, J.B., and G. Hendricks (1967) Automobile Ownership and Residential Density (Survey Research Center). Ann Arbor,Michigan: University of Michigan.

Lee, T.R. (1962) Brennan's Law of Shopping Behavior. Psychological Reports 11: 662.

Lee, T.R. (1964) Psychology and Living Space. Transactions of the Bartlett Society 2: 11-36.

Lee, T.R. (1968) Urban Neighborhood as a Socio-Spatial Schema. Human Relations 21: 241-268.

Lee, T.R. (1970) Perceived Distance as a Function of Direction in the City. Environment and Behavior 2: 40-51.

Lenntorp, B. () A Time-Structured Study of the Travel Possibilities of the Public Transport Passenger. Rapporter och Notiser, 24, Department of Geography, University of Lund :.

Lenntorp, B. (1976) Paths in Space-Time Environments: A Time Geographic Study of Movement Possibilities of Individuals. Lund Studies in Geography, Series B, 44 :.

Lenntorp, B. (1978) A Time-Geographic Simulation Model of Individual Activity Programmes. In T. Carlstein, D.N. Parkes, and N.J. Thrift (eds): Human Activity and Time Geography. London: Edward Arnold, pp. 162-180.

Levin, I., and F. Corry (1975) Information Integration Models of Transportation Decisions, Institute of Urban and Regional Research, Technical Report 61. : University of Iowa.

Levin, I., and M.J. Gray (1977) Analysis of Human Judgement in Transportation. Great Plains Rocky Mountains Geographical Journal 6: 13-21.

327

References

Lewin, K. (1935) A Dynamic Theory of Personality. New York: McGraw-Hill.
Ley, D. (1972) The Black Inner City as a Frontier Outpost: Images and Behavior of A North Philadelphia Neighborhood, Unpublished Ph.D. Dissertation, Department of Geography. : Pennsylvania State University.
Ley, D. (1977) Social Geography and the Taken-for-Granted World. Transactions of the Institute of British Geographers 2: 498-512.
Ley, D. (1983) A Social Geography of the City. New York: Harper and Row.
Ley, D., and M. Samuels (1978) Humanistic Geography. Chicago,Ill.: Maaroufa.
Lieber, S. (1979) An Experimental Approach for the Migration Decision Process. Tijdschrift voor Economiche en Sociale Geografie 70: 75-85.
LLoyd, R., and D. Jennings (1978) Shopping Behavior and Income: Comparisons in an Urban Environment. Economic Geography 54: 157-167.
Looman, J.D. (1969) Consumer Spatial Behavior: A Conceptual Model and an Empirical Case Study of Supermarket Patronage, Unpublished MA Thesis, Department of Geography. Columbus, Ohio: The Ohio State University.
Louviere, J. (1974) Predicting the Response to Real Stimulus Objects from an Abstract Evaluation of their Attributes: The Case of Trout Streams. Journal of Applied Psychology 59: 572-577.
Louviere, J. (1979) Modeling Individual Residential Preferences: A Totally Disaggregate Approach. Transportation Research, B 4: 1-15.
Louviere, J., and D. Henley (1977) Information Integration Theory Applied to Student Apartment Selection Decisions. Geographical Analysis 9: 130-141.
Louviere, J., and D. Henley (1979) Behavioral Analysis of Destination Choice. Institute of Urban and Regional Research, Technical Report 112, University of Iowa 112:.
Louviere, J., and R. Meyer (1976) A Model for Residential Impression Formation. Geographical Analysis 8: 479-486.
Louviere, J., and R. Meyer (1981) A Composite Attitude-Behavior Model of Traveler Decision-Making. Transportation Research B 15: 411-420.
Lowenthal, D. (1961) Geography, Experience, and Imagination: Towards a Geographical Epistemology. Annals of the Association of American Geographers 51: 241-260.
Lowrey, R.A. (1970) Distance Concepts of Urban Residents. Environment and Behavior 2(1): 52-73.
Luce, R.D. (1958) A Probabilistic Theory of Utility. Econometrica 26: 193-224.
Luce, R.D. (1959) Individual Choice Behavior: A Theoretical Analysis. New York: John Wiley.
Lynch, K. (1960) The Image of the City. Cambridge,Ma.: MIT Press.
MacKay, D.B., and R. Olshavsky (1975) Cognitive Maps of Retail Location: An Investigation of Some Basic Issues. Journal of Consumer Research 2: 197-205.

References

MacKinnon, R.D., and P.A. Rogerson (1981) Information Sensitive Migration Models. In D.A. Griffith and R. MacKinnon (eds): Dynamic Spatial Models. Alphen aan den Rijn: Sijthoff and Noordhoff, pp. 67-77.

Marshall, D.R. (1968) Who paricipates in What? A Bibliographic Essay on Individual Participation in Urban Areas. Urban Affairs Quarterly 4: 201-223.

Martensson, S. (1975) Time Use and Social Organization. Rapporter och Notiser, 17, Department of Geography, University of Lund, Sweden :.

Martin, R.L., N.J. Thrift, and R.J. Bennett (1978) Towards the Dynamic Analysis of Spatial Systems. London: Pion.

Maslow, A.H. (1954) Motivation and Personality. New York: Harper.

Maurer, R., and J.C. Baxter (1972) Images of Nighborhoods Among Black,- Anglo,- and Mexican-American Children. Environment and Behavior 4: 351-388.

Mc Cabe, R.W. (1974) Planning Applications of Retail Models. Ontario, Canada: Ministry of Treasury.

Mc Carthy, P.S. (1982) Further Evidence on the Temporal Stability of Disaggregate Travel Demand Models. Transportation Research B 16: 263-278.

McDermott, P., and M. Taylor (1976) Attitudes, Images and Location: The Subjective Context of Decision Making in New Zealand Manufacturing. Economic Geography 52(4): 325-347.

McGinnis (1968) A Stochastic Model of Social Mobility. American Sociological Review 33: 712-722.

Mehrabian, A., and J.A. Russell (1973) A Measure of Arousal Seeking Tendency. Enviroment and Behavior 5(3): 315-333.

Mehrabian, A., and J.A. Russell (1974) An Approach to Environmental Psychology. Cambridge,Ma.: MIT Press.

Menchik, M. (1972) Residential Environmental Preferences and Choice: Empirically Validating Preference Measures. Environment and Planning 4: 455-458.

Meyer, R.J., I.P. Levin, J. Louviere, and D. Henley (1980) Issues in Modeling Travel Behavior in Simulated Choice Environments: A Review, Department of Geography. Iowa: University of Iowa.

Michelson, W. (1966) An Empirical Analysis of Urban Environmental Preferences. Journal of the American Institute of Planners 24: 355-360.

Michelson, W. (1968) Urban Sociology as an Aid to Urban Physical Development: Some Research Strategies. Journal of the American Institute of Planners 34: 105-108.

Moore, G.T. (1970) Emerging Methods in Environmental Design and Planning. Cambridge, Ma.: MIT Press.

Moore, G.T. (1976) Theory and Research in the Development of Environmental Knowing. In G.T. Moore and R.G. Golledge (eds): Environmental Knowing. Stroudsburg,Pa.: Dowden, Hutchinson and Ross, pp. 138-164.

References

Moran, P. (1948) The Interpretation of Statistical Maps. Journal of the Royal Statistical Society, Series B 10: 243-251.

Moser, C., and G. Kalton (1971) Survey Methods in Social Investigation. London: Heineman Educational Books.

Murdie, R.A. (1969) Factorial Ecology of Metropolitan Toronto, 1951-61, Research Paper No. 116, Department of Geography. Chicago: University of Chicago.

Muth, R.F. (1969) Cities and Housing. Chicago, Ill.: University of Chicago.

Nasar, J.L., D. Julian, S. Buchman, D. Humphreys, and M. Mrohaly (1983) The Emotional Quality of Scene and Observation Points: A Look at Prospect and Refuge. Landscape Planning 10: 355-361.

Newton, P.W. (1978) Modelling Locational Choice. New Zealand Geographer 34: 31-40.

Norman, K., and J. Louviere (1974) Integration of Attributes in Public Bus Transportation: Two Modeling Approaches. Journal of Applied Psychology 59: 947-955.

O'Riordan, T. (1973) Some Reflections on Environmental Attitudes and Environmental Behavior. Area 5: 17-19.

Olivier, D. (1970) Metric for Comparison of Multidimensional Scaling. Unpublished Manuscript :.

Olsson, G. (1965) Distance and Human Interaction: A Review and Bibliography. Philadelphia,Pa.: RSRI.

Orleans, P., and S. Schmidt (1972) Mapping the City: Environmental Cognition of Urban Residents. In W.J. Mitchel (ed): Environmental Design: Research and Practice, Proceedings of the ERDA 3/AR8 Conference. Los Angeles,Ca.: Univ. of California,Los Angeles, pp. 1. 4.1-1.4.9.

Osgood, C.E., G.J. Suci, and P.H. Tannenbaum (1957) The Measurement of Meaning. Urbana,Ill.: University of Illinois Press.

Pacione, M. (1976) A Measure of the Attraction Factor: A Possible Alternative. Area 6: 279-282.

Palm, R. (1976) The Role of Real Estate Agents as Information Mediators in Two American Cities. Geografiska Annaler 51B: 28-41.

Park, R.E., E.W. Burgess, and R.D. McKenzie (1925) The City. Chicago, Ill.: University of Chicago.

Parkes, D., and N. Thrift (1980) Times, Spaces and Places. New York: John Wiley.

Parkes, D., and W.D. Wallis (1978) Graph Theory and the Study of Activity Structure. In T. Carlstein, D.N. Parkes, and N.J. Thrift (eds): Human Activity and Time Geography. London: Edward Arnold, pp. 75-99.

Pas, E. (1982) A Methodology for Measuring Complex Travel-Activity Patterns. AAG San Antonio Meeting :.

Peterson, G.L. (1967) A Model of Preference: Quantitative Analysis of the Perception of the Visual Appearance of Residential Neighborhoods. Journal of Regional Science 7(1): 19-32.

References

Peterson, W. (1958) A General Topology of Migration. American Sociological Review 23(3): 256-266.

Piaget, J., and B. Inhelder (1967) The Child's Conception of Space. New York: Norton.

Pickvance, G.C. (1973) Life-Cycle, Housing Tenure and Intra-Urban Residential Mobility: A Causal Model. Sociological Review 21: 279-297.

Pipkin, J. (1981) The Concept of Choice and Cognitive Explanations of Spatial Behavior. Economic Geography 57(4): 315-331.

Pipkin, J.S. (1981) Cognitive Behavioral Geography and Repetitive Travel. In K.R. Cox and R.G. Golledge (eds): Behavioral Problems in Geography Revisited. New York: Methuen, pp. 145-181.

Popper, K.R. (1972) Objective Knowledge: An Evolutionary Approach. London: Oxford University Press.

Potter, R.B. (1976) Directional Bias within the Usage and Perceptual Fields of Urban Consumers. Psychological Reports 38: 988-990.

Potter, R.B. (1977) Spatial Patterns of Consumer Behavior and Perception in Relation to the Social Class Variable. Area 9: 153-156.

Potter, R.B. (1978) Aggregate Consumer Behavior and Perception in Relation to Urban Retailing Structure: A Preliminary Investigation. Tidschrift voor Economiche en Sociale Geografie 69: 345-352.

Potter, R.B. (1979) Perception of Urban Retailing Facilities: An Analysis of Consumer Information Fields. Geografiska Annaler 61B: 19-29.

Poulson, M.F. (1975) Patterns of Residential Movement and Urban Structure. Institute of Australian Geographers Thirteenth Annual Conference,Wollongong :.

Pred, A. (1967) Behavior and Location. Lund Studies in Geography, Series B, Gleerup, Lund .

Pred, A. (1973) Urbanization, Domestic Planning, Problems and Swedish Geographic Research. In C. Board, R.J. Chorley, P. Haggett, and D.R. Stoddart (eds): Progress in Geography, Vol.5. London: Edward Arnold, pp. 1-76.

Pred, A. (1977a) City Systems in Advanced Economies: Past Growth, Present Processes and Future Development Options. London: Hutchinson.

Pred, A. (1977b) The Choreography of Existence: Comments on Hagerstrand's Time-Geography and its Usefulness. Economic Geography 53(2): 207-221.

Pred, A. (1981) Of Paths and Projects: Individual Behavior and its Societal Context. In K.R. Cox and R.G. Golledge (eds): Behavioral Problems in Geography Revisited. New York: Methuen, pp. 231-255.

Quandt, R.E. (1956) A Probabilistic Theory of Consumer Behavior. The Quarterly Journal of Economics 30(4): 507-536.

Quigley, J. (1976) Housing Demand in the Short Run: An Analysis of Polytomous Choice. Explorations in Economic Research 3(1): 76-102.

Rapoport, A. (1977) Human Aspects of Urban Form: Towards a Man Environment Approach to Urban Form and Design. Oxford: Pergamon.

References

Ravenstein, E.G. (1885) The Laws of Migration. Journal of the Royal Statistical Society 48: 167-235.

Recker, W.W., M.G. McNally, and G.S. Root (1982) An Activity-Based Model of Complex Travel Behavior. AAG San Antonio Meeting :.

Relph, E. (1976) Place and Placelessness. London: Pion.

Richardson, G.D. (1979) The Appropriateness of Using Various Minkowskian Metrics for Representing Cognitive Maps Produced by Nonmetric Multidimensional Scaling, Unpublished MA Thesis, Department of Geography. Santa Barbara,Ca.: University of California.

Ritchey, P.N. (1976) Explanations of Migration. Annual Review of Sociology 2: 363-404.

Rogers, D.S. (1970) The Role of Search and Learning in Consumer Space behavior: The Case of Urban In-Migrants, Unpublished MA Thesis, Department of Geography. Madison,Wisconsin: University of Wisconsin.

Rossi, P.H. (1955) Why Families Move: A Study in the Social Psychology of Urban Residential Mobility. Glencoe, Ill.: Free Press.

Rushton, G. (1965) The Spatial Pattern of Grocery Purchases in Iowa, Ph. D. Dissertation, Department of Geography. Iowa City, Iowa: University of Iowa.

Rushton, G. (1969a) Analysis of Spatial Behavior by Revealed Space Preference. Annals of the Association of American Geographers 59(2): 391-400.

Rushton, G. (1969b) The Scaling of Locational Preference. In K.R. Cox and R.G. Golledge (eds): Behavioral Problems in Geography: A Symposium, Studies in Geography, Department of Geography, 117. : Northwestern University, pp. 197-227.

Rushton, G., R.G. Golledge, and W.A.V. Clark (1967) Formulation and Test of a Normative Model for the Spatial Allocation of Grocery Expenditures by a Dispersed Population. Annals of the Association of American Geographers 57(2): 389-400.

Russell, J.A., L.M. Ward, and G. Pratt (1981) Affective Quality Attributed to Environments: A Factor Analytic Study. Environment and Behavior 13(3): 259-288.

Saarinen, T.F. (1966) Perception of the Drought Hazard on the Great Plains. Department of Geography, Research Paper 106, University of Chicago :.

Saarinen, T.F. (1973a) The Use of Projective Techniques in Geographic Research. In W.H. Ittelson (ed): Environment and Cognition. New York: Seminar Press, pp. 29-52.

Saarinen, T.F. (1973b) Student Views of the World. In R.M. Downs and D. Stea (eds): Image and Environment. Chicago,Ill.: Aldine, pp. 148-161.

Sadalla, E.K., W.J. Burroughs, and L.J. Staplin (1980) Reference Points in Spatial Cognition. Journal of Experimental Psychology: Human Learning and Memory 5: 516-528.

Sadalla, E.K., and L.J. Staplin (1980a) The Perception of Traversed Distance: Intersections. Environment and Behavior 12: 167-182.

References

Sadalla, E.K., and L.J. Staplin (1980b) An Information Storage Model for Distance Cognition. Environment and Behavior 12: 183-193.

Schuler, H.J. (1979) A Disaggregate Store Choice Model of Spatial Decision Making. The Professional Geographer 31(2): 146-156.

Seamon, D. (1982) The Phenomenological Contribution to Environmental Psychology. Journal of Environmental Psychology 2: 119-140.

Selye, H. (1956) The Stress of Life. New York: McGraw-Hill.

Shapcott, M., and P. Steadman (1978) Rhythms of Urban Activity. In T. Carlstein, D.N. Parkes, and N.J. Thrift (eds): Human Activity and Time Geography. London: Edward Arnold, pp. 49-74.

Shaw, R.P. (1975) Migration Theory and Fact: Bibliography Series. Philadelphia,Pa.: Regional Science Research Instit.

Shemyakin, F.N. (1962) Orientation in Space. In B.G. Ananyev (ed): Psychological Science in the USSR,1,Report No. 62-11083. Washington, D.C.: Office of Technical Services, pp. 184-225.

Sheppard, E.S. (1980) The Ideology of Spatial Choice. Papers of the Regional Science Association 45: 197-213.

Shevky, E., and W. Bell (1955) Social Area Analysis. Stanford, Ca.: Stanford University Press.

Siegal, A.W., and J.H. Cousins (1983) The Symbolizing and Symbolized Child in the Enterprise of Cognitive Mapping. In R. Cohen (ed): The Development of Spatial Cognition. Hillsdale,N.J.: Lawrence Erblaum Association.

Siegal, A.W., and S.H. White (1975) The Development of Spatial Representations of Large-Scale Environments. In W.H. Reese (ed): Advances in Child Development and Behavior. New York: Academic Press, pp. 10-55.

Simmons, J. (1974) Patterns of Residential Movement in Metropolitan Toronto Department of Geography Research Publications. Toronto, Canada: University of Toronto.

Simon, H.A. (1957) Models of Man. New York: Wiley.

Singson, R. (1975) Multidimensional Scaling Analysis of Store Image and Shopping Behavior. Journal of Retailing Summer: 38-52.

Smith, T.R., and W.A.V. Clark (1980) Housing Market Search: Information Constraints and Efficiency. In W.A.V. Clark and E.G. Moore (eds): Residential Mobility and Public Policy. Beverly Hills, Ca.: Sage Publications, pp. 100-125.

Smith, T.R., W.A.V. Clark, J.D. Huff, and P. Shapiro (1979) A Decision Making Search Model for Intra Urban Migration. Geographical Analysis 11: 1-22.

Smith, T.R., J.W. Pellegrino, and R.G. Golledge (1982) Computational Process Modeling of Spatial Cognition and Behavior. Geographical Analysis 14: 305-325.

Sommer, R. (1969) Personal Space: The Behavioral Basis of Design. Engelwood Cliffs,N.J: Prentice-Hall.

Sorre, M. (1955) Les Migrations des Peuples: Essai Sur la Mobilite Geographique. Paris:.

References

Sorre, M. (1957) Rencontres de la Geographie et de la Sociologie. Paris: Marcel Riviere.

Sorre, M. (1958) La Geographie Psychologique: L'Adoptation au Milieu Elimatique et Biosocial. Traite de Psychologie Appliquee 6(3): 1343-1393.

Spector, A.N. (1978) An Analysis of Urban Spatial Imagery Ph.D. Dissertation, Department of Geography. Columbus,Ohio: Ohio State University.

Spencer, A.H. (1978) Deriving Measures of Attractiveness for Shopping Centers. Regional Studies 12: 713-726.

Spencer, A.H. (1980) Cognition and Shopping Choice: A Multidimensional Scaling Approach. Environment and Planning A 12: 1235-1251.

Stanley, T., and M. Sewall (1976) Image Inputs to Probabilistic Model: Predicting Retail Potential. Journal of Marketing 40: 48-53.

Stea, D. (1965) Space, Territory and Human Movement. Landscape 15(1): 13-16.

Stea, D. (1969) The Measurement of Mental Maps: An Experimental Model for Studying Conceptual Spaces. In K.R. Cox and R.G. Golledge (eds): Behavioral Problems in Geography: A Symposium,Northwestern University Studies in Geography No.17. Evanston,Ill.: Northwestern University, pp. 228-253.

Stevens, S.S. (1956) The Direct Estimation of Sensory Magnitudes-Loudness. American Journal of Psychology 69: 1-25.

Stewart, T.C. (1970) The City as an Image of Man. London: Latimer Press.

Stimson, R.J. (1978) Social Space, Preference Space and Residential Location Behavior: A Social Geography of Adelaide, Ph.D. Dissertation, Department of Geography. Flinders, Australia: Flinders University.

Stimson, R.J., and E.S. Ampt (1972) Mail Questionnaires in the Investigation of Spatial Behavior: The Problem of Respondent and Non-Respondent Differences. The Australian Geographer 12(1): 51-54.

Stopher, P. (1977) On the Application of Psychological Measurement Techniques to Travel Demand Estimation. Environment and Behavior 9(1): 67-80.

Stouffer, S.D. (1940) Intervening Opportunities: A Theory Relating to Mobility and Distance. American Sociological Review 5: 845-867.

Szalai, A., P.E. Coverse, P. Fldheim, E.K. Scheuch, and P.J. Stone (1972) The Use of Time: Daily Activities of Urban and Suburban Populations in Twelve Countries. The Hague: Mouton.

Talvitie, A., and D. Kirschner (1978) Specification, Transferability and the Effect of Data Outliers in Modelling the Choice of Model in Urban Travel. Transportation 7: 311-331.

Tardiff, T. (1980) Definition of Alternatives and Representation of Dynamic Behavior in Spatial Choice Models. Transportation Research Record 723: 25-30.

Taylor, P.J. (1971) Distance Transformations and Distance Decay Functions. Geographical Analysis 3: 221-238.

References

Theodorson, G.A., and A.G. Theodorson (1969) A Modern Dictionary of Sociology. New York: Thomas Coowell.

Thomlinson, R. (1969) Urban Structure: The Social and Spatial Characteristics of Cities. New York: Random House.

Thompson, D.L. (1963) New Concept: Subjective Distance. Journal of Retailing 39: 1-6.

Thorndyke, P.W. (1981) Distance Estimation from Cognitive maps. Cognitive Psychology 13: 526-550.

Thrift, N.J. (1977) Time and Theory in Human Geography. In C. Board, R. J. Chorley, P. Haggett, and D.R. Stoddart (eds): Progress in Human Geography, Vol. 1. London: Edward Arnold, pp. 65-101.

Timmermans, H. (1981) Spatial Choice Behavior in Different Environmental Settings: An Application of the Revealed Preference Approach. Geografiska Annaler B 63: 57-67.

Timmermans, H. (1982) Consumer Choice of Shopping Center: An Information Integration Approach. Regional Studies 16: 171-182.

Timmermans, H. (1983) Non-Compensatory Decision Rules and Consumer Spatial Choice Behavior: A Test of Predictive Ability. Professional Geographer 35: 449-455.

Timmermans, H., R.V. van der Heijden, and H. Westerveld (1982a) Cognition of Urban Retailing Structures: A Dutch Case Study. Tijdschrift voor Economiche en Sociale Geografie 73: 1-12.

Timmermans, H., R.V. van der Heijden, and H. Westerveld (1982b) The Identification of Factors Influencing Destination Choice: An Application of the Repertory Grid Methodology. Transportation 11: 189-203.

Tobler, W.R. (1976) The Geometry of Mental Maps. In G. Rushton and R.G. Golledge (eds): Spatial Choice and Spatial Behavior. Columbus, Ohio: The Ohio State University Press, pp. 69-82.

Tobler, W.R. (1977) Bidimensional Regression,Unpublished Manuscript, Department of Geography. Santa Barbara,Ca.: University of California.

Tolman, E.C. (1948) Cognitive Maps in Rats and Men. Psychological Review 55: 189-208.

Trowbridge, C.C. (1913) On Fundamental Methods of Orientation and Imaginary Maps. Science 38: 888-897.

Tuan, Y.F. (1971) Geography, Phenomenology and the Study of Human Nature. Canadian Geographer 15: 181-192.

Tuan, Y.F. (1974) Topophilia: A Study of Environmental Perception, Attitudes, and Values. Englewood Cliffs,N.J: Prentice-Hall.

Tuan, Y.F. (1976a) Humanistic Geography. Annals of the Association of American Geographers 66(2): 266-276.

Tuan, Y.F. (1976b) Geopiety: A Theme in Man's Attachment to Nature and Place. In D. Lowenthal and M.J. Bowden (eds): Geographies of the Mind. New York: Oxford University Press, pp. 11-39.

Tversky, A., and D. Kahneman (1974) Judgement Under Uncertainty: Heuristics and Biases. Science 185: 1124-1131.

Vernon, M.D. (1962) The Psychology of Perception. Baltimore: Penguin.

References

Wapner, S., and H. Werner (1957) Perceptual Development. Worcester,Ma.: Clark University Press.

Webber, M., and R. Fincher (1985) On Nature of Empirical Research in Human Geography: A Marxist Approach. Unpublished Paper, McMaster University :.

Werner, H., and B. Kaplan (1963) Symbol Formation: An Organismic-Developmental Approach to Language and the Expression of Thought. New York: John Wiley.

Wheeler, J. (1972) Trip Purposes and Urban Activity Linkages. Annals of the Association of American Geographers 62: 641-654.

Wheeler, J., and F.P. Stutz (1971) Spatial Dimensions of Urban Social Travel. Annals of the Association of American Geographers 61: 371-386.

White, G.F. (1945) Human Adjustment to Floods: A Geographical Approach to the Flood Problem in the United States,Research Paper 29, Department of Geography. Chicago,Ill.: University of Chicago.

White, G.F. (1966) Formation and Role of Public Attitudes. In H. Jarrett (ed): Environmental Quality in a Growing Economy: Essays from the Sixth R.F.F. Forum. Baltimore: The John Hopkins Press, pp. 105-127.

Wilson, A.G. (1967) A Statistical Theory of Spatial Distribution Models. Transportation Research 1: 253-269.

Wilson, A.G. (1969) The Use of Analogies in Geography. Geographical Analysis 1: 225-233.

Wilson, A.G. (1970) Entropy in Urban and Regional Modelling. London: Pion.

Wilson, A.G. (1972) Some Recent Developments in Microeconmic Approaches to Modeling Household Behavior, With Special Reference to Spatiotemporal Organization. In A. Wilson (ed): Papers in Urban and Regional Analysis. London: Pion.

Wilson, A.G. (1973) Further Developmetns of Entropy-Maximizing Transport Models. Transportation Planning and Technology 1: 183-193.

Wilson, A.G. (1981) Catastrophe Theory and Bifurcation. London: Croom Helm.

Wilson, R.L. (1962) Livability of the City: Attitudes and Urban Development. In F.S. Chapin and S.F. Weiss (eds): Urban Growth Dynamics. New York: John Wiley, pp. 359-399.

Wingo, L. (1961) Utilization of Urban Land. Papers and Proceedings of Regional Science Association 11: 195.

Wohlwill, J.F. (1968) Amount of Stimulus Exploration and Preference as Differential Functions of Stimulus Complexity. Perception and Psychophysics 4(5): 307-312.

Wolpert, J. (1964) The Decision Process in a Spatial Context. Annals of the Association of American Geographers 54: 537-558.

Wolpert, J. (1965) Behavioral Aspects of the Decision to Migrate. Papers and Proceedings of the Regional Science Association 15: 159-169.

References

Wolpert, J. (1966) Migration as an Adjustment to Environmental Stress.
Journal of Social Issues 22: 92-102.

Wright, J.K. (1947) Terrae Incognitae: The Place of the Imagination in
Geography. Annals of the Association of American Geographers 37(1):
1-15.

Wrigley, N. (1981) Categorical Data Analysis. In N. Wrigley and R.J.
Bennett (eds): Quantitative Geography: A British View. London:
Routledge and Kegan Paul, pp. 111-122.

Wrigley, N. (1985) Categorical Data Methods and Discrete Choice
Modelling in Spatial Analysis: Some Directions for the 1980's. In P.
Nijkamp, H. Leitner, and N. Wrigley (eds): Measuring the
Unmeasurable. Dordrecht: Martinus Nijhoff, pp. 115-137.

Wrigley, N., and R. Dunn (1984a) Stochastic Panel-Data Models of Urban
Shopping Behavior 3: The Interaction of Store Choice and Brand
Choice. Environment and Planning A 16: 1221-1236.

Wrigley, N., and R. Dunn (1984b) Stochastic Panel-Data Models of Urban
Shopping Behavior 2: Multistore Purchasing Pattern and the Dirichlet
Model. Environment and Planning A 16: 759-778.

Zannaras, G. (1968) An Empirical Analysis of Urban Neighborhood
Perception, Unpublished MA Thesis, Department of Geography. Columbus,
Ohio: The Ohio State University.

Zannaras, G. (1973) An Analysis of Cognitive and Objective
Characteristics of the City: Their Influence on Movements to the
City Center, Unpublished Ph.D. Dissertation, Department of
Geography. Columbus, Ohio: The Ohio State University.

Zannaras, G. (1976) The Relation Between Cognitive Structure and Urban
Form. In G.T. Moore and R.G. Golledge (eds): Environmental Knowing.
Stroudsburg,Pa.: Dowden, Hutchinson and Ross, pp. 336-350.

Zipf, G.K. (1946a) Some Determinants of the Circulation of Information.
The American Journal of Psychology 59(3): 401-421.

Zipf, G.K. (1946b) The p1 p2/d Hypothesis: On the Intercity Movement of
Persons. American Sociological Review 11: 677-686.

Index

Index

Index